Translating Time

A JOHN HOPE FRANKLIN CENTER BOOK

Duke University Press

Durham and London

2009

BLISS CUA LIM

Translating Time

Cinema, the Fantastic, and Temporal Critique

© 2009 Duke University Press
All rights reserved.
Printed in the United States of America
on acid-free paper ∞
Designed by C. H. Westmoreland
Typeset in Chaparral
by Tseng Information Systems, Inc.
Library of Congress Cataloging-in-Publication
Data appear on the last printed page
of this book.

TO THE MEMORY OF MY FATHER, MANUEL G. LIM (林荣昌)
AND FOR MY MOTHER, FELICIDAD CUA-LIM (柯淑端)

CONTENTS

ILLUSTRATIONS

ACKNOWLEDGMENTS

One writes alone, but one never writes alone. This book is for my parents, scholar-physicians of the finest stamp, because my first, fathomless debt of gratitude, an *utang na loob* that can only be recognized but never repaid, is owed to them. The many forking paths that led away from medicine to poetry to teaching and cinema, and at last to this book, were roads first opened by their love. In Manila and the United States, across the years, I have enjoyed the unfailing support and encouragement of my family: Val and Boyet, Otto and Don, Jun and Blanca, and not the least, Nila Gregana.

In the earliest stages of this project, when I was possessed with ideas of which I was unsure, Lauren Steimer and Joel David were inspiring interlocutors and patient listeners who made it possible for me to continue to think in the vein of time. I benefited immeasurably from Bibi Tinio's close and careful reading of both the earliest, inchoate drafts of this work and its recent, much-altered incarnations. And I am grateful for the guidance of Chris Straayer, Richard Allen, Zhang Zhen, Robert Stam, Esther Yau, and Ellen Paglinauan, and for the camaraderie-in-writing of Alisa Lebow.

Where my education in politics, teaching, and the cinema is concerned, a long, durative thread binds the completion of this book to several people and disparate times. I am thankful to fiercely brilliant mentors at the University of the Philippines Integrated School and the Department of English and Comparative Literature in UP Diliman: Edel Garcellano, staunch friend and vigilant cultural critic; and Ma. Teresa de Villa, who first infused my understanding of literature with nationalism. I still miss the lively mind and laced humor of the late Concepcion Dadufalza, my first, unforgettable teacher of pedagogy, and the late Maria Luisa Doronila, my first professor of mythology. I consider myself privileged to have learned from luminaries whose loss is still felt in the Philippine cultural scene: Franz Arcellana, Pacita Guevara-Fernandez, and Yolanda Tomeldan. At my first full-time faculty appointment at the University of the Philippines Department of Comparative Literature, the company of Carol Hau, Patricia Arinto, Tonchi Tinio, Nana Mabilangan, and the late Luisa Mallari, among several others, allowed me to experience an intensely formative intellectual and political camaraderie. And at New York University, a climate charged with criticality and cinephilia was forged by several friends in my graduate school cohort, only some of whom are mentioned here: Roger Hallas, Matt Fee, Jason Sanders, Keith Harris, Mia Mask, Linda Lai, Hector Rodriguez, and Barry Long.

Learning how to pose the questions in this book, how to hone and articulate my own political and intellectual stakes in this project, had its own temporality, its own unforeseeable path. I was fortunate to find myself in the company of brilliant friends and colleagues at the Film and Media Studies Department and the Visual Studies Program of the University of California, Irvine, and beyond. Victoria Johnson, Akira Lippit, Anne Friedberg, Ed Dimendberg, Glen Mimura, Adria Imada, Peter Krapp, and Rene Bruckner shared ideas, film screenings, and research materials with me at crucial stages in my writing. I am grateful to Mark Poster, Karen Lawrence, Judith Halberstam, and Jennifer Doyle for their enthusiastic support of my work, and especially to Fatimah Tobing Rony, inspiring scholar-filmmaker and friend, for generously providing me with a transcript of *On Cannibalism* and for permission to reproduce images from that work. I am grateful to Jonathan Hall for his incisive comments on a version of the final chapter and to the members of the Critical Theory Institute for reading and commenting on two chapters of this book. The responses of Dina Al-Kassim, Kavita Philip, and Jared Sexton emboldened me to foreground the ontological-political stakes of my work, proof positive that a generous reading by another can bring what one is arguing into sharpest focus. For gracious, rigorous, and indispensable institutional support at UCI, I am grateful to Vikki Duncan, Virak Seng, and Peter Chang, and to Dianna Sahhar and Daniel Tsang at the Langson Library.

My deepest thanks to Ken Wissoker at Duke University Press for his enthusiasm, encouragement, and patience as I revised this manuscript. I am profoundly appreciative of the incredible rigor, care, and attentiveness the Press's readers brought to my work; their responses prompted me to reformulate the crux of a temporal critique thought through the cinema. I have learned enormously from my graduate and undergraduate students through the years, but I want to especially thank my undergraduate students who participated in my seminars on fantastic cinema in the winters of 2006 and 2007.

Those rarest of moments, the time to think and write, were enabled by research and travel grants from the School of Humanities and the International Center for Writing and Translation at the University of California, Irvine, in 2004 and 2005; research assistance via the Executive Vice Chancellor's New Faculty Initiative Award from 2001 to 2003; a Visiting Research Fellowship at the College of Mass Communication, University of the Philippines, Diliman, in 2005; and a Visiting Research Fellowship at the College of Arts and Letters, University of the Philippines, Diliman, in 2006. I am glad to have had the opportunity to present parts of this book in talks delivered in New York City, Hong Kong, Manila, and Seoul. I benefited greatly from the responses of my hosts and interlocutors at the International Conference for Chinese Film and Cross-Cultural Understanding at the City University of New York Graduate Center in 2002; at the "Hong Kong/Hollywood at the Borders" conference at Hong Kong University in 2004; at a public lecture for the University of the Philippines College of Mass Communication in 2005; and at an international conference on Korean language, literature, and culture at Yonsei University in 2007. At those coordinates, I benefited from the generous, collegial company of Joi Barrios, Gina Marchetti, Nicanor Tiongson, Cindy Wong, Linda Lai, Hector Rodriguez, and Baek Moon Im.

The pioneering efforts and boundless goodwill of two archivist-preservationists associated with the Philippine Society of Film Archivists (SOFIA) have made it possible for me to screen and study films belonging to the dwindling, fragile archive of Filipino cinema. I am deeply grateful to Vicky Belarmino, film archivist of the Cultural Center of the Philippines; for more than a decade she has been a patron saint to my research on Filipino cinema. I am also thankful to Mary del Pilar, film archivist of ABS-CBN, for her tremendous generosity. My research at the University of the Philippines, Diliman, benefited greatly from the knowledgeable guidance of two dedicated librarians: Regina Murillo, head librarian of the College of Arts and Letters; and Wilma Azarcon, head of the Filipiniana serials section at the main library. My heartfelt thanks to Marta Braun for her invaluable help with the Etienne-Jules Marey chronophotographs included herein. I am also grateful to filmmakers Butch Perez, Ricky Lee, and Mike de Leon for permission to reproduce photographs and film stills from their personal collections; Butch Perez and Ricky Lee also generously consented to be interviewed for this project.

Portions of chapter 4 were published in an earlier form as "Generic Ghosts: Remaking the New 'Asian Horror Film,'" in *Hong Kong Film, Hollywood and the New Global Cinema*, edited by Gina Marchetti and Tan See Kam (London: Routledge, 2007), 109–25. Chapter 3 is a revised and expanded version of a prior article, "Spectral Times: The Ghost Film as Historical Allegory," *positions: east asia cultures critique* 9, no. 2 [special issue, Asia/Pacific Cinemas: A Spectral Surface] (fall 2001): 287–329. I am grateful to Gina Marchetti and to Duke University Press for permission to publish those earlier pieces in their present form in this book.

A life lived in many places at different rhythms makes one acutely appreciative of the sustaining presence of old friends. I am grateful for abiding, deep-rooted friendships with Bibi Tinio, Patricia Arinto, Joel David, Lauren Steimer, Tina Baluyut, Charmian Uy, Jasmin Jamora, Anya Leonardia, Alen Shapiro, Liza Gouger, and Emilie Gramlich. Mary Reilly, a once and future collaborator in the fantastic, spurred me at a critical juncture to put out this book. And in the thickets of writing during these last years I am grateful for the kindness, thoughtfulness, and support of Kelly Wolf, Patty Ahn, Karen Tongson, and Napoleon Lustre.

In his poem "Piedra de sol" [Sun stone], Octavio Paz asks:

—and this our life, when was it truly ours?
. . . life is not ours, it is the others'.

So many roads, to arrive at long last to this book, and to pass beyond it; and the last oceanic passage of working, writing, and dreaming would not have been possible without Joya Escobar, and the calm, exhilarating, unshakable course marked by her bright star.

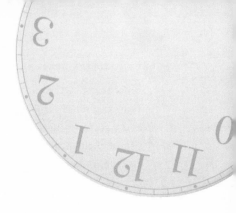

Clocks for Seeing

Cinema, the Fantastic, and the Critique of Homogeneous Time

For our duration is not merely one instant replacing another; if it were, there would never be anything but the present—no prolonging of the past into the actual, no evolution, no concrete duration. Duration is the continuous progress of the past which gnaws into the future and which swells as it advances. And as the past grows without ceasing, so also there is no limit to its preservation.   HENRI BERGSON, *Creative Evolution*

We are too accustomed to thinking in terms of the "present." We believe that a present is only past when it is replaced by another present. Nevertheless, let us stop and reflect for a moment: How would a new present come about if the old present did not pass at the same time that it is present? How would any present whatsoever pass, if it were not past at the same time as present? The past would never be constituted if it had not been constituted first of all, at the same time that it was present. There is here, as it were, a fundamental position of time and also the most profound paradox of memory: The past is "contemporaneous" with the present that it has been.   GILLES DELEUZE, *Bergsonism*

Fantastic cinema incites us to think in dis-accustomed terms about time. Gilles Deleuze, drawing on the philosophy of Henri Bergson, describes the paradoxical countenance of a nonidentical temporality.[1] Overturning the

presentism of the contemporary, Bergson rejects the notion of pure contemporaneity—"there is for us nothing that is instantaneous"—since in
every seeming instant of the present there is already a "continuous thread
of memory," a durative "depth of time."[2] If the past is not dead, but instead paradoxically coexists alongside the present, then the very notion
of contemporaneousness—as a single, self-consistent meanwhile—starts
to fray.

This book espouses a form of temporal critique that takes seriously two
linked issues: first, the persistence of supernaturalism, of occult modes
of thinking encoded in fantastic narratives; and second, the existence of
multiple times that fail to coincide with the measured, uniform intervals
quantified by clock and calendar. The supernatural is often rationalized as
a figure for history or disparaged as an anachronistic vestige of primitive,
superstitious thought. But from an alternate perspective it discloses the
limits of historical time, the frisson of secular historiography's encounter
with temporalities emphatically at odds with and not fully miscible to
itself. Confronted with radical peasant supernaturalisms in the modern-
day Philippines, for example, historian Reynaldo Ileto warns that to dis-
miss such instances as aberrations in a fully secularized national-historical
past would be to deny that *that* world—derided as fanatical, millenarian,
or superstitious—coexists alongside our own. We should not assume that
a profoundly discordant view of time and agency, such as may be found in
a peasant idiom of unrest (a world in which specters provoke rebellions, a
time in which the dead return), is meaningless except for its articulation
within the disenchanted present of modern homogeneous time.[3]

The fantastic unraveling of a unified present comes through powerfully
in a ghost film directed by Mike de Leon, a major figure in the Philippine
New Cinema of the 1970s and 1980s.[4] *Itim* [Black/Rites of May, 1976]
opens with a provincial homecoming: Jun, a Manila-based photojournalist, returns to his ancestral home to visit his paralyzed father and to photograph Holy Week rites in the town of San Ildefonso, Bulacan (fig. 1). In the
Christian liturgical year, Holy Week refers to the last days of Lent, a period
when the devout contemplate the Christian Passion or *pasyon* and a season
in which the mundane time of everyday life intersects with a biblical temporality of sin, repentance, and redemption.

Among Filipino/a Catholics, Holy Week is commemorated through the
procession of *santos* (holy images or statues of biblical characters asso-

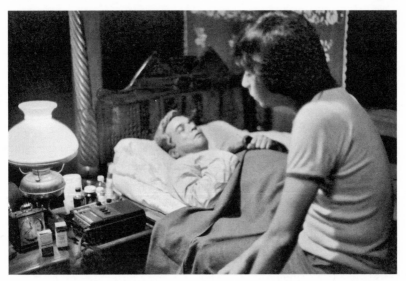

1. In *Itim* [Black / Rites of May, dir. Mike de Leon, 1976], Jun, a photojournalist, visits his ailing father during Lent. Courtesy of Mike de Leon.

ciated with the stages of the pasyon narrative), which are publicly paraded in well-adorned floats or carriages. According to Victor S. Venida, the social institution of *santo* ownership, which continues to this day, appears to have its origins in the mid-nineteenth-century rise of a large municipal native and mestizo elite.[5] In a context in which the inherited social obligation of *santo* ownership confers social distinction on Filipino families who lend the saintly images for Lenten rites, then, two brief scenes in *Itim* become particularly meaningful. The first is an uncanny nightmare sequence in which the protagonist dreams he is being attacked by a roomful of *santos* come to life (fig. 2); the second is when he questions the long-standing expectation that his family contribute several holy images to the town's procession. These small but significant scenes indicate the urbanized hero's disaffection and alienation from the social practices that express and cement the social distinction of the rural aristocracy. This aspect of the film resonates with the director's stated interest in scrutinizing a social world with which he was intimately familiar—Filipino "landed gentry" with a pronounced involvement in film.[6]

In the Catholic pasyon, darkness (*dilim*) and light (*liwanag*)—the selfsame words that haunt the urban protagonist of *Itim* from the first evening

more about how horror represents
social tensions

on which he attends a *pabasa*, a collective oral reading of the pasyon—are visual metaphors for polarities of death and resurrection and of a mystical passage from mortal suffering to heavenly radiance. The language of darkness and light (condensed in the film's title, *Itim*, or "black") was prominent in the idiom of anticolonial peasant dissent that fueled popular Filipino resistance movements from the mid-nineteenth century to the early twentieth. The Christian vocabulary introduced by Spanish evangelical imperialism was appropriated by a host of peasant groups who mounted armed resistance against Spanish authorities. Ileto relates images of light and darkness to two distinct temporal orders or "dimensions of time" that, during the Holy Week and other pasyon-related rituals throughout the year, converged: "a blurring of distinctions between the 'everyday world' and the 'pasyon world.'"[7]

Itim deftly mobilizes this doubled temporal logic, embedding quotidian events (a son visiting his father, a boy meeting a girl) in the otherworldly temporality of the Holy Week's pasyon rites. Set in a provincial Tagalog town, *Itim*'s narrative unfolds over the course of Holy Monday to midnight on Good Friday, a day given over to the contemplation of human mortality and frailty in Catholic dogma. Circularity and doubling structure the film: the father, a physician, has an affair with a young novitiate. When he discovers that she is pregnant, he murders her (fig. 3).

Years later, his son, Jun, a professional photographer, takes a snapshot of the novitiate's sister, now possessed by the dead girl's restless spirit. The slow revelation of the father's murderous act proceeds through two séances that bookend the film. In the first, a spiritist (*spiritista*) correctly predicts that the dead novitiate's spirit will return on Good Friday; in the second séance, at the close of the film, the murdered young woman's restless spirit speaks through the body of her surviving sister, exposing the murderer, Jun's father (figs. 4–6). Fleeing from the ghost's accusations, the father falls down the stairs to his death. By ending on Good Friday, the day of mortality, the plot's temporal reach stops short of the promise of redemption signified by Easter Sunday. De Leon's film closes on the darkness of death, remorse, and frailty named in its title.

The film's title, *Itim*, can be understood, then, as a multivalent reference to, first, the visual metaphors of darkness and light that pervade the pasyon narrative; second, the film's low-key light design, its rich chiaroscuro palette for the ancestral home's state of somber disrepair; and last,

2. Against the backdrop of Catholic Lenten rites, the secular protagonist of *Itim* has a nightmare that a roomful of holy images has come to life. Courtesy of Mike de Leon.

3. The father's brutal killing of a young novitiate in years past slowly comes to light in *Itim*. Lobby card courtesy of Mike de Leon.

4–6. *Itim* opens
and closes with two
séances; in the
climactic séance, the
murdered girl speaks
through her sister to
expose her killer.
Courtesy of Mike
de Leon.

7. Photographic traces of an enduring, bloodstained past come to light in the son's darkroom in *Itim*. Courtesy of Mike de Leon.

the darkroom studio in which photographic traces of an enduring, blood-stained past come to light.

On Jun's first night home, he prints photographs while his ailing father sleeps (fig. 7). The scene makes extensive use of parallel editing, alternating between the old patriarch asleep in a moonlit bedroom and the son at work in a darkroom. The sequence opens with a clock on the father's bedside table that is later graphically rhymed by the darkroom timer that regulates Jun's work (figs. 8 and 9). To audiences familiar with the well-worn conventions of continuity editing, such crosscutting between bedroom and darkroom is an immediately legible cinematic device that gives the spectator spatiotemporal omniscience: we understand the two distinct events unfolding in separate spaces to be occurring in the same "meanwhile." At the end of the scene, however, something unexpected happens: when the son completes a photographic enlargement of a striking young woman he caught on film, his father inexplicably wakes, alarmed.

On the surface, it would seem that the scene is about three characters at one time: Jun, his father, and the freshly printed image of a girl are all juxtaposed in a single simultaneous present, 5:00 in the morning on the last Tuesday of Lent. But *Itim* is a possession film, and the

[handwritten margin note:] cross cutting to show *hegemonic* Time

8, 9. A sequence in *Itim* crosscuts between the father's bedroom and the son's darkroom. Shots of a bedside clock and a darkroom timer evoke the simultaneity codified by parallel editing and its dependence on chronological time.

young girl whose photograph Jun snapped is inhabited by the spirit of her older sister, a woman whom his own father brutally murdered several years before. The duality of romantic involvements (father and son grow enamored of two sisters who are the same dead woman) coincides with a doubled temporal logic (figs. 10 and 11): on the one hand, a modern homogeneous time measured by darkroom timer and bedside clock; on the other, a spectral time of haunting and return, one in which the dead are alive and the past, fully preserved, "lean[s] over the present" and "gnaws" at the future.[8] The two temporal orders are immiscible and fail to coincide. In *Itim*, fantastic cinema, like the aperture of Jun's camera, opens to more than one time.

   In *Camera Lucida*, Roland Barthes calls the camera a "clock for seeing," binding time to sound and vision and writing lovingly of the "noise of Time,"

ghase as p regards of the past

TOMMY ABUEL · CHARO SANTOS
MARIO MONTENEGRO · MONA LISA
Ipinakikilala
ITIM
Pelikula ni MIKE DE LEON
CINEMA ARTISTS Philippines EastmanColor

TOMMY ABUEL · CHARO SANTOS
MARIO MONTENEGRO · MONA LISA
Ipinakikilala
ITIM
Pelikula ni MIKE DE LEON
CINEMA ARTISTS Philippines EastmanColor

10, 11. Dual romantic involvements in *Itim*: father and son become involved with two sisters; later, romances and identities are conflated when the surviving sister is possessed by the spirit of her murdered sibling. Lobby cards courtesy of Mike de Leon.

of the sound of the camera shutter as reminiscent of a clock's auditory time signal.[9] Clocks, one learns from Bergson, are translation machines, instruments for time measurement and time-discipline that render duration (*durée*) as linear succession, converting heterogeneous temporalities into a series of equidistant, uniform intervals: the seconds, minutes, and hours that make up calendrical days and years.[10] From the thirteenth century on, the tolling of public time, of church or civic work bells, has been experienced and resisted by workers as a form of time-discipline, a means of controlling and standardizing the regularity, intensity, and length of periods of labor and intervals of leisure. This temporal discipline is perhaps most keenly felt as the pressure of speed.[11]

In brief, the clock is the exemplar of "homogeneous, empty time," the critique of which, for Walter Benjamin, is the necessary point of departure for dismantling the concept of progress: "The concept of the historical progress of mankind cannot be sundered from the concept of its progression through a homogeneous, empty time. A critique of the concept of such a progression must be the basis of any criticism of the concept of progress itself."[12] Under the rule of the clock, the question "what time is it?" always yields an answer rooted in a standard, instantaneous present ("It's 5 a.m."). The clock graphically represents time as spatial and measurable: a number line is grafted onto its radial face so that the *progress in space* of the clock hand, moving across its circular trajectory, coincides with the *passage of time*. If I go by the clock on my bedside, then yesterday evening—the past—has elapsed and thus has ceased to exist. The future yawns before me, and for everyone else, as a predictable, empty, uniform series of recurring, measured intervals, waiting to be filled with experience. The clock will sound at 5:00 a.m. again tomorrow; Monday will come again next week; next year in February it is likely to be cold. But for the critics of empty, homogeneous time, or what I am calling modern time consciousness, clock time does not tell the truth of duration but exemplifies a socially objectivated temporality, one that remains "indispensable but inadequate"—a necessary illusion that must be exposed.[13]

The emergence of the mechanical clock in late thirteenth-century Europe signals the inception of modern homogeneous time, gradually replacing traditional, unequal hourly divisions handed down since antiquity with abstract, uniform periods severed from the relative length or brevity of daylight, specificities of use, or differences in custom or locale.[14] Since the worldwide adoption of standard time zones by the International Meridian Conference in 1884, modern homogeneous time has come to seem increasingly natural and incontrovertible, assuming the guise of a ready-made temporality. Yet despite the indispensable advantages of synchronizing people, information, and markets in a simultaneous global present, critics point out that modern homogeneous time is an enduring theme of social conflict.[15] Modern time consciousness is a means of exercising social, political, and economic control over periods of work and leisure; it obscures the ceaselessly changing plurality of our existence in time; and it underwrites a linear, developmental notion of progress that gives rise to ethical problems with regard to cultural and racial difference.

Barthes is not alone in construing the camera as a clock for seeing. The cinema and its photographic base have been repeatedly compared to a clock, since both machines represent time and movement as measurable and divisible into uniform intervals. A consummate elaboration of this analogy can be found in Bergson's *Creative Evolution*, in which the cinematograph stands condemned as a figure for the temporal misprisions of our own psychic mechanism. The cinema, like habitual perception, reduces time to the homogeneity of measurable space. Both in filming and projection, the cinema is a kind of clockwork mechanism, exposing and projecting immobile photograms at regular, equidistant intervals — say, sixteen or twenty-four frames per second — producing a convincing illusion for spectators, for whom the frozen frames, in rapid succession, appear to move. Yet the way in which cinema is a clock for seeing, an apparatus that links vision to rationalized time, is only one aspect of the cinema's relationship to temporality. Paradoxically, and often very pleasurably, I argue, the cinema can also provoke a critical reassessment of modern time consciousness.

On the one hand, the cinema as clockwork apparatus belongs to the regime of modern homogeneous time; on the other, fantastic narratives strain against the logic of clock and calendar, unhinging the unicity of the present by insisting on the survival of the past or the jarring coexistence of other times. This tension plays out in that scene from *Itim*: darkroom timer and bedside clock presume a single measurable time, and juxtaposed events unfold in a seemingly unproblematic simultaneity. But the return of the injured dead disjoins contemporaneity: the girl's photograph, and the dark romances evoked, are both then *and* now, exceeding a rational, chronological time. In this fantastic film, the temporal unruliness of haunting is only partially managed by being recast—that is, translated—into a single cinematic meanwhile.

In order to glimpse an "outside" to the regime of modern homogeneous time, one that we might seize as a starting point for more ethical temporal imaginings, this book approaches fantastic cinema as a kind of temporal translation: a translation of thorny and disreputable supernaturalisms into the terms of a modern, homogeneous, disenchanted time. Fantastic narratives, I argue, have a propensity toward temporal critique, a tendency to reveal that homogeneous time translates disparate, noncoinciding temporalities into its own secular code, because the persistence of supernaturalism often insinuates the limits of disenchanted chronology. I refer to traces of untranslatable temporal otherness in the fantastic as *immiscible times*—multiple times that never quite dissolve into the code of modern time consciousness, discrete temporalities incapable of attaining homogeneity with or full incorporation into a uniform chronological present.

Modes and Topoi of Temporal Critique

To argue this theory of immiscible times, I draw on a twofold critical reservoir that is fully explored in the first chapter. First, I look to the work of Henri Bergson, who argues that the cinema is implicated in homogeneous time but also demonstrates that a critique of homogeneous time must, perforce, contend with the cinema. Second, I consider how colonialism and its aftermath underpin modern *historical time* and how, in turn, a view of time as homogeneous, epitomized by the ideology of progress, served as a temporal justification for imperialist expansion. The first mode of temporal critique, Bergsonism, links temporal critique to visuality and the cinema; the second mode, postcolonial thought, binds modern homogeneous time to temporal exclusions—of the primitive, of anachronistic, "superstitious" folk—that found the notion of progress. My critique of homogeneous time, routed through the cinema, is fed by both streams. As I demonstrate in chapter 1, this book does not seek to obviate Bergson's temporal critique but rather to interweave historical and postcolonial analyses of homogeneous time to his visualist ontology. Considered proximately, the two modes of temporal critique—*visual-ontological* and *historical-postcolonial*—illuminate the modernity that grounds Bergson's approach to time and the cinematograph, a historical specificity that belies the unmarked, universal subject presumed by his project. More important, the historical and post-colonial approaches I seek to fold into Bergson's philosophical critique reveal the conditions of emergence of homogeneous time to be shaped not by the limits of "natural" human consciousness and perception but by global historical processes, that is, to the world-historical project of modernity that hinged on colonialism. Apart from underscoring the historically modern aspects of Bergsonism's philosophy of time, a critique of homogeneous time that attends to historical and cultural difference develops and complicates some of the themes already raised in Bergson's philosophy.

By collocating these two modes of temporal critique, respecting their differences while remaining attentive to their crucial points of convergence, I hope to throw into relief three topoi for the critique of homogeneous time: the upholding of plural times (Bergson's "multiple temporal rhythms," Dipesh Chakrabarty's "heterotemporality"), the refusal of anachronisms, and the recognition of untranslatability, that is, the avowal of *immiscible temporalities*.[16]

Temporal Multiplicities

In *Matter and Memory*, Bergson considers time to be, as Deleuze puts it, a "radical plurality of durations," coexisting cacophonously at different rhythms.[17] In *Creative Evolution*, Bergson offers a penetrating analysis of the way in which temporal heterogeneity is spatialized and made linear in a deterministic understanding of time in which "all is given."[18] The teleological time Bergson seeks to unseat—which conceives of "the future and the past as calculable functions of the present"[19]—has a profound affinity to both the temporal logic of colonialism, a linear, evolutionary view of history that spatialized time and cultural difference, and to the preemptive workings of contemporary capitalist governance, which dreams of foreclosing futurity.[20]

Imperialist discourse depended on a temporal strategy in which radical cultural differences brought to light by colonial contact were framed as primitive or anachronistic. Imperialist discourse—whose "discovery" of new worlds was "never in fact inaugural or originary"—framed territories as empty and discoverable by denying their inhabitants were there, "symbolically displac[ing]" the indigene into what Anne McClintock calls "anachronistic space": "According to this trope, colonized people—like women and the working class in the metropolis—do not inhabit history proper but exist in a permanently anterior time within the geographic space of the modern empire as anachronistic humans, atavistic, irrational, bereft of human agency—the living embodiment of the archaic 'primitive.'"[21] Such a temporal strategy presumes empty, homogeneous time to be culture-neutral and universal, hence able to encompass even peoples whose form of time consciousness contravenes notions of linear, uniform, and abstract time. This linear, evolutionary concept of time would, in Bergsonian terms, be considered deterministic and teleological. It is important to note at the outset that Bergson's thinking avoids the pitfalls of a modern historical consciousness that is evolutionary, in the sense of Chakrabarty's discussion of historicism.[22] Bergson's emphatically nonteleological concept of "creative evolution" denotes absolutely unforeseeable becoming, not the uniform, predictable, developmental temporal process denoted by the concept of progress.[23] The colonial trope of time-as-space, of the *globe as a kind of clock*—with the metropolitan center marking the path to progress, while the colonized other remains primitive and superseded—is a version of what Bergson exposes as the "all is given" logic of homogeneous time. To maintain that the future holds the same thing for everyone, that the future is already known (the achievement of progress, secular disenchantment, and rationality), and hence to anticipate that the primitive will one day be like the modern observer ("their" future can be extrapolated from "our" past), would, in Bergsonian terms, amount to a fundamentally timeless view of time.[24]

The Survival of the Past, or the Refusal of Anachronisms

The survival of the past demands serious engagement in any project that hopes to forge a more ethical, less distorting temporal view of otherness. The copresence of older modes of being is often translated as a relic or vestige of a prior developmental stage, something that has been superseded but stubbornly returns. Seen in this way, the survival of the past tends only to shore up the cachet of progress rather than to critique it. But there are other ways to conceive of the survival of the past: for Bergson, the past *is*, alongside the present; for Chakrabarty, the fiction of a single present is a containment of heterotemporalities.

For Bergson, duration is not a process by which the current moment deposes one that came before, for if that were the case, then all we would have is the present. Rather, duration is the "survival of the past," an ever-accumulating ontological memory that is wholly, automatically, and ceaselessly preserved: "Memory, as we have tried to prove, is not a faculty of putting away recollections in a drawer or of inscribing them in a register. There is no register, no drawer; there is not even, properly speaking, a faculty, for a faculty works intermittently, when it will or when it can, whilst the piling up of the past upon the past goes on without relaxation. In reality, the past is preserved by itself, automatically. In its entirety, probably, it follows us at every instant; all that we have felt, thought, and willed from our earliest infancy is there, leaning over the present that is about to join it, pressing against the portals of consciousness that would fain leave it outside."[25]

In Bergson's buccal figure, it is because the past never subsides that we feel the "bite of time."[26] Deleuze writes: "one of the most profound, but perhaps also one of the least understood, aspects of Bergsonism [is] the theory of memory. . . . We have great difficulty in understanding a survival of the past in itself because we believe that the past is no longer, that it has ceased to be. We have thus confused Being with being-present."[27] The Bergsonian survival of the past requires that we desist from our habit of "thinking in terms of the present." We believe that the present is all that exists and that the past has elapsed and is gone. Resisting such presentism, Bergson insists that the past *is*: it has not elapsed; it is not over and done with. Rather, it coexists alongside the present as the latter's absolute condition for existing.[28] The past survives regardless of human consciousness or memory, regardless of how much or how little we remember it, since pure recollection, the open register on which duration is inscribed without interruption, is not an individual or subjective psychological faculty but an "immemorial or ontological memory," a "Being-memory" that belongs to matter itself, to everything and no one.[29]

Bergsonism's paradoxical view of temporality — "the past is contemporaneous with the present it has been" — resonates with Chakrabarty's insistence that older modes of being are never entirely surmounted. Bergson, on the one hand, argues that the illusion of an instantaneous present occludes the very real survival of the past, and hence, the truly heterogeneous character of duration. Chakrabarty, on the other hand, reveals that the charge of anachronism — the claim that something out of kilter with the present really belongs to a superseded past — is a gesture of temporal exclusion. Bergson's argument is ontological (a Being-memory); Chakrabarty's critique is likewise ontological (heterotemporalities characterize human existence), but it is also historical and disciplinary. While Bergson insists on the coexistence of the past and the present, refusing the idea of the past as simply left behind, Chakrabarty and Johannes Fabian, in their anticolonial critiques of historiography and anthropology, contest the rhetoric of anachronism as the antipode to progress.

In a temporal move that Johannes Fabian calls a "denial of coevalness," nineteenth-century anthropology refused to recognize the ethnographiable subject as the modern observer's contemporary (to wit: this other is a savage, a living anachronism, a throwback to a prior stage of human evolution).[30] Postcolonial thinkers have called our attention to those processes by which ways of being in the world that were profoundly different from those of European colonizers were represented as anachronisms—premodern, primitive, and superstitious. Worlds that contained spirits and other enchanted beings remained untranslatable to colonial discourse and modern time consciousness: this impasse of untranslatability was resolved temporally, through, as Vicente Rafael puts it, "wishful mistranslations."[31] In sixteenth-century colonial missionary accounts, nineteenth-century anthropology, ethnographic cinema, and modern historiography, one repeatedly encounters examples in which intractable differences are *temporally managed* by being positioned as already known and surmounted precursors, not something disturbing that persists alongside and within the modern but as relics of superseded chronological antecedents.

For both modes of temporal critique, to presume pure contemporaneity and an entirely surmounted past would be to deny the copresence of multiple but noncoinciding temporalities. Bergsonism and postcolonial temporal critique both share a refusal of anachronism, of a past left behind; they impel us to think in terms other than the present in order to see beyond seeming obsolescence. This requires going "beyond the turn," further than the practical convenience of living our lives by clock and calendar, as though the past were finished, the present uniform, and the future given or ready-made.[32]

Untranslatability

> In short, the word with well-defined outlines, the rough and ready word, which stores up the stable, common, and consequently impersonal element

in the impressions of mankind, overwhelms or at least covers over the delicate and fugitive impressions of our individual consciousness. To maintain
the struggle on equal terms, the latter ought to express themselves in precise words; but these words, as soon as they were formed, would turn against
the sensation which gave birth to them, and, invented to show that the sensation is unstable, they would impose on it their own stability.   BERGSON,
Time and Free Will

For Bergson, all attempts to articulate pure duration are betrayed by language. Articulations of temporal heterogeneity invariably strain against
what he calls "the language of common sense," since this language natu-
ralizes the misconstrual of time as space.[33] The "rough and ready word" reduces sensation to the lowest common denominator of known experience,
making the ineffable into something stable and resulting in a colorless,
degraded experience of life.[34] Multiple temporal rhythms, newness of becoming, and the experiences and emotions registered in the depths of the
self, are all objectified and made equivalent by language. These intertwined
themes of reification and untranslatability are given poignant expression
by Bergson: "We fail to translate completely what our soul experiences:
there is no common measure between mind and language."[35] In *Time and
Free Will*, he frames the misconstrual of heterogeneous time as homogeneous space—which leaves us unable to recognize our own freedom and
duration—as a problem of translation, the difficulty of trying "to express
the idea of freedom in a language into which it is obviously untranslatable."[36] Language—whether that of mathematics, science, or everyday
usage—can only express time insofar as it is past, accomplished, and objectified (time flown, not time flowing).[37]

Bergson repeatedly posits heterogeneous temporalities as fundamentally
untranslatable, betrayed by language, since the "rough and ready word"
works via abstraction.[38] From another critical perspective, Chakrabarty,
drawing on the work of Vicente Rafael and Gayatri Spivak, likewise discerns in homogeneous time the problem of translating radically different
times and ways of inhabiting the world into the language of secular historiography. Questions of temporal translation are a particularly fraught issue
for subaltern historians, who often have to translate the lived experience
of different temporal worlds into the code of a secular, disenchanted, historical time. Both ontological and postcolonial critiques of homogeneous

time, then, alert us to the consequences of taming and translating plural times into homogeneous chronology.

The Language of Disenchanted Time

> The moment we think of the world as disenchanted, however, we set limits to the ways the past can be narrated.   CHAKRABARTY, *Provincializing Europe*

> As becoming shocks the habits of thought and fits ill into the molds of language, they declared it unreal.   BERGSON, *Creative Evolution*

This picture of empty homogeneous time—as spatialized, abstract, chronological, measurable, and premised on a logic of temporal exclusion—is nearly complete. Chakrabarty adds a last, crucial dimension to this book's consideration of modern historical time. The title of his essay "The Time of History and the Times of Gods" indicates that homogeneous historical time is secular and disenchanted; it follows that ways of being in the world that admit of supernatural agency will present a problem of translation for homogeneous time.[39]

Modern homogeneous time is a language ("a dialect backed up by an army," as Chakrabarty ironically puts it) whose hegemony is naturalized as universality.[40] It rests on the assumption that its own conception of time—as "godless, continuous, empty and homogeneous"—is a natural "structure of generality." This explains why even the nonsecular and the nonmodern can be relegated to a position in this history. "The naturalism of historical time lies in the belief that everything can be historicized. So while the nonnaturalness of history, the discipline, is granted, the assumed universal applicability of its method entails a further assumption: that it is always possible to assign people, places, and objects to a naturally existing, continuous flow of historical time." It becomes feasible to retrospectively position peoples and cultures who do not share this time consciousness as forerunners to modernity in a universal, linear narrative of human history. Modern time is thus projected in every direction to include even what exists outside of or prior to its minting as a concept, entertaining an "ideal of objectivity," a belief that its conception of history is the "overarching language," the universal narrative to which all specific instances can be subsumed. Like the time of Newtonian science, the time of history is one in which heterogeneity is translated into homogeneity in order to govern unsettling, radical difference. Such temporal translations are naturalized—so that we forget that we are even translating very different temporalities into the modern one—yet they belie a "radical untranslatability." Secular historiography claims to mediate and translate supernatural or ghostly accounts, but ghosts and gods cannot be seen within a horizon of sameness when they "belong to a field of differences."[41]

As Chakrabarty brilliantly demonstrates, recasting the nonmodern as a precursor to modernity involves an *act of translation*. However necessary and expedient this translation is to the way we live our lives according to the stable past, present, and future of modern calendars, Chakrabarty exhorts us not to forget that translation is at work whenever we speak of supernaturalism or precapitalist worlds in relation to modern time:

> The prefix *pre* in "precapital" . . . is not a reference to what is simply chronologically prior on an ordinal, homogeneous scale of time. "Precapitalist" speaks of a particular relationship to capital marked by the tension of difference in the horizons of time. The "precapitalist," on the basis of this argument, can only be imagined as something that exists within the temporal horizon of capital and that at the same time disrupts the continuity of this time by suggesting another time that is not on the same, secular, homogeneous calendar (which is why what is precapital is not chronologically prior to capital; that is to say, one cannot assign it to a point on the same continuous time line). This is another time that, theoretically, could be entirely immeasurable in terms of the units of the godless, spiritless time of what we call "history," an idea already assumed in the secular concepts of "capital" and "abstract labor."
>
> . . . Subaltern histories are therefore constructed within a particular kind of historicized memory, one that remembers History itself as a violation, an imperious code that accompanied the civilizing process that the European Enlightenment inaugurated in the eighteenth century as a world-historical task. It is not enough to historicize "history," the discipline, for that only uncritically keeps in place the very understanding of time that enables us to historicize in the first place. The point is to ask how this seemingly imperious, all-pervasive code might be deployed or thought about so that we have at least a glimpse of its own finitude, a vision of what might constitute an outside to it.[42]

Although it remains a practical necessity to translate different worlds and temporalities into the terms of modern time consciousness, Chakrabarty asks those who work on subaltern pasts to keep the "finitude" of secular time constantly in mind. It is necessary to retain a sense of "scandal in every translation" so that the requisite paraphrasing of other worlds and temporalities as premodern and precapitalist—when these were not so much prior to as outside of, other than, and unassimilable to modern time—never goes entirely unchallenged.[43]

Chakrabarty describes himself as a historian of labor in modern South Asia who has repeatedly come up against the problem of having to translate nonsecular worlds into the codes of secular historiography. The disciplinary limits of sociology and history, for example, structure the expectation that a historian will demystify peasants' claims that their gods called on them to revolt.[44] The discrepancy between these nonsecular worlds and the codes of disenchanted historiography prompts Chakrabarty to pose the following question: "How do we conduct these translations in such a manner as to make visible all the problems of translating such diverse and enchanted worlds into the universal and disenchanted language of sociology?" He responds by calling for a scandalous uncanniness: "An ambiguity must mark the translation of the tool-worshiping jute worker's labor into the universal category 'labor': it must be enough like the secular category 'labor' to make sense, yet the presence and plurality of gods and spirits in it must also make it 'enough unlike to shock.' There remains something of a 'scandal'—of the shocking—in every translation, and it is only through a relationship of intimacy to both languages that we are aware of the degree of this scandal."[45]

As is clear from the discussion thus far, Chakrabarty's work has pivotal significance for this study of cinema and the fantastic, though he writes from a different set of disciplinary concerns, those of sociology and history. I would characterize one focus of his book *Provincializing Europe* and of an essay that preceded it, "The Time of History and the Times of Gods," as a redemptive critique of the supernaturalism of peasant and subaltern worlds. From the perspective of the "single, homogeneous, and secular historical time" of modernity, "a peasant-but-modern political sphere . . . not bereft of the agency of gods, spirits, and other supernatural beings" can only be an anachronism.[46] The refusal to see worlds in which ghosts and other supernatural forces exist as coeval or contemporaneous with the modern at once excludes the peasant (and a whole host of frequently feminized "superstitious" others) while naturalizing modern historical time as universal.[47] As Chakrabarty wryly notes: "One empirically knows of no society in which humans have existed without gods and spirits accompanying them. Although the God of monotheism may have taken a few knocks—if not actually 'died'—in the nineteenth-century European story of 'the disenchantment of the world,' the gods and other agents inhabiting practices of so-called 'superstition' have never died anywhere. I take gods and spirits to be existentially coeval with the human, and think from the assumption that the question of being human involves the question of being with gods and spirits."[48]

So fierce and finely accomplished a critique of modern time consciousness, from the perspective of a postcoloniality alive to ghosts, was an invaluable resource for my thinking about fantastic cinema. His forceful, but never dismissive, critiques of homogeneous, modern time as "indispensable but inadequate"—indispensable to our daily lives and to emancipatory projects of political and intellectual modernity, yet inadequate to diverse ways of being in the world—led me to think of the fantastic as a form of temporal translation: narratives that represent enchanted worlds within the framework of secular modern homogeneous time but intimate a sense of discrepant temporality. The ethical, political, and scholarly stakes of a temporal critique of the fantastic are much like the problems posed by gods and spirits to the writing of history: the real issue is not so much belief but rather ways of recognizing and translating a plurality of worlds and times, while resisting the tendency to refuse supernaturalisms, or their supposedly superstitious adherents, contemporaneity.

The superstitious primitive is the foil that sets off the modern to best advantage. This is why, in Max Weber's famous 1917 lecture, "Science as a Vocation," savages—the "Red Indian or a Hottentot"—are invoked to reveal the true meaning of "scientific progress":

> Let us first of all clarify what this intellectual rationalization through science and scientific technology actually means in practice. Does it perhaps mean that today we—for example, everybody who is sitting in this room—have a greater understanding of the conditions under which we live than a Red Indian or a Hottentot? Hardly. Not one of us who travels on trams has any idea of how trams come to move unless he is a physicist. . . . It means something else—the knowledge or the belief that, *if one only wanted to*, one *could* find out any time; that there are in principle *no mysterious, incalculable powers at work*, but rather that one could in principle master everything through *calculation*. But that means the disenchantment of the world. One need no longer have recourse

to magic in order to control or implore the spirits, as did the savage for whom such powers existed. Technology and calculation achieve that, and this more than anything else means intellectualization as such.[49]

Though Weber is not the first in German intellectual history to employ the notion of *Entzauberung*, or disenchantment, it is in Weber's characterization of modernity as a process of disenchantment that "the term gains definitional status."[50] Disenchantment refers to the ways in which enchantment—the felt mysteriousness and fundamental unknowability of the world—has given way to calculative knowledge. The rational mastery and progress exemplified by science displaces the magical means of "the savage, for whom such mysterious powers existed." The sphere of modern disenchantment is thus demarcated by contrast to the racialized imaginary of "Red Indian" and "Hottentot" worlds.[51] The colonial encounter— framing the other *in terms* of the primitive, encountering the indigene as an anachronism—is constitutive of the Weberian disenchantment thesis. To do its work, the disenchantment thesis as a historical enframing must always call up the specter of the savage.

There are compelling reasons to regard the disenchantment thesis less as an accurate characterization of modernity than as an exclusionary temporal gesture and a mechanism for social stratification that began to attain decisive historical ascendancy in the eighteenth century. Who is fenced out by the disenchantment thesis? For Chakrabarty, it is the superstitious third world peasant; for Lorraine Daston and Katharine Park, it is the vulgar European populace.

According to historians of the early modern, the late sixteenth century and early seventeenth constitute a "period that can be called with justice an age of wonder," as "books of marvels poured off the printing presses of Europe."[52] The "vogue for the marvelous" gripped European culture across nations and spheres of activity—literature, visual arts, music, drama, theology, natural sciences, philosophy—in the late-Renaissance and Baroque periods. Etymologically, wonder and marvel were linked: in Italian *meraviglia*, in French *merveille*, in German *wunder*. Marvels and wonders included "fabulous creatures of folklore, supernatural phenomena with apocalyptic associations, and the miraculous powers of holy relics or religious images," as well as the "fabulous human races" of the New World.[53] Thus "the Age of the Marvelous" looks forward to modernity: from Marco Polo's late thirteenth-century accounts of exotic lands to the voyages of

Columbus, Magellan, and Vespucci, in the late fifteenth century and early sixteenth, these travels to the Orient, the Americas, the Middle East, and Africa yielded much-coveted exotica for cabinets of curiosities or *wunderkammern*. The marvelous thus referred not only to objects but to native peoples in the wonder-tinged, racialized imaginary forged by the voyages of colonial expansion. As Joy Kenseth points out: "of all the wonders to be found in the New World . . . the native inhabitants aroused the greatest curiosity."[54]

But by the eighteenth century, one writer declared that "the marvelous is not made for us," signaling that though wonders persisted in fairgrounds, in cabinets of curiosity, and in popular publications, for the urban-oriented intellectual vanguard of eighteenth-century Europe, "the star of the marvelous had indeed waned." Daston's and Park's illuminating discussion of this period discounts the scholarly commonplace that the rise of rational science swept the marvelous away. Rather, they trace a historical shift whereby the marvelous becomes a merely popular entertainment, banished from elite intellectual discourse, derided as the vulgar preoccupation of uneducated folk.[55] According to Daston and Park, the vulgar were those most "susceptible" to being deceived by marvels: "Women, the very young, the very old, primitive peoples, and the uneducated masses, [formed] a motley group collectively designated as 'the vulgar.' In the works of the learned, the vulgar stood as the antonym of the enlightenment; they were barbarous, ignorant, and unruly. When, in the early eighteenth century, the 'love of the marvelous' also came to be seen as a hallmark of the vulgar, it was a sure sign that enlightenment and the marvelous were no longer compatible."[56]

The hierarchy between reason and the marvelous corresponds not just to a cultural valuation but to the stratification of the socially powerful vis-à-vis the socially marginal; the Enlightenment aversion to marvels was also an exclusion of vulgar classes and popular cultural forms, a discourse of both "metaphysics and snobbery."[57]

Daston and Park characterize Weberian disenchantment as a variant of what they call "the wistful counter-Enlightenment" tradition, the argument that science and post-seventeenth-century rationalism are responsible for the demise of the marvelous. In contrast, Daston and Park suggest that elite discreditation and disparagement of the marvelous—not a scientific debunking of wonders—is what put an end to the age of wonders by the eighteenth century.

The wistful counter-Enlightenment tradition is simultaneously patronizing and nostalgic for the lost world of the marvelous. "Its nostalgia for an age of wonders, supposedly snuffed out by an age of reason, is rooted in an image of Enlightenment as the cultural and intellectual analogue of the transition from childhood to adulthood." This disenchantment paradigm, mingling condescension and nostalgia in equal parts, is also based on a teleological rhetoric of anachronism. Casting the Enlightenment as a cultural adulthood for the human race, the marvelous is seen to belong to a premodern childhood, something to be "outgrown" as well as yearned for once we moderns "mature into rationality." The marvelous comes to be defined "by the negative and anachronistic criterion that no educated adult now credits them. To outgrow wonders is to mature into rationality, a process that is, for this tradition of cultural criticism, as sadly irreversible as adulthood." In their trenchant critique of the disenchantment narrative, Daston and Park point out that in the early modern period, marvels were not trifles for children but matters of scholarly debate for natural and preternatural philosophy; marvelous prodigies and miracles were capable of inciting civil unrest, leading both lay and religious figures in the late seventeenth century to denounce superstition and regulate miracles. Thus, instead of rehearsing the conventional story of empirical science's dramatic ascendancy in an increasingly demystified world, Daston and Park offer a compelling, alternative historical account whereby elite disparagement from the eighteenth century onward discredits the marvelous, a marvelous that is not superseded but continues to thrive vigorously in popular culture.[58]

What one learns from their provocative counterhistoriography is that disenchantment as a world-historical process is not so much the unequivocal triumph of rationality as it is a trajectory of *temporal elitism* (the marvelous is cast as a premodern childhood of vulgar superstition), *popularization*, and *exclusion* (monsters survive, but they are consumed by culturally disparaged audiences). Far from dispelling enchantment, moderns have merely devalorized it. The social and cultural history of the supernatural in our age is not the heroic tale of a truer, rational, skeptical schema's triumph over premodern superstition; rather, it is a story of temporal elitism and temporal exclusion, of how supernaturalism came to be fenced out from highbrow, urbane, and educated thinking. Marvels persist in our own day; their generic home, however, is no longer learned philosophical treatises but horror, science fiction, tabloids, and a host of other disreputable genres. Indeed, popular culture, from freak shows to what one critic calls "occult TV," remains the undisputed stomping ground of the marvelous in our own age.[59] The Enlightenment is defined in contradistinction to supernaturalism not because the world has been completely disenchanted but because enchantment is now derided as a state of cultural provincialism.

In *Provincializing Europe*, Chakrabarty briefly and intriguingly mentions an alternative to translating radically different worlds into the language of disenchanted, homogeneous time: an "antisociological" mode of narrating supernaturalism that is best suited to fiction and the cinema: "It is obvious that this nonsociological mode of translation lends itself more easily to fiction, particularly of the nonrealist or magic-realist variety practiced today, than to the secular and realist prose of sociology or history. In these fictive narratives, gods and spirits can indeed be agents."[60] Or again: "this mode of translation is antisociology and for that reason has no obligation to be secular. The past is pure narration, no matter who has agency in it. Fiction and films, as I have said, are the best modern media for handling this mode."[61] Though he does not further clarify what he means by "pure narration," I remain fascinated by his suggestion that film as well as certain genres — fiction in a "nonrealist or magic-realist mode" — that is, cinema and the fantastic, hold out the possibility of a scandalous, nonsociological translation of plural, enchanted worlds. Fantastic cinema, I argue in the next section, can productively be conceptualized as a mode of translation that retains, in Spivak's apt phrase, an uncanny quality of "contained alterity,"[62] an intimation of otherness that exceeds the confines of secular, homogeneous time.

"History cannot represent, except through a process of translation and consequent loss of status and signification for the translated, the heterotemporality of that world."[63] What Chakrabarty refers to as heterotemporality is precisely what remains recalcitrant to translation by historical time. But, as I suggest below, it is precisely this trace of untranslatability, of *immiscible temporalities*, that fantastic narratives, in contrast to secular historiography, might be best able to explore.

A Modal Approach to Genre

An interest in the fantastic leads into the thickets of a double disreputability: on the one hand, genre criticism has, as Fredric Jameson points out, been undervalued by a particular variant of the "ideology of modern-ism" that stresses originality and invention over convention and repetition.[64] On the other hand, as Robert Scholes remarks in his foreword to Tzvetan Todorov's canonical book on the subject, the fantastic is one of the "humbler literary genres."[65] S. S. Prawer notes, with understated wit: "An interest in the uncanny does lead us into some bad or indifferent company."[66]

Despite the pervasive devaluation of both genre study in general and the fantastic in particular, I propose an understanding of the fantastic that underscores the important contribution both can make to our ways of thinking and unthinking time. The fantastic can disclose a starting point for temporal critique, one that is enmeshed in the very idiom of homogeneous time yet strains against it, producing a quality of uncanniness.

Cinema's temporal critique is not possible only through the fantastic; neither is the fantastic confined to film. The supernatural worlds so often thematized by fantastic cinema are frequently articulated through both media specificity and media convergence.[67] The critique of homogeneous time is reducible to neither the cinema nor the fantastic; compelling temporal critique has been elaborated in anthropology, historiography, philosophy, experimental video, and elsewhere. This book does argue, though, that the fantastic has a *propensity* toward temporal critique, a tendency to reveal that homogeneous time is not "reality" but rather a translation, because the persistence of supernaturalism tends to insinuate the limits of disenchantment.

Jameson demarcates two approaches to the study of genre: the structural or syntactic approach, which constructs a textual model, and the semantic approach, which regards genre as a mode.[68] Todorov's influential structuralist theory of the fantastic, which I will discuss in depth in chapter 2, belongs to the first method. In *The Fantastic: A Structural Approach to a Literary Genre*, Todorov erects a textual paradigm for the mechanisms at work in a fantastic narrative, providing a precise formula for the production of an implicit reader's hesitation in the face of an anomalous event: the presence of two worlds (natural and supernatural), discursive ambiguity, and the banning of allegorical or poetic readings.[69]

The approach to genre I adopt in this book belongs to the second variant: a semantics of the fantastic that explores its "form of being-in-the-world," the "generalized existential experience" the fantastic encodes.[70] In an extremely incisive essay on film genre theory, Christine Gledhill defines "generic verisimilitude" as "what is expected of a particular kind of *fictional* world."[71] In keeping with her formulation, one may say that the generic verisimilitude of the fantastic brings *worldness* into sharp relief.

Jameson argues that magical narratives contemplate being-in-the-world. For Jameson, magical narratives are a literary form in which "the *world-ness* of *world* reveals itself. . . . *World* in the technical sense of the transcendental horizon of my experience becomes precisely visible as something like an innerworldly object in its own right, taking on the shape of *world* in the popular sense of nature, landscape, and so forth."[72]

What does it mean to say that the "world-ness of world reveals itself" in the fantastic? For Martin Heidegger, the world is not a tangible space in which things are "objectively present" (e.g., a chair that is in a classroom in a school on Earth) where things are both "in" space and "at" a location. The chair, the classroom, the school, that "world-space," and all material things construed to be objectively present "in" the world are entities that can only be encountered insofar as they have been disclosed by that overarching interpretive fore-conception that is the world.[73] If we discover things, it is in the ontological context of their involvement with human possibility, their place in the set of assignations we ourselves construct. We are not objects that can be found within the world; rather it is human understanding that constitutes the world as a totality of relevances or involvements that we apprehend in relation to our own possibilities. What we can know or perceive is thus subject to the world we are familiar with, to that dwelling-in or worlding the world that is the very precondition for our encountering things like chairs and books in their readiness-to-hand. Though we frequently misinterpret ourselves as entities within the world, the world is rather something that we ourselves disclose. Our worlding is the precondition for our knowing about things within it; the world is thus not a thing outside us but that horizon in which we move.[74]

For Jameson, what makes the magical narrative a special type of generic world is that world, in the Heideggerian sense, is concretely represented as an actual place, a physical setting. Adapting Jameson's conceptualization of the magical narrative to fantastic cinema, I suggest that competing epistemological frameworks—secular and enchanted worlds, for example—have, in the fantastic, become "objects of representation," *concretized in the mise-en-scène*. In most genres (with the exception, perhaps, of the emphatically antiquotidian world of the film musical), world as "that supreme category which permits all experience or perception in the first place," as Jameson notes, "cannot normally be an object of perception in its own right."[75] This is because "conventional narrative realism" portrays the world as an objectively existing environment in which people act and events occur, rather than as an experiential horizon.[76] In contrast to realist narratives, the fantastic is precisely that genre in which antithetical forms of worlding are concretely figured as physical setting, as mise-en-scène: enchanted forests and haunted houses are diegetic objectifications of experiential fore-structures that admit of supernatural agency.

I adopt from Jameson and Gledhill a modal view of genre; in the broadest terms (which I refine below), this study conceptualizes the fantastic as a narrative that juxtaposes two (or more) radically different worlds.[77] The encounter with a forked world is registered within the narrative as an experience of limits, whether these be limits of epistemological certainty, cultural transparency, or historical understanding. Because the unfamiliar world most often takes the form of a supernatural realm in which the linear chronological time of clock and calendar does not hold, the fantastic has a propensity to foreground a sense of temporal discrepancy that cannot be entirely translated into the terms of modern homogeneous time.[78]

Mode has a particular relationship to a historical consideration of genre. Jameson clarifies that mode is "not bound to the conventions of a given age, nor indissolubly linked to a given type of verbal artifact, but rather persists as a temptation and a mode of expression across a whole range of historical periods, seeming to offer itself, if only intermittently, as a formal possibility which can be revived and renewed."[79] Mode, then, is a transhistorical category: a modal approach to the fantastic does not confine the genre to a particular national tradition nor to a particular historical period (that is, it does not begin and end, as Todorov and others assert, with late eighteenth-century and nineteenth-century European fantastic literature). Nevertheless, a modal approach to the fantastic enables historical understanding by tracking how its forms of expression and aesthetic possibilities are spoken by particular works in specific circumstances. That is, historical specificity is actualized through the transhistorical possibilities offered by a mode. Though mode may appear at first glance to offer an ahistorical method, in modal genre criticism the question of history is asked in a particular, and to my mind, productive, manner: how does the historical instance speak through a given aesthetic lexicon, a discursive universe of possibles? The fantastic is thus a reservoir of formal, affective, and semantic possibilities; but the ways that each work articulates, transforms, or renews those possibilities are contingent on specific junctures of emergence, reception, and circulation. This means that fantastic narratives are not always the same thing to every public: they may cause Todorovian hesitation, for example, or they might not.[80] As I demonstrate in the coming chapters, modal criticism opens up genre scholarship to the crosscurrents of historical transformation and shifting horizons of transnational reception.

Immiscible Times: The Fantastic as Temporal Translation

The translation of supernaturalisms into homogeneous time, a translation that must contend with generic conventions, is where my chief interest in the fantastic lies. Every temporal reinscription is an inextricably generic act; it must engage the horizon of expectations codified by genre. For a historian like Chakrabarty, the temporal translation of the "times of the gods" is subject to the conventions and expectations that underpin the genre of secular historiography. In contrast, fantastic cinema's temporal translation of supernaturalism occurs within a generic mold centrally concerned with the epistemological crisis posed by an inexplicable event, since, in a purportedly disenchanted world, the possible existence of the supernatural transgresses against received knowledge.

Todorov's enormously influential theory of the fantastic identifies three things at the "heart" of the genre: (1) an "apparently supernatural event," one that appears to confound all explanations that accord with the laws of "our familiar world"; (2) an affective response: hesitation. The inexplicable event causes the reader (and sometimes, the fictional characters) to become doubtful or hesitant as to the right way to perceive the event and, by extension, the world; and (3) the temporality of affect: the fantastic as "the duration of this uncertainty," the duration of hesitation.[81]

For Todorov, the fantastic is a drama of disbelief in which we waver between two competing perspectives: either the world is charged with wondrous events that the laws of nature are inadequate to explain (the marvelous), or the impossible event is an illusion that scientific explanation

can dispel (the uncanny). In Todorov's spatialized and temporalized definition, the fantastic is flanked by two adjacent genres: the uncanny (the
supernatural demystified by rational explanation) and the marvelous (the
supernatural accepted, repudiating the laws of nature). Todorov provides
the following diagram. The neighboring genres, poles antithetical to the
pure fantastic, are given to the extreme left and right (uncanny and marvelous). The subgenres closest to the fantastic (fantastic-uncanny and
fantastic-marvelous), characterized by a hesitation resolved in favor of
either pole, are represented as interior terms. Strikingly, the fantastic has
no territorial span, and it appears in Todorov's map only as the borderline
between the fantastic-uncanny and the fantastic-marvelous:

uncanny	fantastic- uncanny	fantastic- marvelous	marvelous

DIAGRAM 1. In *The Fantastic: A Structural Approach to a Literary Genre*, Tzvetan
Todorov maps the relationship of the fantastic as pure borderline to neighboring
genres and subgenres.

Explaining this diagram, Todorov writes: "The fantastic in its pure state
is represented here by the median line separating the fantastic-uncanny
from the fantastic-marvelous. This line corresponds perfectly to the nature of the fantastic, a frontier between two adjacent realms."[82] Todorov's
emphasis on perceptual hesitation spatializes the fantastic as an "evanes-
cent" dividing line between a hesitant dismissal of the supernatural and a
grudging acceptance of it.[83] As the term *evanescence* and his spatial illustration suggest, for Todorov the fantastic is a genre whose purity—unalloyed
hesitation, never resolved in favor of skepticism or credulity—results in a
transient, imperiled state: "The fantastic . . . lasts only as long as a certain
hesitation. . . . [It] leads a life full of dangers, and may evaporate at any moment. It seems to be located on the frontier of two genres, the marvelous
and the uncanny, rather than to be an autonomous genre."[84] The fantastic
as pure boundary line is a result of Todorov's emphasis on generic purity,
to the point that most texts are fantastic only for a certain duration of
reading, while the reader is still in the grips of uncertainty.

Todorov is the great contemporary cartographer of the fantastic, stak-
ing out the perimeters of contiguous but discrete genres. His approach to

the fantastic exemplifies Gledhill's keen insight into the engine of genre studies as a preoccupation with borders: "Genre is first and foremost a boundary phenomenon. Like cartographers, early genre critics sought to define fictional territories and the borders which divided, for example, western from gangster film, thriller from horror film, romantic comedy from the musical. . . . Not surprisingly, the process of establishing territories leads to border disputes."[85]

A cartographic approach to genre is driven by the linked desires for generic purity and scholarly mastery, the desire for genre study to yield a definitive, historically invariable answer to a question posed in the singular: What *is* the fantastic? In this book, I suggest that the value of genre scholarship might be related less to questions of purity and historical stasis than to the question of generic transformation. Jameson asks, for example, "What happens when plot falls into history?"[86] In a similar vein, Gledhill compellingly argues that the productivity of genre studies lies in tracing "the life of films in the social."[87]

Considered from the perspective of the fantastic as a mode of temporal translation, Todorov appears as a grammarian-cartographer of the fantastic, one who made explicit its rules, erected a taxonomy, and, from within the genre's presumption of the normativity of homogeneous time, conceptualized the fantastic's thematizing of difference. As I argue in chapter 2, ensuing critics who grafted Todorov's synchronic model onto a diachronic line (the marvelous corresponds to the pre-Enlightenment, the uncanny to the post-Enlightenment) accurately described the workings of this genre from within the hegemony of homogeneous time. What one perhaps misses in these accounts is a recognition of the genre's capacity to point outside temporal normativity, to intimate the breakdown of chronological historical time as such, to allude to the heterogeneity of times in excess of the uniform intervals measured by clock and calendar.

This book argues that the fantastic as temporal translation is a kind of *mistranslation* operating between two asymmetrically ranked codes; this is translation in the politicized context of hierarchy. One temporal code (the homogeneous time of Newtonian science and modern historical consciousness) is positioned as universal, while others (the heterogeneous times of the supernatural, the folkloric, and the popular) are devalued as merely local and archaic.[88] Although fantastic translation enables the communicative breaching of a gap, a fording of differences, it does so at the cost of misapproximation, with a host of power effects that may prop up a particular social order or signal elements of resistance, counterappropriation, or evasion.

The fantastic as a mistranslation of heterogeneous temporalities into the universalizing code of homogeneous time nonetheless hints at the violence of this translation. The fantastic narrative translates the plural times of worlds that affirm the existence of the supernatural into the secularism of modern homogeneous time. But this is, in Gayatri Spivak's parlance, "wholesale translation," a betrayal obedient to "the law of the strongest,"[89] that standard time that emerged victorious at the end of the nineteenth century. Nonetheless, this mistranslation of supernaturalism's temporal otherness into the logic of homogeneous time preserves a hint of untranslatability. The fantastic as temporal translation can, at its most uncanny, allude to the "always possible menace of a space outside language," of a world outside our familiar time. The uncanny here is that eeriness that Spivak describes in a translation that provokes a sense of "contained alterity," of a world unlike our own narrated for ourselves, in *this* time.[90] That uncanny hint of untranslatable times, that trace of containment and excess, is what I am calling *immiscible temporality*.

The adjective *immiscible*, from the Latin *miscibilis* ("that can be mixed"), means "incapable of mixing or attaining homogeneity." The immiscible pertains to the commingling of oil and water, for instance, which can never yield a true solution. Immiscibility — which, I am arguing, is both an epistemological problem disclosed by translation and an ontological property of plural times — belongs to the ontology of cinema as well. As Akira Mizuta Lippit points out, the enabling material-chemical condition of photography, the *photographic emulsion*, is by definition an immiscible mixture: "By fixing visible light and other forms of radiation on chemically treated photosensitive plates — in the first instances with a silver compound held in suspension in collodion or gelatin — the photograph holds the image between surface and atmosphere, film and air . . . Suspended between two dimensions and arrested in time, the photograph appears as an effect of the interstice opened by the immiscible mixture."[91] Chakrabarty speaks briefly of immiscibility when he calls for a recognition of untranslatability in the writing of postcolonial histories, urging us "to work out the ways these immiscible forms of recalling the past get juxtaposed in our negotiations of modern institutions."[92] Spivak also gestures at immiscibility when she writes evocatively of a translation in which the seams show, where the "selvedges of the language-textile" come partly undone, so that the translation shows signs of "fraying."[93] She is writing about a loving translation open to unraveling, a translation that cares for the source, that does not engulf it. The fantastic as temporal translation of heterogeneity into homogeneity, in contrast, is an act of containment and ideological legitimation, preserving the cachet of homogeneous time by translating alterity as anachronism. Nonetheless, the fantastic, a genre defined by its encounter with anomaly and limit, does expose the seams of temporal translation. Under the selvedge, one catches sight of a kind of fraying, an undoing of the universalizing terms of the translation.

To glimpse temporal immiscibility means to ask how the fantastic, in the seams and selvedges of its translation, gestures at temporal differences that cannot be fully homogenized. How does the fantastic disclose the untranslatability at the heart of its temporal translation, the uncanny excess lurking behind reassuring chronology, a nonincorporative remainder able to interrupt our complacency toward homogeneous time?

This book is not asking: How does the fantastic dramatize the return of surmounted modes of thought? How does this genre shore up our sense of modernity by foregrounding skepticism toward the vestiges of premodern supernaturalism?[94] Those questions remain within the purview of homogeneous time; they are premised on the belief that there are no really intransigent temporal differences in ways of inhabiting the world. To such a view, everyone, and all ways of being, shorn of unruliness, can be positioned in a single, linear unfolding toward progress. Modern time, despite being so recently invented, is so universal and so empty that it can contain all apparent differences, because in translating them, it transcends them. In contrast, if one writes from the position of temporal critique, then another view of genre appears. This study discerns in the fantastic traces of worlding immiscible to homogeneous time. Its line of inquiry insistently mines the genre for traces of temporal alterity, for refractory difference. Temporal critique does not begin by asking how the genre dramatizes the return of or encounter with surmounted modes of thought but rather: how does this genre allow immiscible worlds and times to rise to my notice? The trace of immiscibility is that kernel of protest lodged in the heart of narratives that thematize the supernatural but presume the ascendancy of homogeneous time.

Organizing Logics and Chapter Analyses

The form of temporal critique I am describing sits uneasily within established frames of reference in film and media studies. To take one example: national cinema is a productive analytical lens frequently employed in this book—as in the third chapter's discussion of spectral figures in the Philippine New Cinema and what I call the "national cinema effect" of the Hong Kong New Wave—but it cannot found the book's organizing logic. This is because national cinema, however enabling in some respects as a regulatory discursive fiction, depends on imagined coherences that are at once cultural and temporal. The fiction of a homogeneous national culture, as Andrew Higson points out, underpins the idea that a national cinema is somehow expressive of the uniqueness of the national character. (One familiar variant of this theme discovers in national cinema traditional values assailed by modernization.) Apart from the premise that a national cinema is necessarily coextensive with the territorial span of the nation-state in which certain film industries and markets are geographically located,[95] the imagined unity of a national cinema also crucially presumes a temporal unity. The fiction of a homogeneous national culture is founded on the ascendancy of homogeneous time. "Nation" depends on the fiction of calendrical coincidence, a shared, simultaneous present in which all citizens live and move, even as it is haunted by stubborn temporal paradoxes: the modernity of the nation as a political form vis-à-vis claims that the nation has always existed, merely conferring a new name for a community rooted in immemorial antiquity.[96] For these reasons, temporal critique attentive to immiscible times in cinema cannot treat "nation" and "national cinema" as unproblematized organizing categories, since, as I discuss in chapters 2 and 3, a linear national present is precisely what splinters when *aswang* and ghosts return.

Neither can this study adopt accepted definitions of genres like horror and the fantastic or assume their interchangeability. As I elaborate in chapter 2, distinctions between the natural and the supernatural, and a particular story of how the world became secular and rational (the disenchantment thesis), underpin prevailing definitions of the fantastic, but the historicity of the concepts of nature and the supernatural have been repressed in such accounts. As I explore in some detail in the coming chapters, the Todorovian fantastic, national cinema, and Asian horror—each productive analytical rubrics to a certain extent—would be of limited use as overarching organizing principles for temporal critique precisely because the coherence of each category—national, regional, or generic—starts to come apart once the self-evidence of homogeneous time erodes.

The term *genre*, as Rick Altman has shown, is really shorthand for an intersection of interests that may agree or be at cross-purposes with one another: formal conventions, audience expectations, formulas for production and marketing, and critical and historical perspectives (which are often at odds with film-industrial classifications).[97] The two genres foregrounded in this book, horror and the fantastic, are often regarded as adjacent, but their areas of convergence are perhaps less interesting than the tensions between them. The fantastic receives its fullest and most influential elaboration in European literary theory, in reference to nineteenth-century gothic texts. Horror, in contrast, shares some of the terrain of both gothic and fantastic literature but is also an immediately legible contemporary category for transnational film production and distribution (used in everything from pitching scripts to labeling films for ancillary markets), able to bring certain types of audiences to theaters and drive international adaptation and exchange. In the final chapter, I explore the way in which fantastic cinema, for all its propensity for temporal critique, has also become enmeshed in highly profitable global practices of adaptation and de-racination (to wit, from 2001 to 2005, Hollywood remade "Asian horror" at a very brisk rate). Temporal critique of and through the cinema must come to grips with the temporality—the sheer speed—of such forms of transnational generic borrowing and exchange. But this study can only undertake such a consideration precisely insofar as it does not take globalist-regionalist marketing labels such as "Asian horror cinema" at face value.

This book is not about a genre in a national cinema at a historical period (although it draws heavily on my core field of specialization, contemporary Philippine cinema, and my research and teaching on various Asian national cinemas). Rather, the various chapters and the book's overall argument unfold as an explication of the book's method, the modes and topoi of temporal critique.

I want to emphasize from the outset that critiques of homogeneous time provoked by immiscible temporal worlds are not the sole province of colonial or postcolonial histories of modernity. If I concentrate on filmic examples and historical circumstances from the Philippines, and to a lesser extent, genre films from other Asian national cinemas, it is because my relative intimacy with these screen texts and cultural coordinates enables that cognizance of translation entailed by the consideration of the fantastic as a form of temporal critique. The book's focus on the specters that suffuse Asian screen texts is emphatically not an exceptionalist claim regarding the way in which these films, and their cultural and historical contexts of emergence and circulation, are the sole, or privileged, sites of plural temporalities. As I explain in greater depth in the final chapter, claims of exceptionalism (succinctly conveyed by a *New York Times* article entitled "Why Asian Ghost Stories Are the Best") are suspect, since the differences being espoused are never differences that arise from specificity but are very often fantasies of cultural essence that serve only too well the logic of global capitalism.

One very welcome development in film and media scholarship is the small but growing area of inquiry into cinematic temporality, a body of work that rigorously engages Bergsonian duration. Books as diverse and accomplished as Marta Braun's *Picturing Time* (1992), David N. Rodowick's *Gilles Deleuze's Time Machine* (1997), and Mary Ann Doane's *The Emergence of Cinematic Time* (2002) are emblematic of an upsurge of scholarship exploring the vital stakes of temporality for film and video studies, influenced in no small measure by Deleuze's long-standing Bergsonism.

It is not that temporal critique *of and through* the cinema is obligated to grapple with Bergson's discussion of perception as cinematographic. What motivates my own return to Bergson is the fascination exerted by a critique of homogeneous time cast in unmistakably visual terms. The first chapter of this book attempts to answer the following question: *How can the cinema undertake a critique of homogeneous time when it is arguably an instantiation of it?* The first chapter contextualizes Bergson's condemnation of the cinema and his suspicion of spectatorship in light of the medium's own unforeseeable becoming. Bergson's critique of the cinematograph, published in 1907, equates cinematic temporality with the spatialized time of the apparatus itself. A century later, the cinema—a media-convergent global industry, a vast social network of film workers and spectators—comprises temporalities that can no longer be reduced to the mechanisms of camera and projector.

Each chapter attempts to wrestle with multiple analytical concerns. The first chapter, for example, delineates the dual character of the book's temporal critique: on the one hand, Bergsonism's ontological, visualist appraisal of cinema as enmeshed in homogeneous time; and on the other, a historical and postcolonial consideration of the emergence of modern time consciousness. The productive dovetailing of both modes — the ways in which cinema can both uphold and contest the racialized rhetoric of anachronism — is illustrated by a case study that closes the first chapter. Fatimah Tobing Rony's 1994 experimental video, *On Cannibalism*, a metacommentary on the fantastic premises of Merian Cooper's and Ernest Schoedsack's *King Kong* (1933), offers a powerful rejoinder to the time machine of early ethnographic cinema.

The second chapter elaborates the role of genre as a lens for temporal critique by likewise juxtaposing twinned concerns: first, a counterreading of Todorov's structuralist model of the fantastic, premised on the disenchantment thesis, and of his theory's reliance on an ideal reader immanent to the text; and second, a close look at the ways in which fantastic texts encounter noncontemporaneous audiences. If the first chapter explores an expanded understanding of *the time of cinematic production* as heterogeneous and irreducible to the cinematographic apparatus, then the second chapter insists on the *multiple temporalities of reception*, especially with regard to fantastic films that adapt supernatural narratives of centuries-old provenance.

To insist on the survival of the past — as translated by the fantastic — requires a temporally nuanced consideration of reception: the question of the *noncontemporaneous audience*. On the one hand, extraordinarily long-lived texts encounter new readers, listeners, and spectators; on the other, the "contemporary" filmgoing audience is also temporally disjoint, belonging to more than one time. Immiscible temporalities surfaced conspicuously when supernatural sightings of a winged nocturnal monster — an *aswang* in the slums of Manila, preying on the urban poor — disrupted the 1992 Philippine presidential elections. The second chapter looks closely at a Filipino horror film cycle that sought to exploit the tremendous popular currency of the aswang in the early 1990s. Though newspapers reported the proliferation of aswang accounts "during" the 1992 elections, the presumed calendrical coincidence of these two worlds — those to which aswang and modern political processes belong — came undone. The media-convergent nature of the aswang event drew on reserves of colonial and neocolonial translations of fantastic accounts, ranging from sixteenth-century Spanish missionary ethnologies of "native superstitions," to the discourse of twentieth-century anthropology, to a cynical American CIA operative's implantation of aswang rumors in a "psy-war" ruse against Filipino/a Communist guerillas in the 1950s.

The first two chapters uncover two sets of analytical problems for a temporal critique of film genre. First, *cinematic time*: the Bergsonian account of the temporality of the cinematographic apparatus, as well as the film-historical contexts subtending Bergson's encounter with the new medium in the period of its emergence. Second, the *times of reception and rearticulation* of a cross-generic, media-convergent event: the aswang as a condensation of conflicted times, worlds, and interests, colonial and neocolonial involvements as well as peasant idioms of protest.

The third chapter, on ghost films, looks at the spectral time of haunting and the affective temporality of nostalgic allegory. Through a close analysis of spectral figures in the New Cinema movements of Hong Kong and the Philippines, the chapter underscores the tensions and paradoxes that arise when ghosts become the linchpin of a historical allegory: allegory's capacity to vivify a nearly forgotten past is coupled with ghost narratives that obstinately allude to nonhistorical temporalities. In chapter 3, I consider Stanley Kwan's *Rouge* (1987) alongside Antonio "Butch" Perez's *Haplos* [Caress, 1982]. Both films invite consideration in relation to the film culture fields that constitute the New Cinema movements of Hong Kong and the Philippines. New Hong Kong Cinema and the Hong Kong New Wave are two near-synonymous film-historical namings, though periodization and the inclusion of canonical directors varies with the critic. Kwan's ghost film, *Rouge*, has been repeatedly approached through the same interpretive paradigms that founded the naming of the Hong Kong New Wave: auteurism, localism, urbanism, and a reflectionist reading of Hong Kong art cinema in relation to the 1997 handover. While *Rouge* has received wide international distribution and is consequently familiar to North American film scholars, *Haplos*, a work belonging to what has been called the Second Golden Age of Filipino cinema, has enjoyed neither national nor international commercial release on DVD formats (it was briefly available on commercial VHS release locally) and is consequently best known only among Filipino/a cinephiles with access to film archives or to limited releases in film retrospectives and on local television. Yet despite such asymmetries, these two ghost films, drawn from two roughly contemporaneous New

Cinema movements in Southeast Asia, both work to disrupt the rubric of national cinema that subtends scholarly analyses of these film movements. Specters are strongly contrarian to cultural, historical, and national homogenization; the ghost film partly undermines the culture-binding function of auteurist film movements by foregrounding spatiotemporal discrepancy. While the first two chapters consider cinematic temporality and the times of reception, the third chapter looks at fantastic disruptions of *national time* alongside the use of a sexualized politics of nostalgia that reins in the more unsettling aspects of spectral temporality. Like aswang, ghosts bring out the contours of a third issue for temporal critique: the fantastic unsettles the fantasy of a single calendrical present shared by all citizens through an *occult splintering of the national meanwhile.*

The third chapter also complicates Bergsonism's critique of homogeneous time-as-space by closely considering the question of *heterogeneous space.* In his later writing, Bergson maintained that quantifiable, detemporalized, uniform extensity is not the true character of space. Homogeneous space, like homogeneous time, is an abstraction, a necessary illusion well suited to the demands of social life and to a consideration of our possible action upon things. The ghost film, however, diverges strikingly from homogeneous space. Places have long memories; space is neither static nor solid but vibrates with both permanence and becoming. In narratives focalized through a specter's gaze on the world, space is revealed to be crosshatched with various temporal rhythms. The durative plurality of space in ghost films recalls the Bergsonian image of a kaleidoscopic, vibrational universe, one that changes ceaselessly, while the past abides.

In the fourth chapter, this study of time, cinema, and genre comes full circle by shifting methodological gears, directly addressing what scholars have called the inevitable mismatch between theoretical and industrial genres. For all its potency as a lens for temporal critique, the fantastic, unlike a proximate and sometimes overlapping genre, horror, is not a film-industrial category. In this final chapter, I identify a fourth set of analytical problems: the *times of transnational generic exchange.* Through a consideration of Takashi Shimizu's *Ju-on: The Grudge* (2003), remade as *The Grudge* (2004), and Kim Jee-woon's *A Tale of Two Sisters* (*Janghwa, Hongryeon,* 2003), whose DreamWorks remake, *The Uninvited,* was released in 2009, the chapter retraces the remarkable celerity of transnational practices of film (re-)production, distribution, and circulation. By tracking a recent film cycle—global Hollywood's remakes of "Asian horror films" (a regionalist appellation referring primarily to films originating in Japanese, South Korean, and Hong Kong film industries)—I examine both the multiple temporal rhythms of generic repetition (the practice of "remaking" films) and the *speed* with which Hollywood studios appropriate and deracinate the cinematic signatures of rival national cinemas.

In 1907, Bergson's critique of homogeneous time figuratively engaged an emergent technology, the cinematographic apparatus. A century later, temporal critique thought through the cinema is obliged to confront the reticulated character of transnational genres and global film industries, markets, and audiences. The various moments of this study move from considerations of modern time in the service of capital and empire to the velocity of global Hollywood's deracinating strategies of cultural appropriation; that is, from homogenizing temporal misprisions to cinematic translations that attempt to blunt the hard edges of cultural difference.

Political and historical film genre criticism—by which I mean, in the best sense, scholarship attuned to racial, sexual, cultural, and historical difference—has been disparaged by detractors as mere "ideological criticism" whose ultimate goal is to decide on the progressive or conservative bent of screen texts.[98] Yet temporal critique offers another way to look at the politics of genre, that is, to conduct genre studies in a manner that is attuned to complex, historically overdetermined differentials of power among diverse, noncontemporaneous audiences, without pigeonholing screen texts into either-or pronouncements of ideological persuasion.

For Jameson, genre is a *combinatoire* of three "reciprocally permutational" elements: the individual text, its intertextual horizon, and its historical conditions of emergence. This modal combinatoire enables a historical consideration of genres that avoids the pitfalls of reflectionist accounts (the problematic positing of social or historical change as directly causing, or being mirrored by, cultural texts). In contrast, to regard genre as combinatoire is to consider how contexts of emergence and circulation function as "limiting situations" or "conditions of possibility" that constrain the manner in which formal and semantic elements can be deployed and transformed.[99]

The temporal critique of the fantastic I pursue in the pages that follow can be broadly understood as tracing a combinatoire that engages temporalities of production (not just the temporality of the apparatus but also historically changing definitions of what counts as cinema), reception (the encounter with temporally fractured audiences), and distribution (genre cinemas and global capitalism), as well as fragmented fantasies of a singular national time. Throughout the work, I presume that the fantastic is not equivalent to horror, but neither is horror merely "as conservative as a Republican in a three-piece suit," a genre in which monstrosity only ever upholds the status quo.[100] Supernatural narratives, I argue, are not one thing or another, neither eclipsed nor overcome by modern homogeneous time. Rather, they stage immiscible encounters that play out in fascinating ways, as temporal polarities fail to conciliate or dissolve. The tensions that pervade this method of temporal critique echo the contradictions of the fantastic as well: a historical approach, no matter how carefully pitched, sees its limits, its necessary acknowledging of the possibility of error, in a genre that fervently contemplates an outside to historical time.[101] Throughout this book, genre is construed as a mode of cinematic repetition and return, a ghostly revenant through whose eyes we might glimpse not only vexed histories of contestation and containment but also the fantastic's recalcitrance toward homogeneous time and, perhaps, the beginnings of more ethical temporal imaginings.

CHAPTER 1

Two Modes of Temporal Critique

Bergsonism and Postcolonial Thought

The cinema is a legatee of modern homogeneous time. This argument finds its fullest elaboration in the work of Henri Bergson; nevertheless, cinema's entanglement in modern time consciousness is latent in historical accounts of cinema's emergence amid a host of technologies that ushered in profound changes in our apprehension of time and space. The cinema belongs to the shared genealogy of mechanical clock, wireless telegraph, and railroad, that is, to the tendency toward the technical denaturalization, homogenization, and standardization of time.[1]

This chapter is composed of two main sections, the first of which explores the ontological critique of homogeneous time elaborated by Bergson. Beginning with *Time and Free Will*, written in the years from 1883 to 1887 and published in 1889, Bergson offers a critique of spatialized time contemporaneous with the railroad industry's successful promulgation of standardized public time in the closing decades of the nineteenth century, a rationalized temporality that is still part of our global inheritance today. Bergson offers a *corrective* theory of time, one that disrupts our habit of thinking time in spatial, numerical terms. Bergson's corrective philosophy of time is emphatically visualist, a visualism that can be grasped in two ways: first, as a suspicion of seeing and of optical technologies. Bergson argues that in order to regard time as homogeneous, one must first visualize an empty space in which increments of time can be laid out for measurement. Similarly, Bergson repeatedly equates spectatorship—watching the clock or the moving images of a cinematograph—with our failure to apprehend the heterogeneity of true duration. We misrecognize our own duration as coinciding with the trajectory of the clock hand, or the movement-in-general of the cinematographic apparatus. Yet Bergsonian visualism, I argue in this chapter, also has a second valence, one that holds out the possibility of forging an alternate route through Bergson's suspicion of vision and the cinema.

Drawing on David N. Rodowick's discussion of Deleuze's *Cinema* books, I suggest that the visual analogues that suffuse Bergson's writing—photograph, cinematograph, spectatorship—should be construed as historical "images of thought."[2] Such figures are not merely conceptual objects of denunciation; rather, visual analogies enable Bergson's temporal critique and ground the modernity of his approach. Deleuze asks a crucial question of Bergson: has the cinema always been with us? Is it, as Bergson maintained in *Creative Evolution*, a cipher for the age-old flaws of human perception? Or, to ask Deleuze's question in a different way, could Bergson's temporal critique have been possible prior to the advent of the cinema? An alternative path through Bergson begins with a consideration of the cinema's historicity, its own unforeseeable "creative evolution." Bergson's searing treatment of the cinematograph appeared in print in 1907; a hundred years later, we feel the enduring force and relevance of that critique but are well aware that Bergson's cinema—as *reducible to the cinematographic apparatus*—is no longer our own. Our global cinema—predominantly narrative, industrialized, and media-convergent, a social institution circulating among diverse publics—is not the mechanical novelty Bergson encountered in the medium's earliest years.

The second part of this chapter traces the emergence of modern time consciousness, a reified time that for Karl Marx levels the qualitative heterogeneity of human labor into abstract labor time; homogeneous labor time lies concealed at the heart of the commodity form. Though the concept of progress, according to Reinhart Koselleck, is minted in the eighteenth century, the decisive ascendancy of a world-historical homogeneous time can be traced to late nineteenth-century and early twentieth-century transformations in the experience of time and space. In the United States, national standard time was operationalized by railway managers in 1883;

the following year, the International Meridian Conference inaugurated the worldwide adoption of twenty-four standard time zones calculated from the Greenwich Prime Meridian.

Like Benjamin, Koselleck sees progress as the defining attribute of modern historical consciousness. Both concepts—modern historical time and its central feature, progress—were fired in the furnace of global imperialism from the late fifteenth century onward. In the crucible of empire, the emerging ideology of progress was twinned with its obverse: anachronism. Again and again, colonial expansion and the European encounter with radically heterogeneous worlds were temporalized. Though intractable differences divulged by culture contact always threatened to expose the fiction of a single homogeneous present, such differences were *temporally managed* by distancing the indigene from the colonizer's present. Koselleck's "contemporaneity of the noncontemporaneous," Fabian's "denial of coevalness," and Chakrabarty's "anachronism" are names for allochronic gestures, tactics of temporal distancing that translate heterogeneity into the terms of homogeneous time.[3]

The cinema is implicated in this modern temporal elitism. As filmmaker-theorist Fatimah Tobing Rony demonstrates, early ethnographic cinema is a kind of time machine that transports the primitive to a "faraway present." This chapter closes with a discussion of Rony's experimental video *On Cannibalism*, a work that dislodges the rhetoric of anachronism by upholding the force of lived experience. Rony's video exposes the ruse of temporal exclusion and brings both the nineteenth-century ethnographic imagination and the contemporary spectator into the ambit of temporal copresence and accountability toward those encountered as savages.

By orchestrating a conversation between two ways of mounting a critique of homogeneous time—Bergson's ontological method and a postcolonial challenge to modern time consciousness—this chapter interweaves visuality, plural temporalities, a refusal of anachronism, and a recognition of untranslatability, uncovering topoi of temporal critique that will be elaborated in the rest of the study.

Part One. Bergsonism

Bergsonian Dualisms and the Corrective Philosophy of Time

In *Time and Free Will*, Bergson introduces us to the founding dualisms of his philosophy: the distinction between heterogeneous time, or pure duration, and homogeneous time, or time-as-space.

Pure duration is Bergson's name for an authentic understanding of time, a time "free from all alloy," that is, purified of spatiality. To pure duration Bergson accords the experience of our ego when it "endures," that is, when it experiences "succession without distinction," when time is lived as an organic whole, an interpermeating, indivisible, and hence, nonnumerical multiplicity. Bergson's figures for pure duration are often musical or aural: he compares pure duration to the memory of a musical phrase in which "we recall the notes of a tune melting, so to speak, into one another." Bergson contrasts to pure duration a second, habituated and erroneous, conception of time as a "homogeneous medium." Homogeneous time consists of "project[ing] time into space," inaccurately representing time as a simultaneous juxtaposition of distinct instants.[4]

As Deleuze has remarked, Bergson's method, *intuition*, is dualistic (opposing duration to space, heterogeneous to homogeneous, quality to quantity) and fixated on purity ("pure duration" or "pure heterogeneity").[5] Deleuze points out that the dualisms of Bergson's method are rooted in the realization that our experiential reality is ruled by composites. Commonsensical perception yields neither pure time nor pure space but spatialized time, the time of clock and calendar. Thus, Bergson's emphasis on purity stems from the desire to go further than surface experience in order to recover our capacity to intuit a difference in kind between the two pure tendencies, time and space.[6]

The Bergsonian philosophy of time is strongly corrective in thrust: the dualism between space and time figures spatial thinking as an "intrusion" into an authentic understanding of time as duration.[7] In Bergson's early work, his corrective theory of time proceeds largely at the cost of a devalorization of space, though at moments he acknowledges that homogeneous space is a perception, an "act of the mind," rather than the true nature of space.[8] As Deleuze notes, in *Time and Free Will* duration had been "confused with duration as a psychological experience." Bergson subsequently moved away from this early idea of duration as the sole property of the consciousness that endures (an entirely human-centered notion of time, since there would be no time without consciousness); in *Creative Evolution*, Bergson characterizes himself as crafting "a philosophy which sees in duration the very stuff of reality."[9] This evolution in Bergson's thinking forced a reassessment of space as well: no longer the mere repository of impure homogeneous time, space would be conceived as heterogeneous and authentic, just as the former human-centered duration would be recast as a generalized ontological duration.[10]

Time is at the core of all of Bergson's philosophical work, forming the heart of his method (intuition is thinking in terms of time rather than space) and grounding its founding dualisms (the dichotomy duration-vs.-space is implicated in all the other Bergsonian dualisms).[11] For Bergson, ordinary knowledge, like science, cannot adequately come to grips with real duration: "We do not think real time. But we live it, because life transcends intellect." Time cannot easily be thought, but it is always lived, felt, intuited. Here he explicitly moves away from the ground of intellect, which often ends by objectifying time, to the realms of feeling and intuition, the register of his methodology. For this reason, Bergson writes that the work of philosophy must be to interrupt our "habitual method of thought."[12] Bergson's attentiveness to ordinary perception is complemented by his rigorous fascination with science. Elizabeth Grosz writes that Bergsonism "is a conceptual reflection on the accomplishments and limits of the sciences, concerned with the production of its own unique concepts, but perhaps required by the sciences if they are to gain self-understanding." Instead of "making philosophy a form of passive acceptance of the givenness of the discourses or practices of the sciences," Bergson retains a critical, never obeisant, perspective on scientific claims. Bergsonism functions both "alongside" and "underneath the sciences, making explicit their unacknowledged commitment to philosophical and ultimately ontological concepts."[13]

Whether in our everyday practices or in Newtonian science, both of which treat time as a measurable, calculable factor, the consequences of misconstruing time as homogeneous are, for Bergson, far-reaching. The misprision of homogeneous time involves a blindness to "that heterogeneity which is the very ground of our experience";[14] in the cinematographic character of our ordinary perception, Bergson argues that this temporal misprision leads to a false apprehension of movement, as discussed in some detail below. But most crucially, for Bergson, homogeneous time must be resisted because it obfuscates our sense of our own freedom.[15] For Bergson, freedom is inextricably *durative*, both because the whole of our past informs each decision we make and because our future is completely unlike anything that has gone before, entirely insusceptible to calculation. If we liberated our conception of time from its objectification by language, science, and mathematics (one glimpses here a Bergsonian variant of the concept of reification), then we would recognize the truth of our own duration—our ceaseless transformation, our ever-new invention and becoming—as well as that of the universe.[16]

Why does Bergson declare that homogeneous time "is nothing but space, and pure duration is something different"?[17] Notions of chronology always entail a concept of space. Conceiving of ordered events in time means taking each element as a distinct unit that can be assigned a position in relation to the others, implying a spatial-conceptual juxtaposition. Hence notions of temporal order—of a chronological past, present, and future, of before, during, and after—are always spatial and quantifying in spirit.[18]

Similarly, an understanding of time as numerical, measurable, or calculable (clock or calendar time) is necessarily homogeneous and spatialized. Bergson points out that the concept of number is homogenizing by definition: to count is to regard discrete things as identical, to elide differences in order to total them up. Number, he insists, is no mere "collection of units"; it always already implies a way of thinking in homogeneous terms. "It is not enough to say that number is a collection of units; we must add that these units are identical with one another, or at least that they are assumed to be identical when they are counted."[19] For Bergson, time is multiplicity but not sum: this is because sum proposes a tally of identical elements, whereas duration is heterogeneous succession. As is evident in this discussion of time as number, Bergson's critique is not leveled only at commonsensical thinking but at scientific and mathematical accounts of time as well, which regard time as a measurable quantity.[20]

The scientific and mathematical view of homogeneous time that Bergson disputes is the legacy of Newton's clockwork universe. In 1687, Isaac Newton's classical mechanics declared time to be absolute, uniform, and mathematical. The notion of time as number founded the spatialized, measurable time to which Bergson so strongly objected, time atomized into divisible units. As Stephen Kern puts it, "No motif gives as graphic a reminder of the atomized nature of time as a clock."[21] With the special theory of relativity of 1905 and the general theory of relativity in 1916, Einstein would challenge the Newtonian view of empty, uniform time irrespective of events by proposing that time was not absolute but relative to the observer's motion; in effect, there could be no singular, absolute clock time in the universe.[22] In the sciences, the Newtonian temporal legacy has been contested by relativity theory, quantum mechanics, and thermodynamics.[23]

Bergsonian Visualism

Though the visualism inherent in Bergson's critique of homogeneous time would be fully elaborated in his critique of the cinematograph in *Creative Evolution*, Bergson's suspicion of vision as bound up with homogeneous time can be seen as early as *Time and Free Will*, where he argues that the homogeneity of number necessarily involves a visualization of space. Counting time (ever-accreting seconds, minutes, and hours tallied toward a measurement of elapsed time) presumes that "an instant of duration" "waits" in space to be counted. At least until habit allows one to perform calculations by rote, the concept of quantity requires a picturing of number, a visual representation of accretion or diminution in an ideal space. "In order that the number should go on increasing in proportion as we advance, we must retain the successive images and set them alongside each of the new units which we picture to ourselves: now, it is in space that such a juxtaposition takes place and not in pure duration."[24] Thus, for Bergson, the imagined homogeneity of quantifiable time is rooted in the spatial and the visual: "Every clear idea of number implies a visual image in space."[25] In an analog clock face or the tabular grid of a calendar, time is measured and divided into uniform segments. These units of time are spatialized as distinct and nonpermeable increments, equidistant and separated from the other, like points on a number line or links in a chain.[26]

The pervasive visualism of Bergson's philosophy of time often takes the form of equating spectatorship with a misconstrual of duration: in *Time and Free Will*, Bergson describes the deceptive experience of simultaneity that results from watching a clock or a shooting star; in *Creative Evolution*, the occlusion of authentic duration by abstract movement is exemplified by an apparatus, the cinematograph. To be clear, I use the term *visualism* in relation to Bergsonism in two ways: first, visualism designates Bergson's suspicion of vision and visual technologies as implicated in homogeneous time. Second, through an alternate route I trace through Bergson later in this chapter, visualism is also understood as enabling Bergson's critique of homogeneous time. This alternate meaning of visualism might be encapsulated in the Deleuzian "image of thought" as explained by Rodowick. Applied to Bergsonism, the suffusive visualism of his images of thought alerts us to the fact that Bergson's temporal critique is not merely *leveled at* the visual; rather, Bergson's arguments for heterogeneous temporalities are, in a very historically specific way, enabled by, and *thought through*, modern visual technologies.

In *Time and Free Will*, Bergson argues that we misrecognize our own inner duration as corresponding to clock time. He begins with a quotidian example of watching the clock: "When I follow with my eyes on the dial of a clock the movement of the hand which corresponds to the oscillations of the pendulum, I do not measure duration, as seems to be thought; I merely count simultaneities, which is very different." Bergson proceeds to disabuse readers of the misleading sense that the ticking hand of the clock we are watching corresponds directly to our own inner experience of time. It seems to us that the clock, an external object in space, "endures" as we endure, that the period of elapsed duration we have registered in our psyche is the selfsame period through which the clock, outside, in space, has likewise persisted. In *Time and Free Will*, space knows no duration, only the present or, to be precise, only simultaneity: the current position of the clock hand on the dial. "Outside of me, in space, there is never more than a single position of the hand and the pendulum, for nothing is left of the past positions."[27]

As I have noted above, a far more complex understanding of space as heterogeneous emerges in Bergson's subsequent writing (I explore the notion of heterogeneous space in chapter 3). Duration, in Bergson's later work, is no longer conceived solely as psychological (the perceiving consciousness of the spectator) but becomes ontological, the stuff of universal being: "we live the duration imminent to the whole of the universe," writes Bergson almost two decades later.[28] But in the earlier *Time and Free Will*, Bergson posits pure duration as an attribute only of the human consciousness: temporal succession is known solely to the ego that endures. In the visualist example Bergson provides, pure duration exists not for the clock on which the spectator has fixed his or her gaze but only for the spectator's consciousness: "succession exists solely for a conscious spectator who keeps the past in mind."[29] In keeping with the dualisms that found his theory, Bergson posits, outside, space without duration; inside the spectator's consciousness, duration without numerical measure. In this example, the two (pure duration within, clock time without) sync up in the *simultaneity of spectatorship*. That is, watching the clock, the spectator misrecognizes the clock as enduring while he does, and misapprehends, too, the interpenetrating succession of his own inner duration as corresponding to the discrete numerical intervals of a timepiece. (The unnamed subject of Bergson's philosophy is assumed to be masculine.)[30] The spatial position of the hand of the clock and the temporal duration of inner consciousness coincide in the spectator's perception of simultaneity: "duration thus assumes the illusory form of a homogeneous medium, and the connecting link between these two terms, space and duration, is simultaneity, which might be defined as the intersection of time and space."[31] Simultaneity in this discussion means two things. First, it refers to the incremental understanding of time as a position in space. Simultaneity is another name for what Bergson calls instants or immobilities. A spatialized misconstrual of time treats it as divisible into units, as opposed to the interpenetrating succession of true duration, which has no instants, no moments, no incremental divisions.[32] Second, simultaneity refers to the familiar-but-false sense of correspondence or synchronicity between the inner duration of consciousness and the homogeneous time of the clock.

In another discussion of spectatorship, Bergson's example of watching a shooting star, he notes that the movement of the shooting star is not identical to the space that the star traverses. The unity of the star's movement belongs to our consciousness of pure duration, whereas space yields only position, the distance that the star travels but not the unity of the event. The space traversed is a homogeneous, divisible, measurable quantity; in contrast, movement itself is pure duration, existing only in the consciousness of the spectator who watches the star's advance. Only to the spectator is there a past and a present; in external space, there is no capacity for duration, no "*comparing* the present with the past."[33] Though Bergson would later abandon this equation of duration with human psychology, in *Time and Free Will*, the wholeness of motion has no reality except in consciousness, which preserves a sense of the past.

For Bergson, the reduction of time to space and number is at work in the confusion between movement and the space traversed. Science can measure simultaneities (incremental positions on a line, the starting and end points of a movement), but it cannot reconstruct the movement itself, the qualitative changes that take place in the interval between the two points. Disregarding what happens in the intervals between two moments in time, science and mathematics (and arguably, modern modes of transport from railway travel onward) are "concerned only with the ends of the intervals and not with the intervals themselves."[34]

The instant is what Bergson calls any unit of homogeneous, abstract, divisible time. In contrast, authentic duration implies succession and continuity: not the units of measurement, the edges or "extremities" of moments, but the interval that joins one to another. The interval "connects" the present to the past; the interval is the "real persistence of the past in the present," yet it is precisely what cannot be measured, since the number line is concerned with the points on the line, not with what lies between them.[35] It follows, then, that homogeneous time, being a quantification and spatialization of duration, is actually a timeless time: "All our belief in objects, all our operations on the systems that science isolates, rest in fact on the idea that time does not bite into them."[36]

Bergson cautions that "we cannot make movement out of immobilities." When one measures movement, treating temporalized motion as though it were divisible space, one has not captured motion. Instead, one has calculated the distance spanned by the movement; that distance, however, is motionless.[37] Bergson conveys his critique of homogeneous time almost scathingly: "duration, as duration, and motion, as motion, elude the grasp of mathematics: of time everything slips through its fingers but simultaneity, and of movement everything but immobility."[38] This distinction between the duration of movement on the one hand, and quantifiable but immobile space on the other, prefigures his critique of the cinema.

When Bergson speaks of scientific thinking as a reification of duration—"instantaneous and motionless views taken at intervals along the continuity of a movement"—we already hear behind his words a photographic analogy. For Bergson, scientific and commonsensical views of time are frozen, like the photograph, into an instant, and cannot represent the duration of an interval. Human perception, being oriented to action, takes in the ceaseless becoming of life and duration only as an instantaneous photograph: "the intellect, like the senses, is limited to taking, at intervals, views that are instantaneous and by that very fact immobile of the becoming of matter." These "instantaneous views" are of those moments "plucked out of duration" that are relevant to our virtual action, but they render us "unable to perceive the true evolution, the radical becoming." Hence Bergson laments that "of becoming we perceive only states, of duration only instants, and even when we speak of duration and of becoming, it is of another thing that we are thinking. Such is the most striking of the two illusions we wish to examine. It consists in supposing that we can think the unstable by means of the stable, the moving by means of the immobile."[39]

Life, defined by Bergson as constant becoming, is condensed by human perception into a series of "forms" or "stable views." Perception registers only a fraction of the ceaseless transition of being, as when it detects the sudden movement of an object that was previously at rest. In actuality, nothing is ever at rest, since the vibrational universe moves and changes ceaselessly. (It has been noted that Bergson was "remarkably prescient" as regards subsequent discoveries in physics.)[40]

In a passage that recalls series photography and early motion studies—the immediate antecedents to Auguste and Louis Lumière's *cinématographe*—Bergson, in a fascinating turn of phrase, describes the way in which the human intellect condenses change or mobility into a "single mean image," averaging out, through a sequence of snapshots, the ceaseless flux that occurs between each frozen image:

> In reality the body is changing form at every moment; or rather, there is no form, since form is immobile and the reality is movement. What is real is the continual change of form: form is only *a snapshot view of a transition*. Therefore, here again, our perception manages to solidify into discontinuous images the fluid continuity of the real. When the successive images do not differ from each other too much, we consider them all as the *waxing and waning of a single mean image*, or as the deformation of this image in different directions. And to this mean we really allude when we speak of the essence of a thing, or of the thing itself.[41]

What we perceive as a particular state or quality is in reality already a series of interpermeating successive states, a constant change that exceeds form. Our mental faculty, though, grasps instead a sequence of instants. Each instant is an abstraction: Bergson's "single mean image" is an abridged and averaged visual instant of movement. Perception, then, condenses the movement and duration of reality into a series of instantaneous images. Instead of perceiving the infinite number of movements that compose a foot-long stride, our intellect serializes the indivisibility of movement into several frozen images so that we see only intermittently, at intervals, fragments of the stride begun, in midstep, and finally, completed. In his figurative evocation of photographic motion studies, we see foreshadowed Bergson's analogy between human perception and the cinematograph, which substitutes abstract movement and intermittent, flickering images for the heterogeneity and fluidity of real motion.[42]

Perhaps the best example of the impulses of visualization, spatialization, and measurement in instantaneous photography's depiction of homogeneous time and movement are furnished by the work of Etienne-Jules Marey, whose *chronophotographe*, developed in 1882, was a crucial precursor to the Lumière cinematograph. Marta Braun's careful framing of Marey's motion studies at the Station Physiologique in France reminds us that Marey was not primarily a photographer but rather a physiologist who used the camera as one of many scientific instruments to study and visually describe the mechanics of locomotion.[43]

In 1878, Marey's better-known Anglo-American contemporary, Eadweard Muybridge, published photographs taken by multiple cameras that sequentially reconstituted the illusion of movement. In contrast, Marey's chronophotography used a single camera to decompose human and animal movement in instantaneous exposures. Braun explains: "With a single camera that he both devised and constructed to make multiple images on a single plate and from a single point of view, he photographed movement in a way that did more than just stop time. He captured ongoing phases of movement and spread them over the photographic plate in an undulating pattern of overlapping segments."[44] In Marey's chronophotography, these exposures were then recomposed, not in sequential frames that would reproduce the illusion of successive movement but in a single image in which a succession of overlapping moments (the passage of time) were broken down for analysis, made visible in the space of a single plate. As Braun incisively puts it: "Marey was spatializing time with his camera so that he could analyze motion."[45]

What is particularly interesting here is that Marey's creation of a series of "mean" or average images to capture the succession of time not only converts, in Bergsonian terms, duration and movement into immobilities (a series of frozen instants); the passage of time also unfolds, as Braun notes, via spatial juxtaposition. For example, in Marey's chronophotographic series from 1887, *Flight of a Pelican* (figs. 12 and 13), one may, reading from left to right, attempt to retrace with one's eyes a sequence of stages in the bird's recorded flight. This is the spatialization of time and movement, the translation of successive duration into a single image of frozen time, movement equated with space traversed. Marey's chronophotography allows us to apprehend the entire arc of the movement as one simultaneous image: the prior as well as later moments of the bird's descent are juxtaposed. The temporality of movement is portrayed not as a successive unfolding in time but as a spatial simultaneity, given as an "all at onceness."[46]

We know that the history of cinematography, like that of photography, is a history of "parallel invention."[47] The cinematograph that the Lumière brothers unveiled to the public in 1895 had its technological basis in Marey's chronophotographe, with its single lens, slotted-disk shutter, and spooled light-sensitive film; but the Lumière cinematograph incorporated the crucial improvements of perforated film (first introduced in Emile Reynaud's projecting praxinoscope in 1888) and employed a tooth-and-claw mechanism, inspired by the sewing machine, to assure equidistant and uniform movement (Marey never solved the problem of equidistance).[48] The cinematograph could do what photographic motion studies could not do: reproduce the illusion of movement by projecting a series of still images at a speed sufficient to make them appear to the human mind to be moving. Thus, on celluloid, each frame is static; once projected at a certain rate, the photograms, succeeding each other, take on the semblance of moving pictures.

Bergson's well-known discussion of the cinematograph in *Creative Evolution* reads:

> In order that the pictures may be animated, there must be movement somewhere. The movement does indeed exist here; it is in the apparatus. It is because the film of the cinematograph unrolls, bringing in turn the different photographs of the scene to continue each other, that each actor of the scene recovers his mobility; he strings all his successive attitudes on the invisible movement of the film. The process then consists in extracting from all the movements peculiar to all the figures an impersonal movement abstract and simple, *movement in general*, so to speak: we put this into the apparatus, and we

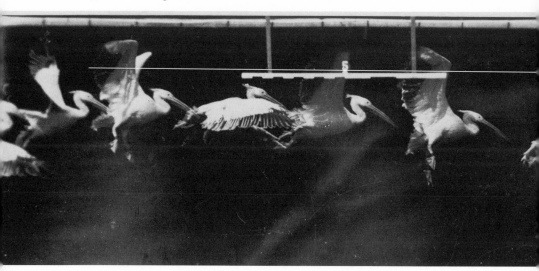

12, 13. Etienne-Jules Marey, *Vol du Pélican* (1887), Collège de France: move-ment and time, the unfolding duration of a pelican's flight, are represented as spatial simultaneity.

reconstitute the individuality of each particular movement by combining this nameless movement with the personal attitudes. Such is the contrivance of the cinematograph. And such is also that of our knowledge. Instead of attaching ourselves to the inner becoming of things, we place ourselves outside them in order to recompose their becoming artificially. We take snapshots, as it were, of the passing reality, and, as these are characteristic of the reality, we have only to string them on a becoming, abstract, uniform and invisible, situated at the back of the apparatus of knowledge, in order to imitate what there is that is characteristic in this becoming itself. Perception, intellection, language so proceed in general. Whether we would think becoming, or express it, or even perceive it, we hardly do anything else than set going a kind of cinematograph inside us. We may therefore sum up what we have been saying in the conclusion that the *mechanism of our ordinary knowledge is of a cinematographical kind.*[49]

As we know, to watch a film being projected means that we do not actually "see" uninterrupted movement. At a frame rate of twenty-four frames per second, for example, twenty-four different still images are projected each second, passing quickly and successively in front of our eyes. As Richard Barsam puts it, "As the projector moves one of these images out of the

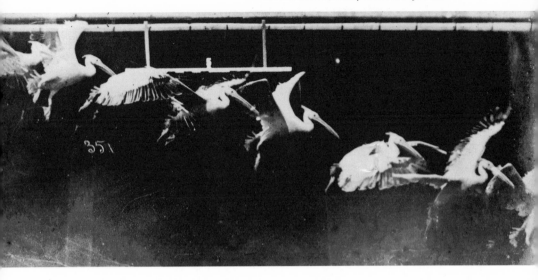

frame to bring the next one in, the screen goes dark. . . . We spend a good amount of our time in movie theaters sitting in complete darkness, facing a screen with nothing projected on it at all!"[50]

Bergson thus accurately describes the cinematograph as a machine for making apparent movement out of stillness. Concrete movement—in Bergsonian terms, duration, the very fabric of being—is absent, present only as omission. To paraphrase Bergson in the vocabulary of Christian Metz's imaginary signifier, the cinema's absent presence is movement itself, the imaginary movement that exists only as an ellipsis between photograms.[51] Rene Bruckner, drawing on Bergson, has argued that the cinema's visual regime is a "logic of disappearance," since cinematic movement "appears by disappearing" into the interval, the darkness between the frames.[52]

The Lumière cinematograph was three machines in one: a camera, a developer, and a projector. The cinematograph, as camera, drains the specificity of the actual movement of whatever is in front of the camera, "decomposing" movement into still images or film frames when it records the profilmic event. Later, as projector, the cinematograph replaces and "recomposes" the lost particularity of profilmic movement (the differences between a man sneezing, a train arriving, and a horse galloping) through the smooth and regular "movement-in-general" of the apparatus that advances the roll of film in front of the projector lamp, so as to project these still images onto a screen at a rate rapid and uniform enough to create an illusion of movement.[53] But Bergson argues that in recomposing movement by adding the homogeneous time of the cinematographic apparatus to immobile frames, one actually "miss[es] the movement," as Deleuze puts it, since "movement will always occur in the interval between the two [instants], in other words behind your back."[54]

The moving picture, therefore, is a mechanical illusion that substitutes abstract movement for the real, specific movement of pure duration. Thus the cinema, like human perception, is a mechanism of substitution: the mechanical substitution of discontinuity (a given number of frames per second) for real existential continuity. Bergson's analysis of the cinematograph in *Creative Evolution* also recalls his earlier discussion of the simultaneity of spectatorship in *Time and Free Will*. The experience of spectatorship is again faulted with fostering a mistaken view of time: watching the clockwork mechanism of the cinema, we misconstrue the temporality of the cinematograph as corresponding to pure duration. For Bergson to have said, then, that "the mechanism of ordinary knowledge is of a cinematographical kind" is to describe the flawed but useful working of human perception as follows: the "inner becoming of things" is "recomposed artificially" by a machine. This abstract, uniform, in a word, homogeneous temporal movement then replaces the concrete duration and movement of the profilmic event.

Bergson refers to "the movement, always the same, of the cinematographical film, a movement hidden in the apparatus and whose function it is to superpose the successive pictures on one another in order to imitate the movement of the real object." The cinematic apparatus is for Bergson a figure for the automatism of habituated perception. To grasp true duration and the consequent reality of our freedom, we must give up habituated thinking; Bergson calls us to "escape from the cinematographical mechanism of thought."[55] To become aware of heterogeneous duration requires a break with habituated thinking so radical as to "do violence to the mind"; for Bergson, this is precisely the work of philosophy.[56]

In his consideration of the cinematograph, Bergson implicitly advances an explanation for the unprecedented realism of the cinema: the convincing quality of its illusion is rooted in the way in which it mirrors the conditions of our own perception. That is, the cinema's verisimilitude does not originate in its faithful depiction of the real; rather, the cinema feels so realistic because of its resemblance to the character of our own perception. In this way Bergson's account of the cinema—as mirroring not reality but human perception—is surprisingly close to some of the arguments advanced in the 1970s apparatus theory of Jean-Louis Baudry.[57]

Bergson traces a through-line between the "cinematographical mechanism of the intellect," modern science, and the ancient Greek philosophy of ideas: "Modern, like ancient, science proceeds according to the cinematographical method."[58] Each resembles the other in that they subscribe to "the stable view taken of the instability of things," the conversion of movement into a fixed immobility.[59] Like the homogeneous time of the cinematograph, modern science and ancient philosophy see "extremities," not "intervals." "So the cinematographical method forces itself upon our science, as it did already on that of the ancients."[60]

Both ancient philosophy and modern science exemplify cinematographical thinking, but they differ in one important respect: "ancient science thinks it knows its object sufficiently when it has noted of it some privileged moments, whereas modern science considers the object at any moment whatever."[61] Ancient philosophy selects the "privileged," "quintessential" moment; modern science, however, regards time as infinitely and indefinitely divisible: "We can, we ought to, divide it as we please. All moments count. None has the right to set itself up as a moment that represents or dominates the others."[62] The representative or privileged moment of ancient philosophy is thus replaced by a modern ethos of the quotidian moment. The distinction between the modern and the ancient view of time is for Bergson "a difference of degree rather than kind." Modern science (exemplified here by photography) has achieved "higher precision": "It is the same cinematographical mechanism in both cases, but it reaches a precision in the second that it cannot have in the first."[63]

That Bergson posits an essential homology between the modern apparatus of the cinematograph and ancient philosophy is not too surprising given that his argument is not historical but figurative, an analysis that considers the motion picture apparatus as metaphorical "mental cinema," a way of thinking time that predates the historical emergence of the medium as such.[64] Bergson uses the cinematograph as a figure for the universal, natural character of human intellection. Yet his condemnation of the cinematograph remains unsettling because it runs so conspicuously against the grain of other aspects of his philosophy. Arguably, the ways in which Bergsonism enriches our understanding of the cinema can take other routes, paths that consider cinema in terms of its own "creative evolution."

Has the Cinema Always Been with Us?
Alternate Paths through Bergson

In his first Bergsonian commentary in *Cinema 1: The Movement-Image*, Deleuze notes that in characterizing the cinema's reliance on any-instant-whatever, Bergson has actually "forcefully demonstrated" the modernity of the cinema. But Bergson then "hesitates between two paths." The first, as we have seen, judges the cinema to be essentially the same as both ancient philosophy and natural perception. But Deleuze also discerns a second path in Bergson's analysis, which suggests that the cinema is an "essential factor" in a new, modern philosophy, that it "has a role to play in the birth of this new thought, this new way of thinking." Thus there are two routes through Bergson's analysis of the cinema: the first, explicit in Bergson's discussion, recasts the cinema in the image of the eternal, as "the perfected apparatus of the oldest illusion." But Deleuze here gestures at a second path that is only implicit in Bergson's analysis, though it actually represents the more properly Bergsonian position of time as a ceaseless process of invention. This alternate route through Bergson sees what is modern about the cinema as "the organ for perfecting the new."[65]

Deleuze astutely remarks that "it is strange that Bergson should give the oldest illusion such a modern and recent name."[66] For Bergson, the "cinematographic mechanism of thought" encompasses not only the false movement of the motion picture apparatus but also the misconceptions of natural human perception common to both modern science and ancient Greek philosophy. In so doing, Deleuze rightly points out, Bergson, who challenged us to think the new rather than the eternal, ends by denying what is new about the cinema. "Does this mean that for Bergson the cinema is only the projection, the reproduction of a constant, universal illusion? As though we had always had cinema without realizing it?"[67]

Has the cinema always been with us? Deleuze's apposite question lays bare the limits of Bergson's cinematographic argument. To maintain that we have always had the cinema runs counter to Bergson's own emphatic adherence to newness, invention, and becoming. To suppose that the cinema always already belonged to the universal human psyche and to the ancients is to subscribe to another version of the "all is given" thesis. This contradiction is acknowledged in Deleuze's Bergsonian protest against Bergson himself: "The essence of a thing never appears at the outset, but in the middle, in the course of its development, when its strength is assured. Having transformed philosophy by positing the question of the 'new' instead of that of eternity (how are the production and appearance of something new possible?), Bergson knew this better than anyone."[68] In *Creative Evolution*, Bergson argued that newness and becoming reveal the limits of ready-made concepts: "The idea that for a new object we might have to create a new concept, perhaps a new method of thinking, is deeply repugnant to us. The history of philosophy is there, however, and shows us the eternal conflict of systems, the impossibility of satisfactorily getting the real into the ready-made garments of our ready-made concepts, the necessity of making to measure."[69] This is the Bergsonian path not taken by Bergson himself: a temporal critique made to the measure of cinema in its own unforeseeable becoming.

The course Deleuze charts out of Bergson's universalizing condemnation of the cinema takes the form of restoring its historicity. Deleuze posits that the cinema, in Bergsonian terms, must also be seen as a becoming: a transformation from the static shot to mobile camera and montage.[70] In short, Deleuze reminds us that Bergson's cinema, in those years immediately preceding *Creative Evolution*'s first publication in France in 1907, is no longer our own.

Thus, in considering Bergson's deprecation of the cinema, one notes that two alternatives are possible. On the one hand, there is the path that reveals the central irony that Deleuze identifies: Bergson, the radical philosopher of the new, who insisted that repetition is impossible if time is invention, falls victim to the very illusion he critiques, in which the new is mistaken for the same old thing. The cinema in its irreducible historicity, having transformed prior ways of thinking and seeing, appears to Bergson to be a reiteration of the age-old illusion of natural perception.

A second path through Bergson is also possible, one that recognizes that several of Bergson's own precepts are ratified, in hindsight, by his position on the cinema. *Creative Evolution*, read today, bears (to use Bergson's own buccal metaphor for the mark of temporality) the bite of history's tooth: it was written at that moment in cinema's infancy when it was regarded primarily as an apparatus, a technical achievement. The cinema for Bergson is the cinematograph: a scientific apparatus for the reproduction of motion. But that solely machinic cinema is no longer our own. For us the cinema is not one thing but many: a globalized, heterogeneous set of industrial as well as amateur practices—inviting questions of history, ideology, cultural value, audiences, and genres—as well as synergistic relationships to new technologies. Mary Ann Doane cautions against the reduction of cinematic temporality to the time of the apparatus; our notion of cinematic time must remain supple enough to consider the distinct temporalities of reception and narration.[71] The ways in which cinema has "creatively evolved" are very much in keeping with Bergson's emphasis on duration as the production of the unforeseeably new. Thus we might speculate that, without being able to anticipate what cinema would become, Bergsonism in this alternate account already expected the cinema not to repeat itself, to become, in the course of time, something other.

Our own globalized and remediated cinema, a ubiquitous presence in popular culture and everyday life, can no longer be for us a site of defamiliarization that readily enables a critique of habituated thinking. In contrast, at the time of Bergson's writing, the cinema's revelatory power, its equidistant, serially exposed and projected photograms, its instants and intervals, were so newly discovered, so modern, that the cinema could in fact offer Bergson a provocative image of thought, a figure through which issues are conceptualized and worked out. Despite Bergson's explicit aversion to the cinema in *Creative Evolution*, his philosophy of duration in *Matter and Memory* (1896) reveals a pervasive and productive visualism. His evocative figures for ontological duration, human perception, and freedom—of a luminous, reflective universe, of matter as image, of the photograph snapped at all points in space, and his thinking through the cinematograph—are clearly inseparable from visual technologies. Such figures shape Bergson's philosophical problematic.[72] There is, in short, no Bergsonism without the contemporaneous optical technologies through which its temporal critique is thought through. As Deleuze notes, "Bergson is startlingly ahead of his time: it is the universe as cinema itself, as metacinema."[73]

Read as a historically specific intervention on temporality in relation to visual technologies, one could argue that Bergson's philosophy would not have been possible a hundred years earlier, without the cinema.[74] The visual technologies that were Bergson's contemporaries—photography and the cinematograph of his day—were thought-figures, critical engines that made possible the thinking through of a powerful critique of homogeneous time. This is very much consistent with Vivian Sobchack's discussion of figures as shaping and transforming the very problematic they embody;[75] here the cinematograph as figure, a pivotal Bergsonian image of thought, is part and parcel of the historical specificity of Bergson's philosophy.

Cinema/Cinematograph: 1907

As noted above, Bergson's critique of the cinema was first published in France in 1907. The years in which Bergson was writing *Creative Evolution* thus belong to the earliest years of the new medium, what historians of early cinema have called the period of cinema's emergence.

This period witnessed the unveiling and refinement not only of a machine that generates an illusion of movement but, as Charles Musser elaborates in *The Emergence of Cinema: The American Screen to 1907*, the rise of a distinct nexus of modes of reception, representation, and production. From 1895 to 1907, American audiences were rarely presented with a story they did not already know in advance; in order to screen familiar material, the cinema in the era of its inception borrowed heavily from other media—theater, novels and short stories, newspapers, popular music, and folklore. This mode of reception is characterized by the importance of the exhibitor in framing cinematic meaning, whether in the form of live narration, a lecture presentation, or additional sound. In the earliest years of the medium's development, the cinema's representational strategies were, as Musser puts it, "presentational" in style, highly "indicative," and somewhat restricted.[76] In the presentational style, cinematic temporality was "non-linear" rather than "verisimilar," often employing overlapping, repetitious editing and exceedingly compressed offscreen time. Parallel editing and linear continuity would develop only in ensuing years.[77]

In France, the four years that followed the first public screening of the Lumière cinematograph in December 1895 have been characterized by Richard Abel as a period in which the "technological novelty of the cinema apparatus held sway."[78] Two of the major companies involved in the cinematograph business in this volatile period of emergence, Lumière and Gaumont, were chiefly concerned with exploring the "technological possibilities of cinema."[79] In retrospect, Bergson's appraisal of the cinema seems to belong to this earliest period of its inception, between 1896 and 1902, when the cinema was above all a novel apparatus, the cinematograph. Yet in the next five years the cinema would rapidly become far more than an apparatus for simulating the illusion of movement. From 1904 to 1907, the cinema, which had developed from series photography's reproduction and analysis of motion, developed narrative forms (with the French firm Pathé-Frères at the forefront of the production of story films), as authorship and editorial control of films slipped from the hands of exhibitors to those of production companies. By 1907, when Bergson's *Creative Evolution* first appeared in print, the cinema, both in France and in the United States, was no longer only the cinematographic apparatus: it had become an industry.

Likewise, in the American context, 1907 is in many ways a historically significant year, since it lies on the cusp of two formative periods in early cinema. First, it marks the end of the period of cinema's inception, stretching from 1895 to 1907; the latter is a year of significant organizational transformations in the U.S. film industry, such as the formation of patent-based alliances that preceded the founding of the Motion Picture Patents Company in 1908.[80] Second, 1907 immediately precedes the beginning of what has been called, in the U.S. context, early cinema's "transitional period," from 1908 to 1917.[81] Both eras were marked by vigorous, often volatile, transformations in every aspect of film: as mode of production, as formal system, and as a set of exhibition and consumption practices.

The intense pace of such transformations can be seen in the French context as well. In 1900 the Pathé-Frères cinema division was run on an artisanal workshop model. By 1906 to 1907 it was, as Abel puts it, an "image factory," producing films in a "director-unit" system employing twelve hundred mostly female workers in its cinema division and producing more than forty thousand meters of positive film stock daily. The story of Pathé-Frères in the years immediately preceding 1907 is the story of that company's dominance not only in the French film industry but worldwide, spearheading important changes in the distribution and exhibition sectors.[82] This was the period of Pathé's confident global advance: in October 1906, Pathé accounted for a third to a half of the lucrative American nickelodeon market; it had agencies in European cities (Russia was a particularly important market for its exports), and in distant regions opened up by imperialism: India, Southeast Asia, Central and South America, and Africa, confirming Abel's insight that the development of national film industries in the early cinema period is inextricable from the world-economic context of European and U.S. colonial conquests.[83] In ensuing years, 1907 to 1914, the French film industry's dominance in international markets was challenged and ultimately dislodged by the United States, while in France itself, the rapid proliferation of permanent cinemas shifted the primary sites of film exhibition away from fairgrounds, enabling cinema to replace café-concerts as the "most popular urban spectacle."[84] Along the way, such industrializing tendencies marginalized pioneers such as Georges Méliès, whose trick films and roots in magical theater defined an earlier age. Méliès's company, Star-Films, peaked in 1903 and 1904; a decade later, a nearly bankrupt Méliès took his leave of the industry.[85] In the period covered by Abel's book, *The Ciné Goes to Town: French Cinema 1896–1914*, then, the cinema metamorphosed from apparatus to global industry, from one of many novel public entertainments to an increasingly legitimized social institution shaping mass culture in France and across the rest of the globe.

In retrospect, what is most striking about Bergson's view of cinema as apparatus is not that it yields no glimpse into aesthetic and industrial transformations in cinema contemporaneous with his writing. Rather, what stands out is his universalizing approach to cinema as a figure for natural mental faculties. Despite its emphasis on cinema as a model for individual psychic life, Bergson's philosophy is curiously subjectless in the sense that this subject, being universal, remains undifferentiated and unmarked. Reading his analysis of the cinematograph today, with the luxury of hindsight and a wealth of film-historical scholarship, one is struck by how much at odds Bergson's universalizing approach was with the powerful social and collective cast of the new medium of his day. Historians of early American cinema tell us that 1905 to 1907, the early nickelodeon era, saw the rise of both "a new kind of specialized spectator, the moviegoer," and working-class audiences that included a significant number of women and youths. Such audiences, far from conforming to the subjectless, de facto masculine spectator imagined by Bergson's analysis, were very much transected by social differences (class, gender, race, profession, generation) and were drawn to the new sexual and class egalitarianism of filmgoing, which had become an enormously popular and affordable amusement. As Musser puts it, "The cinema was rapidly becoming a site of mass entertainment and mass consumption."[86] Whether greeted by pleasure or consternation, cinema in the period immediately preceding the publication of *Creative Evolution* was no solitary experience of spectatorship. It was undeniably becoming a significant force in public, collective forms of everyday life.

Temporal Multiplicity

In *Matter and Memory*, spectatorship and visualism open onto radical temporal plurality. In another visual object lesson, Bergson cites the multiple temporalities at work in the everyday experience of looking at a color. To our eyes it takes but a moment to see the color red. Yet in reality red light, which possesses the longest wavelength in the color spectrum, completes 400 billion successive vibrations per second. Given the limits—or more accurately, the different temporal rhythm—of human perception, it would take us more than 250 centuries to pick out these successive vibrations. Bergson adduces: "We must distinguish here between our own duration and time in general."[87] In contrast to the human-centered duration of *Time and Free Will*, and the limited temporal pluralism of *Duration and Simultaneity*, in *Matter and Memory*, everything endures, and the universe is composed of a multiplicity of coexistent but noncoinciding times, a radical temporal heterogeneity. The time of spectatorship (a fraction of a second to take in a color or an image) may not always coincide with the temporal rhythm of the object of our gaze. Human perception contracts an image that possesses a much different duration into the terms of our own temporality. We "seize," in perception, something that "outruns perception itself."[88] There is therefore no one empty homogeneous time but an overabundance of heterogeneous temporal rhythms.

In another striking example of temporal multiplicity from *Creative Evolution*, Bergson writes about having to wait for sugar to melt in a glass of water:

> If I want to mix a glass of sugar and water, I must, willy nilly, wait until the sugar melts. This little fact is big with meaning. For here the time I have to wait is not that mathematical time which would apply equally well to the entire history of the material world, even if that history were spread out instantaneously

in space. It coincides with my impatience, that is to say, with a certain portion of my own duration, which I cannot protract or contract as I like. It is no longer something *thought*, it is something *lived*.[89]

This lived time is one in which all elements of the whole have changed—I have aged, the sugar has dissolved into the water, things in the world have endured with me. The passage serves as a key illustration of Bergsonian duration as belonging to the whole of the universe, of the universe itself as an open, relational whole, in Deleuze's words, "neither given nor giveable," in contrast to teleological or determinist conceptions of time.[90] Thus, becoming for Bergson is incapable of repetition and is always new. This newness means that the future is entirely open, impossible to anticipate or foresee. For Bergson, this absolutely unforeseen future, if only we could become aware of it, is freedom's purview.[91]

In *Cinema 1*, Deleuze writes that duration, the ever-changing, unforeseeable openness of the whole of relations, is the meaning of Bergson's famous example of waiting for sugar to melt. Change is not the sole property of the one who waits impatiently for the sugar to dissolve. What changes or endures through the duration of waiting is not only the one who waits but everything.[92]

Moreover, this apparently prosaic example of waiting impatiently for sugar to dissolve in water illuminates yet another facet of our temporal being, represented in this case as the duration of our impatience. Impatience is, by definition, one's unwillingness to endure, yet in Bergson's example one endures still. For Deleuze, while we wait impatiently, we become (somewhat painfully) aware not only of our duration but of the multiple durations outside of our own: "my own duration, such as I live it in the impatience of waiting, for example, serves to reveal other durations that beat to other rhythms, that differ in kind from mine."[93] The deepest significance of Bergson's sugared water is that one's duration, when authentically recognized, opens up to other temporalities "above and below" one's own. Intuition is the name for the Bergsonian method that allows my duration to come into view and for other durations, whose rhythms are entirely different from mine, to rise to my notice.

Yet temporal multiplicity is not limited, in Bergson, to the plural temporal rhythms that coexist in the "present" that is seemingly shared by the sugar, the water, and the one who waits. In *Matter and Memory*, the temporality of perception already at work in the various examples considered thus far (watching the clock, a shooting star, the cinematograph, sugar dissolving) is a perception fully immersed in memory. This thread in Bergson's thinking represents his most decisive challenge to chronological, homogeneous time, disclosing a temporal heterogeneity characterized by the coexistence of past and present.

Bergson puts it lyrically: "There is no perception which is not full of memories." The rapidity of human perception relies on our memories to "supplant our actual perceptions" with the already-known or already-seen.[94] Recollection allows us to immediately recognize things, but it does so at the cost of illusion or misreading. Thus perception for Bergson is a question of time, a cognizance of the past that bears on the speed of cognition in the present. Perception always occupies duration, since memory aids perception by prolonging one moment into another. All immediate perception is "cloaked" with memory, "contracting a number of external moments (recollection) into a single internal moment (perception)." The subjective cast of our perception is owing to the fact that perceiving is always intertwined with remembering; consciousness always involves a contraction of duration.[95]

Bergson defines memory as "the survival of past images" that "constantly mingle with our perception of the present." Memory temporalizes perception by "at every moment complet[ing] our present experience, enriching it with experience already acquired; and, as the latter is ever increasing, it must end by covering up and submerging the former."[96] Memory overwhelms the experience of the present, thus lending perception its subjectivity. Thus for Bergson nothing in perception is instantaneous; all is linked to the work of memory. "Perception ends by being merely an occasion for remembering."[97] Choice, the unforeseeable exercise of our free will, is underpinned by memory. In this way freedom is linked to duration, and through our choices, the future is linked to the past. In short, Bergson temporalizes freedom: the greater and lesser intensities of memory ("to retain in an ever higher degree the past in order to influence ever more deeply the future") correspond to greater and lesser degrees of freedom; freedom consists in bringing duration, a consciousness of one's own becoming, to bear on choice.[98]

Part Two. Postcolonial Critiques of
Modern Time Consciousness

> My way of getting out of it [the scholasticism of postwar French academic
> philosophy] at that time, was, I really think, to conceive of the history of
> philosophy as a kind of buggery or, what comes to the same thing, immacu-
> late conception. I imagined myself getting onto the back of an author, and
> giving him a child, which would be his and which would at the same time be
> a monster. It is very important that it should be his child, because the author
> actually had to say everything that I made him say. But it also had to be a
> monster because it was necessary to go through all kinds of decenterings,
> slips, break ins, secret emissions, which I really enjoyed. My book on Berg-
> son seems to me a classic case of this.   DELEUZE, *Dialogues*

In these arresting, witty remarks to Claire Parnet, Deleuze describes,
with enormous wit, his engagement with Bergson in terms both sacred
and queerly profane. In language at once droll, sexualized, and self-astute,
Deleuze describes a kind of freeing, passionate engagement with those
thinkers that one is drawn to yet differs with. Significantly, this engagement does not come under the sign of a devotee's fidelity but is depicted
as a creative monstrosity: it is at once an offshoot of a close attentiveness
to the thinker one engages ("the author actually had to say everything that
I made him say") and also a prodigy issuing from rupture and diremption
("all kinds of decenterings, slips, break ins, secret emissions"). Rodowick
adverts to this same passage to explain his own approach to Deleuze: "Reading philosophy means less understanding or interpreting what the 'mas-
ters' mean than producing something new out of an encounter motivated
equally by Eros and aggressivity. There is no better reason to read than to
discover an intellectual desire and to create something new from it."[99]

My path through Bergson is likewise not directed by an ideal of faithfulness but rather by a desire to work through what it is that fascinates
me about his writings, even where I may have strong differences with his
positions. The productive encounter I seek to stage between Bergson's critique of homogeneous time (situated on the scale of the universal, natural
faculties of human consciousness) and anticolonial critiques of homogeneous time (implicated in questions of power, legitimation, and exclusion)
could find no ready footing in a faithful exegesis of Bergsonism. Thus what

I hope might result is a play of departure and convergence that is, in the Deleuzian sense, "monstrous," inviting the volatility of the new.

For Bergson, we are our own lifework, the "artisans" of the temporality of our lives, "creating ourselves continually."[100] The Bergsonian themes of freedom, duration, and self-creation belong to a theory of the self—of the human being as a corporeal agent exercising freedom—that is not a theory of subjectivity, if we mean by the latter Michel Foucault's notion of a self constrained as well as produced by disciplinary power, or Judith Butler's mechanisms, at once violating and enabling, of subjectivation. Rather, to become free, in Bergson's account, one must radicalize one's understanding of time in order to grasp more consciously the ways in which duration always bears on the present and the future. Memory leans over the exercise of our freedom, but at the same time, this freedom inclines toward a future that is radically indeterminate, unanticipated, unforeseen. For all its beauty and intuitive force, Bergsonism gives us a philosophy of temporalized freedom, not a theory of social power.

In the most general sense, one learns from Deleuze how a historical approach to Bergson—the cinema as an era's image of thought, the modernity of cinema's any-instants-whatever—can be productively incorporated into Bergson's philosophy. In this second part of the chapter, I orchestrate a historical consideration of certain Bergsonian themes (the critique of homogeneous, quantifiable time-as space, the upholding of an open future, temporal multiplicity, and untranslatability) to point up the ways in which history writing has itself been implicated in homogeneous time. Finally, this chapter ends by opening onto cinematic means of keeping temporal heterogeneity in view. The consideration of these two modes of temporal critique, the visual-ontological and the historical-postcolonial, attempts to uncover a critical rubric with which to seize on those occasions in the cinema in which the dominance of homogeneous time is unsettled.

The Emergence of Modern Time Consciousness

The homogeneous time Bergson railed against, a time that "answers better the requirements of social life," is what Thomas Luckmann refers to as "socially objectivated time." Social life requires a continual realignment of our inner times with abstract categories of public time. Luckmann refers to this continual "adjustment" between the self and the social as "synchronization," the work of modulating inner time to the socially constituted temporality that is superimposed on it. Socially constituted time is abstract and anonymous; it is not so much generated from our own interactions with others but is "ready-made" in the sense that this time appears to "have a degree of social objectivity." Ready-made, standard time allows disparate events to become equivalent and comparable by synchronizing them in accordance with the "universal" time of clock and calendar. This standard, public, objectivated time has become so dominant that it has entered into the "social stock of knowledge."[101]

Historians remind us that this socially transmitted, homogeneous time has not always been universal, though the dominance of modern time consciousness is now so complete that it appears to us in the guise of a ready-made temporality. Its practical utility in social life—synchronization at the cost of homogenization—was, in a variety of ways, strongly resisted, as we will see below. Over the course of several hundred years, from the late thirteenth century to the nineteenth, modern time consciousness—today's planetary, standardized, homogeneous time—was very slowly emplaced.

In Bergsonism, as well as in accounts of the emergence of modern time consciousness, the rule of homogeneous temporality is characterized as abstract, objectified, quantifiable, and exchangeable, uniting the globe in synchronicity and equivalency. In such descriptions we already glimpse the Marxist theory of reification. The dualisms that structure the critique of homogeneous time—heterogeneity and homogeneity, quality and quantity, concrete and abstract—recall Marx's account of the commodity as the abstraction of qualitatively different forms of human labor. It is "human labour in the abstract" that gives the commodity its exchange value, and this value is quantified temporally as labor time: "The quantity of labour, however, is measured by its duration, and labour-time in its turn finds its standard in weeks, days, and hours." This labor time, as Marx demonstrates, is not that of the individual worker but is an average, uniform, socially necessary time: "The labour-time socially necessary is that required to produce an article under the normal conditions of production, and with the average degree of skill and intensity prevalent at the time."[102] The abstract time that renders the heterogeneity of concrete labor equivalent, suppressing differences in use value as well as qualitative differences in human labor, is unveiled by Marx as the secret at the heart of the commodity: "The determination of the magnitude of value by labour-time is therefore a secret, hidden under the apparent fluctuations in the relative values of commodities."[103]

In their discussion of "socially necessary labour time," Michael Neary and Glenn Rikowski point out that the capitalist drive to increase surplus value underpins the pervasive sense of time pressure in modern life, what they describe as the tyrannical "speed of life in capitalist society."[104] Doane has noted that that, at the close of the nineteenth century, "modernity was perceived as a temporal demand" across the spheres of visual culture, philosophy, literature, and everyday life.[105] In a related vein, Neary and Rikowski interpret this modern temporal pressure as the "social form of time in capitalist society," rooted in the regulation of social labor as social time: "As the pressure is constantly to expand the amount of surplus value being extracted, there is corresponding pressure to reduce the amount of socially necessary labour time in the production of commodities . . . Socially necessary labour time becomes the measure of the speed of human activity: *the speed of life.*"[106]

Homogeneous time, as Marxist critique underscores, is a labor relationship, one that involves not only production but also consumption and pervasive reification under capitalism. In his classic treatment of labor and time-discipline, E. P. Thompson writes, "Time is the employer's money"; Jean Baudrillard conceptualizes the commodity as crystallized time; and in different ways, they, like Theodor Adorno, trace the subjugation or growing impossibility of "free" or leisure time.[107]

In "Reification and the Consciousness of the Proletariat" (1923), Georg Lukács writes that the commodity structure pervading every aspect of social life must be resisted because it subordinates human beings to machines and results in a profound alienation of self from self, and of self from others: "a relation between people takes on the character of a thing."[108] In Marxism, the alienation of the worker from the possibility of an autonomous control of time is unveiled as a characteristic feature of capitalism. In an argument that recalls Bergson's critique, Lukács declares that the commodity structure "reduces space and time to a common denominator and degrades time to the dimension of space." Lukács quotes Marx's acrid assessment of the worker as entirely effaced by abstract labor time, by the rule of the clock: "the pendulum of the clock has become as accurate a measure of the relative activity of two workers as it is of the speed of two locomotives. Therefore, we should not say that one man's hour is worth another man's hour, but rather that one man during an hour is worth just as much as another man during an hour. Time is everything, man is nothing; he is at most an incarnation of time."[109]

These remarks are from Marx's *The Poverty of Philosophy*, written in 1847; the prior discussion of the commodity is taken from the first volume of *Capital*, written in 1867. Likewise, Bergson began writing *Time and Free Will* in 1883, the very year in which American railroad managers instituted a standard public time. Both Bergson's temporal critique and Marx's treatment of clock and locomotive as epitomizing a temporal regime subservient to capital were penned in the very era in which the linked technologies of mechanical clock, railway travel, astronomy, and telegraphy came together in the institution of a globally standardized modern time. Despite the universalizing, ahistorical cast of Bergson's philosophy of time, then, it remains important to appreciate the historical position of Bergsonism as an impassioned response to what Doane calls "the pressure to rethink temporality" in the face of a pervasive rationalization and abstraction of time in modern life.[110]

Several scholars have described the complex transformations in concepts of time and space that took place from the late eighteenth century to the early twentieth. On local, national, and global scales, discrepant notions of time and space were changing as railroads, telegraphy, telephony, automobiles, electricity, and, not least, the cinema became ubiquitous in modern life. Technology, as we will see throughout this study, bears crucially on notions of time and space, though it is never alone in shaping them.

What we learn from historians of modern temporality is that homogeneous time is far from natural. The mechanical clock emerged in the late thirteenth century, but it was not until the rapidly modernizing nineteenth century that a single standard time would be promulgated throughout the world. First called forth in the medieval period by the needs of an orderly life of religious work and devotion, and later disseminated through the collusion of capitalist interest and technological advance in the nineteenth century, the institutionalization of modern, homogeneous time as we know it was a gradual, centuries-long shift. Tremendous effort was required to unseat the cacophony of durations that confronted homogeneous time. But once installed, clock time becomes, as we have seen, naturalized, invisible, expected.

To take one nationally circumscribed example: in the United States, between the 1830s and the 1880s, astronomical time, via telegraphed time signals from observatories, came to define public time. Slowly, more individuated chronometric modes, such as the sundial and the almanac, declined. Astronomically determined, telegraphically disseminated time had a wide range of applications: it allowed the determination of longitude for maritime navigation; enabled colonial expansion in the surveying of territories and the resolution of boundary disputes; and provided uniform times by which the workings of industry, and in particular, railway travel would become rationalized.[111] A National Observatory was established in 1834, and many others followed in that decade. By the 1840s, several railroad companies looked to astronomers for standardized time signals communicated via telegraph; the regional time standard for New England rail, for example, was supplied by the Harvard College Observatory.[112]

In *Keeping Watch: A History of American Time* Michael O'Malley documents the collusion of science, capital, and nation in the promulgation of standard time. O'Malley argues that the felt need for a "scientific public time" was primarily rooted in the drive for American commercial expansion; unifying a spatially vast nation, standardized time allowed for the synchronization of markets, news and postal systems, travelers, and consumers. Railway travel best exemplified the business interest in a synchronized exchange of goods and information and the technological means of accomplishing such synchronicity by rapidly traversing distance.[113]

As Wolfgang Schivelbusch has shown, the mechanization of travel in the industrial age—enabled by the technical development of the steam engine in the eighteenth century—ushered in profound changes in the modern perception of space and time. First, denaturalization: the substitution of locomotive engine for animal power represents a "capitalist emancipation from the limits of organic nature," as well as an erosion of the previously mimetic relationship between nature, space, and human travel: "ships drift with water and wind currents, overland motion follows the natural irregularities of the landscape and is determined by the physical powers of the draft animals." In contrast, mechanized travel is homogenizing in the Bergsonian sense: "the mechanical motion generated by steam power is characterized by regularity, uniformity, unlimited duration and acceleration," writes Schivelbusch.[114] The starkest account of the locomotive's constitutive role in the shaping of modern time consciousness emerges in Schivelbusch's well-known discussion of the nineteenth-century topos of the annihilation of time and space:

Steam power, inexhaustible and capable of infinite acceleration, reverses the relationship between recalcitrant nature (i.e., spatial distance) and locomotive engine. Nature (i.e., spatial distance), which had caused the animal "locomotive engines" to strain themselves to exhaustion, now succumbs to the new mechanical locomotive engine of the railroad that, in a frequently used metaphor, "shoots right through like a bullet." "Annihilation of time and space" is the *topos* which the early nineteenth century uses to describe the new situation into which the railroad places natural space after depriving it of its hitherto absolute powers. Motion is no longer dependent on the conditions of natural space, but on a mechanical power that creates its own new spatiality.[115]

This new spatiality is linked to speed, a temporal diminution that is registered as a shrinkage or overcoming of space. Actual distances are not annihilated; rather, prior experiential or perceptual paradigms relating time and space to human potentiality are eroded. The topos of travel yokes time and space in homogenizing terms, especially in the measurement of spatial distance as travel time, with important consequences for the synchronization of industries and markets, a reconfiguring of the national imaginary around both a new proximity to the metropolitan center and the rise of suburbanization.[116] The railroad also actualized the homogeneous space of Newtonian mathematics, approximating the Newtonian idea of a frictionless road—smooth, hard, level, and straight. Such a road made it difficult for animal hooves to achieve traction but was well suited to overcoming the friction between wheel and road, machine surface and irregular terrain.[117]

Yet the topos of the annihilation of time and space was haunted by heterogeneity. In the 1850s, proponents of standard time noted that the swift advance of the locomotive, in conquering space, repeatedly ran up against the problems of local time—that is, with the problem of heterogeneous, place-bound temporalities, as well as with disparate modes of timekeeping among the various railroad and steamship lines.[118] Stephen Kern points out that "around 1870, if a traveler from Washington to San Francisco set his watch in every town he passed through, he would set it over two hundred times."[119]

As such remarks illuminate, the much-touted overcoming of space by modern technologies led to trouble with heterogeneous time. Paradoxically, the modern experience of speed and simultaneity inaugurated by the telegraph, which communicated information instantaneously and lent new immediacy to "current events" unfolding far away, heightened the per-

ception of chaotic local times, of conspicuous gaps between local heterogeneity and the rationalized synchronicity sought by regional standards.
For instance, the completion of the transnational railroad in Utah in 1869
was simultaneously signaled by telegraph to various American cities — but
this simultaneity met up with profound nonsynchronism. The supposedly
"exact," singular moment was recorded differently according to local time
standards: "at Promontory the telegraph clicked around 12:45 p.m., in Vir-
ginia City at 12:30; San Francisco had 'precisely' either 11:46 or 11:44:37,
depending on which paper one read, while in Washington, 2:47 seemed ap-
proximately right."[120] To our eyes today, the decades before the adoption of
standard time afford a fascinating look at the way in which homogeneous
and heterogeneous public temporalities brushed up against each other. It
was a period in which the discovery of simultaneity failed to correspond
to synchronicity; instead, the new technologically enabled experience of
simultaneity was forced to contend with plural, competing, noncoinciding
"presents."

   In 1849, the New England Association of Railroad Superintendents met
to recommend the adoption of a telegraphically communicated standard
time by all the companies operating in New England; this determination
by railway men was the origin of the first regional time zone in the United
States, though a national standard time was not established until 1883.
The results of resolutions adopted by railway men, in hindsight, were far-
reaching: the new standard time ushered in by the railways cut the links
between time, nature, and custom and between the accepted hour and the
place-bound, routinized, diurnal rhythms of the solar day. Scheduling the
train according to the clock at a time when private watches were not yet
widely available made the train's comings and goings, in effect, the authori-
tative public timekeeper. As Henry David Thoreau noted in *Walden* (1854),
the train, ruled by the clock, regulated social life, becoming itself the public
timepiece of industrial society.[121]

   The four-zone system presented by William Allen to the General and
Southern Railway Time Conventions in 1883 was one based on Greenwich
zone standards, but its regional boundaries were cut to the measure of the
railroad industry's needs and designed to preempt state or federal intervention into time standardization (Connecticut had set a legal precedent
for state-standardized time the year before). Allen believed that railroads
would teach local folk to base their time not on local practice but on the

train lines that spanned the vast nation.[122] Just to be sure, and in advance of the scheduled time change, Allen lobbied various observatories, corporations, and public officials in several states to win their support prior to the railroads' new time standard. Nevertheless, protests and disputes persisted for years to come—among the urban elite and rural working class folk alike, as well as across the pages of newspapers, especially in places where the standardized time change meant more than a few minutes' difference from the old customary times and a distinct variance with the local sun, or for states on the borderline between two zones. Federal legislation remained silent on the new temporal standard raised by the railroads, though standard time became an issue that Supreme Courts in several states decided to either disregard or uphold. Some forms of dissent were rooted in the refusal to allow a single industry to arbitrarily set the order of daily life or in a distaste for mechanical regulation of an increasingly automatic human existence; other forms, as in the Populist resistance to standard time, were grounded in a suspicion of industrial uniformity and a championing of agricultural ways of life.[123]

In the years immediately preceding 1883, the adoption of the Greenwich Prime Meridian as the yardstick for world standard time had achieved growing consensus among international scientists. In October 1884, the International Meridian Conference led to a resolution by twenty-five nations to adopt Greenwich as the initial meridian extending from the North to the South Pole; from this zero longitude, twenty-four time zones, each separated by an hour, were calculated; all countries were to embrace a universal twenty-four-hour day. Despite this international resolution, Greenwich time would still provoke nationalistic resentment from some countries, like France, which saw no reason to adopt an "unpatriotic" temporal standard—the English Royal Observatory at Greenwich. After the International Meridian Conference in October 1884, worldwide adoption of Greenwich time advanced only gradually.[124] Nonetheless, the eclipsing of local times was well under way once the first global time signal was transmitted via wireless telegraph from the Eiffel Tower in July 1913.[125]

Wireless telegraphy, which had been conceptualized in 1864, was in widespread use among news services and seafaring vessels by 1903. As Kern has shown in *The Culture of Time and Space*, the wireless telegraph revolutionized the modern world's understanding of the present. The older notion of the present as composed of a sequence of local experiences was replaced by a particularly modern, global view of the present as an over-arching *simultaneity* through which events in separate, even remote, places could be shared by different people at the same time. Benedict Anderson, in his acclaimed analysis of the nation as an imagined political unity, *Imagined Communities*, underscores the importance of simultaneity: "So deep lying is this new idea that one could argue that every essential modern conception is based on a conception of meanwhile."[126] Nothing brought this home more grippingly than the plight of the *Titanic* on April 14–15, 1912, as it sank in a North Atlantic ice field with 1,522 passengers on board. The vessel wirelessly communicated a distress signal at 12:15 a.m. to ships too distant to come to its aid. Tragically, the only ship close enough to respond to its signal failed to do so because its wireless operator had retired for the night. About an hour later, and into the wee hours of the morning, news dispatched wirelessly and by cable allowed the rest of the world to learn of the unfolding disaster—a newly achieved simultaneous present experienced by survivors at sea, mariners in faraway ships, and wireless operators and news services in distant lands.[127]

Kern refers to the period stretching from 1880 to the outbreak of the First World War as "the culture of time and space." The notion of homogeneous time, though championed by railroad men and astronomers, was also coming under attack by other scientific developments, such as Einstein's theory of relativity. Likewise, Euclidean geometry—the basis of classical physics—began to be questioned. Various challenges to homogeneous space were mounted from 1860 onward in the form of non-Euclidean geometries, Einstein's relativity theories, developments in the natural and social sciences, and modern art's departures from Renaissance perspective.[128]

Despite such challenges to homogeneous space in the sciences and the humanities, in everyday life in Europe and the United States the experience of modernity seemed to affirm rather than undermine spatial homogeneity. Technologies of speed and simultaneity were also, by their very nature, technologies for territorial conquest. As distance was reconfigured by cinema, telephone, and automobile, the thirst for spatial expansion grew, and the unified globe felt like a smaller and smaller place.[129]

Imperialist rhetoric assumed that the conquest of space (crucially aided by new technologies in this period) signified national power and distinction. Yet imperialist expansion resulted in a prominent fin de siècle motif:

nostalgia over the loss of "empty space," with the once "open" spaces of Asia and Africa fully colonized, the American frontier closed in 1890, and the threatened disappearance of the last wild, unexplored places on Earth.[130]

Simultaneity, Anachronism, and Noncontemporaneity: Imperialism and the Modern Present

In *The Practice of Conceptual History* and in *Futures Past: On the Semantics of Historical Time*, Reinhart Koselleck characterizes modern time as a secular experience of history, in contrast to the Christian vantage point encapsulated by the book of Ecclesiastes ("there is nothing new under the sun"), a biblical temporal perspective that persisted into the seventeenth century.[131] "It was only when Christian eschatology shed its constant expectation of the imminent arrival of doomsday that a temporality could be revealed that would be open for the new and without limit."[132] What makes this modern concept of time a properly historical time (or, as Koselleck puts it, a "temporalization of history") is that its defining attribute, progress, is not derived from prior theological or mythological temporal structures. Recalling similar arguments by Jürgen Habermas, modernity for Koselleck is conceptualized as self-grounding, taking its definition not from retrospective temporal structures but from its own palpably different present and its emphatically new future.[133]

Koselleck grants that it is difficult to locate the precise epochal threshold of modernity—some propose 1500 (the conquest of America, the beginning of a worldwide slave economy, the development of the printing press) or 1800 (the widespread impact of the industrial revolution, as well as other far-reaching political changes in Europe).[134] Nonetheless, based on a careful lexical survey of German historiography, Koselleck proposes that the eighteenth century be understood as the advent of the specific temporal categories of modernity. Slowly coming into use after 1700, by 1800 the two words *neue Zeit* (new time) appear more and more frequently to periodize the current epoch as one that began around 1500.[135] The composite of the two words, *Neuzeit* (modernity), first emerges in 1870.[136] The end of the eighteenth century is also the moment when the term *progress* was first coined in German. Koselleck writes, "Progress (*der Fortschritt*), a term first put forth by Kant, was a now a word that neatly and deftly brought the manifold of scientific, technological, and industrial meanings of progress, and finally also those meanings involving social morality and even the totality of history, under a common concept."[137] Our current usage of *progress* as a collective singular noun, one of many collective singular terms that proliferated in the late eighteenth century, is the result of specific lexical processes. First, universalization: the "subject of progress" is no longer a specific field like science or art but humanity itself. Second, the attribution of historical agency: progress is considered as an active historical agent in its own right, as in the phrase "the progress of history." These developments led to the now-dominant practice of using *progress* as a collective singular term, "progress itself," "a subject of itself."[138]

Progress would encapsulate the widening gap between past experience (what Koselleck calls the "space of experience") vis-à-vis the future ("the horizon of expectation"), giving modernity its new, epochal significance as an accelerating, directional advance. The experience of an ever-accelerating pace of technological change and the corollary need to adjust prior knowledge gives the future an open quality, defined precisely and unforeseeably as that which had been impossible in the past.[139] The relationship between the space of experience and the horizon of expectation is never fixed, but in modern time consciousness that differential between experience and expectation, past and future, has escalated, and the latter (expectation/future) has come to be privileged over the former (past/experience).[140] The concept of progress, according to Koselleck, is the name for this "differential experience of past and future." It refers to an experience of a modern, sped-up time in which the lessons of the past seem to be outmoded ever more quickly (to wit, Goethe's complaint that we are obligated to relearn things every five years). The future as open and radically new can no longer be reliably and completely extrapolated from what is known from the past; the future is not exhausted by patterns of recurrence.[141]

Koselleck's conceptual history makes clear, from quite a different perspective than the one Deleuze offered, that Bergson's philosophy of time as openness to the new is a specifically modern one.[142] Proceeding from Deleuze's insight that Bergson's critique of the cinema distilled what was specifically new about this technology, one could speculate that Bergson's way of thinking temporality would not have been possible a century earlier, without the cinema. Moreover, in light of Koselleck's discussion, it becomes clear that, though Bergson's objective was to describe certain universal, age-old aspects of being, the conceptual vocabulary he employed was a thoroughly modern idiom.

The future as unforeseeably new and absolutely open is taken up in Bergsonism as an ontological question and never becomes incorporated into evolutionary, teleological understandings of chronological time. The ideas of the new and of the open future are approached in a very different way by Koselleck, not as existential, universal aspects of being but as categories of a specifically modern understanding of history. Despite such differences, we can delineate the following areas of convergence between Bergson's ontological temporality and Koselleck's account of modern historical time. First, Koselleck, like Bergson, maintains that all attempts to visualize or represent time lead invariably to space: "when one seeks to form an intuition of time as such, one is referred to spatial indications, to the hand of the clock or the leaves of a calendar that one pulls off every day. . . . All the examples that are intended to render historical time visible refer us to the space in which humans live."[143] The second shared argument, already anticipated by the first, is the theme of untranslatability, the noncoincidence of time and its visual or linguistic representation: "language and history depend on each other but never coincide."[144]

The third and fourth thematic convergences and differences between Bergsonism and Koselleck's account of the emergence of modern historical time are the most important for this discussion. The notion of the open future, for Bergson an aspect of duration and becoming as unceasing invention, is for Koselleck the mark of an epochal threshold, the inauguration of a specifically modern concept of history marked by progress and acceleration. Finally, both thinkers recognize the coexistence of multiple, divergent times but point to different implications. (Here, the differences between philosopher and historian are far more significant than their initial resemblances.)

For Koselleck, the notion of temporal multiplicity is not considered ontologically (as with Bergson) but historically. Koselleck argues that the disconcerting discovery of multiple, simultaneously coexisting and yet radically different temporalities is a specifically modern experience, prompted above all by European colonial expansion and the encounter with intractable cultural difference. A *contained recognition* of temporal multiplicity, a contemporaneous noncontemporaneity, is a specific historical experience constituted by imperialism.

Koselleck argues that the development of modern time consciousness in the eighteenth century depended crucially on the perceived "noncontemporaneousness of diverse, but in the chronological sense, simultaneous histories" that arose from imperialist global expansion. He directs us to the exclusionary temporal politics of the modern concept of simultaneity (or in Anderson's analysis, the *meanwhile*) and its obverse, anachronism (Fabian's "denial of coevalness"). The modern dynamic of contemporaneity and its antinomy, anachronism, is a strategy of temporal containment. It attempts to manage a recalcitrant "field of differences" by presuming a totalizing historical movement applicable to all peoples and cultures and labeling certain forms of difference as primitive or anachronistic. Temporal contradictions are already signaled in the language used by various thinkers to describe the dynamic of contemporaneity/anachronism, whether in Marx's "uneven development" or Ernst Bloch's "nonsynchronism."[145] Koselleck shows that the imperialist project called for a strategy of temporal containment—the "contemporaneity of the noncontemporaneous"—that relied on a (mis)translation of difference-as-anachronism. This temporal management of troublesome heterogeneity under the rubric of modern homogeneous time is the imperial move that postcolonial scholars vociferously refute. I quote his argument at some length here because it illuminates several themes explored in this half of the chapter:

> The geographical opening up of the globe brought to light *various but coexisting cultural levels which were*, through the process of synchronous comparison, *then ordered diachronically. Looking from civilized Europe to a barbaric America was a glance backward.* . . . Comparisons promoted the emergence in experience of a world history, which was increasingly interpreted in terms of progress. A constant impulse leading to progressive comparison was drawn from the fact that individual peoples or states . . . were found to be in advance of the others. From the eighteenth century on, therefore, it was possible to formulate the postulate of acceleration; or conversely, from the point of view of those left behind, the postulate of drawing level or overtaking. This fundamental experience of progress, embodied in a singular concept around 1800, is rooted in the knowledge of *noncontemporaneities which exist at a chronologically uniform time.* . . .
>
> The contemporaneity of the noncontemporaneous, initially a result of overseas expansion, became a basic framework for the progressive construction of the growing unity of world history. Toward the end of the century, the collective singular "progress" was coined in the German language, opening up all domains of life with the questions of "earlier than" or "later than," not just "before" and "after."[146]

Koselleck calls the Enlightenment "a time when the plurality of historical times was made conscious for the first time."[147] In the eighteenth century the multiplicity of times revealed by imperialist expansion became conceptualized as an experience of noncontemporaneousness. The "contemporaneity of the noncontemporaneous" was cast in terms of a universal history in which some were advanced and others backward, resulting in politically charged ideas about looking forward, being overtaken, catching up, or feeling left behind.

Though Koselleck's "contemporaneity of the noncontemporaneous" is unwieldy, the very unwieldiness of this oxymoronic phrase signals the contested process of (mis)translating the heterogeneous multiplicity of other ways of being in the world into a homogeneous, developmental idea of a single world history, a new "geopolitical concept of time."[148] This evolutionary view of world-historical progress is exactly the move Bergsonism's antiteleological consideration of temporally plural being avoids. In contrast to Bergsonism's affirmation of radical temporal multiplicity, the colonial rhetoric of progress begins with a recognition of multiplicity and coexistence ("the savage is my contemporary") but moves quickly to impute anachronism ("the savage I encounter now is really from a prior stage of history"). Thus, an anticolonial critique of modern time consciousness takes up several Bergsonian topoi of temporal critique — translation, multiplicity, and coexistence — but engages these in a very different way. In particular, an anticolonial critique of homogeneous time points out that the modern notion of progress and its corollary, the accusation of noncontemporaneousness, translate multiple ways of inhabiting the world into a single, homogeneous time. This translation is arguably a deliberate *mistranslation* in that the allochronic gesture — the appraisal of the other as an anachronism — served as a potent temporal justification for the colonial project.

Imperialism's "discovery" of noncontemporaneous, plural times is a striking aspect of what Koselleck calls the modern "temporalization of history," a sense of the world-historical unfolding of a single (diachronically ordered) but plural (culturally noncontemporaneous) time.[149] Yet even in a postcolonial era, contemporaneity and anachronism continue to structure ideological rhetoric, wherever we hear the temporal cast of claims to legitimacy: politically, in the terms *progressive* or *conservative*, in thinkers who are "ahead of" or "behind" the times, and with regard to style, the ideas of being "hip" or "current" as opposed to that which is "dated" or "passé." The ideology of progress is built on the temporal logic of anachronism because one can only be forward-looking or progressive in contrast to those who, while seeming to be one's contemporaries, have already been left behind.

It is important to note that, while the contemporaneity of the noncontemporaneous finds its condition of possibility in the planetary experience of European colonialism, this temporal logic of exclusion has never been aimed solely at the "non-Western" other. In the 1870s, for instance, Samuel Langley, while striving to promote standard observatory time, warned the unconvinced citizens of Pittsburgh that their customary local times were a "relic of antiquity," vestiges of an outmoded past.[150] What comes through so clearly from Langley's rhetoric of noncontemporaneity is the gesture of temporal elitism that Koselleck's account emphasizes. The rhetoric of anachronism is consistently employed by proponents of homogeneous time whenever a stubborn heterogeneity is encountered. One comes to expect that wherever anachronism is shouted, conflicting, coexistent times are being hastily denounced.

To have noted that modern time consciousness was underpinned by the experience and legitimation of colonial conquest is precisely to insist on the global character of modernity rather than subscribing to an "internalist" account of modernity as a European invention that slowly spread to its "elsewheres." As Chakrabarty persuasively argues, this is yet another variant of the linear, uniform, evolutionary time he refers to as historicism, which believes modernity to have been invented in Europe and from there slowly disseminated to the rest of the world. The temporality of the statement "first in Europe, then elsewhere" is once again spatial: time becomes an index of cultural difference, the perceived backwardness of the non-West in relation to the European center.[151]

Ironically enough, to decry modern time consciousness as solely European time consciousness is to perpetrate, as Enrique Dussel has provocatively argued, another kind of Eurocentrism, a Eurocentrism that attributes modernity uniquely to Europe on account of supposedly exceptional internal attributes that enabled the West to develop modernity and then to spread it throughout the world:

> Two opposing paradigms, the Eurocentric and the planetary, characterize the question of modernity. The first, from a Eurocentric horizon, formulates the phenomenon of modernity as exclusively European, developing in the Middle Ages and later on diffusing itself throughout the entire world. . . . According to

this paradigm, Europe had exceptional internal characteristics that allowed it to supersede, through its rationality, all other cultures. . . . The chronology of this position has its geopolitics: modern subjectivity develops spatially, according to the Eurocentric paradigm, from the Italy of the Renaissance to the Germany of the Reformation and the Enlightenment, to the France of the French Revolution; throughout, Europe is central. . . . [This] is an ideological and deforming organization of history; it has already created ethical problems with respect to other cultures. . . .

The second paradigm, from a planetary horizon, conceptualizes modernity as the culture of the center of the "world-system," of the first world-system, through the incorporation of Amerindia, and as a result of the management of this "centrality." In other words, *European modernity is not an independent, autopoietic, self-referential system, but instead is part of a world-system: in fact, its center. Modernity, then, is planetary*. It begins with the simultaneous constitution of Spain with reference to its "periphery" (first of all, properly speaking, Amerindia: the Caribbean, Mexico, and Peru). Simultaneously, Europe . . . will go on to constitute itself as center (as a super-hegemonic power that from Spain passes to Holland, England, and France over a growing periphery). . . . Modernity, then, in this planetary paradigm is a phenomenon proper to the system "center-periphery." *Modernity is not a phenomenon of Europe as an independent system, but of Europe as center. . . . The centrality of Europe in the world-system is not the sole fruit of an internal superiority accumulated during the European Middle Ages over against other cultures*. Instead, it is also the fundamental effect of the simple fact of the discovery, conquest, colonization, and integration (subsumption) of Amerindia. This simple fact will give Europe the determining comparative advantage over the Ottoman-Muslim world, India, and China. . . . The human experience of 4,500 years of political, economic, technological, and cultural relations of the interregional system *will now be hegemonized by a Europe — which had never been the "center," and which, during its best times, became only a "periphery."*[152]

Dussel proposes a radical rethinking of modernity as a planetary phenomenon that grows out of a particular world-historical system in which Europe tried to manage the "world" as its imperialist center. What is finally debilitating about an East versus West understanding of modernity is that it forgets that colonialism, and the modernity of the cultural center that managed it, is not an independently European but a planetary dynamic. The development of modernity as the culture of the European center

emerges not autochthonously but as a technology for managing and establishing the relation, center-periphery, of a Europe that was annexing and
expropriating other territories and peoples for its benefit. That is, European modernity was not the result of an exceptional innate superiority
that allowed Europe to dominate the rest of the world but was a specific
set of (temporalized and spatialized) management strategies that emerged
in the course of Europe's establishing itself as a superhegemonic center
to its colonized peripheries. To draw attention, as Chakrabarty and Koselleck do, to the colonialist underpinnings of modern time consciousness is
not to impute that modernity is simply European and that only postcolonial nations have endured the violent incursions of modernity (as Schivelbusch, Kern, and O'Malley show, the homogenization of time and space
was vigorously resisted in the United States and Europe as well) but rather
to characterize the global nature of this world-historical consciousness.

This characterization of modern time consciousness as forged in the
global crucible of colonialism—particularly in the temporalized framing
of imperialism's conquest of space and its encounter with cultural difference—echoes similar points made by Fabian on the evolutionary time espoused by nineteenth-century anthropology. Fabian's well-known critique
of the uses of anthropological time, the modern observer's "denial of coevalness" to the cultural and racialized other, established the links between
secular time, evolutionary thinking, and spatial-as-temporal distance.
Fabian's analysis of tactics of temporal elitism is one that other postcolonial critiques of homogeneous time adapt and explore: "Beneath their bewildering variety, the distancing devices that we can identify produce a
global result. I will call it a denial of coevalness. By that I mean a persistent
and systematic tendency to place the referent(s) of anthropology in a Time
other than the present of the producer of anthropological discourse."[153]

Fabian's "auto-critique of anthropology," *Time and the Other*, sheds light
on anthropology's historical and epistemological roots in "an allochronic
discourse; it is a science of other men in another time." To speak of others
as though they were temporally behind oneself is to remove them from
one's own present. Fabian concludes: "This 'petrified relation' is a scandal.
Anthropology's other is, ultimately, people who are our contemporaries."[154]
Koselleck's noncontemporaneity and (as we will see in a moment) Chakrabarty's anachronism are alternate names for the allochronic gesture that
Fabian detects in countless ethnographies, a "temporal distancing" that

casts the empirically present other as somehow absent, belonging to a time anterior to the anthropologist's own.[155] Fabian mounts a forceful critique of the judgment of noncontemporaneity, the refusal to see the other as coeval with the modern observer.

According to Fabian, nineteenth-century anthropology's insistence on the noncontemporaneity of the savage provided the temporal justification for imperialism, positioning the other in a prior evolutionary stage in the development of human history. "It promoted a scheme in terms of which not only past cultures, but all living societies were irrevocably placed on a temporal slope, a stream of Time—some upstream, others downstream."[156] This recalls Koselleck's acute description of the temporalizing colonial gaze: "looking from civilized Europe to a barbaric America was a glance backward."[157] As Fabian demonstrates, the colonizer did not encounter primitives; instead, he encountered colonial others *in terms of the primitive*, that is, in terms of a temporal strategy of containment that (mis)translates difference as chronologically prior in a homogeneous concept of time.[158]

The Ethnographic Time Machine

Drawing on Fabian's work, filmmaker-theorist Fatimah Tobing Rony calls ethnographic cinema and photography a "time machine" that transports indigenous subjects into a "displaced temporal realm," converting performers who share a space and time with the filmmaker into native specimens from an earlier age.[159] In the broadest sense, ethnographic cinema is aimed at explaining one culture (that of the subjects being filmed) to another culture (that of the filmmaker and audience). Early ethnographic cinema—whose episteme is still at work in popular forms today—was most visibly defined through its subject matter: indigenous peoples, foreign exotic others. For Rony, the ethnographic imaginary defined by early European and North American practitioners from 1895 to the 1930s is a broad continuum including scientific films and popular cinema. From the "ethnographic romanticism" of Robert Flaherty's *Nanook of the North* (1922) to the "pastiche exotic film" *King Kong* (1933), by Merian Cooper and Ernest Schoedsack, films of this period that drew upon the ethnographic imaginary were "time machines into a faraway present which represented a simple, savage past."[160] As Rony's suggestive phrase, "faraway present" indicates, the primitive as ethnographiable object, though interacting with the filmmaker in a shared filmic space, was not considered coeval with the latter's historical subjectivity. Thus in the ethnographic time machine, spatial, cultural, and racial difference were converted into temporal distance.[161]

In the comparative anatomical studies of the eighteenth and nineteenth centuries, the dissection of deceased indigenous "specimens" like Saartje Bartman by European scientists reached obsessive proportions. Rony astutely remarks, "Anthropology was a science strewn with corpses, one obsessed with origins, death, and degeneration."[162] The morbidity of nineteenth-century anthropology carried over into the temporal logic of the ethnographic film. Salvage ethnography, for example, idealized rather than scorned the "vanishing primitive" it hoped to record for posterity but nevertheless betrayed a similarly embalming temporal logic. *Nanook of the North*'s salvage ethnography did not depict Inuits as they were at the time of filming; rather, the film portrayed Inuits as Flaherty imagined they had been.[163] Rony refers to this as ethnography in the taxidermic mode. Whereas the taxidermist stuffs, mounts, and otherwise prepares the dead animal in a way that makes it appear to be alive, the ethnographic filmmaker as taxidermist, Rony suggests, presents the living as though they were already dead: "The character of Nanook, with his disciplined hard work and industriousness, is simultaneously an embodiment of the 'living dead' and a dramatically heroic evolutionary 'ancestor' for the Western viewer to identify with." As she astutely notes, Nanook's elegiac realism "made the dead look alive and the living look dead."[164] By turning a funereal gaze on thriving cultures, taxidermic ethnographies, nostalgic for the supposedly more authentic ways of life of the "vanishing primitive," ended up denying the crucial fact that indigenous peoples, despite the ravages of modern colonial incursion and exploitation, had actually survived.[165] In this respect, the denial of coevalness as an anachronizing discourse is also a discursive *doing-to-death* of living but radically different worlds. Taxidermic-ethnographic time, despite its collocation with revenants and ghosts, is actually the antinomy of what, in chapter 3, I call spectral times. In the spectral logic of ghost films, the temporality of haunting is that of a betrayed past that returns to call the living to ethical accountability. In contrast, in the time machine of ethnographic cinema, the living other's copresence is refused via a cinematic death-doing; that is, the coeval other is done to death by being filmed as a primitive, as though already dead.

Toward a Critique of Noncontemporaneity: On Cannibalism

As Habermas demonstrates in *The Philosophical Discourse of Modernity*, modernity's self-understanding is that of a radical break from the past, preserved in words like *revolution, emancipation,* and other concepts of dynamism. This means that modernity cannot define itself by recourse to other eras and prior models; modernity must ground itself. Habermas characterizes modernity's myth of self-grounding in these terms: "Modernity can and will no longer borrow the criteria by which it takes its orientation from the models supplied by another epoch; *it has to create its normativity out of itself.*"[166] Similarly, strategies of temporal management-via-exclusion (the logic of anachronism, noncontemporaneity, and the denial of coevalness) are attempts to preserve modernity's cachet as "self-grounding," as a "true present" that has invented itself with only a negative debt to its forerunners, thus accomplishing a radical break with the past (hence the insistence on modernity's having surmounted or superseded its precursors).[167] The charge of noncontemporaneity or anachronism is thus a definitive, structural feature of homogeneous time, a necessary fiction if the evidence of "heterotemporality," as Chakrabarty puts it, is to be suppressed:[168] "In the awakening of this sense of anachronism lies the beginning of modern historical consciousness. Indeed, anachronism is regarded as the hallmark of such a consciousness. Historical evidence (the archive) is produced by our capacity to see something that is contemporaneous with us — ranging from practices, humans, institutions, and stone-inscriptions to documents — as a relic of another time or place."[169]

From Chakrabarty's discussion of anachronism as foundational to modern homogeneous time, we learn that this allochronic gesture does several things at once: it converts something that is our contemporary, something that cohabits our present and attests to the diversity of that present, into something that is "noncontemporaneous," a relic of the past. The charge of anachronism is not only the production of a temporal distance — you do not belong in my present; you are actually a remnant of the past — but also the production of an epistemological distance between subject and object, familiar from the objectifying gaze of ethnography. To objectify cultural difference as anachronistic is to insert a gap between the observer and the observed, to deny the lived experience that binds the observer to the belief, practice, or person she or he is presently observing. Chakrabarty defines anachronism as the denial of *lived relations* with the other:

If historical or anthropological consciousness is seen as the work of a rational outlook, it can only "objectify"—and thus deny—the lived relations the observing subject already has with that which he or she identifies as belonging to a historical or ethnographic time and space separate from the ones he or she occupies as the analyst. In other words, the method does not allow the investigating subject to recognize himself or herself as also the figure he or she is investigating. It stops the subject from seeing his or her own present as discontinuous with itself.[170]

It is lived experience that often dismantles the objectifying temporal distance of the ethnographic gaze. Lived experience is foregrounded to great ironic effect in Rony's experimental video *On Cannibalism*, a highly germane example for this book, since it functions as a metacommentary on the collusions between the imagination of nineteenth-century anthropology and the fantastic premises of a venerable Hollywood jungle-horror film, Cooper's and Schoedsack's *King Kong*. Though exhibiting little of the hesitation that Todorov identified as the hallmark of the fantastic, *King Kong* does exemplify one of the genre's defining traits: the admixture of two temporally discrepant worlds.[171] Spectators are introduced to the primitive, ahistorical world of Skull Island. Carl Denham, the diegetic filmmaker, describes it as an uncharted isle in latitudes "way west of Sumatra." On this island, the director and his crew encounter savages who "have slipped back, forgotten higher civilization" and who sacrifice women to appease a gigantic ape. Counterpoised to Skull Island is the world of New York City, from which the filmmaker and his crew set out and to which they eventually return, with King Kong in chains. Though Kong and those who worship him are copresent with the filmmakers, they are spatially and temporally distanced: Skull Island is a remote, uncharted island off the coast of Sumatra, a place where time has literally come to a temporally confused stop: the enormous primate, Kong, battles a dinosaur. Kong and the primitives who worship him are therefore anachronistic contemporaries of the diegetic filmmakers (and, implicitly, of the extradiegetic spectator).

In a remarkable eight-minute riposte to that film, Rony's 1994 experimental video *On Cannibalism* begins with the memory of spectatorship. On the soundtrack, Rony's voice-over narration recounts that as a child, she had heard that her mother's people, the Batak of North Sumatra, had been cannibals. Years later, as she was flipping through television channels, an old black-and-white monster movie came on: Cooper's and Schoedsack's

King Kong. Watching, Rony suddenly realized that the anonymous, superstitious natives who worshipped Kong as a god on the uncharted Skull
Island "west of Sumatra" were speaking an Indonesian language: "I don't
remember how it happened, but somehow, I heard that—someone told
me that—people said that—my mom's people had been cannibals. It was
probably my dad who told me. When I was older, much older, I sat up one
night switching television channels. I found myself watching the middle
of a Hollywood jungle film with island savages. Suddenly, I realized that I
understood what these savages were saying. They were speaking some kind
of strange Indonesian. Suddenly, I realized that *I was a savage.*"[172]

It is this first moment of recognition—Rony is an Asian American filmmaker of Sumatran descent—that ruptures the temporal distancing of the
natives and Kong as part of an anachronistic, primitive world. *King Kong*,
she convincingly asserts, is a movie about the making of an ethnographic
film, and the ape is patently a placeholder for the racialized subjects of the
ethnographic gaze.[173]

The resonance of Rony's title, *On Cannibalism*, is best appreciated when
read alongside Anne McClintock's discussion of the trope of cannibalism in
colonial cartography: "Graham Greene noted how geographers traced the
word 'cannibals' over the blank spaces on colonial maps." McClintock reads
the motif of cannibalism as a "fear of engulfment": "the fear of engulfment
by the unknown is projected onto colonized peoples as *their* determination to devour the intruder whole."[174] *King Kong* offers a potent staging
of this imaginary, beginning from the skipper's evocative description of
an uncharted island "way out of any waters I know"; the film expedition
that follows on Skull Island confirms that the fearsome prospect of engulfment does await explorers in the blank spaces of colonial cartography.
Rony looks at the trope of cannibalism from the opposite door: not from
Denham's perspective of encountering cannibals but from the realization
that she is being encountered *as* a cannibal.

Rony's video uses the structure of the compilation film—an important
aesthetic device to which feminist documentary film and video have often
turned—in the service of counterethnography. The compilation film was
first explored by Soviet filmmaker Esther Shub in films like *The Fall of the
Romanov Dynasty* (1927), in which preexisting documents, mostly news-
reels and stock footage, were edited together with intertitles. Shub devised
this structural form as a solution to the problem of representing revolutionary ideas using "counter-revolutionary material."[175] As Rony's *On Can-*

nibalism brilliantly demonstrates, the formal-ideological strength of the compilation structure is rooted in its capacity to resignify and even reverse the semantic polarity of the footage, sounds, and materials it quotes via reediting, rephotography, voice-over, and a disruptive use of sound and image. The video juxtaposes footage of *King Kong* against family photographs and archival images of indigenous subjects exhibited throughout the nineteenth and early twentieth centuries in World's Fairs, animal shows, zoos, and museums: Saartje Bartman (the "Hottentot Venus"), Ota Benga, Igorots, Wolofs. Rony disrupts the objectifying gaze of both Hollywood monster movies and the ethnographic imagination that underpins them by insisting on the *lived experience* of a woman of Indonesian descent, a spectator who, late one night, jarringly recognized herself to be the living descendant of the imputed primitives represented on film. With an admixture of incredulity, irony, and understated indignation, Rony takes up the place of nonidentification foreclosed by this classical Hollywood film. That is, as a disaffected, racialized spectator, she identifies oppositionally with a barely seen character whose screen time in *King Kong* consists of one brief medium shot: the native "Bride of Kong," the female savage eclipsed by the blonde white beauty, Ann Darrow.[176] In *The Third Eye: Race, Cinema, and Ethnographic Spectacle*, Rony gives this mode of defiant spectatorship a name:

> For a person of color growing up in the United States, the experience of viewing oneself as an object is profoundly formative. Reflecting on an indelible childhood memory, W. E. B. DuBois describes the double consciousness that a young person of color is forced to develop. DuBois explains that one day, a young white girl gave him a glance, and in that glance he recognized that he was marked as an Other. As DuBois describes it, the internalization of this recognition gives one "the sense of always looking at one's self through the eyes of others," or of seeing "darkly as through a veil." The experience of the third eye suggests that DuBois's insight can be taken one step further—the racially charged glance can also induce one to see the very process which creates the internal splitting, to witness the conditions which give rise to the double consciousness described by DuBois. The veil allows for clarity of vision even as it marks the site of socially mediated self-alienation.[177]

What Rony calls the "third eye" is a breakage in the visual circuit of a racially charged, asymmetrical exchange of looks. It is, for a moment, to

14. In this shot of the filmmaker against a reticular grid to establish scale and position, the mise-en-scène deliberately evokes the conventions of anthropometric photography and early motion studies. *On Cannibalism* (dir. Fatimah Tobing Rony, 1994).

"float above" the limits of one's own gaze (a moment of "self-alienation" or "internal splitting") in order to witness the entire circuit of looks between oneself and another. This is the mode of DuBois's "double consciousness," a defining "experience of viewing oneself as an object." The third eye is the recognition of one's objectification by the look of another, a resistant assertion of a denied subjectivity against the power of a racializing gaze.

Rony's video, a brilliant send-up combining outrage and humor, counters the modern historical time underpinning ethnographic and jungle horror films via graphic matches that overlay her own image in the present with that of photographed savages, or against a reticular grid to establish the scale and position of the subject in front of the camera (fig. 14). Such mise-en-scène deliberately recalls the conventions of anthropometric photography and early motion studies, as well as the obsession with scientific measurement typified by Felix-Louis Regnault's chronophotography of West African performers, which often included "a painted scale on the ground to measure the duration of a subject's step."[178]

To incongruous, witty effect, her voice-over's challenge to the logic of evolutionary time is paired with footage of contemporary anthropological exhibits depicting human evolution, from primitive to modern, under

15–17. Superimpositions and graphic matches in *On Cannibalism* produce a video palimpsest that layers the filmmaker's photographic portrait onto that of her great-great grandfather. Rony marshals lived experience to insist on the contemporaneity of imputed savages and expose the durability of the nineteenth-century ethnographic imagination.

the heading, "Our Place in Time." The visual track moves across complex human taxonomies, accounts of the evolution of the "family of man," from primates to modern human; on the audio track, Rony's voice-over narration alludes to the polygenetic versus monogenetic debates—the question of whether people from various races belong to the same species. These debates were constitutive of the nineteenth-century invention of race and underwrote the scientific racism of that era's studies in comparative anatomy and biology.[179] At a key moment, Rony's voice-over narration makes use of a second-person address that calls the gaze of the ethnographer-voyeur (into whose shoes the spectator is uncomfortably cast) into account: "You came in droves in the nineteenth and twentieth centuries to colonize us, and then to photograph us. You *anthropologists*. You *scientists*. You *doctors*. Suddenly you understood deviance. You understood time. For after all, history was a race. Those who did not vanquish would vanish. We were the primitives to you. The first ones. The first ones to go. You imagined us, and you captured us, and then you devoured us."

The emphasized words become far worse names than *cannibal* in Rony's stinging delivery, resonating with a deeply historical indignation. Both sound and image forge an oppositional identification between the anachronistic savage and the contemporary, disaffected spectator, thus telescoping the primitive into the present (figs. 15–17). Like the use of direct address in the voice-over, graphic matches and superimpositions condense her own photographic portrait onto that of her great-great-grandfather ("*Ompung* of my *ompung*"). Such devices powerfully insist on the contemporaneity of the savage and highlight the durability of the nineteenth-century ethnographic imagination, which lives on in twenty-first-century popular culture.[180] Rony's use of compilation video and photographic palimpsest disrupts the visual representation of the racialized other as "relic" via an outspoken insistence on the filmmaker's copresence. Interrupting the exclusionary framing of the Indonesian savage as an anachronism, a primitive from another time, with anecdotes about her family and her experiences as a spectator, Rony's *On Cannibalism* marshals the temporal force of a lived experience whose copresence refuses to be denied.

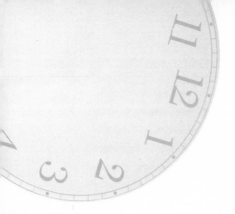

CHAPTER 2

The Fantastic as Temporal Translation

Aswang *and Occult National Times*

The belief in asuangs is too firmly established in the minds of most of the people to be easily shaken, and is sometimes the cause of great mischief, as the asuang is a mortal, in many respects like themselves—indeed, may be one of their neighbors. The chief characteristic of the asuang is his liking for human flesh, especially the livers of young children.   MILLINGTON AND MAXFIELD, "Philippine (Visayan) Superstitions" (1906)

Recent studies in Philippine culture have come up with some unexpected finds. One of these is that the ancient Philippine deities, discredited after successive religious conversions and long considered dead, still circumscribe the lives of peasants and city-dwellers alike. . . . Today, vestiges and variations of these beliefs and practices still exist.   RAMOS, "Belief in Ghouls in Contemporary Philippine Society" (1968)

Welcome to Tondo, circa 1992. It looks like 400 years of Catholicism and 50 years of Hollywood have not quite succeeded in erasing pre-colonial beliefs. The recent uproar over the *manananggal* in Tondo has had such a grip in the imagination that people believe the *manananggal* to be now either flying all over Metro Manila or to have multiplied—there are now reported sightings of *manananggal* in Valenzuela, another in Marikina, and still another in Antipolo—the fare that keeps the tabloids selling briskly these days. SICAM, "'Manananggal' Season" (1992)

Aswang sightings and rumors flared suddenly into prominence about a month before the May 1992 national elections that would hand the Philippine presidency to Fidel Ramos.[1] Favored by the United States, Ramos was a West Point–trained general who had been chief of the Philippine Constabulary under the authoritarian regime of former president Ferdinand Marcos. On the eve, as it were, of Ramos's accession to the presidency, media coverage of a winged nocturnal monster in the slums of Tondo, preying on the urban poor under cover of darkness, captured the city's popular imagination. *Manananggal* overshadowed "the biggest elections in Philippine history" to that point, with voters selecting a new president, vice president, members of Congress, and seventeen thousand local officials from a roster of more than eighty-five thousand candidates. What one Reuters item dubbed "*manananggal* fever" swept the city of Metro Manila as aswang sightings proliferated, providing a "spine-chilling diversion from [the] polls."[2]

The viscera-eating manananggal is only one type of aswang; the latter appears in many guises and can be either male or female, though viscera suckers are persistently feminized. Maximo Ramos defines the "aswang complex" as a "congeries of beliefs" incorporating the aspects of five creatures: witch, self-segmenting viscera sucker, were-beast, bloodsucker, and corpse eater.[3] Aswang are recorded in the earliest Spanish missionary accounts of the Visayan and Central Luzon regions of the Philippines, appearing in Miguel de Loarca's 1582 description of Visayan funerary practices, published sixty-one years after Magellan's fateful arrival in the Port of Cebu in 1521 and seventeen years after the Spanish Crown's "active imposition of sovereignty" on the islands.[4] In 1731 Tomas Ortiz, a Spanish Augustinian priest who exhorted other missionaries to stamp out native superstitions in the Philippines, proffered this definition of "the witch called asuang, which, flying, passes by the houses of those who are in childbirth. . . . It places itself on the roof of a neighboring house, and from thence extends its tongue in the form of a thread that passes into the body of the child. . . . With it he draws out the bowels of the child and kills it."[5]

Ortiz's characterization of the aswang—a winged monster whose long threadlike tongue enters the body of a pregnant woman to suck out the unborn child in her womb—is the aswang's most durable and immediately recognizable guise, as depicted in the 1992 film *Aswang* (figs. 18–20). Perched on the thatch roofs of houses or concealed under the floorboards, the nocturnal aswang is also seen in the guise of a manananggal or self-

18–20. In *Aswang* (dir. Peque Gallaga and Lore Reyes, 1992), the monster appears in its most recognizable guise: perched on a thatch roof at night, eyeing its prey—an unborn child.

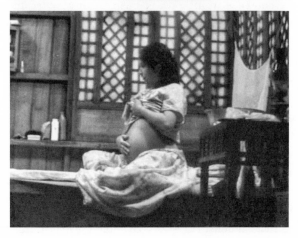

segmenting viscera sucker, "an attractive woman by day, buxom, long-haired, and light-complexioned" who, on its nightly hunt, "discards its lower body from the waist down and flies" in search of human prey.[6]

This chapter looks closely at a Filipino horror-film cycle that coincided with the tremendous media prominence of aswang—in tabloid and broadsheet news, radio and television programming, and literary fiction—during the 1992 national elections. Todorov's structuralist theory of the fantastic, which I explore in the first section of this chapter, hinges on the hesitation of an implied reader, not an actual historical audience. Textual auto-referentiality also underpins Todorov's concept of the supernatural as a linguistic figure of pure literality.[7] In contrast, my consideration of aswang narratives proceeds from the premise that cultural texts demand to be read in relation to disparate horizons of emergence and reception. I argue that the fantastic in our age cannot be understood through the lens of textual autoreferentiality; a tangled skein of reception characterizes centuries-old supernatural narratives that outlive their original audiences. Likewise, contemporary fantastic narratives are not reducible to the cinema or any single medium; instead, their social existence is characterized by what Lisa Cartwright calls "media convergence."[8] Lastly, in this chapter on aswang narratives, and the following chapter on ghost films, I suggest that supernatural accounts are at once fraught with historical inscription *and* insinuate the limits of homogeneous national-historical time.

The second section of this chapter embeds the early 1990s aswang films by directorial team Peque Gallaga and Lore Reyes in the horizons of reception that greeted the manananggal sightings of 1992. Aswang narratives are not well served by a Todorovian approach largely because the recounted supernatural event does not occur solely within the confines of a fictional genre. First recorded in sixteenth-century colonial missionary accounts, aswang glide between journalistic reportage, sociological analysis, popular film, and literary fiction. Moving across the veridical regimes of genres, aswang highlight the porosity of story and history, confirming Trinh T. Minh-ha's reminder that "literature and history once were / still are stories."[9]

The range of affective responses such supernatural narratives provoke includes but is not confined to Todorovian hesitation. Though aswang accounts do meet with skeptical incredulity among some audiences, the aswang is, as one prominent anthropologist put it, a "living belief" in cer-

tain regions and interpretive communities in the Philippines and overseas. Among Filipino/a middle-class commentators in 1992, manananggal
accounts met with two intertwined responses: first, a form of secular disparagement that was strongly temporalized and class-inflected; second,
a deciphering of their supposedly superstitious-delusional structure as
a kind of social allegory. Aswang films of this period thematized social
audiences and media convergence as the domain of the aswang itself and
visualized the porosity of rural, urban, peasant, and middle-class worlds in
their mise-en-scène.

As I noted above, the aswang has been dubbed a "congeries of beliefs."
Where the supernatural is concerned, however, the question of belief is
often a smokescreen for intransigent temporal differences. The Todorovian
approach to the fantastic as a drama of disbelief, a wavering between rational skepticism and credulity toward the supernatural, has not only occluded the temporal immiscibility that the fantastic foregrounds but also
has lent itself to a teleological understanding of a necessary trajectory that
begins from premodern superstitious belief and ends in modern rational
skepticism. This emerges, as I show below, in the well-meaning attempts
of subsequent critics to reintroduce the question of history to Todorov's
structuralist approach to the fantastic. The unfortunate consequence of
the dominant conceptualization of the fantastic as a question of belief versus skepticism is a rigid antinomy between enchantment and disenchantment. As I explain in this chapter, that dichotomy entails a historical forgetting of the ways in which both terms are constitutively intertwined: the
marvelous is always already at the heart of the modern. This is why I think
the question of the fantastic is insoluble if put in terms of belief and skepticism. Bergsonism emphasizes that the framing of one's questions has a
bearing on the answering knowledge produced: "the problem always has
the solution it deserves, in terms of the way in which it is stated (i.e., the
conditions under which it is determined as a problem), and of the means
and terms at our disposal for stating it."[10] In this vein, I am suggesting that
the Todorovian reduction of the fantastic to a question of belief or disbelief
in the supernatural is, in the Bergsonian sense, a "false problem" that fails
to take temporal heterogeneity into question. Commonsensical analyses
of supernatural belief are underwritten by notions of anachronism and
primitivism: certain folks, in this account, have yet to be disabused of their
belief in ghosts. This phrase, "yet to be disabused," signals the teleological
foreclosing of futurity, the all-is-given premise that those who begin by be-

lieving in marvels will, with the proper enlightenment, eventually outgrow them. This is why I propose that belief is often a way of evading the thorniness of temporal immiscibility on the one hand, while smuggling in telos in the form of a temporalized judgment of supernaturalism on the other. Approaching the fantastic from the perspective of temporal translation is motivated by my hope of posing or inventing the problem anew.

Accordingly, the third part of this chapter considers not congeries of belief but "congeries of translations." I trace the many guises of the aswang, first articulated by Spanish evangelist-imperialists, "decrypted" by the functionalist paradigms of twentieth-century anthropologists, and cynically deployed in the 1950s by an American CIA operative assigned to the Philippines, Edward Lansdale, who implanted an aswang rumorscape in a "psy-war" maneuver against Communist guerillas. These densely reticulated webs of temporal translation continue to circulate because the various articulations of the aswang across the centuries, preserved in print and other media, constitute what Stephen Greenblatt calls "mimetic capital."[11] The mimetic capital of the aswang is a durable "stockpile" of colonial and postcolonial representations in which imperialist stratagems collide with peasant idioms of protest.

To approach the fantastic through the porosity of its generic worlds and through the lens of temporal translation reveals temporal multiplicity and heteroglossia to be the very stuff of the aswang's conflicted cultural biography. The fourth and last section of this chapter argues that aswang and manananggal expose immiscible times that disrupt the nation's illusory temporal homogeneity. If, as Benedict Anderson suggests, newspapers bind the nation through the calendrical coincidence of an empty, disenchanted, homogeneous time, then tabloid and broadsheet coverage of aswang in 1992 point to an occult interruption of the national meanwhile, an acknowledgment of enchanted temporalities hidden in the penumbra of national time.

Part One. The Todorovian Fantastic and
Histories of Disenchantment

> In a world which is indeed our world, the world we know, a world without devils, sylphides, or vampires, there occurs an event which cannot be explained by the laws of this same familiar world. The person who experiences

the event must opt for one of two possible solutions: either he is the victim of an illusion of the senses, of a product of the imagination—and the laws of the world then remain what they are; or else the event has indeed taken place, it is an integral part of reality—but then this reality is controlled by laws unknown to us.

The fantastic occupies the duration of this uncertainty. Once we choose one answer or the other, we leave the fantastic for a neighboring genre, the uncanny or the marvelous. The fantastic is that hesitation experienced by a person who knows only the laws of nature, confronting an apparently supernatural event. TODOROV, *The Fantastic*

Apart from its conceptual rigor and cogent clarity, the Todorovian conception of the fantastic is well worth revisiting because it illuminates the genre's core conceit: an epistemological crisis as to the nature of the world, since the narrative posits the existence of two diametrically opposed orders of events, the natural and the supernatural. Unlike studies that conceptualize the genre around a reality/fantasy binary, Todorov recognizes that the fantastic throws the very givenness of that dichotomy into question.[12] In contrast to what Neil Cornwell calls a "history of critical imprecision" that conflates fantasy with the fantastic, Todorov's formulation broaches prior questions about our capacity to apprehend the world in the first place, how ideas of reality and unreality are constituted, and the correctness of the yardstick we use to evaluate the real.[13] For Todorov, at issue in the fantastic is finding an appropriate way of knowing and of taking one's bearings when the certainties that govern the known, familiar world suddenly appear limited or questionable.[14]

Yet despite the highly productive aspects of Todorov's formulation—identifying the epistemological crisis provoked by conflicting worlds in the fantastic—one limitation of his structuralist approach lies in the extreme autoreferentiality he ascribes to the textual system. For Todorov, literature has achieved an absolute autonomy; words no longer refer to an "external reality," and writing is only about writing: "Words are not labels pasted to things that exist as such independently of them. . . . If I write, I write about something, even if this something is writing."[15] An extreme textual self-enclosure envelops two key areas in his study of the fantastic: the implicit reader immanent to the text and a supernatural that for Todorov exists only in language, two issues I will consider in turn.

Todorov's Implicit Reader

In *The Prison-House of Language*, Fredric Jameson opposes the "auto-referentiality of narrative" posited by structuralism and issues a call to "reopen text and analytic process alike to all the winds of history."[16] The "paradoxical self-designation" imputed to the literary text is for Jameson the "return of form upon itself," the very imprisonment in the house of language that gives his study its title and explains his characterization of structuralism as a "philosophical formalism."[17]

Jameson's critique of structuralism provides an important starting point for a revaluation of Todorov's theory of the fantastic. As José B. Monleón has noted, the implied reader in Todorov's fantastic is a problematic gambit: "the weight of the definition resides in the reader—a conclusion that must necessarily create tension with the underlying structuralist premises of the book. Todorov solves the conflict by resorting to the conception of the implicit reader in the text. Yet such a formalization of the problem does not adequately address the initial epistemological proposition, since surely the characteristics of such an implicit reader would depend on the historical determinants that framed the text."[18] As Monleón points out, Todorov's theory of the fantastic pivots on the reader's response; but instead of pointing outward to the audience that the narrative addresses, the formalism and autoreferentiality of Todorov's genre theory fold the text onto itself, addressing not a historical, social other but a reader frozen within.[19] Todorov writes: "The fantastic therefore implies an integration of the reader into the world of the characters; that world is defined by the reader's own ambiguous perception of the events narrated. It must be noted that we have in mind no actual reader, but the role of the reader implicit in the text."[20] Todorov's implicit reader is a means of limiting the question of the fantastic to the text alone. Fantastic hesitation, however, inevitably gestures outside the confines of the text by posing the question of "the existence of an extra-linguistic signified."[21]

Jameson has talked about the Saussurean "circuit of discourse" as "the concrete structure of speech" formed in "a relationship between two speakers."[22] But in Todorov, this concrete circuit of discourse becomes a purely immanent aspect of the text, addressing a reader within itself. For Todorov, the genre's circuit of discourse, both "the person who emits the text" and "the person who receives it," involves "an image implicit in the text, not a real author or reader."[23] The implicit reader is one facet of the autodesignation, the fenced-in quality of Todorov's model of the fantastic: the work, in effect, is talking to itself.

A serious difficulty with the notion of the implicit reader is that the theorist's reading protocols are naturalized as any historical reader's competencies and proclivities. This move shrouds the critic's own particular reading and overdetermined subject position in the anonymity of an ideal reader immanent to the text. In *Toward an Aesthetic of Reception*, Hans-Robert Jauss argued against the reduction of the historical reader into a "perceiving subject who follows the directions in the text," a merely passive decoder of textual prescriptions rather than a productive force in the text's own history. Jauss writes, "The historical life of a literary work is unthinkable without the active participation of its addressees."[24] The social is the begged question, the undercurrent to the image of the implied reader. The implied reader tends to abridge an otherwise complicated consideration of legibility and taste, providing an easy answer to these questions: For whom is the genre pleasurable? To whom are these generic conventions legible? A paradigm of genre criticism that answers such questions with the implied reader rests on a reassuring tautological circuit: the implied reader is the perfect operationalization of the codes discovered by the genre critic, an obeisant reader projected by the textual structure who validates the scholar's detection of textual cues through the presumption that these cues always work.

In contrast to a text-immanent concept of genre, this book's approach to the fantastic is strongly colored by Jameson's view of genre as a social institution, a tacit contract between producers and audiences bound in a circuit of exchange.[25] This social and institutional view of genre is to my mind one of the great conceptual benefits of Jameson's method. Another is his keen understanding of the fragility of the generic contract. Whereas most genre critics presume the success of a genre when they propose a definition (for Noël Carroll, the horror film terrifies by confronting us with the threatening or impure; for Todorov the fantastic provokes hesitation),[26] genre for Jameson is always prone to failure. In short, the horror film may fail to scare all viewers; the fantastic may neither arouse perceptual disquiet nor provoke a recognition of temporal immiscibility. The ever-present possibility of a genre's failure is the gap between a work's generic conventions (textual prescriptions regarding the proper response to the work) and what social audiences actually *do* with a given work. For Jameson, generic conventions attempt to prescribe and thereby foreclose the text's horizon of reception, a foreclosure of social use and significance that is, from the outset, impossible.[27] This resonates with Altman's "pragmatic" approach to film genres, the "exponentially increasing 'use indeterminacy' factor" surrounding every film.[28] A genre theory open to use, to pragmatics, to success or failure with social audiences, casts an entirely different light on the problems inherent in Todorov's reliance on the implicit reader. Acknowledging the fragility of generic prescriptions and the diversity of spectatorial responses highlights, by contrast, the docility of Todorov's implied reader and the problematic assumption of a genre's success. Genre as a social institution demands that readers, spectators, and consumers are recognized as more than a single implied reader or a mere theoretical mechanism for carrying out procedures prescribed in the text, whether these relate to affective response or narrative sense-making.

Histories of the Natural and the Supernatural

A second focus of historical critiques of the Todorovian fantastic has been his ahistorical dichotomy between the laws of nature (which Todorov uses interchangeably with "laws of our world" and "laws of reason") and the supernatural.[29] The autoreferential concept of literature that underpins his notion of the implicit reader likewise results in an ahistorical notion of the supernatural as pure literality. Todorov writes: "The supernatural is born of language, it is both its consequence and its proof: not only do the devil and vampires exist only in words, but language alone enables us to conceive what is always absent: the supernatural. The supernatural thereby becomes a symbol of language, just as the figures of rhetoric do, and the figure is, as we have seen, the purest form of literality."[30]

These aspects of Todorov's work on the fantastic have drawn criticism from several scholars. In his analysis of Irish fantastic literature, Chris Morash elaborates on the limitations of Todorov's theory when brought to bear on supernatural narratives in colonial and postcolonial contexts: "What is 'real' is not a simple unqualified fact of nature, but the product of a complex set of power relations . . . The 'laws,' as Todorov calls them, 'of this same familiar world' are recognized in a colonial context to have been produced by a set of political relations whose power resides in the ability to say what is real and what is not, so that in a colonized society the nature of reality is one of the main issues under dispute."[31] Todorov's reliance on an antinomy between natural law and supernatural anomaly has also been questioned by Andras Sandor: "The trouble with Todorov's theory lies with his concepts of nature, the natural, and the supernatural on the one hand, and with his aestheticist concept of poetry/literature as self-referential on the other."[32] Identifying the need for a broader historical understanding of the dichotomy between the supernatural, on the one hand, and the laws of nature, on the other, which Todorov understood as static literary categories, Monleón writes: "'In a world which is indeed our world,' says Todorov, 'there occurs an event which cannot be explained by the laws of this same familiar world.' But what must we understand by the laws of our world? Should a story written in the Middle Ages be considered according to the concept of nature upheld in those times or according to our current understanding of reality? Should the genre of a work change as the history of humanity modifies the idea of nature?"[33]

Both Monleón and Sandor ask a prior question: are the laws of nature and the notion of the supernatural historically immutable? If those ideas themselves have a complex genealogy, history rears its head in the very heart of Todorov's synchronic, autoreferential study. If nature and the supernatural are terms susceptible of historical mutation, then the definition of the fantastic, being a genre pinned to these concepts, must also be historically variable.

Today, Todorov's understanding of the supernatural as the antithesis of scientific laws of nature is commonsensical, allowing him to advert to "a world which is indeed our world, the world we know."[34] Yet such a conception of the natural as the diametrical opposite of the supernatural presupposes a historical forgetting of the very basis of modern science in natural theology, in the belief that God is at work in nature. The roots of the now-familiar natural laws that govern the physical world are to be found in the fourteenth century, when English Franciscan William of Ockham and other philosophers developed a voluntarist, theistic conception of the laws of nature. This "new metaphysics and philosophy of nature" continued to influence seventeenth-century science and is evident, for instance, in the theism of Descartes's mechanical philosophy.[35] The concept of nature as ordered by laws was first grounded in the supernatural agency of God as a divine lawgiver who created the world ex nihilo and directly and continually sustains the natural world. As John R. Milton puts it:

Once the idea of laws of nature had become generally accepted, it was possible (for those who so wished) to reject the theological standpoint which had originally made the idea acceptable. . . . By the middle of the eighteenth century, if not before, the concept of a physical law of nature had become one of those most basic of all concepts, which apparently require no metaphysical justification for their use and which are therefore employed with complete confidence. The idea of laws of nature could now appear to be natural; the slow changes of thought that had led to its genesis could be forgotten.[36]

The idea of nature as the antipode of the supernatural is consequent upon a thoroughly historical forgetting of their linked genealogies. As Daston observes, moderns would sooner oppose culture, rather than the supernatural, to nature.[37] The dichotomy Todorov invokes — supernatural versus natural — belongs to a much older continuum of concepts. According to Daston and Park, from the thirteenth century to the sixteenth, Europeans "did not treat natural and supernatural causes as mutually exclusive," in contrast to the "comparative coarseness of the modern distinction between the natural and the supernatural."[38] In the early modern period, nature was conceived alongside a set of collocated categories: the preternatural, the unnatural, and the artificial, among others. For the purposes of the present discussion it is the triangulation between the natural, the supernatural, and the preternatural that is most germane, especially since, as Daston points out, "in the current metaphysical vernacular . . . the supernatural has shrunk to a philosophical possibility . . . and the preternatural no longer exists at all."[39]

The thirteenth-century theologian Thomas Aquinas distinguished between two types of violations of the natural order: either via God's direct intervention in the form of a supernatural miracle or via "unusual occurrences" that were not God's doing but were "beyond nature" or "preternatural" (from Aquinas's phrase *praeter naturae ordinem* "apart from the order implanted [by God] in natural things").[40] For Aquinas, miracles demonstrate that God may violate the laws of nature that he himself established, exemplifying the way in which the creator is "above nature," that is, literally, supernatural. In contrast, the preternatural is not above but merely beyond nature. The key distinction to be made between the two categories rests on the agency and authority of the causative agent: in the case of the supernatural miracle, there can only be one causative actor: God, the Creator; in the case of preternatural anomalies, there are many possible causative agents, ranging from demons and angels to human magicians and nature itself. In practice, as the history of witchcraft trials painfully attests, distinctions between the supernatural and the preternatural, the work of God and the work of the devil, were notoriously difficult to adjudicate.[41] In Todorov's twentieth-century usage, the category of the preternatural has been evacuated and conflated with the supernatural.

What would it mean to take up the challenge posed by the history of science in order to think of the supernatural and the natural not as oppositions but as co-constitutive, historically mutable categories? To historicize these terms would open the fantastic to Jameson's winds of history. For example, nature from the standpoint of European thinkers in the medieval and early modern periods is characterized by regularity, but it is not equivalent to the modern conception of inviolable laws of nature, a natural order no longer "porous" to miracles or marvels that emerged in late seventeenth-century and eighteenth-century Europe.[42] While the notion of laws of nature grew in prominence from the Middle Ages to the seventeenth century, the laws of nature held by voluntarist thinkers, including Descartes and Bacon, did not in principle discount marvels from the order of nature. The mechanical philosophy of Bacon and Descartes was not fully disenchanted, since nature was thought to be governed by God's will. The eighteenth-century order of nature, a nature impervious to the marvelous, required a further refinement on the older terminology of *leges naturae*: the laws of nature came to be understood as "immutable," "always regular and uniform," a nature characterized by economy and moderation in cause and effect. The opposition between natural and supernatural, current in our own time and reflected in Todorov's assumptions, inherits (but forgets) the historical legacy of this early modern redefinition of the order of nature, the historical emergence of what Daston and Park call "the new metaphysics of uniform nature."[43]

The fantastic narrative is distinguished by its contemplation of temporalized being; the genre's key semantic codes are temporal likeness and temporal otherness.[44] The temporal alterity of the unfamiliar world can sometimes be simply a function of differences in temporal order, that is, a difference of chronological position in a linear, homogeneous time. This may explain why so many critics of late eighteenth-century and nineteenth-century fantastic literature subscribe to a chronological mapping of the two worlds depicted in the fantastic, with the marvelous a placeholder for medievalism, while the uncanny corresponds to Enlightenment or post-

Enlightenment skepticism. Such a view is, strictly speaking, not inaccurate where certain films are concerned. There are several examples of films that rehearse this linear, historical rendering of temporal alterity. This is perhaps most explicitly (and self-reflexively) acknowledged in Terry Gilliam's *The Adventures of Baron Munchausen* (1988), which begins with intertitles ironically announcing the disenchanted world's temporal setting—"18th Century. The Age of Reason. Wednesday."—into which the Baron, a figure from the pre-Enlightenment past, intrudes.

In contrast, aswang narratives foreground differences in temporal being so fundamental and so insurmountable that the attempt to linearize or homogenize the other world in terms of modern time consciousness results in an immiscible solution. The attempt to frame the discrepancy between two worlds, natural and supernatural, or urban and provincial, as a difference in chronological historical time feels, in aswang films, like a poor translation.

In advocating a historical consideration of Todorov's categories of the natural and the supernatural—which, in turn, underpin his definition of the uncanny and the marvelous—I am not advocating a historical trajectory that locates the fantastic as a midpoint in the progression from medieval supernaturalism to the disenchanted world of post-Enlightenment rationality. This kind of historical mapping, to which I am opposed, is given clearest articulation in the work of Tobin Siebers, who recasts Todorov's marvelous, fantastic, and uncanny as an evolutionary historical progression from superstitious acceptance to rational rejection of the supernatural. In *The Romantic Fantastic*, Siebers writes:

> The progression from the Pure Marvelous, Fantastic Marvelous, Pure Fantastic, and Fantastic Uncanny to the Pure Uncanny charts the rhapsodic transformation of supernatural representation in historical time. Folklore and fairytales, in which the supernatural reigns unchecked and unquestioned, represent the attitude of belief found prior to the crisis of Reason. They are pre-Rational forms of representation, although this does not preclude the possibility of recreating them at any point in time. . . . The Pure Uncanny represents belief apparently overcome by skepticism, where the inexplicable events formerly relegated to the supernatural are placed in limbo to await further investigation.[45]

Siebers's historical narrative charts a universal, linear course from mythic credulity to rational skepticism. This argument redresses the ahistorical quality of Todorov's model but delivers it to telos, thus missing the genre's

capacity to call into question the presumption of an evolutionary historical time. What Chakrabarty might call the scandalous quality of temporal untranslatability posed by supernatural narratives is here converted
into a predictable trajectory of historical supersession, when what is most
provocative about the fantastic is its capacity to insinuate the *failure* of
modern disenchantment to completely supplant nonmodern worlds. The
kind of argument that Siebers's analysis typifies, with its assumption that
the modern stands for a completely desacralized and internally consistent
worldview, is the historicist basis for definitions that engage the fantastic
via the trope of disenchantment, the survival of myth in a demythologized
age.[46]

The fantastic as the articulation of a superseded ethos bears a striking
resemblance to Freud's uncanny as the apparent confirmation of animistic
beliefs that have been repressed or should have been surmounted: "We—
or our primitive forefathers—once believed that these possibilities were
realities, and were convinced that they actually happened. Nowadays we
no longer believe in them, we have surmounted these modes of thought;
but we do not feel quite sure of our new beliefs, and the old ones still exist
within us ready to seize upon any confirmation."[47]

For Freud, those who are susceptible to the uncanny have not left the
"primitive" thinking of their "forefathers" "completely and finally" behind.
Hence one's vulnerability to the uncanny—which, defined as surmounted
modes of thought, closely resembles the notion of the fantastic as mythic
survival—is in inverse proportion to one's capacity to "rid" oneself of
primitivism. As I argued in my introduction, this collocation of savagery
and enchantment is constitutive of the disenchantment thesis.

The disenchantment thesis underwrites prevailing conceptions of the
fantastic as staging the supersession of outmoded, premodern schemata
by "progressive" rational paradigms. In this view, narratives of supernatural agency are merely the persistence of surmounted thought, a form of
mythic survival, a relic of a prior age. Such attempts to interject a historical
dimension to an understanding of the fantastic regrettably end by repeating the gestures of temporal exclusion characteristic of historicism.

  Chakrabarty defines historicism as

> the idea that things develop in historical time, that this time is empty and
> homogeneous, that history is layered and contains what Marx called the "un-
> vanquished remnants of the past." . . . Because of its openness to certain kinds

of "evolutionism" and its association with the logic of bureaucratic decision making, [it is] an inherent modernist elitism that silently lodges itself into our everyday consciousness.

Historicism, as Heidegger explained in his critique, consists in a very particular understanding of the question of contemporaneity: the idea that things from different historical periods can exist in the same time (the so-called simultaneity of the non-simultaneous) but belong to different worlds. Thus we may have a "medieval" object before us, but it is [a] relic from a past world that is no longer there. One could, in historicism, look at peasants in the same way: as survivals from a dead world. This is a fundamental characteristic of historicist thought. It is what allows us to think that the "agency of the supernatural" is a problem from the past surviving, for good and understandable historical reasons, in a disenchanted present.[48]

As Chakrabarty demonstrates, historicism is a kind of "modernist elitism" that has seeped into our commonsensical ideas about history, a temporal elitism at work in the rhetoric of writers who argue that fantastic narratives encountered in the present are actually vestiges of a prior, eclipsed world. This historicist gesture, so palpable in the idea of the fantastic as the residue of demythologization, manages to say to accounts of the supernatural: "you appear to be here and now but you are really there and then." The erasure of something that confronts us with its contemporaneous presence—whether it be a fantastic account or, in Chakrabarty's example, a "superstitious" third world peasant—by claiming that it is actually the tenacious remnant of a dead world, amounts to Fabian's denial of coevalness.

To take seriously the coeval, vigorous presence of supernatural narratives in global popular culture is to depart from Todorov's understanding of the fantastic as coextensive with late eighteenth-century and nineteenth-century European fantastic literature. Toward the end of his book, Todorov makes explicit the historical scope of his study: "It appeared in a systematic way around the end of the eighteenth century with Cazotte; a century later, we find the last aesthetically satisfying examples of the genre in Maupassant's tales." Raising the question, "Why does the literature of the fantastic no longer exist?," Todorov concludes that the death of the fantastic was brought on by psychoanalysis: "psychoanalysis has replaced (and thereby has made useless) the literature of the fantastic."[49] Todorov's remarkable study ends, in effect, by embalming its object.

Despite Todorov's pronouncement of the ·death of the fantastic, on screens across the globe, not to mention a host of other genres and media forms—ranging from literature to popular film and television—supernatural narratives that trigger epistemological crises persist. Todorov's somewhat premature declaration that the fantastic came to an end in the late nineteenth century would, if accepted, cast contemporary supernatural narratives as a vestige of an earlier century's literary paradigm, now secularized and surmounted by psychoanalysis.

But another path, suggested by Todorov himself, consists of following the fantastic experience of limits outward, beyond the textual frame. Having completed his synchronic description of the genre, Todorov turns, in the fascinating last chapter of his study, to another methodological route. This other course leads to a consideration of the social significance and historical constitution of genre: "Our investigation has hitherto been located within the genre. We have sought to produce an 'immanent' study of the fantastic, to distinguish the categories by which it might be described, supported by internal necessities alone. We must now, in conclusion, change our perspective. Once the genre is constituted, we may consider it from the outside—from the viewpoint of literature in general, or even of social life—and ask our question again, though in another form: no longer 'what is the fantastic?' but 'why is the fantastic?'"[50]

Considering the fantastic "from the outside," Todorov suggests that the "social function of the supernatural" consists of a "license to transgression": "the fantastic permits us to cross certain frontiers that are inaccessible so long as we have no recourse to it." The fantastic offers a way of breaching taboos, particularly in relation to sexuality: "the function of the supernatural is to exempt the text from the action of the law, and thereby to transgress that law."[51] If, following Todorov, the fantastic is considered as a license to transgression, one glimpses the play of what Spivak terms "contained alterity," the tension between containment (license, permission) and unruly difference (transgression).[52] That is, one catches sight of the genre's character as translation, of writing otherness back to acceptable forms.

In my admittedly differential reading of Todorov, the law that the fantastic pushes to its limit is not only sexual—though, as we will see in chapter 3, sexuality is also often conscripted for strategies of temporal management and dissent—but temporal. The sanction, then, that the fantastic is licensed to transgress is frequently the rule of modern, secular, homogeneous time.

Part Two.
Stereoscoping Times: Aswang and Media Convergence

Aswang, circa 1992

When news of manananggal gripped the Philippine capital in 1992, journalists repeatedly drew parallels between electoral violence and fraud, on the one hand, and supernatural sightings, on the other, as two contemporaneous forms of bloodletting, secular and occult. "Come election day," a *Manila Chronicle* writer quipped, "you can expect sightings of *manananggal* hovering over polling precincts, and God forbid, people sighting *manananggal* spiriting off with ballot boxes."[53] Originating in the rumorscape of Metro Manila's impoverished slums, aswang narratives were disseminated by tabloids, covered by "sober broadsheets and otherwise clearheaded columnists," and reported by foreign correspondents, prompting one journalist to declare: "Everybody's batty these days."[54] This double entendre was an insinuation that the entire city, gripped by terror and fascination with the creature, had gone quite mad; such a pronouncement was of a piece with the secular consternation that greeted the phenomenon, a disparagement that was simultaneously class-inflected and strongly temporalized.

The *Manila Chronicle*, a newspaper with an elite urban readership, glossed the terrific popular currency of the aswang with ironic flourish: "Welcome to Tondo, circa 1992. It looks like 400 years of Catholicism and 50 years of Hollywood have not quite succeeded in erasing pre-colonial beliefs."[55] To anyone who has encountered analyses of aswang tales, beliefs, and practices across a wide range of fields—the ethnologies of early Spanish missionaries on the islands, the folklore studies of American observers in the colonial period, and the scholarship of the first wave of Filipino anthropologists and sociologists writing for American mentors and interlocutors—the temporalized condescension of this journalist is entirely typical.[56] The exclusion of aswang and their audiences from the modern present proceeds swiftly from a recognition of contemporaneity ("Welcome to Tondo, circa 1992") to the imputation that the worlds in which aswang move belong to another time ("pre-colonial beliefs" that have almost, but not quite, been erased). The charge of anachronism applies not only to supernatural creatures but to the "batty" tabloid readers who believe, or half-believe, in them. As I have argued, the accusation of noncontemporaneity, the claim that a present phenomenon really belongs to a prior, premodern time, is a way of managing intractable difference by denigrating it as outmoded. Rather than pursue the implication that "Tondo, circa 1992" might be traversed by multiple times and heterogeneous worlds, the homogeneity of modern time is upheld by excluding the enchantments of popular culture.

Aswang have figured prominently in Philippine cinema since the silent film *Aswang* (1932), starring Monang Carvajal; since the mid-1980s, they have become the mainstay of a twenty-year-old horror-film cycle initiated by the directorial team of Peque Gallaga and Lore Reyes, arguably the most prominent and prolific horror directors in the contemporary Filipino film industry. Their profitable horror-comedy franchise, the *Shake, Rattle and Roll* films — each one an omnibus of three episodes by various directors — began in 1984; the first outing featured a segment entitled "Manananggal." Aswang and manananggal were featured as well in *Shake, Rattle and Roll 2* (1990; "Aswang" episode), *Shake, Rattle and Roll 4* (1992; "Ang madre" [The Nun] episode), *Aswang* (1992), and in a slew of other horror movies since.[57] Featured in tabloids and broadsheets and flickering across film and television screens, aswang in the early 1990s confounded the generic borders between hearsay, fantastic fiction, and journalistic reportage; they were also the locus of emphatic media convergence. Self-conscious and defensive about their indulgence in marvels, various media institutions accused one another of a kind of figurative vampirism: respectable broadsheets characterized the manananggal craze as a sensational tabloid affair while disavowing the similarly profit-oriented, presentist interests that fueled their own coverage.[58] When, in 1992, Regal Films announced that *Aswang* would hit movie theaters by the end of the year, one writer remarked that executive producer "Mother Lily" Monteverde "must be cackling with glee," implicitly equating profit-hungry film producers with diabolical creatures.[59]

Screening Aswang

Aswang (1992), directed by Peque Gallaga, Lore Reyes, and Don Escudero, begins with a supernatural ritual of transfiguration, as a wizened old hag transforms herself into a comely young woman. Walking along the out-skirts of the town, the seductress lures a drunken man into the woods. He expects a tryst but instead meets his death at the hands of a feral were-beast. Following a frantic attack, we see the man's final moments, half-devoured, his entrails splattered across the grass. This opening set piece of rural supernatural violence cuts abruptly to an uppercase intertitle—MANILA—as the Philippine capital is introduced via a crane shot of the city by night, its thoroughfares crowded with cars.

Another grisly series of events unfolds. The child Catlyn and two domes-tic servants charged with her care narrowly escape death when the family home is robbed by a gang of criminals. The thieves brutally murder the other servants and Catlyn's mother, but Catlyn, her nanny (Veron), and the family driver (Dudoy) manage to get away. With the killers in hot pur-suit, the three leave Manila for the safety of Dudoy's provincial hometown, Talisay (shot on location in Tiaong, Quezon Province), there to await the return of Catlyn's father from overseas. The hoped-for safety of a provin-cial refuge turns out to be an illusion, however, since Talisay is being rav-aged by the slakeless hunger of an aswang—in this film, an amalgam of viscera sucker, shape-shifting witch, and were-beast.

To battle the supernatural threat, the urbanites quickly absorb the rudi-ments of aswang detection and expulsion. When Catlyn learns that aswang can take on the guise of other people at will, she peeks out from behind the viewfinder of a point-and-shoot camera and, wide-eyed, asks how it's possible to make copies of other people (fig. 21).

The film persistently likens visual technologies to supernatural aswang (both are able to reproduce appearances). This analogy is made most ex-plicit when an aswang-hunter plays back, in slow motion, a video recording of a pretty girl walking in the forest. The video footage alternates between a young woman and an old crone; diegetic protagonists and filmic audience alike are treated to indisputable visual evidence of the two guises of the same woman, a chameleon-like aswang (figs. 22–27).

On one level, the diegesis is here upholding the capacity of optical tech-nologies—the video camera, to be precise—to pierce the veil of enchant-ment, to see the buxom young woman for what she really is: an ancient aswang. On another, perhaps even more compelling level, the sequence is a defamiliarized review of the powers and pleasures of the cinema's con-tinuity system and invisibility editing. Despite the visible presence of two

21. The child protagonist of *Aswang* learns that aswang can
copy human appearances. The scene explicitly links the aswang's
ability to mimic human guise with photographic reproduction.

different actresses, our perception of the same aswang revealed in forked
guise as she walks through the woods is fostered by the strong impression
of continuity forged by the directional aspects of each figure's movement
and glance. These are combined with carefully controlled aspects of the
mise-en-scène to match the quality of natural light with location setting,
camera angle, and distance of framing in the footage of both women. Continuity hides profilmic artifice and the cut and delivers a single aswang's
doubled stride into the forest.

The economical retooling of invisibility-editing-as-special-effect is also
a return to the spare elegance of one of the oldest formal devices in the
cinema's fantastic arsenal: the doubled aswang on video recalls the substitution splice pioneered by Georges Méliès, in which the seamless continuity of the projected film, along with a controlled homology of framing,
makes a magical transformation come to seem both abrupt and seamless,
accomplished, as it were, in the blink of an eye. Méliès's famous *trucage*
is a kind of optical magic that diegetically conveys the presence of enchantment and, reflexively, displays the novel powers and pleasures of the
cinema.[60] If it works, that is, if the film trick is convincingly amazing, then
it makes spectators, for a moment, doubt the evidence of their own eyes,
while whetting their appetite for further visual marvels.

22

23

25

26

24

22–27. In *Aswang*, slow-motion video footage of a single aswang walking in the woods exposes her doubled guise, alternating between a beautiful young woman and an old crone.

27

In terms of its spatial and temporal politics, *Aswang* is the middle ground between two poles of Gallaga's and Reyes's depictions of aswang. In 1990, two years before the manananggal scare gripped Metro Manila, *Shake, Rattle and Roll 2* included a segment entitled "Aswang." The segment retells folk narratives about an urbanite's entrapment in rural space. A student from Manila, invited to vacation in a classmate's provincial hometown, is nearly devoured when the classmate and the rural villagers turn out to be aswang.[61] The motifs of betrayed friendship, as well as the reversal of a host's ethic of care toward a guest, are linked to a phobic imaginary that conflates class, space, and position in evolutionary time. As I have noted elsewhere, "the episode is most transparently a spatialized sketch of a wealthy urbanite's fear of the provincial, understood as the site of a feral primitivism that confounds modern rationality. The . . . Manila youngsters are wholesome and God-fearing, whereas the peasants are pagans who practice the black arts of human sacrifice and cannibalism."[62]

By 1992, the "Ang madre" episode of *Shake, Rattle and Roll 4*, in attempting to capitalize on the aswang rumorscape of earlier months, profoundly shifted the spatial and temporal character of the onscreen aswang. Whereas both the *Aswang* episode of 1990 and the full-length feature film *Aswang* in 1992 dramatized an urban bourgeoisie assailed in the backwoods, the ripped-from-the-headlines narrative of "Ang madre" centered on the vulnerability of the urban poor in Metro Manila, ravaged by manananggal posing as middle-class social workers. The male physician and Catholic sister who run a charity clinic in an impoverished neighborhood by day turn out to be bloodsucking predators by night. Whereas the set pieces of earlier aswang films by Gallaga and Reyes equated class privilege with virtue (bourgeois protagonists retreating to shiny cars and well-appointed houses locked tight against aswang threatening to break in), in "Ang madre" the slum dwellers are the far more vulnerable heroes, sleeping only in flimsy carts or *cariton*, wheeled hovels that offer precious little by way of defense from a manananggal attack.

In one scene, the cart-pushers warn one another to shut themselves in as tightly as possible for the night but note wryly that, unlike the rich, they have nothing worth stealing and cannot hide behind the security of high walls and guard dogs. Someone replies that even the poor have something worth taking: their lifeblood. Such dialogue defines personhood as corporeal self-ownership, the only form of property to which unpropertied indigents can lay claim. In scenes like these "Ang madre" thematizes the horizon of reception that greeted the 1992 manananggal attacks in the slums of Metro Manila: the aswang sightings were widely glossed by middle-class writers as an allegory for the victimization and vulnerability of the urban poor.

In "Ang madre," the monstrosity of the aswang is explicitly likened to the hypocrisy of middle-class do-gooders; the Catholic nun gently chastises her impoverished patients for being superstitious, saying, "We create our own fears; the reason why we never see progress in our lives is that we are even now tied to mistaken beliefs." Teleological time is implicit in her reproach, opposing the old mistaken beliefs to progress (*asenso*). Ultimately, as the episode title "Ang madre" [The Nun] highlights, the eponymous Christian *religeuse* who espouses rational skepticism is exposed as the fearsome manananggal herself; her colleague, the kindly medical doctor, is likewise a creature of the night.[63] At the end of the segment, the virtuous protagonist, Puri (literally, "purity"), filled with the righteous indignation of the downtrodden, rebukes the aswang: "You pretend to help us, to heal us, to be kind, but you are nothing but devils in disguise!"

The social evils of pretense or hypocrisy (*pagpapanggap*) on the part of elites who purport to improve the lot of the underclasses literalize a conspicuous aspect of the horizon of reception for aswang sightings in 1992. The crosshead in a *Manila Chronicle* article reads: "This story is about the blood-suckers who are flying, not running for office," alleging a one-to-one correspondence between the manananggal craze and the national elections the phenomenon was overshadowing.[64] Middle-class commentators in English-language periodicals vacillated between characterizing manananggal and politicians as competing for national attention *and* asserting a metaphoric equivalency between politicians and supernatural viscera suckers, since both disguise their true nature while preying on the very poor.

Likewise, short fiction published in the literary sections of weekly magazines during this period made explicit the allegorical correspondence between aswang attacks and an electoral process marked by widespread violence and fraud. In Felix Fojas's short story "Manananggal," Mayor Timoteo Sangre (Spanish for "blood"), an inveterate gambler and corrupt politician, turns out to be a manananggal himself. As the number of supernatural killings mount, the local government responds to townsfolks' demands that the monster be apprehended by framing an innocent derelict. On election night, the mayor-manananggal's lackeys arrange for a power outage to occur an hour after the elections to enable ballot-switching; when the town is plunged into darkness, the young human rights lawyer running in opposition to the mayor, who is leading in the ballot count, is abducted and killed. A month after the elections, a farmer surprises a manananggal on his roof and kills it with a bamboo spear. The crowd that gathers beside the slain aswang recognize the mayor's face on the winged creature and realize that politician and monster were one and the same: "venting their pent-up rage upon the dying bloodsucker, the citizens closed in for the kill."[65]

Like Fojas's story, "Ang madre" reverses the generic conventions of aswang narratives in terms of class and temporalized space — the aswang is drawn from the ranks of the middle classes, no longer confined to the supposedly anachronistic world of the rural peasant as in the previous Gallaga and Reyes films. The embrace of populist sensibilities in "Ang madre" also led to a shift in the directors' racialized politics of casting. The relatively unknown, dark-skinned, older actress Lilia Cuntapay had played witches and aswang in prior Gallaga and Reyes films ("Yaya" [The Nanny] in *Shake, Rattle and Roll 3* [1991]; and in *Aswang* [1992]), but in "Ang madre" casting practices were reversed. Fair-skinned, attractive mestizo stars Aiko Melendez and Miguel Rodriguez starred as bourgeois manananggal, while Lilia Cuntapay played a kindhearted elderly recluse mistaken by a vindictive crowd for an aswang. The film's object lesson — not to make aswang accusations based on appearances — is directed against the diegetic mob but also implicitly calls into question the directorial team's racialized, class-inflected casting choices to that point, their conflation of the physical appearance of dark-skinned, older peasants with aswang physiognomy.

In an essay on film noir, Vivian Sobchack offers an original approach to the question of history in genre films. Departing from figurative readings of genre, Sobchack demonstrates that historical specificity can be inscribed in the form of actual historical spaces visible in the mise-en-scène.[66] A consideration of mise-en-scène in terms of historical inscription is well suited to "Ang madre." The self-conscious attempt to make the horror-comedy speak, to a certain extent, in the register of docudrama, to convey a "ripped-from-the-headlines" quality of relevance and urgency, results in a mise-en-scène that closely resembles journalistic and tabloid accounts of manananggal sightings in the 1992 electoral season and unwittingly recalls the politicized use of urban location shooting in the Philippine New Cinema of the 1970s.

Recounting a May 6 incident in which a manananggal was chased down by a crowd in Tondo, a writer for the *Sunday Inquirer Magazine* writes: "the object of pursuit glided over lamp posts, electric lines and TV antennas and sailed toward the schoolhouse."[67] At an April 13 sighting, a crowd of hundreds gathered so thickly around one home that an onlooker was reminded of the February Revolt of 1986, when massive political demonstrations held on EDSA (E. de los Santos Avenue) called for the ouster of Ferdinand Marcos.[68] As if literalizing this analogy, "Ang madre" begins with a high-angle establishing shot of EDSA at night, the blur of automobile headlights dwarfed by huge neon billboards. The downward tilt of the mobile crane shot is continued in the vertical descent of the tracking shot that follows; the initially distant aerial gaze gives way to an intimate on-the-ground view of one depressed neighborhood in the densely populated capital.

Most striking, however, are the daytime establishing shots in "Ang madre," location footage meant to ground the fictional narrative in the historical, place-bound specificity of the 1992 manananggal attacks. In this shot, probably taken in Mandaluyong, where later sightings were reported, the camera hovers well above the rusting iron-roof sheeting of the squatter colonies, the disorderly tangle of electric lines and TV antennas (fig. 28).[69]

This mise-en-scène—the skyline of some of the poorest districts in Metro Manila—is the new stalking ground of the aswang, no longer confined, as before, to rural environs. Such establishing shots refer directly to the manananggal fever that began in Tondo but also (perhaps unconsciously) link the film to the visual vocabulary of the critically acclaimed social-realist city films of the 1970s. Describing director Lino Brocka's 1975 film *Maynila: Sa kuko ng liwanag* [Manila: In the Claws of Neon], the film that marked the inception of an aesthetically compelling, politically charged New Cinema in the Philippines, one film reviewer astutely drew attention to Brocka's practice of shooting on location in Tondo: "Brocka's unpatronizing sympathy for the underclasses has brought him to shoot, time and again, in Tondo, Manila's worst slum. The films made there . . . are exempt from any facile proletarianism."[70] First Lady Imelda Marcos, concerned about the national image under the Marcos regime, barred location shooting in Tondo in 1981. By 1992, with the Marcos regime toppled and Corazon Aquino's presidency about to give way to the Ramos administration, slums were once again open to film crews. A key difference, of course, is that in Brocka's 1970s films and studio classics like *Anak Dalita* [Child of

28. The mise-en-scène of establishing shots in "Ang madre"
(from *Shake, Rattle and Roll 4*, dir. Peque Gallaga and Lore
Reyes, 1992) recalls newspaper coverage of the manananggal
attacks on Metro Manila slums in 1992 and the politicized
use of location shooting in Lino Brocka's social realist films.

Sorrow] (Lamberto Avellana, 1956), urban squatter colonies epitomize the
bleak disillusioned realism of national allegories in which the housing crisis
of the urban poor (composed largely of provincial migrant workers barely
eking out a living in Manila) is metonymic of the country's ills. In contrast,
the tenor of *Shake, Rattle and Roll 2*, like all of Gallaga's and Reyes's collabo-
rative horrors—a campy horror comedy punctuated in equal measure by
gross-out and moments of levity—depicts slum dwellers as indefatigably
cheerful and heroic in the midst of want.

As I argued in my introduction, the fantastic is a genre whose forked
worlds—two radically different orders of events, or experiential forestruc-
tures—are represented as concrete places within the film frame. This is
why mise-en-scène in fantastic cinema is so frequently invested with significance; both filmmakers and viewers know that setting, light, color, and
the look of the figures onscreen literalize the otherness of *that world* in
comparison with the world of everyday life. In Gilliam's *Baron Munchausen*,
for example, epistemic struggles between enchantment and reason are signaled by shifts in color. The world of reason looks drab; in contrast, pleasure, exuberance, and youthfulness are the province of the marvelous,

which explains both the ornate vibrancy of the magical worlds within the frame and the notoriously high production costs Gilliam accumulated off-screen. But in Gallaga's and Reyes's episode "Ang madre," the mise-en-scène of the fantastic centers on the slums of Metro Manila, visualizing motifs of enchanted-but-modern rooftops and tangled television and electric cables familiar from tabloid and broadsheet coverage of the manananggal sightings in early 1992. The mise-en-scène of "Ang madre"—a decrepit urban skyline—unwittingly recalls the New Cinema's social realist tradition of location shooting while shifting the aswang film cycle's place-bound notions of enchantment from province to city, making the aswang a figure for the porosity of rural and urban modes of being, the blurring of spatially demarcated, class-delineated worlds.

For me the most memorable image in "Ang madre" is the moment when the manananggal, fleeing the scene of her latest kill, snags her wings in television antennas atop the hammered-metal shingling of the slum residences (figs. 29–31). Diegetically, the aerial wires nearly impale her; extra-diegetically, the scene reads as a figuration of the media-saturated career of the aswang, her infamy soaring through the airwaves to radio and television audiences.

"Ang madre" is visibly preoccupied with the question of popular audiences; this emerges most interestingly in its characterization of the protagonists as themselves members of a collective media public. In one scene, two street kids use a newspaper for a blanket. A closer shot reveals that it is *People's Journal Tonight*, the largest-circulation tabloid in the Philippines, notorious for its coverage of the 1992 manananggal scare (figs. 32 and 33).

The two boys are literally sleeping under the cover of rumors. Like the off-screen diegetic sound of radio hosts cracking manananggal jokes in an expository scene, such shots bring home the fact that the diegesis centers on slum dwellers who are collectively constituted as a tabloid-reading public, co-tellers of stories heard on the street, listeners to radio broadcasts about the manananggal. Television coverage is troped as well: in "Ang madre," the scene in which an elderly woman confronts an angry mob recalls news footage of "a dozen young men, accompanied by a television crew, [who] barged into the home of Teresita Beronqui, to investigate rumors that she was the dreaded manananggal. ABS-CBN showed a terrified, elderly woman trying to explain that she was not the manananggal."[71] Violence

29–31. In "Ang madre," the manananggal entangled in television antennas and spotted by slum residents is a figure for both media convergence and media audiences.

32, 33. In
"Ang madre,"
two street
kids sleep
under tabloids
reporting
manananggal
attacks.

was averted when Beronqui, in front of a national television viewership, unflinchingly touched a stingray's tail (*buntot ng pagi*), thus acquitting herself of suspicions that she was a manananggal.

Benedict Anderson has persuasively argued that the newspaper (and other forms of print capitalism, like the novel) plays a vital role in cementing the imagined temporal coincidence that binds the nation in a fantasy of community. The fact that every newspaper will be outdated by tomorrow imposes the expectation that it will be read within today's remaining span. "The obsolescence of the newspaper on the morrow of its printing," Anderson points out, "creates this extraordinary mass ceremony: the almost precisely simultaneous consumption ('imagining') of the newspaper-as-fiction. . . . What more vivid figure for the secular, historically clocked, imagined community can be envisioned?"[72]

The newspaper in Anderson's analysis is a kind of ticking clock in print, a book certain to be outdated by tomorrow. A strongly temporally circumscribed commodity, the newspaper delivers a fantasy of "simultaneous consumption" in a collective present: today, in other parts of the country, others are reading the very newspaper I am holding. Such an experience of "calendrical coincidence" fosters an imagined national meanwhile. Anderson writes: "The date at the top of the newspaper, the single most important emblem on it, provides the essential connection—the steady onward clocking of homogeneous empty time."[73] In this light, the manananggal's heavily mediatized presence in 1992 becomes even more fascinating, since the role of tabloid and other media cultures (not only the newspaper but television journalism and popular films alluding to newspaper accounts) did convey a sense of simultaneity for a national audience; however, this temporality was not the homogeneous time of the modern nation but an unwieldy, occult splitting of national time, a *heterogeneous meanwhile*.

Tabloid newspapers not only bound a collective readership in thrilling accounts of supernatural menace; they also exemplified perceived differences, as well as the interpermeability, of classed reading publics purportedly held apart by taste and cultivation, on the one hand, and gullibility and sensationalism, on the other. One journalist remarks, "The rumorscape is fascinating and while strange in this day and age—the dawn of the 21st century to be exact—it makes even the most cynical and educated of us curious (just observe how many motorists buy the tabloids with manananggal stories splashed on their front pages), and to even reflect."[74] Chula Sicam interpellates the readers of the *Chronicle* as "cynical and educated" people like "us," who are nevertheless drawn in by supernatural curiosities. The motorist tempted to pick up a tabloid featuring manananggal emerges as a frequently invoked figure of class contagion. In one particularly colorful example, Rene Pastor, writing for *Malaya*, paints this scene: "Tabloids featuring the latest exploits of the rapidly multiplying creature are snapped up in the Makati financial district by socialite matrons in air-conditioned Mercedes Benzes."[75]

Such characterizations were meant to play on the incongruity of the well-educated rich stooping to consume the pulp fictions enjoyed by their supposed social underlings; instead, these writers betrayed anxiety-ridden middle-class responses to the aswang's popularity. The conventional, classed notions such writers invoked—for instance, the purportedly cultivated tastes of the wealthy—are exposed as fictions. The tabloid-obsessed socialite revealed that the well-heeled are not necessarily inured to marvels; superstition is not symptomatic of ignorance, nor are these two qualities synonymous with particular classes.

The Porosity of Generic Worlds

> Those who live in the towns laugh at these superstitions, yet it would be difficult to find any one who does not believe at least some of them.
> MILLINGTON AND MAXFIELD, "Philippine (Visayan) Superstitions"

Despite persistent assumptions that aswang stories, beliefs, and practices belong to a fixed nexus of time, place, and class—the premodern world of the rural peasant—aswang insistently demonstrate the permeability of disparate worlds. From centuries-old folk narratives to the manananggal reports that shook Metro Manila in 1992 and the horror-film cycle that ensued, it becomes clear that aswang belong to more worlds than one: as much to the gossip of public markets as to a middle-class readership; as much to the city's mediascape as to deep forests and remote villages. Weaving story and history, the aswang actualizes generic porosity and exchange. Its domain is neither fiction nor nonfiction but the equivocal character of rumor, hearsay, and the repeatedly retold account. Writing on Chinese classical tales of the strange (*zhiguai*), Judith Zeitlin similarly refuses to characterize strange tales as fiction, proposing instead a nuanced consideration of the slippery veridical status of hearsay, which operates on ambiguity, not incredulity: "The ambiguity that the pretext of hearsay creates is of utmost importance to accounts of the strange, for the burden of truth is partially suspended: the claim becomes in some sense that the story was told, not that the events in the story occurred."[76] Like the zhiguai's enactment of the veridical instability of hearsay, the horizons of reception in which aswang circulate fuse belief, skepticism, and suspended judgment; their ambit bridges the presumed urban-rural divide and demonstrates that the fantastic narrative may often straddle the borders of history and fiction.

The exposition of the film *Aswang* is governed by a strict principle of spatial alternation that contrasts two forms of violence: the occult dangers of a rural town vis-à-vis the ever-present menace of homicidal crime in the urban center. The split but porous worlds of the fantastic are visualized as setting in the mise-en-scène. In *Aswang*, the two worlds, rational and supernatural, are at first spatialized and rigidly demarcated as the respective domains of city and province. As the film progresses, however, the two worlds-as-places — disparate epistemic horizons as physical locales — grow more permeable. The sleepy rural town is drawn into ever-widening circles of urban crime, and the Manileños in Talisay are attacked by aswang. The narrative takes for granted that many of Manila's citified residents are themselves first-generation provincial migrants who now live and work in the nation's capital.

In an interview with Saurabh Dube, Chakrabarty gives a concrete example, drawn from his own life history, of the porosity of middle-class and rural peasant worlds. He suspects that his experience belongs to the "collective biography of the Indian middle classes":

> In the case of the specific histories of the Indian middle classes, there is an interesting phenomenon. At least until now, we have never been very far from peasant or rural modes of orienting ourselves to the world. This is partly because [of] our practice of employing domestic servants who are often of peasant stock. This is a very complicated part of our collective biographies. . . . Most of us as children have intimate relations of proximity to members of the class we later come to see as objects of pedagogical exercise. In our childhood, however, these people are often our teachers. Through the stories they tell when looking after us, through the affections they shower on us in our childhood, they impart to us orientations of the world we often later disavow. I did not have to read the history of plague riots of 1898 to understand the opposition of subaltern classes to hospitalization or modern medicine. When we were kids, the city authorities used to send vaccinators to our homes to vaccinate against cholera, typhoid, smallpox, and other diseases. Who would hide under the bed for fear of the needle? It would be my sister and me, and our adult servant. My father would drag us out of there. While we the children got a modernizing lecture on public health and hygiene, the servant was bullied into submission. I have often wondered if subaltern studies did not have some roots in this aspect of the collective biography of the Indian middle classes.[77]

In this anecdote the analytic and the lived are intertwined, and Chakrabarty deals candidly with the problems inherent in the middle-class intellectual's dispassionate stance, a scholarly position that often involves objectifying members of other classes — as peasants, as masses — when, in childhood, they had been one's caregivers and teachers. I am struck by this passage, partly because the social practice of employing domestic servants who usually hail from the provinces is a long-standing aspect of life for the urban middle classes in the Philippines. The dynamic Chakrabarty recalls here, in which the middle-class child grows up in the city but is also enmeshed in the worlding of caring domestic helpers from rural towns, is not only validated by my childhood in Metro Manila but also by a slew of fantastic films that link the presence of the supernatural to a child-nanny dynamic, to the vicissitudes of the cross-class, cross-place relationship Chakrabarty describes. *Aswang*, as noted above, begins with caring domestic servants from the provinces rescuing their ward from the clutches of would-be kidnappers. To elude criminals in Manila, they take Catlyn to Dudoy's provincial hometown, but there they come upon aswang. In this fantastic narrative, the movement from human malevolence to supernatural threat is accomplished precisely by the intersection of worlds enabled by the shared affection between the urban middle-class child and her peasant caregivers. Manilyn Reynes, the actress who plays the virtuous nanny Veron in *Aswang*, appears in several of the *Shake, Rattle and Roll* films and a slew of horror films in the 1990s. The most visible star of that decade's Filipino horror films, her star persona became indelibly linked to the role of provincial migrant, embodying the intersection of rural and urban worlds so frequently narrated by aswang films.[78]

Rural-to-urban labor flows are a submerged motif of the manananggal sightings of 1992, and this is not only because the aswang's emergence in Tondo reemphasized the lack of adequate housing for the urban poor, many of them workers recently arrived from the countryside. In newspaper accounts, an oft-repeated origin story for the sightings centers on two domestic servants, Luz and Lucille, who worked for a middle-class family in Tondo. The two girls were romantic rivals who quarreled over a tricycle driver. Luz lost both her boyfriend and her job and uttered a malediction against Lucille before leaving for her hometown in Negros. Two months later, on April 13, a disfigured Luz was seen hovering over the house of her former employers; neighbors took her for a manananggal.[79]

The anthropologist Raul Pertierra's functionalist analysis of the aswang complex suggests that aswang accounts articulate patriarchal anxieties over female labor migration and the sexual freedoms enjoyed by women far from home. For Pertierra, the work patterns of young Visayan women leaving for urban employment in the service industries raise concerns over uncontrolled female sociality.[80] More compelling, perhaps, is another noted Filipino anthropologist's cautionary warning against reifying "rural" and "urban" as rigid antinomies, since for many Filipinos, the two place-bound affiliations are intertwined even in a single life history. In response to an interviewer's asking whether or not the aswang "appear[s] only to the lumpen," F. Landa Jocano replies:

> Not necessarily. It appears not only in a lower group but also among the educated, because there are teachers, lawyers, doctors who believe in aswang. I would not say depressed area or poorer neighborhood, but rather a marginalized community where interpersonal relationships and social interactions are particularly strongest. . . . The inroads of rural beliefs find themselves in urban places like Tondo where the population are recent migrants, squatters who are rural people. But I would hardly correlate this belief with poverty, ignorance, illiteracy, but rather with recency of rural migration to the urban center. When people move to urban areas they carry their beliefs with them, and that is the reason for this upward movement of this aswang phenomenon from the Visayas to Manila. Any traditional system of the rural areas can be magnified in an urban setting, if only for the reason that many urban dwellers were rural people 10 years ago, and that is not even one generation.[81]

Published in the same year of the 1992 sightings, Nerissa Balce's short story "Manananggal" opens with the first-person narrator, a university professor, cringing at the sight of her eleven-year-old son regularly poring over tabloid reports on the manananggal craze: "seeing naked starlets on the front pages of *People's Tonite* over milk, bread, and luncheon meat at breakfast disturbed me."[82] At one point, the short story takes a decidedly cinematic turn, evoking a montagelike juxtaposition of manananggal tales told by her son, as his mother, the narrator, keeps one eye on televised updates of the electoral tallies.

The narrator both tells and listens to stories: in one scene, the radio is broadcasting news of electoral fraud; in another, a university colleague recounts the death of her activist sister, a victim of the Marcos government's violent suppression of leftists. "The General" running for president had, in the 1970s, ordered the activist's death. (This is a clear allusion to Fidel Ramos, who enforced the repressive violence of martial law under the

Marcos regime in 1972; he defected in 1986 and would emerge victorious in the 1992 presidential elections.) Set against the backdrop of such stories is the central plight of the professor-narrator's laundrywoman, Asuncion, whose philandering husband, an unemployed alcoholic, habitually beats his wife. Balce's story evokes a metaphoric correspondence between two forms of patriarchal power and violence. On the one hand, the story of the murdered female activist points to covert, state-sanctioned violence in the public sphere; the laundrywoman's plight points in the other direction, to domestic abuse in the private realm of marital life. One day, Asuncion confides to her employer, our narrator: "It would be easier to kill him."[83] Soon after, the abusive husband is found dead, his stomach rent open and his intestines diced; neighbors conclude he was victimized by an aswang.

The manananggal becomes, in Balce's story, a figure of female retribution: Asuncion, we infer, is a copycat murderess who dispatches her husband in the manner attributed to viscera suckers. The domestic servant's cunning stratagem manages to decisively turn the tables on heteronormativity and shifts the story to a bifurcated level of social allegory. In Balce's story, the rapacious viscera sucker is allied on the one hand with the patriarchal power of both the corrupt militarized state and the abusive husband; on the other hand, the aswang is also the guise assumed by a woman who rescues herself from sexual-economic subordination. In this second sense, the manananggal enables an imagined mode of exacting reparations by violent means, of visiting outraged, long-deserved punishment on patriarchal power.

Balce's story also underscores the permeability of diverse worlds, which intersect in the tabloids' conspicuous presence in the family life of a university professor, providing unsavory topics for conversation at breakfast or over dinner; and in the shared intimacies between middle-class professionals and the working-class domestic servants they employ. Notably, it is through these two routes—tabloid cultures and the social institution of domestic help—that manananggal enter the world of the secular middle-class urbanite.

Part Three. "Congeries of Translations"

In a 1949 essay, Frank Lynch, an American pioneer of sociology and anthropology in the Philippines, wrote: "In the Bicol region—as throughout

most of the Philippine lowlands—belief in the asuwang is a living belief."
His essay was based on data collected from 1946 to 1948 in the Bicol region
of southeastern Luzon, where the existence of aswang, though doubted
or invalidated by some, was "accepted as true by most."[84] Sociological accounts of the aswang have been dominated by functionalist approaches:
for Lynch, aswang beliefs in Bicol enforce social discipline among both children and adults.[85] The thematic of social control is echoed by F. Landa Jocano, who mentions aswang in his work on the Malitbog of Panay, drawing
on fieldwork conducted in the mid-1950s and 1960s. Jocano's *Growing Up
in a Philippine Barrio* approaches supernatural narratives from the perspective of "childhood training practices," a form of managing children through
fright. His study depicts Malitbog society as "invariant and regular"; in
this context, aswang contribute to the production of docile adults.[86] More
recently, Raul Pertierra has defined the aswang as a conceptual complex or
idiom that both explains and articulates "threats to conceptual and moral
orders" experienced in "times of personal and communal stress."[87]

In broadsheet coverage of 1992, the functionalist paradigms of prior decades were recycled and reduced to a slogan. "Manananggal!," Sicam tells us,
was in reality a "cry of confusion, of help" on the part of the impoverished
masses.[88] Such analyses erect a causal model: in response to social crises,
the aswang is likely to be mobilized as an idiom for expressing collective or
individual stress. In this view, the aswang complex mistranslates modern
experiences—of poverty, of sexual unruliness—into a pre-Christian language of supernaturalism that anthropologists, fictionists, and journalists
confidently decode in order to uncover their real social significance.

I am not opposed to approaching the aswang complex as analogous to
language, as Pertierra does when he conceptualizes it as a social idiom.
I suggest, however, that if one wants to speculate that aswang translate
electoral violence, class resentments, or sexual anxieties into a superstitious code, then one should also self-reflexively acknowledge the converse.
Anthropological accounts are likewise translations of aswang and manananggal narratives, experiences, and practices. Because the early Spanish chroniclers' ethnologies and the anthropological studies that drew on
them claim to operate on a level of detached universality, their renderings
of the manananggal into Christian or social-scientific terms are regarded
as transparent record and largely go unrecognized as translations. Conversely, acknowledging that the process of transposing something into an-

other code is common to both superstitious discourse and modern schol-arly analyses—with neither language granted universality—would open both translations to the possibility of error or a lack of exhaustiveness. The ideal of "getting it right" in relation to some ever-receding ideal of truth about aswang is chimerical because both translations are converting ex-periences that are on some basic level untranslatable to the other idiom.

Bearing in mind Chakrabarty's critique of the premodern or precapital-ist, there is a distinction to be made between, on the one hand, the ob-servation that aswang antedate Spanish colonialism and Christianity in the Philippines and, on the other, the assumption that aswang are there-fore prior in the evolutionary sense to Christianity and Western thought. Aswang belong to a world that is not a developmental stage, a primitive belief that will first cede to Christianity and finally give way to secular rationality, but another mode of worlding that is contemporaneous with and heterogeneous from the other two terms; their amalgam is a cross-hatched, never fully homogenized experience of times, spaces, and worlds that intermingle but whose differences are never fully dissolved.

Secular accounts of the aswang complex purport to decrypt supernatu-ral "belief systems" as communal expressions that fail to accurately grasp social reality. In this view, the social violence engendered by the super-natural accusation is dissent acted out on imaginary adversaries and bug-bears, instead of calling real social actors to account (for example, hunting down aswang instead of opposing corrupt politicians and the class inter-ests they serve). From a disenchanted perspective, the aswang is an alien-ated social idiom poorly suited to the realities of political modernity, in contrast to parliamentary action, class struggle, and democratic models of political engagement. But if this indictment is to be leveled against the aswang complex as a superstitious-delusional idiom, then the same charge must also be entertained with regard to the detached, secular, "objective" account. Representations of the aswang complex as an outmoded pre-Christian throwback, a mere developmental antecedent to both Catholi-cism and secular political modernity, are likewise translations no closer to the truth. Both translations are unlikely to achieve perfect correspondence or transparency because, although their worlds are permeable, their terms, their times, their knowing are not the same. An awareness of various non-coincident translations subtending aswang narratives recalls Trinh Minh-ha's point that truth lies in the interval: "On the one hand, each society has its own politics of truth; on the other hand, being truthful is being in the in-between of all regimes of truth."[89]

Enchanted Capital

What to make of the tangled webs—social, cultural, political, economic, historical, epistemological—of aswang and manananggal? Aswang are entangled in a dizzying, conflictual play of worldings, myths systematized into folklore and mythology, explained by sociological accounts and spoken by media convergences and everyday life: newspaper, tabloid, and television journalism; popular movies and literary fiction. How does one begin to craft an understanding of the aswang's webs of appearing that is neither dismissal nor reduction, however sympathetic, of "beliefs in supernaturalism" into the supposedly more real realities of social disenfranchisement?[90]

While struggling with these questions, I came across Jean and John Comaroff's fascinating work on what they call "the enchantments of capital" in the north and northwestern provinces of rural South Africa in the 1990s, where accounts of zombies circulated in everyday conversation, the local press, labor disputes, and legal and governmental spheres. In 1995, the Northern Province administration established the "Commission of Inquiry into Witchcraft Violence and Ritual Murders" to look into "an 'epidemic' of occult violence, [and] reported widespread fear of the figure of the zombie."[91]

Through the term "enchantments of capital" and other similar phrases ("phantom history," "spectral economy," and South Africa's "phantasmagoric history of labor") the Comaroffs tease out the lived contradictions of what they call "millennial capitalism," that is, late twentieth-century neoliberal capitalism in a global vein. If, in the late eighteenth and nineteenth centuries, production had been capitalism's defining feature, by the close of the millennium the emphasis on consumption, finance markets, and speculation had "eclipsed" production, not in real terms but in terms of production's "*perceived* salience for the wealth of nations."[92] (In several passages this rhetoric of false appearing is directly linked to the enchantments of capitalism.)

The Comaroffs argue that increasingly, global neoliberal capitalism gives rise to an "experiential contradiction": "the fact that it appears to offer up vast, almost instantaneous riches to those who control its technologies, and simultaneously, to threaten the very livelihood of those who do not." This contradiction is especially conspicuous in circumstances where the move from "tightly regulated material and moral economies" to laissez-faire capitalism has been jarringly sudden.[93] In their study, the enchantments of capital primarily refer to two ideas: first, the mysterious and mystified (that is, obscured or occluded) relation of consumption to production; and, more particularly, the abrupt appearance of new wealth and an abundance of commodities side by side with the absence of job opportunities. Amid glaring asymmetries—conspicuous consumption accompanied by rampant unemployment—wealth appears to be a product of enchantment. The enigmatic appearance of "wealth without work"—a very real contradiction that belies the neoliberal emphasis on consumption—is felt by the disenfranchised in particular to be opaque, occult, spectral.[94]

The figure of the zombie in rural postapartheid Africa at the end of the millennium is, for the Comaroffs, an embodiment of this enchanted capitalism, of "mounting local fears about the preternatural production of wealth" in the context of widespread joblessness. Zombies are the resurrected dead, including those who were murdered for this very purpose. Working only at night, and disappearing once sighted, zombies are mute, their tongues having been severed by the witches who raised them from their graves. In rural South Africa, some suspect that a "spectral workforce" of zombies is to blame for the scarcity of available employment.[95]

The Comaroffs compellingly demonstrate that enchantment is an idiom of profound disaffection, a lived and felt register of resistance to the contradictions of millennial capitalism. Their figural reading of zombies in relation to anxieties about work and immigration confirms the suggestiveness of politically engaged readings of the occult. I am not averse to figural, historical, and political approaches to specters, as is evident in the following chapter on ghost films, which I read as nostalgic historical allegories that insinuate the inadequacy of historical time. But I would like to also emphasize another facet of the Comaroffs' argument, one I find particularly relevant to the present study.

Near the end of their essay they call attention to the finitude, the limits, of a purely functionalist account of supernatural agency as "cultural fantasy": "How, furthermore, do we make sense of the particular poetics of these fantasies, whose symbolic excess and expressive exuberance gesture toward an imaginative play infinitely more elaborate than is allowed by a purely pragmatic, functionalist explication?" And further on: "Although we have tried to subdue the fantasy of labor by recourse to historical reason, its animus still eludes us. What, finally, are we to make of its symbolic excess?" Their conclusion astutely recognizes that the postulate of enchantment as a misrecognition of the social real cannot account for the no-less-real social agency afforded by ontologies of the supernatural, which force even the state to respond.[96]

Taking up the route suggested by the Comaroffs' remark that enchantments exceed or elude historical reason, I would suggest that specters do not belong only and entirely to the logic or life history of capital but remain, in some sense, outside it. In *Provincializing Europe*, Chakrabarty delineates two histories of capital in Marx. On the one hand, what Chakrabarty terms "History 1" denotes "capital's antecedent posited by itself," a past posited by capital itself as its precondition. "History 2," on the other hand, is "affective history": these are the pasts that capital encounters as antecedents, though they are not forms of its own "life-process," pasts that did not work themselves out as the "logical presuppositions" of capital.[97] Chakrabarty argues that supernatural agency is not premodern but, in keeping with the second historical trajectory, rooted in lifeworlds that are nonmodern; such worlds are not capital's precursors but something other. The translation of another past in terms of the history of capital is bound to produce what the Comaroffs refer to as "symbolic excess."

Though aswang in Tondo have been linked to labor migration, the former are not entirely subsumed by the history of the latter. I read "enchantments of capital" not only in the sense of a disenchanted critique of the occult as a mystification of capital's contradictions, though such contradictions are likely to be involved. Along with this first sense of the term, I wish to also underscore a second aspect of enchanted capital. The spectral alerts us to the contiguity—rather than the subsuming—of diverse ways of inhabiting the world. One worlding admits the active force of the supernatural; the other moves in the realm of instrumental rationality. To critique homogeneous time is to insist that people dwell in more than one world and one time. Thus, instead of considering enchantment solely as a function of capitalist contradiction, I would rather say that diverse modes of being are intermingling. Social inequities are translated into the code of the occult, and conversely, the history of labor secularizes the phantasm as figure. These translations are each very real and very useful to those who advert to them, whether they be peasants, historians, anthropologists, or government workers, but neither translation can produce a wholly miscible solution. Aswang, like zombies, now move in a capitalist world, but they do not belong to the genealogy of capital, to its life history; they were not forms entertained by the so-called primitive mind on the way to the inevitable world-historical triumph of rationality.

Colonial Translations: The Aswang's Mimetic Capital

Aswang are exceedingly long-lived, appearing in many guises in some of the earliest Spanish missionary accounts in the Philippines. In 1582, Loarca, in "Relación de las Islas Filipinas," describes the Visayan natives' watchfulness against creatures that eat the innards of the young and the bodies of the recently deceased.[98] According to Maximo Ramos, Loarca mistranslates corpse-eating aswang as "*los bruxos*," witches wanting to touch rather than devour the corpse. Reports by Spanish clerics are marked not only by such mistranslations; they are also characterized by a distanced writing style that keeps native practices at arm's length. Jose Maria Pavon's 1830s description of West Visayan precautions against aswang, for example, maintained a properly Christian distance from the "pagan" rituals he recorded. Ramos observes that writers like Loarca and Pavon possessed an incomplete understanding of the indigenous rites they observed; they "often irresponsibly filled in the lacunae," covering "gaps in [their] data with European preconceptions."[99]

A compelling feminist critique of Spanish missionary depictions of native *supersticiones* appears in folklorist Herminia Meñez's study of the manananggal's persistent feminization.[100] In contrast to other Southeast Asian cultures in which viscera suckers appear as ungendered animals, the Filipino/a manananggal is typically (though not always) a woman. To explain the feminization of the Filipina viscera sucker, Meñez revisits early Spanish chronicles that complain of *baylanes*, religio-political priestesses who defied Spanish sovereignty. Meñez provocatively argues that the feminization of the Filipina viscera sucker is a result of the colonial demonization of baylanes. The figure of the viscera sucker was retooled to discredit and disenfranchise female shamans who vigorously resisted Spanish evangelical imperialism: "I suggest that this symbol, directly or indirectly, was formulated or transformed as a result of the colonial encounter between the most powerful native women—the *bailanes/babaylanes* . . .—and Spanish priests whose mission was to eradicate indigenous religions throughout the archipelago."[101] Spanish attempts to control the political and sexual threat posed by the baylanes resulted in the decline of women's agency in the sexual, political, and religious spheres. Meñez argues that the gendered dichotomy between private and public spheres in the Philippines may be a consequence of Spanish colonization: by the late nineteenth century, all leaders of the revolution in lowland Christian areas were male, and women had been reduced to healers:

> By the revolutionary period, the great majority of leaders of millenarian movements that challenged Spanish rule were all male. In Bicol and the Visayas, especially, the new warriors also appropriated shamanistic roles. Female shamans in the Hispanized lowland communities were reduced to curers and midwives. No longer did they lead community-wide rituals nor exhort their men to fight. . . . It was no mere coincidence then that once known for their tradition of female priesthood, Bicol and the Visayas gained a reputation as the home of viscera-suckers. . . . Viewed historically, the viscera-sucker represents a process of disenfranchising the most powerful Filipino women and a politics of gender that has deep roots in the Spanish conquest of the Philippines.[102]

Meñez's approach stresses ethnic and regional differences; she is not concerned with "nationaliz[ing]" the aswang but attends instead to its uneven prevalence in the Philippine archipelago. Aswang beliefs do not have national compass in the Philippines but are found predominantly in lowland Christian communities that were "the first to be intensively missionized" by Spanish colonizers. In non-Hispanicized communities (the highlands of northern Luzon and the Islamic regions of Mindanao in the South), the aswang is relatively unknown. Meñez considers the region-specific gender politics of the viscera sucker in relation to the vicissitudes of colonial contact between indigenous peoples and Spanish evangelists.[103]

Meñez's argument is corroborated by Juan de Plasencia's *Los costumbres de los Tagalogs*. Plasencia's 1589 account lists several types of aswang— viscera-eating *silagan*, self-segmenting *magtatangal*, and flying, flesh-eating *osuang*. He recounts that a Spaniard was disemboweled by a viscera sucker in Catanduanes: "Let no one, moreover, consider this a fable; because, in Calavan, they tore out in this way through the anus all the intestines of a Spanish notary, who was buried in Calilaya by father Fray Juan de Merida." One of the first Franciscan missionaries in the Philippines, Plasencia, a linguist and ethnologist, asserted an equivalence between native priestesses who resisted the Spanish and the various aswang listed above, gathering them under a single category: Tagalog "priests of the devil."[104]

This account recalls Greenblatt's example of a sixteenth-century Huguenot pastor who wrote that the rites of native women he witnessed in Brazil were analogous to witches' sabbaths in Europe, as both Brazilian women and European witches were servants of Satan.[105] Such imagined correspondences were apparent in colonial clerical accounts of the Philippines as well, for instance in the translation of indigenous female shamans and aswang into the Spanish missionary's ethnoracial vocabulary of witches and priests of the devil.[106]

By the nineteenth century, three hundred years into Spanish colonization, the aswang no longer belonged solely to indigenous practices but circulated in European representations of the native other as an abiding form of mimetic capital. In his study of early colonial accounts of the New World, Greenblatt calls early modern discourses of the colonial other a highly durable form of "mimetic capital," "a stockpile of representations, a set of images and image-making devices that are accumulated, 'banked,' as it were, in books, archives, collections, cultural storehouses, until such time as these representations are called upon to generate new representations."[107]

As evidenced by the way in which contemporary Philippine historians, anthropologists, and folklorists continually return to early Spanish missionary sources, European representations of contact with "radically unfamiliar human and natural objects" enjoy lasting influence as a result of their preservation in print. The mimetic capital generated by early Spanish denunciations of native superstitions possesses immense "reproductive power" and is exceedingly durable.[108] Hence, the mimetic capital of the aswang, though linked to peasant anticolonial histories, has also been repeatedly enlisted in the opposite direction, as a means of stamping out native resistance. This occurred not only in the early period of Spanish encroachment but also in mid-twentieth-century struggles against American dominance in the Philippines.

In the early 1950s the aswang was conscripted in the cold war waged by the United States on Philippine soil. Colonel Edward Lansdale, a CIA operative, was instrumental in the election of Filipino president Ramon Magsaysay, the anti-Communist, pro-American congressman who catapulted to victory in 1953. Lansdale skillfully orchestrated Magsaysay's publicity and covertly sourced campaign funding from the CIA and multinational corporations with a vested interest in a strong American presence in the Philippines.[109] From Lansdale's own accounts, it is clear that one sore point in his fabled friendship with Magsaysay was the latter's "superstitious" beliefs in what Lansdale called "the ghosts and ghouls of the provinces." Lansdale derided the superstitious peasant within the modernizing, pro-American Philippine president but did not hesitate to use superstition in his own counterinsurgency "psy-war" stratagems against the Huks — short for *Hukbo ng Bayan Laban Sa Hapon* or Anti-Japanese People's Army — a peasant nationalist guerilla movement that incorporated socialist and Marxist tenets.[110] Despite the CIA's acknowledgment of the revolutionary movement's basis in "the legitimate grievances of tenant farmers," in the eyes of American foreign policy the Huks were essentially no different from Stalinists; they were part and parcel of the cold war imaginary of a monolithic Communist threat.[111]

Lansdale is notorious for the "fantastic methods" he resorted to in his three-year campaign against the Huks, from 1950 to 1953. Lansdale enlisted the aswang in a counterinsurgency campaign that used "psychological warfare" instead of relying exclusively on military force. The result was a CIA stratagem that was as cynical and sinister as it was inexpensive. Lansdale claims to have sent psy-war teams into a village in order to spread rumors that an aswang was on the loose in the Huks' turf. Following the implantation of this rumorscape, a captured Huk guerilla was killed; the psy-war team put two holes in the dead Huk's throat and drained his corpse of blood. Huk guerillas encountered the apparently vampirized body and, according to Lansdale, dispersed in terror. Historian Jonathan Nashel is unsure as to the credibility of Lansdale's account, which appears in the latter's memoir, but reads it as an example of the self-promotional myth Lansdale cultivated in Washington and in the field, proof of Lansdale's cynical orientalism. Well-known for his amateur ethnography, Lansdale collected information on indigenous practices and cannily retooled them in the service of American interests.[112]

Part Four. Generic Worlds and Occult National Times

Coming full circle, this chapter arrives at last in 1992, when the memory trace of the aswang's roles in histories of political conflict reemerged during the May elections. Both the *Manila Chronicle* and the *Philippine Daily Inquirer* reported rumors attributing the sudden presence of manananggal to the Aquino government's anti-insurgency campaigns: "Rumors have it that soldiers had raided a 'stronghold' of manananggal in Capiz, causing them to seek refuge in Manila; that a boatload of them had been dumped on Manila's shores."[113] This fascinating aspect of the manananggal rumorscape in 1992 implicitly chided the government's violent militarization of the provinces as resulting in current urban crises but also rehearsed a centuries-old correspondence between rebels and aswang drawn from the mimetic repository of Spanish colonial and American neocolonial representations of nationalist guerillas as viscera suckers. The rumor's reference to manananggal forced by government soldiers to flee the Visayan province of Capiz makes this place-bound origin story a dense palimpsest of historical allusions. In folklore studies, "Capiz is generally regarded as the home of vampires,"[114] and historical evidence lends credence to Meñez's argument that aswang narratives are thickest in areas like Capiz, where resistance to Spanish colonialism was particularly intense. Capiz is the site of some of the first Spanish military settlements in the sixteenth century, and by the late nineteenth century it was a hotbed of anticolonial revolts in the Visayas, with religio-political groups like the *Pulahan* challenging colonial dominance and agitating for social reforms.[115]

The manananggal sightings that gripped Metro Manila during two feverish summer months in 1992 bear out Anderson's incisive discussion of national time, but they also point to an uncanny outside to the secular homogeneous time of the nation. For Anderson, the new modern experience of simultaneity, whose roots I traced in chapter 1, is indispensable to the imagined community of nation. A simultaneous meanwhile that takes place in an empty, homogeneous time is essential, because clock and calendar afford a "transverse, cross-time" experience of "temporal coincidence" that binds the imagined community in an experience of "deep, horizontal comradeship." That is, the citizen's capacity to imagine the horizontal fellowship of the nation (despite vertical inequities of class, sexual, and racial subordination, for example, and the fact that one will never meet all of one's anonymous countrymen face to face) is bound by the "cross-time" coincidence of a shared calendrical present.[116]

To remark that aswang sightings swept the city *during* the violence-ridden 1992 electoral season—with *during* signifying precisely that calendrical coincidence Anderson described—bears out Anderson's meanwhile effect, a kind of meanwhile fostered primarily by tabloid and broadsheet newspaper coverage. The newspaper binds disparate items of news occurring in various places in the world via an assumption of temporal juxtaposition. Events reported by a newspaper, however arbitrary and unrelated, occurring all over the country and the globe, are temporally united in that they are *current events*, occurrences in an unproblematic, unified present.[117] By way of summarizing the historical contexts of the aswang rumorscape, I might say: "In the Philippines, during the presidential elections of 1992, fantastic narratives concerning aswang and manananggal gripped the nation across a broad range of media." But such a presumption of contemporaneity is already a temporal translation, since elections and aswang attacks do not belong to the same order of time.

The aswang rumorscape that began in Tondo can be assigned a calendrical date, but the worlds in which the aswang moves do not all belong to the disenchanted, homogeneous time of the nation. The aswang acts instead like a prism that both refracts and disperses the light—splitting homogeneous time into a spectrum of discrepant forms of worlding—so that a seemingly monologic figure gains a kind of inordinately stereoscopic depth of time.

Similarly, fantastic narratives of aswang in popular media are also temporal and spatial translations because they presume to nationalize worlds that are *imagined* to be coterminous and coextensive with the territorial span of the nation. As Michael J. Shapiro notes, "the spatial discourse of citizenship is uneasily articulated with a temporal one." National time produces and presumes a shared cultural field, but this narrative of a homogeneous culture coextensive with the territorial span of the nation "belies the ways in which citizen-subjects are temporally disjunctive."[118]

Newspaper coverage notwithstanding, it remains unclear to what degree the aswang scare gripped the nation, rather than simply circulating within particular media publics in the national capital region of Metro Manila. More significant are the problems raised by nationalizing the aswang. Anticolonial nationalist revolutionaries in the late nineteenth-century Philippines adopted the territorial span invented by the Spanish colonial state, but as historians point out, under different circumstances the islands might well have come under other colonial powers. Under Dutch or English rule, for example, the Philippine archipelago, named for Felipe II, might have been carved up differently, incorporated into nineteenth-century Singapore or Malaya.[119] Conquistadors, as Anderson points out, ruled as much via a temporal ordering of the colonized zones as by a spatial mapping that carved out, invented, and designated a sphere of governance for imperial rule. The aswang-fearing *indios* whose "customs" the clerics scrupulously described in the late sixteenth century were not (yet) Filipinos, and not all the natives scattered across the seven thousand islands of the archipelago recognized that species of supernatural being we now know as aswang. Spanish priest-ethnologists, however, encountered divergent worlds under the single category of the newly "discovered" territory on which the sovereignty of the king of Spain was to be imposed. Over time, their accounts of Tagalog and Visayan practices became coextensive with Filipino folklore and superstition as such, regardless of the fact that the aswang complex, for example, could not claim adherents among the Islamic communities of Mindanao. The abiding power of the geographical mapping of colonial states, inherited by postcolonial governments and anticolonial nationalisms, is what Anderson refers to as the emblematic function of the map, which "penetrated deep into the popular imagination, forming a powerful emblem for the anticolonial nationalisms being born."[120] The power of such emblematic mapping to homogenize the enduring diversity of worlds under the rubric of nation emerges in anthropological accounts. Faced with the uneven distribution of the aswang, its conspicuous prevalence and marked absence in certain regions of the archipelago, anthropological discourse has insisted on nationalizing the aswang, presuming the "homogeneity of the Philippines as a culture field" in order to demonstrate the appropriateness of Filipino culture as an ethnological object.[121]

Any attempt to discover in the aswang the authentic mind of the precolonial indigenous "folk" is bound to fail because the earliest primary sources are spoken by the colonizers themselves. Castilian missionaries provide our only glimpse into the worlds that aswang inhabited at the time of first contact with the Spanish, and these ethnologies, as Rafael and Meñez have shown, were mistranslations that served the ends of imperial evangelism. Nor does the aswang belong only to folklorists, ethnologists, and anthropologists. As we have seen, the aswang—mistranslated as analogous to the European vampire that leaves two fang marks in the victim's neck or throat—was conscripted in the service of cold war ideology, assuming a brief starring role in the CIA's counterinsurgency campaign against the Huks.

In all of this, a definitive, authentic aswang complex in the singular cannot be found; instead, we are caught in densely webbed histories of asymmetrical translation and untranslatability. The aswang complex is akin to a palimpsest (a concept developed in the following chapter on ghost films), in which overwritings remain visible, as well as partially obscured; each writing cannot be retrieved intact without implicating the others, yet it is clear that the various inscriptions do not all belong to one voice or hand. Permeability is twinned with immiscibility. To put this in visual terms, I would suggest that looking exhaustively, as we have just done, at the persistence and transformation of the aswang complex is like looking at a suspension in which particles and liquids of various densities are mingled and yet never completely coalesce to the point of full dissolution. The suspension of so many elements, some of which are at cross-purposes with one another, prevents the aswang from becoming a fully homogenized figure, a single cohesive blend. The aswang remains monstrous and suggestively impure because the discrepant historical moments and interpretive communities evoked by aswang call attention to the selvedges, fissures, repurposings, and adaptations that are stereoscoped into this never-singular figure, carrying with them the index of multiple and incompatible worlds, historical periods, and nonhistorical temporalities.

Generic Worlds and Times

> Genres construct fictional worlds out of textual encounters between cultural languages, discourses, representations, images, and documents according to the conventions of a given genre's fictional world, while social and cultural conflicts supply material for renewed generic enactments. Heteroglossia and dialogism are built into the genre product's need both to repeat, bringing from the past acculturated generic motifs, and to maintain credibility with changing audiences by connecting with the signifiers of contemporary verisimilitude, including signs of struggles to shift its terms in the name of the real, of justice, of utopian hope.   GLEDHILL, "Rethinking Genre"

> My position would be something like this: capitalist production may be a relatively recent phenomenon but the subject who lives with and under the sway of capital is not made solely by capital itself. The struggle to be at home by making a world out of this earth—a struggle that admits of no permanent resolution—both intersects with and diverges from the logic of capital.   CHAKRABARTY, in Dube, "Presence of Europe"

As Gledhill's compelling formulation of the worlding of genres indicates, genres stage an encounter between disparate reservoirs of mimetic capital and the urgency of social and cultural conflicts; it is at once heteroglossic and heterotemporal, pulling from the disparate accretions of the past while attempting to speak credibly to changing publics. The realm of reception and influence is the domain of the aswang itself, a densely crosshatched spectrum of responses, mediations, and reappropriations by various publics—tellers and listeners, chroniclers and readers, soldiers and guerillas, spectators and filmmakers, authors and critics—in diverse times, places, and languages. The aswang's horizons of reception are irreducibly conflicted because the horizons of experience through which aswang enter—via tale, belief, practice, newspaper account, television interview, popular film, or experimental video—were themselves contradictory, despite being closely interwoven. The aswang is a deceptively singular name for plural forms of worlding, those of indio, Spanish colonial missionary, American imperialist, contemporary anthropologist, urbanite and provincial, elite and disenfranchised.

Stereoscoped into the aswang's visage is an intractably disparate, nonlinear succession of receptions whose heterogeneity is indivisible from duration, a duration characterized by what Jauss calls the "perpetual mediation of the past." The durative character of the aswang belies any illusion of a single, conclusive, timeless meaning ably decoded by an implied reader, listener, or spectator. "A literary work is not an object that stands by itself and that offers the same view to each reader in each period," writes Jauss. "It is not a monument that monologically reveals its timeless essence. It is much more like an orchestration that strikes ever new resonances among its readers and that frees the text from the material of the words and brings it to a contemporary existence."[122]

The aswang attests to the survival and coexistence of a cacophonous past, itself composed of several immiscible times; the aswang on film in 1992 is really, in this view, only the infinitely contracted tip of that fractious past. The aswang has been spoken in many tongues and has lived countless lives in accounts by sixteenth-century Catholic fathers, 1950s cold war operatives, and contemporary historians, anthropologists, and feminists. Thus, to approach fantastic narratives historically is not to confine our understanding to a moment of textual emergence, as texts outlive the audiences to whom they were first addressed; rather, enduring supernaturalisms demand a durative look at genre that remains alive to the ways in which the supernatural exceeds the frame of historical time. The long, shape-shifting careers of aswang as they flew between tellers and audiences remind us that whenever a narrative comes across as fantastic, it does so from a particular perspective and to a particular interpretive community.

Aswang are an overt embodiment of mediatized orchestration or, as Lisa Cartwright puts it, of "media convergence." For Cartwright, media convergence names a broad set of transformations that became especially apparent in the closing decades of the twentieth century: more and more, we watched cinema on television, via home video, DVD, or the Internet, even as film production itself (from special effects to editing and projection) became digitized, and corporate conglomerates moved synergistically across industries and global markets. As Cartwright succinctly puts it, "Convergence of the media raises important issues for those of us in film studies. We find the defining object of our field—film—disintegrating into, or integrating with, other media." Yet, as she and others have noted, media convergence is not really new, having characterized the cinema since its inception, though the last four decades have witnessed an emphatic acceleration of these trends.[123]

Crucially, Cartwright argues that "with media convergence, film studies becomes a study of something else: a different configuration of media, different conditions of experience and subjectivity. . . . Film studies has never been about film (the medium, its social contexts, its spectator) alone, but has always been about conditions of sensory experience in modernity."[124] Temporality is a key aspect of these modern sensory experiences, not only in terms of Bergsonian cinematic time but also in terms of the profitable reproduction and circulation of centuries-old texts, images, and ideas as global media commodities that reach noncontemporaneous audiences. Heavily remediated and discrepantly temporalized, aswang belong both to quotidian hearsay and to a wide-angle, durative view of the political, exceeding the properly aesthetic. The conflicted cultural biography of the extraordinarily long-lived aswang is *eventful* precisely in that its effects are felt even by those who encounter it centuries after it first comes into view, who respond by retelling, appropriation, mimicry, or challenge.[125] The aswang complex, in its heterogeneously durative, media-convergent eventfulness, thrives and fascinates, continually *experienced and remade* by publics inhabiting different-but-porous worlds and times.

Discrepant forms of worlding allow the Jamesonian theory of genre and Chakrabartian heterotemporality to meet. Where Jameson brought Heideggerian worlding to bear on genre studies, Chakrabarty mobilizes the same for a postcolonial critique of time. In an interview, Chakrabarty remarks, "I do not regard life-worlds as constituting hermetically sealed entities. Nor do I see people as being marked by their belonging to only one life-world. Life-practices for anybody are manifold and would resist being summed up in the description of one life-world. There is for instance an academic life-world you and I share, and that is irrespective of from where our parents came. People move in and out of life-world, and life-worlds, as I think of them, are permeable entities."[126]

This notion of plural worlds through which even a supposedly unified community moves offers a productive consideration of the fantastic, beyond the hermeticism of Todorovian autoreferentiality and the anthropological demystifications of superstition. If we posit that there are diverse, coexisting, never insulated forms of worlding, we might avoid the problems of applying a sociology of religion or magic to supernaturalism. The difficulty with such sociological translations is that they presume and valorize a supposedly homogeneous modernity over so-called traditional enchantment. Secular demystifications of supernaturalism often naturalize the hegemony of homogeneous time as a universal code "lying above" other merely local ways of worlding, assuming that "the analytic holds the key to what's 'real' about the preanalytic world."[127] In contrast, I have argued that it might be productive to approach the fantastic through another route: not the cul-de-sac of credulity and skepticism but the open terrain of immiscible temporalities. I begin from the premise that people live in more than one world and time and that what is reified as "modernity" and "enchantment" are names for heterogeneous, co-implicated modes of worlding, each with its own history.

Returning to the second epigraph to this section: If those who dwell "under the sway of capital" are not solely constituted by it, but may also simultaneously dwell elsewhere—a way of inhabiting and being interpellated by a capitalist "present" that does not proceed only from that history—then fantastic narratives do not merely dramatize the persistence of anachronistic supernaturalisms in a disenchanted age. Instead they offer a glimpse of heterogeneity, pragmatic but incomplete translations, and the enormous effort required to forge tractable subjects of capital, since, while we are undoubtedly subjects of capital, that may not exhaust all we are. As the abiding popularity of aswang and the durable hold of supernaturalisms disclose, we may, in fact, on occasion be very poor modern subjects: unruly, superstitious, disaffected, or outright rebellious.

Aswang attest that fantastic narratives cannot be considered via auto-referential models of fiction, since they always exceed the confines of page or screen. I write from a conviction that the fantastic is locked in a fascinating and pronounced relationship to historical analysis, with one foot in historical time and the other outside it. This makes for an irreducible tension that this study can acknowledge but not resolve: namely, that every historical consideration of the fantastic, any attempt to open it to the winds of history, inevitably reveals the limits of a historical narration premised on a disenchanted, homogeneous time. Because the supernatural is intransigent to chronological historical time, aswang, like ghosts and other fantastic revenants, make for a fraught and fascinating inscription of history.

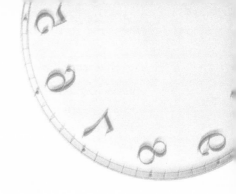

CHAPTER 3

Spectral Time, Heterogeneous Space

The Ghost Film as Historical Allegory

Ghosts call our calendars into question.[1] The temporality of haunting—the return of the dead, the recurrence of events—refuses the linear progression of modern time consciousness, flouting the limits of mortality and historical time. In my introduction, I touched on the ghost film's troubling of contemporaneity with reference to *Itim*. The present chapter deepens the elaboration of spectral time by linking it to affect and to an undoing of homogeneous space. For Johannes Fabian, "relationships between the living and the dead, or relationships between the agent and object of magic operations, presuppose cultural conceptions of contemporaneity" and hence challenge scholars to "establish relations of coevalness with the cultures that are studied."[2] This chapter suggests that ghost films contain the seeds of such culturally resonant theories of temporal coevalness and inhabit the elusive, heterogeneous space posited by Bergsonism.

The two ghost films at the heart of this chapter, *Haplos* [Caress] (Antonio "Butch" Perez, 1982) and *Rouge* (Stanley Kwan, 1987), are both nostalgic historical allegories from roughly concurrent New Cinema movements in the Philippines and Hong Kong. Both bear the hallmarks of "art films" whose critical reception or conditions of production assure them a place in canonical national cinema paradigms. (As I elaborate in the last section of this chapter, much of the critical reception of Hong Kong cinema has generated a "national-cinema effect" that spectral time in *Rouge* partly enables but also unravels.)

Rouge is regarded by Ackbar Abbas as an emblematic work of the New Hong Kong Cinema. It has been the subject of several scholarly analyses that approach the film through the critical paradigms that greeted the Hong Kong New Wave: auteurism, localism, and a reflectionist reading in relation to the 1997 handover. The "New Hong Kong Cinema" and the "Hong Kong New Wave" are distinct terms employed by different critics and film historians, but certain areas of overlap are evident. Similar critical approaches have been brought to bear on these works; moreover, Stanley Kwan, the director of *Rouge*, figures in both the "second New Wave" (as delineated by Stephen Teo) and the New Hong Kong Cinema (as described by Abbas, who considers Kwan one of its vanguard directors).[3] For its part, *Haplos* is penned by Ricky Lee, arguably the foremost screenwriter-auteur of what Joel David calls the "Second Golden Age" of Philippine cinema, and its director, Butch Perez, is a maverick within mainstream Filipino filmmaking. Lee's prizewinning script won the 1981 screenwriting contest sponsored by the Experimental Cinema of the Philippines (ECP), the single most important government film institution for the funding, production, and exhibition of the Philippine New Cinema.[4] The Filipino "New Cinema" or the "Second Golden Age" refers to a paradoxical flourishing of cinematically accomplished, politically engaged films under the repressive Marcos regime, a period of artistic distinction beginning in 1975 (three years after President Ferdinand Marcos's declaration of martial law) and ending in the February 1986 "People Power Revolution" that ousted him from power.[5] Significantly, both *Haplos* and *Rouge*, as New Cinema works, fuse formal innovation to generic repetition. New Hong Kong Cinema exhibits an uneasy, differential relationship to paradigms of national cinema and national culture, while ghosts in the Philippine New Cinema have the effect of splintering and gendering national time.

In *Rouge* and *Haplos*, nostalgia and allegory coalesce, making an almost-forgotten history newly meaningful through haunting. Accordingly, the second and third parts of this chapter consider the dovetailing of nostalgic allegory and ghost film. Each film draws from a culturally specific reservoir of phantoms: in *Haplos*, the folkloric interferes with the modern, interweaving phantoms from the Japanese occupation in World War II with the guerilla conflicts of the 1980s. The haunting repetition of a traumatic past comes to be experienced with the "singularity" of a "first time," renewing our sense of responsibility and solidarity toward the injustices endured by those long dead. For its part, *Rouge*'s deft allusions to classical Chinese ghost literature frame the spectral heroine as a resonant figuration of nostalgia for the end of an era, an affective allegorical cipher for the demands of a radicalized historical consciousness. The notion of historical accountability espoused by these nostalgic allegories resonates with Jacques Derrida's discussion of justice as a "being-with specters" and Walter Benjamin's attentiveness to an oppressed past's unfulfilled horizons of expectation.[6] But, as the last two sections of this chapter detail, the ghost film's departure from notions of progress and historical chronology are collocated with, and somewhat contained by, a sexual politics of nostalgia. In these films, nostalgia serves to gender national time by valorizing the supposedly traditional, anachronistic (that is, patriarchally circumscribed) femininity of the ghost heroines.

Ghost films that are historical allegories make incongruous use of the vocabulary of the supernatural to articulate historical injustice, referring to "social reality" by recourse to the undead. If, from the standpoint of modern historical consciousness, "'supernatural' forces can claim no agency in our narratives,"[7] then the use of ghosts for historical allegory is ensnared in contradiction—unless, that is, the history represented is ghostly in the first place, already recalcitrant to linear chronology. An interest in immiscible times and heterogeneous spaces activates several of the most powerful motifs in the last decade of Hong Kong film scholarship and criticism, underscoring the ways in which Hong Kong's cultural and political situation on the eve of its return to governance by mainland China did not conform to diachronic, nativist understandings of decolonization. The juxtaposition of *Rouge* and *Haplos* sheds light on a significant undercurrent shared by the two films, explored in the final section of this chapter: the recalcitrance of new cinemas' specters to notions of national cinema and national time.

Spectral Time and Heterogeneous Space

A ghost is a special kind of revenant, one whose return breaches the sequential temporal order of calendrical time. Jacques Derrida writes emphatically of the specter: "One cannot control its comings and goings because

it *begins by coming back*."[8] The ghost's affront to conventional temporal expectations prompts Hamlet's declaration that "the time is out of joint."
Specters "disjoin the living present," collapsing departure and return, presence and absence, seen and unseen, death and survival.[9] The apparition
can be grasped "only in a dislocated time of the present, at the joining of
a radically dis-jointed time, without certain disjunction. Not a time whose
joinings are negated, broken, mistreated, dysfunctional, disadjusted, according to a *dys-* of negative opposition and dialectical disjunction, but a
time without *certain joining or determinable conjunction*."[10] Derrida's ghostly
time, uncertain and indeterminate, is far more than the return of a house-
broken past that merely persists in the present. Rather, haunting is unruly:
it is "a spectral moment, a moment that no longer belongs to time, if one
understands by this word the linking of modalized presents (past present,
actual present: 'now,' future present). We are questioning in this instant,
we are asking ourselves about this instant that is not docile to time, at least
to what we call time. Furtive and untimely, the apparition of the specter
does not belong to that time, it does not give time, not that one."[11] Presuming one could stop a ghost to ask the time, the specter's response would be
unlikely to allude to "that one time," that obvious present to which we are
accustomed.

Derridean spectrality is, as Jameson puts it, "what makes the present
waver." This wavering is the inscription of fantastic scandal at the limits of
modern time's field of vision. As Jameson puts it, "Spectrality does not involve the conviction that ghosts exist or that the past (and maybe even the
future they offer to prophesy) is still very much alive and at work, within
the living present: all it says, if it can be thought to speak, is that *the living
present is scarcely as self-sufficient as it claims to be*; that we would do well
not to count on its density and solidity, which might under exceptional
circumstances betray us."[12]

In contrast to thinkers who regard specters as profoundly disruptive
of modern time consciousness, Bergson, in *Time and Free Will*, enlists the
ghost as a figure for homogeneous "time as space"—measurable, empty,
and uniform.[13] In one intriguing sentence, Bergson resorts to a figurative
vocabulary of haunting: "Time, conceived under the form of an unbounded
and homogeneous medium, is nothing but the ghost of space haunting
the reflective consciousness."[14] For Bergson, the ghost of space lurks behind the misconception that time can be quantified; he likewise refers to
our false selves, unaware of the temporalized openness of our freedom,

as spectral. For the most part, Bergson writes, "we live outside ourselves, hardly perceiving anything of ourselves but our own ghost, a colorless shadow which pure duration projects into homogeneous space."[15]

In a work in which Bergson consistently valorizes pure duration over homogeneous space, there are, however, moments in which he allows for the possibility of *heterogeneous space*, suggesting that homogeneity is an illusion owing to the human faculty for abstraction and to the pragmatic requirements of social existence. In such passages Bergson notes that, just as pure duration is misrecognized as homogeneous time, so concrete extensity is occluded by homogeneous space.[16] In his later work, *Matter and Memory*, Bergson states this explicitly: "Homogeneous space and time are the mental diagrams of our eventual action upon matter; they are not the properties of things."[17]

If homogeneous space and time are not essential properties, why do such concepts arise? Bergson holds that homogeneity springs from "the utilitarian work of the mind."[18] The mental utilitarianism of human consciousness performs processes of "abstraction," "solidification," and "division" on the "moving continuity of the real in order to obtain there a fulcrum for our action."[19] Conceiving of space and time as fixed and measurable makes them far more amenable to human intervention.

Bergson not only critiques homogeneity; he also defamiliarizes it. Bergson's defamiliarizing critique is one of the most refreshing aspects of his ontology. Whereas spatiotemporal homogeneity has become a habituated premise for everyday life in modernity, Bergson holds this commonsensical premise at arm's length, noting how deeply it contravenes sensory experience: "the conception of an empty homogeneous medium is something far more extraordinary, being a kind of reaction against that heterogeneity which is the very ground of our experience."[20]

In the passage below, Bergson elaborates a fully sensorialized "ground of experience" through sight and touch; he also redresses his earlier denigration of vision as always enlisted in the service of homogeneous space.[21] To the realm of *ideas* and *abstraction*, which produce the illusion of homogeneity, Bergson, in *Matter and Memory*, opposes visual and tactile *experience*:

> The data of sight and touch are those which most obviously have extension in space, and the essential character of space is continuity. . . . As soon as we open our eyes . . . the whole field of vision takes on colour; and, since solids

are necessarily in contact with each other, our touch must follow the surface or the edges of objects without ever encountering a true interruption. How do we parcel out the continuity of material extensity, given in primary perception, into bodies of which each is supposed to have its substance and individuality? No doubt the aspect of this continuity changes from moment to moment; but why do we not purely and simply realize that the whole has changed, as with the turning of a kaleidoscope? Why, in short, do we seek, in the mobility of the whole, tracks that are supposed to be followed by bodies supposed to be in motion? A moving continuity is given to us, in which everything changes and yet remains: whence comes it that we dissociate the two terms, permanence and change, and then represent permanence by bodies and change by homogeneous movements in space?[22]

Against our habit of abstracting space as a static container for movement, Bergson beautifully intuits an experiential notion of space as a kaleidoscopic whole, a *moving continuity* that fills our gaze without interruption the moment we open our eyes. Confirming the evidence of our eyes, the surfaces of our bodies brush up against the world incessantly without ever finding a break in it, only an uninterrupted succession of difference, passing, and permanence, a durative extensity "in which everything changes and yet remains."

Human consciousness, oriented toward possible action, believes the universe to be ready-made, fixed, and motionless. Empty space is presumed to exist prior to motion, while motion, in turn, is reduced to a divisible quantity. As I pointed out in chapter 1, Bergson holds that in homogenizing space and time, movement is rendered immobile, a mere measurement of distance, direction, and velocity. In abstract space, there is only ever a single instant, the present, sans qualitative continuity with the past. But, Bergson insists, if we turned away from such pragmatic abstractions and strove instead for true knowledge of duration and extensity, we would find not measurable and divisible intervals of time and space but an ever-moving universe in which everything is bound to everything else, nothing is solid or still, and the past and the present, subject and object, all interpermeate each other.[23] As Ronald Bogue explains:

Frequently Bergson insists on the illusory nature of the corpuscular view of matter, according to which the world is made up of various combinations of solid, impenetrable bodies. (The atomistic theory is one such corpuscular view of matter.) Our most basic experience of the world, however, is one of constant change, movement, and flux, and this experience Bergson finds increasingly confirmed in the developments of physics (the tendencies of which he discerns in 1896 and 1907 with remarkable prescience . . .). Physicists recognize the existence of a universal interaction of forces, such that the separation of entities into discrete and autonomous units is called into question, and explorations of the microscopic constituents of matter suggest that there are no irreducible bodies in the world, simply "*modifications, perturbations,* changes in *tension* or *energy,* and nothing else," no things but only actions or movements.[24]

Bergson maintains that there are no static, irreducibly solid, impermeable things (the corpuscular view of matter) but rather a universe composed of movement, interpenetration, and flux: a vibrational universe. Writing in 1911, Bergson perceived that physics, in drawing nearer and nearer to the atom, allows us to rediscover movement underneath the veneer of seemingly solid, impenetrable objects. As force is materialized and matter is regarded less as solidity than as movement, science, for Bergson, recovers its understanding of universal continuity.[25]

Space lacks solidity, and everything moves: Bergsonism's conductive, vibrational universe evokes with uncanny precision the elusiveness of place in ghost films. Whereas, in *Time and Free Will,* homogeneous time is merely "the ghost of space haunting the reflective consciousness," the mise-en-scène in *Haplos* and *Rouge* visualizes the heterogeneous space and time explored in *Matter and Memory.* Haunted forest ruins and eerie city streets are not just static settings in which human actions unfold. Instead, homogeneous space dissolves into a spectral palimpsest of permanence and change, a kaleidoscopic space haunted by immiscible times.

Nostalgic Allegory

In *Haplos,* a man, recently returned to his provincial hometown in the Philippines, unwittingly falls in love with the restless spirit of a woman who died in World War II. At the threshold of the forest (*bukana ng gubat*), he discerns a charming old-fashioned mansion where others see only ruins. Inside this phantom house, he and his spectral sweetheart hear gunshots: the man assumes it is the sound of present-day crossfire between government troops and insurgent guerillas; but the ghost, for whom the forest is alive not with Communists but with colonizers, believes she hears Japanese soldiers nearby.

In *Rouge*, the ghost of a courtesan who seeks her lost lover among the living weeps at the drab sight of Hong Kong's former red-light district, Shek Tong Tsui, in 1987. In one of the film's most telling images, the revenant walks past a shop window, and we see reflected in it, as if on a screen, the shadowy performance of an old Cantonese opera at the theater that the storefront has replaced. In a visual palimpsest, this film sequence depicts one space splintered yet whole: an antiseptic shopping mall in the late 1980s, in whose dark glass we glimpse the warm glamour of the demolished Tai Ping theater (figs. 34 and 35).

These two moments, from two rather different films, are arresting for their nostalgic inscription of postcolonial histories within the context of the ghost narrative. These ghost films are paradoxical, being historical allegories that exceed a disenchanted historical time. To the ghostly heroines of these films, space is a spectral surface of only limited opacity, behind which other times and places are poignantly apparent. For these anachronistic women, and for those who come to love them and partake of their spectral vision, there can be no absolute sense of time and place. Locales are "spatial palimpsests" traversed by divergent temporalities,[26] and time does not merely move forward; it is subject to repetition and return.

It has been suggested that "the paradigm for the allegorical work is the palimpsest" because, like the palimpsest, allegory is a textual doubling that allows one stratum to be construed via another. For Craig Owens, "allegory occurs whenever one text is doubled by another" or, more precisely, when "one text is *read through* another, however fragmentary, intermittent, or chaotic their relationship might be." Typically operating in the perception of a gap, allegory's most "fundamental impulse" is to "rescue from historical oblivion that which threatens to disappear," that is, to alleviate a sense of historical estrangement. At the core of the allegorical mode, then, is an attempt to "redeem for the present" a past whose relevance is in danger of vanishing by inscribing it anew.[27]

Rouge and *Haplos* are allegories in which the past is copresent, exercising an often unseen but nonetheless determining force on everyday life. The spectral past, depicted as both a return and a permeating presence that was never really put aside in the first place, allows these allegories to speak powerfully of times immiscible to modern historical chronology, whether

34, 35. Spatial palimpsest in *Rouge* (dir. Stanley Kwan, 1987):
across a window in a 1980s shopping mall, a shadowy glimpse
into a Cantonese opera performance from decades past.

in spatial memento mori, like the ruined forest mansion of *Haplos*, or the
mirage of an opera house materializing across a shop window in *Rouge*.

Whether in urban Hong Kong, where the frenzied pace of construction
"suggest[s] that space is almost like a kind of very expensive magnetic
tape which can be erased and reused," built over with ever more lucrative
skyscrapers,[28] or in a rural Philippine town, where decaying architectural
styles are briefly glimpsed in their old splendor by a ghost-besotted man,
spatial transience is quintessentially allegorical. To Benjamin, the allegorical exemplar is the ruin: "Allegories are, in the realm of thoughts, what

ruins are in the realm of things." *Haplos*'s ruined old house, slowly disintegrating into the surrounding brush, and *Rouge*'s opera house, materializing across the window of the shop built over it, exemplify Benjamin's idea that in the ruin, temporality is inseparable from spatiality: "In the ruin history has physically merged into the setting. And in this guise history does not assume the form of the process of an eternal life so much as that of irresistible decay . . . In the process of decay, and in it alone, the events of history shrivel up and become absorbed in the setting."[29]

The allegorical imprint of history on setting is realized in the fantastic mise-en-scène of both *Haplos* and *Rouge*, so that seemingly opaque spaces reveal themselves to be underwritten by transience, traces, remains. Allegory reveals the knowledge that has "settled" in obsolete artifacts, which is why Benjamin described allegorical interpretation as a "mortification of works,"[30] a deciphering of history in what is necrosed or buried under the new. One of the few modern champions of the allegorical mode, Benjamin maintained that the decisive distinction between allegory and symbol was the "category of time." Whereas the synecdochical symbol yields its meaning in an "instantaneous present," allegory's "temporal mode is one of retrospective contemplation." Allegory rescues the pagan pantheon deposed by Christianity by making dead gods personifications of abstract ideas, salvaging them through an interpretation later Christians can understand. With its roots deep in the kind of exegesis that proved the relevance of the Old Testament to Christianity by "rewriting the Jewish textual and cultural heritage in a form usable for Gentiles," allegory's temporality is retrospective and redemptive.[31] Though in a sense, allegory's retrospective gaze at the past does adhere to the chronological linearity of modern time, its emphasis on copresence, on animating rather than surmounting the old, pulls allegory in the direction of temporal heterogeneity. Thus allegory's time is not one but many: a time of decrepitude as allegorically contemplated and vivified through the lens of another.

In both *Rouge* and *Haplos*, this allegorical contemplation of one time through another may be characterized as nostalgic, that is, as infused with the pain and pleasure of remembering what is gone beyond recovery. *Nostalgia*, from the Greek words νοστος ("nostos," return home) and αλγος ("algos," pain or sorrow), was originally a seventeenth-century medical term for pathological sadness among exiles that was caused by the desire to return home, a condition that could potentially be remedied. (This original sense is preserved in an English synonym, *homesickness*). Later, it became a more generalized condition, a "yearning for childhood itself" that was "chronic, inconsolable, and incurable," becoming so widespread as to seem the "defining condition of modernity itself."[32] Nostalgia's formerly spatial dimension (a longing for a place) gradually became compounded by a temporal dimension (a desire to return to a lost time).

Nostalgia is frequently denounced for being a distanced, idealized remembrance that "appropriates" its object "for an alien time and place." Yet the distorting distance of nostalgia is not always detrimental. As one critic insightfully remarks, "Both absence and presence distort relations: absence distorts with nostalgic aestheticization while unmediated presence distorts with familiarity." If proximity, as much as distance, is a distorting relation, then nostalgia offers an antidote to a view tainted by too much intimacy, proffering the longer view of things, a perspective "invigorated through absence."[33] Like allegory, nostalgia straddles the line between homogeneous and heterogeneous time: it betrays a kinship to a linear, teleological time, depicting a stable past at a remove from the present. But its appropriative revisiting of the past also pulls away from the notion of chronologically ordered, separate times and tends toward a plural understanding of temporal cohabitation and co-implication.

Nostalgia in *Haplos* and *Rouge* centers on bygone historical periods that neither the human protagonists nor the majority of the films' audience members have lived through. This resembles what Arjun Appadurai calls "imagined nostalgia," "forms of mass advertising [that] teach consumers to miss things they have never lost," thus generating "nostalgia for things that never were."[34] While the success of either of these films might be indebted to some degree to the pervasiveness of nostalgia as a merchandising ploy that has conditioned audience responses, I argue that in *Rouge* and *Haplos* a redemptive kind of imagined nostalgia radicalizes historical consciousness by recognizing the persistence of a past that teeters on the brink of forgetting. Despite the widespread commodification of nostalgia as an effective merchandising trend, in *Rouge* and *Haplos* nostalgia offers the possibility of taking Benjamin's "tiger's leap into the past" in order to see that the past is never merely outmoded.[35] Female apparitions in these ghost films call to mind Benjamin's figurative argument that the *facies hippocratica* (the appearance of the human face in a deathly state) reveals the very countenance of history.[36]

Nostalgia, then, like allegory, is a kind of doubling—not one that restores an original meaning but one that operates from a distance (for Walter Benjamin, the distance requisite to allegory is death, which might explain why ghosts are so rife with allegorical significance).[37] The selfsame distance that allows nostalgia to appropriate the affective value of an object for another time is that very distance that enables allegorical objects to be seized, rescued, and invested with new meanings, thereby reclaiming concerns so estranged or remote as to have almost vanished from memory. This is why, in both *Haplos* and *Rouge*, nostalgia and allegory engender an intense appreciation for spaces that have been built over or have decayed. It is no accident that these films cultivate historical consciousness through the lens of both allegory and nostalgia: the point to redeeming the value of something at a distance, just as it has declined, is that there is no way to apprehend it objectively, without distortion. In these films, nostalgia is not mere distortion but a position, an allegorical one, from which to read and revalue the ruins around which ghosts have gathered.

Ghost Films

Haplos and *Rouge*, two ghost films that thematize romances between ghosts and mortals, revolve around female specters who return to redress a past grievance (the betrayal of lovers or death by sexual violence). In these films, the living and the dead become placeholders for an antichronological meeting of divergent temporalities and frames of consciousness. The renewed legibility of the ethos of 1930s Hong Kong in *Rouge* or of wartime conflict in *Haplos* is made possible by our nostalgic fascination with ghostly women, whose long memories and deep grievances make nearly forgotten injustices palpable once more. These ghost films realize nostalgic allegory's capacity to raise the specter of history. As one spectral heroine remarks to her mortal lover, meeting a ghost can make the dead seem more alive than the living. In the nostalgic allegory of ghostly return, what is dead and long past comes to life, old concerns acquire a new urgency and relevance, and a radicalized historical consciousness fathoms the past's entanglement with immediate concerns.

Haunting, or the specter's act of returning from death, is a refusal to complete the sentence, a worrying of historical knowledge that undermines the capacity of death to resolve the undecidability of life in semantic coherence.[38] By repeating (via haunting) events thought to have been finished or laid to rest, the ghost film has the generic potential to unsettle the linear time of conventional narrative. Whereas most stories serve up a beginning that is different from its ending, the ghost narrative has a tendency to transgress the principles of linearity without becoming antinarrative (as in avant-garde and experimental films). Its fragmentation of time still lies within the purview of the spectator's narrative engagement, because the plot (which conventionally follows the actions of a character) is merely tracing the movements of a ghost, yet in so doing follows the ghost's cyclical, spectral temporality, one that departs from linear story time.[39] *Haplos*'s director has said that for him *Haplos* was a means of exploring themes of "repetition and time" that the cinema, with its capacity to play with temporality by means of editing, is best suited to explore.[40] More recently, he has remarked that "*Haplos* is not a ghost story; it's a time warp."[41] Thus, like Derrida's specter, the ghost film's stories "begin by coming back"; this is literally what ghost films like *Haplos* and *Rouge* depict, because in them a betrayed past confronts its future (our present), and discovers that it is other than what had been hoped for. The ghost film allows characters (and those spectators who identify with them) to experience *time with the ghost*. It is to the specific contours of these spectral times that I now turn.

Haplos: *Local Spirits and Returning Lovers*

In the provincial Filipino town of Buendia, Al, newly returned from migrant work in Saudi Arabia, begins a romantic affair with a childhood friend, Cristy, recently returned from Manila to establish a government "family planning" center.[42] Cristy's first scene with Al depicts her as a vibrant, assertive "modern woman" educating the public on contraceptive use, a former leftist turned government social worker. The film thus characterizes Buendia as a town in the grips of modernizing change, its town square freshly transformed by the offices of a telephone company and a population control center, its surrounding areas increasingly militarized by the Philippine Constabulary (PC). Cristy and Al, fresh from Manila and Saudi Arabia, are agents and embodiments of the town's experience of change and of new patterns of departure and return from both center and periphery. They are linked by their status as "tourists in their own home"

36. Auring, the demure and beautiful specter, is at the cemetery. *Haplos*
(dir. Butch Perez, 1982). Photograph courtesy of Antonio Jose "Butch" Perez.

(in Al's wry phrase), or "*balik*-Buendia" (returned to Buendia, which is how
a friend describes them, punning on *balikbayan* [back to the homeland], a
common term for returned Filipino/a overseas workers).[43] Their flirtatious
banter centers on a shared nostalgia for the Buendia of their childhood,
so that they epitomize "the anguish of an urbanite without a hometown,
or of one robbed of a hometown."[44] Al and Cristy are similar but different: she is a Manila-educated leftist who is now implementing politically
suspect government measures to regulate sexuality and population.[45] Al,
for his part, admits to being motivated only by personal economic gain,
having left Buendia for better financial prospects in Saudi Arabia. Al is no
political activist but rather a returned overseas laborer (in his own jocular
words, a believer in "brain drain" and "Filipinos for export" as a form of
population control) who cannot decide on whether to stay in Buendia or
go back abroad.[46]

   Al and Cristy fall in love, but their budding romance is complicated by a
third figure of return. While visiting his mother's grave, Al meets Auring,
a beautiful, demure woman dressed in white (fig. 36).[47] Al is powerfully
drawn to her, increasingly forsaking the town and Cristy in favor of the
river route to Auring's elegant, old-fashioned mansion in the woods.

Auring's reserved femininity and vulnerability contrast sharply with Cristy's worldly, female-empowered candor. Cristy is thus the perfect foil for the ghost, in that her line of work, family planning through contraception, is a rational, secular attempt at a contained, controlled, and ordered entry into the future, quite the opposite of the historical perspective evoked by Auring. It is revealed that Auring is the ghost of a woman who had been brutally raped and killed in the forest by Japanese soldiers at the end of World War II, as her wounded sweetheart, Basilio, watched, powerless to help. Basilio, a nationalist guerilla, survived and became the town's old drunk, now known as "Mang Ilyong" (an avuncular diminutive for Basilio). Ilyong increasingly spends time with Cristy, using his old guerilla knowledge of the remote regions of Buendia to help the population commission's outreach program, while conversely, Al is constantly with Auring. The love triangle/quadrangle between Al, Cristy, and Auring (with Mang Ilyong as a submerged fourth player whose age bars him from romantic overtones) reaches a crisis when Al and Cristy discover Auring's true identity.

Al finds he cannot choose between the two women. In a tension-filled denouement, Auring hears crossfire between present-day Communist insurgents and the PC, runs terrified into the forest, and relives her wartime rape and murder at the hands of Japanese soldiers, this time with Al looking on. Al sees her house burning, the work of nationalist guerillas punishing her parents for collaborating with the Japanese colonizers. When Al is rescued by townsfolk, he is in shock and uncommunicative. Desperate to help him, Cristy goes back to the forest, walks into Auring's phantom house (now magically whole again), and pleads for the ghost's assistance in Al's recovery.

The last images of the happy modern couple reunited preserve a core of disquiet because Cristy has had to enlist Auring's aid. The pivotal scene, with Cristy donning Auring's garb and manner and ending with the mortal couple's final embrace, depicts Cristy's voluntary possession by the spirit of her rival.[48] The television broadcast version of *Haplos* closes with this possession ending, which preserves the love triangle under the aegis of the couple (spiritual possession is not without sexual undercurrents). The final scene thus chooses to eclipse Cristy, the strong, autonomous, sexually vibrant woman, with Auring, the epitome of an emphatically conventional femininity, a substitution of gender roles to which Cristy herself is shown to aspire (fig. 37).

Cristy's desire to possess and be possessed by Auring implies that, on

VILMA SANTOS/CHRISTOPHER DE LEON/RIO LOCSIN

in

Haplos

Mirick Films
International's
Official Entry
to the
1982 Metro Manila Film Festival

DELIA RAZON·J. EDDIE INFANTE·REZ CORTEZ & JUAN RODRIGO
screenplay: RICARDO LEE/music: JUN LATONIO/ production design: LAIDA LIM-PEREZ
editing: JARLEGO/cinematography: ROMEO VITUG
directed by ANTONIO JOSE PEREZ

37. A publicity image frames *Haplos* as a romantic triangle between ghost and mortals. Photograph courtesy of Ricardo Lee.

some level, nostalgia for the past has led both Cristy and Al to an uncritical preference for a patriarchal femininity fettered in the home. The happy resolution is thus only a smokescreen for an ending steeped in despair.[49] The modern couple who embrace the ghost are both deeply vexed characters: Al is an exponent of troubled masculinity, by virtue of his entry into the vicissitudes of migrant labor; and Cristy, the politically compromised former activist, is facing the consequences of her "new morality" with an unwanted, illegitimate pregnancy in a prudish town. For such characters, at variance with themselves and with their life choices, the nostalgic longing for Auring's seemingly uncomplicated femininity indicates a frustration with their own unsatisfying options in the present and their fantasy of recovering lost (and deeply patriarchal) sexual mores.

Multiple-character films like *Haplos* very often give us a social microcosm, a snapshot of a whole society in miniature, by having each of the many characters stand in for a social type.[50] But unlike the usual multiple-character film, the ghost film's protagonists can include widely divergent social figures, exploiting the historical gap or estrangement between characters from very different eras. *Haplos* is structured around distinct, mutually implicated times and places: the 1940s and the 1980s, the Philippines and Saudi Arabia, Buendia and Manila, rebel-infested ghostly forest and law-abiding urbanized town. Al, the returned overseas worker, is both a newcomer and a familiar face. His early conversations in the film cue us to the film's subtle understanding of place: whenever he is asked about Saudi Arabia, he gives a different answer, and his divergent evocations of that country are clearly determined by his ties to different people. In response to his friend Gorio's eager questions about Al's sexual adventures overseas with "white leghorn" (a racist, sexist epithet for white women), Al says soberingly: "Women are forbidden to us in Saudi, so I didn't get much sex. We would pretend we were sick because there was an Australian nurse in the hospital who slept with the patients, out of pity for them, she said. . . . But once, she was caught with a Filipino patient. . . . She was decapitated. The man was castrated."

Al's account of the sexual policing of Filipino men working in the Gulf adheres closely to the anecdotes of male Filipino overseas workers returning from the Middle East, accounts that document the physical and psychological costs of their ventures into global labor. From 1975 to 1983, the time in which *Haplos* is set, Saudi Arabia was the top recruiter of Filipino contract labor, largely employing male workers in construction or menial services, workers who were vulnerable to unfair labor practices overseas. The male migrant worker's narratives of personal crisis in the Gulf attest to a severe undermining of the worker's sense of masculinity, already worn thin by the lack of gainful employment at home, and stigmatized as an "unclean," "contaminating," "unruly carnality" in a racially hierarchized workplace privileging Euro-Americans and foreign Arabs.[51]

Returned overseas workers did not speak often about what they had endured. Al's account of Saudi Arabia makes no mention of the strict regulatory practices he recounted to Gorio. Rather, Al depicts Saudi as a "lonely desert" watched over by the same night sky he remembers from the Buendia of his childhood. That Al's account of working in the Gulf should differ so dramatically across gender lines typifies the silence of returned male migrant workers regarding their dehumanizing experiences abroad, an understandable attempt to preserve their cultural cachet, their community's high estimation of overseas workers as well-traveled and cosmopolitan.[52]

When Auring, a woman of the 1940s in the Philippines who has no conception of the Middle East, asks Al to describe it, he tells her that the desert is like a cemetery, its vastness a sublime closeness to death. The ghost is impressed by Al's intimacy with death and his remembrance of his mother. "Sometimes, people long dead seem more alive to us than anyone else," she concurs. As a revenant she is the most literal figure of return in the narrative, because while Cristy and Al have returned to Buendia from other places, she returns from another time and from the grave. Like Al and Cristy, the borders Auring crosses are geopolitical, but they are also thresholds of history and mortality.

Al's various evocations of Saudi Arabia—a (missed) opportunity for illicit sexual escapades with white women, a space for recollecting childhood, and a figurative proximity to the grave—underscore the film's espousal of a relational, rather than absolute, sense of place. The film's relational sense of place and its corollary, spatial transience, is best disclosed by the revenant Auring. A beautiful female apparition dressed in white, Auring is kin to the "white lady" of Tagalog urban legend, a seducer of men whose ruined mansion appears, to spellbound eyes, in all its former magnificence. But the motifs of seduction and a spectral forest residence in *Haplos* point to other folkloric beliefs, those concerning the *ingkanto*—from *encanto*, the Spanish word for enchantment—*spirits of a place* whose "characteristics are related to their locale."[53] Ingkanto narratives typically involve an encounter with a beautiful stranger as a result of the trespass of some territorial taboo; the enchantress's victim "disappears into the forest" and beholds her splendid home where others perceive only wreckage. The ingkanto experience does not usually provoke the hesitation vis-à-vis the supernatural that for Tzvetan Todorov characterizes the modern fantastic. Scholars of Filipino folklore note that "encounters with spirits are not themselves considered abnormal"; though some urbanites may respond to ingkanto accounts with concerned incredulity, "as a rule, supernatural encounters are not viewed as pathological" unless the seduced mortal chooses to "remain in the spirit world."[54] In *Haplos*'s ingkanto experience, the crucial question is not whether one ought to believe in the existence of ghosts; rather, the question concerns the dangers of being taken in by a phantom courtship.[55] When Ilyong and Cristy intervene, it is not to doubt what Al has seen but to caution against choosing death over life, one world and time over another, however captivating these alternatives might be.

Auring's terror of the "chaotic times" (*magulong panahon*) in which she lived (the 1940s), and her vain hopes of escaping from its dangers through love, segue into the townspeople's perception of their own tumultuous circumstances (the 1980s). This analogy between two historical moments marked by guerilla conflict is effected by the phantom's vivid memories, so that the present's ability to remind us of the past attains a profound resonance, ultimately destabilizing the borders between past and present by showing these to be porous. Hearing gunfire and voices in the dense foliage, Auring thinks they are caused by the clash of the Japanese Imperial Army and the Huks (Hukbo ng Bayan Laban sa Hapon, or People's Anti-Japanese Army, the selfsame targets of Lansdale's aswang campaigns, examined in the previous chapter). Al and the others, though, assume that it is an exchange of gunfire between the Communist guerillas (the New People's Army or NPA) and the PC. Although perceived parallels and continuities between the two conflicts are encouraged by the film's metaphor of palimpsest—of one set of events being written on another, with both inscriptions legible—it is important not to overlook the profound ambivalence at work in this dissonant evocation of time and place.

The Huks, a resistance army, were organized by the Communist Party of the Philippines (CPP) during 1941 and 1942 to oppose the Japanese Imperial Army. The CPP, intent on harnessing broad support, adopted united-front tactics and played down its own role in the Huks so as not to alienate non-Communist sympathizers.[56] The Huks were involved in a queasy alliance with the American military in retreat (the United States Armed Forces in the Far East, or USAFFE, under the command of General Douglas MacArthur), because the Japanese colonizers were a threat both to Filipino nationalist and American colonial interests. Though the returning USAFFE troops and the Huks fought side by side to end Japanese occupation from 1944 to 1945, in the final months of liberation the USAFFE, as well as Filipino landlords and elite, turned against the Huks. Once heralded as heroes of the resistance, the Huks became stigmatized as Communists and bandits and were attacked by American troops and government forces. In the postwar period, the guerilla army became an insurgent army, a peasant rebellion.[57]

These continuities between the anti-Japanese guerillas and modern-day

Communist forces (NPAs) are prominent in *Haplos*. The use of the term *hapon* in *Haplos* has a double signification: it is at once the Filipino word for Japanese and also a code word among NPA guerillas for Philippine government troops.[58] The two conflicts then—between Japanese soldiers and resistance fighters in the 1940s and between the NPA and the PC in the 1980s—are linked by a historically motivated linguistic slippage (*hapon* can stand for both the foreign colonizers and the national constabulary). The linguistic transposition surrounding *hapon* signals the way in which a foreign race and nationality (the Japanese, here essentialized by means of racism as imperialist) becomes collapsed onto the current opponents of the NPA.

Historical parallels in *Haplos* are conspicuous and insightful, and certainly the ghost narrative, by giving a doubled, dislocated vision of two moments, provides access to the prior conflict (the Huks' campaign in World War II) through the lens of the current one (the clash of military and Communist rebels). Yet the film complicates this surface analogy; strict binary correspondences between past and present are difficult to sustain. Although the Japanese Imperial Army is always cast in a negative light owing to the viewers' sympathy for Auring, the narrative is much more ambivalent about taking sides in the 1980s conflict. The film betrays a profound ambivalence regarding the question of who is to be feared in the forest (ghosts? Japanese soldiers? the NPA? the military?), an ambivalence that arises narratively from the ghost film's invocation of various battles on the same contested terrain.

Haplos's screenwriter has remarked that the ending, in which Cristy takes on Auring's characteristics in the ghost's absence, is really meant to underscore the film's theme of "transience—what is there and what is not there."[59] The director has likewise stated that the doubling between the two couples from the 1940s and the 1980s involves a play with time: "the present contains the past."[60] In the last scene, ghostly possession allows the two female protagonists to converge so that both are visible while simultaneously being occluded: Cristy is and is not herself; Auring is both present and absent in the other woman. In this sense, the four protagonists of *Haplos* epitomize the out of place (*wala sa lugar*) quality of Buendia itself. For Lee, the town raises the same questions that ghostly women do: have old things passed away in the town, or do they remain? Do things long dead persist among the living?[61]

Allegorical palimpsests, or multiple spatiotemporal inscriptions, are nowhere more apparent than in the film's frenetic climax, as the characters converge on the forest scene of the central traumatic event: the phantom repetition of Auring's rape and execution by soldiers of the Japanese Imperial Army in retreat at the close of World War II. The sequence begins with Al's inability to choose between Auring and Cristy, which causes the heartbroken ghost to run, sobbing, into the forest. But other ghosts await her: Japanese soldiers of another time set upon her, and Al, arriving unarmed and too late, helplessly witnesses Auring's traumatic reliving of her sexual violation and death. Through parallel editing, Auring's flight into the forest and her demise are rhymed fourfold: by Al's pursuit of Cristy; by Cristy's pursuit of Al; by Ilyong's failed attempt to rewrite events by rescuing Auring from the Japanese soldiers; and, at the furthest remove, by the townsfolk who follow Cristy into the forest to protect her from Communist rebels — Cristy's mother, the priest, and the Philippine Constabulary. As the film compellingly demonstrates, all the key players in the narrative head for the "same" place at the "same" time, but their experiences of events in the forest are discrepant and incommensurable, animated as they are by different motives rooted in different worlds and times. Parallel editing conveys a cinematic "meanwhile" in which everyone is "simultaneously" running toward the forest, yet this chronological simultaneity is fractured by intractable noncontemporaneity, as the characters' discrepant experiences of that disjointed moment in the forest (so that some see wartime ghosts while others see Communist insurgents) force the insight of calendrically noncoincident, dislocated times and spaces. Whereas crosscutting is conventionally a cinematic device that denotes a "meanwhile and elsewhere" — a chronologically single time in which two lines of action, usually in different places, unfold — the ghost film refuses the notion of a selfsame time. Modern simultaneity gives way to plural, noncoinciding temporalities, and the forest becomes a heterogeneous, splintered space much-visited by spirits.

Parallel editing here is so effective because, in the cinema, editing is equivalent to tense and focalization in verbal language.[62] In the scene of Auring's forest violation, both tense (as parallel editing) and focalization (as point-of-view editing) combine to show us that Auring's "past" is being lived immiscibly as Al's "present" — both of them "see" the Japanese soldiers; "meanwhile," montage gives us the other "present(s)" of the government troops rushing into the forest.

The spectral restaging of Auring's death and violation is the most arresting moment of *Haplos* because it can evoke a split experience of temporality on the part of the spectator. Because the film's graphic retelling of already-accomplished events proceeds as an unfolding in the viewer's present, the knowledge that a tragedy has already come to pass is combined with the urgent feeling that the past has yet to happen. Roland Barthes calls this feeling a "vertigo of time defeated," an uncanny and conflicted sense of temporality generated by old photographs of people who are now "alive" only in the photos. We feel, with a pang, that the dead have yet to die:

> I read at the same time: *This will be* and *this has been*; I observe with horror an anterior future of which death is at the stake. By giving me the absolute past of the pose (aorist), the photograph tells me death in the future. What *pricks* me is the discovery of this equivalence. In front of the photograph of my mother as a child, I tell myself: she is going to die: I shudder . . . *over a catastrophe which has already occurred.* . . . This *punctum*, more or less blurred beneath the abundance and the disparity of contemporary photographs, is vividly legible in historical photographs: there is always a defeat of Time in them: *that* is dead and *that* is going to die.[63]

This multiple and self-contradictory experience of time on the part of the spectator is due to the ghost film's ability to stage the vivid return of past events. Watching with dread as the soldiers lay hands on Auring, we think, "She is going to die; she is already dead," experiencing as an impending tragedy a violation that has already happened. This temporal disorientation in *Haplos* is the crux of what Derrida understands to be the ghost's multiple invocation of time: "Repetition and first time: this is perhaps the question of the event as question of the ghost. *What is* a ghost? What is the *effectivity* or the *presence* of a specter, that is, of what seems to remain as ineffective, virtual, insubstantial as a simulacrum? . . . Repetition *and* first time, but also repetition *and* last time, since the singularity of any *first time* makes of it also a *last time*."[64]

In *Haplos*, history as haunting allows the viewer to experience the rehearsal of the past as a "first time," to see the already known in its moving singularity rather than reciting history by rote or, as Benjamin put it, "telling the sequence of events like beads in a rosary."[65] In this ghost film, haunting is most poignant when the spirit relives the traumatic past, making the repetition of hopes thwarted and injustices committed truly spectral in their splitting of national historical time. Ghostly temporality's retelling of historical injustice retains the power to outrage, the inordinate singularity of a first time.

The title of the film, which can be translated as "touch" or "caress," pertains to ordinary people who have a brush with a local spirit. The ghost's caress sensitizes the characters to the forked, immiscible, but mutually articulated times and places of Buendia itself: past and present, forest and town, local and global. Auring's house at the opening of the forest, which the contemporary lovers enter only to emerge transformed, is a potent figure for standing on the threshold of remembrance, of awakening to the contestations of history.

Rouge: *The Spectral Courtesan*

Rouge tells the story of Fleur, the ghost of a courtesan who died in a suicide pact with her lover in 1934. Having waited fifty-three years for her lover in the underworld, to no avail, she resurfaces among the living to find him. When she first discloses her identity to a journalist, Yun Wing-ding, he responds with terror and confusion. "I failed history at school," he confesses and begs to be left alone. The claim to have failed one's own history through forgetfulness or lack of familiarity is the journalist's first response to the demands of the ghost of the past.

Eventually, Wing-ding and his journalist girlfriend, Ling Chor Gun, resolve to assist Fleur. Chor Gun's initial suspicion that the ghost might pose a threat to her relationship with Wing-ding subsides. Yet a love triangle remains in *Rouge*: both journalists become smitten with the ghost. In her compelling reading of the film, Rey Chow points out that *Rouge* is "not only the story of a ghost talking nostalgically about a past romance, but is itself a romance with Ruhua, a romance that is nostalgic for superhuman lovers like her" (fig. 38).[66]

Learning that Fleur's cowardly lover did not fulfill his end of their suicide pact, the journalists attempt to locate him and orchestrate a reunion for the long-separated couple. The reporters grow more and more captivated by the ghostly Fleur, touched by her coquettish grace and her superlative *"chi qing,"* her "excessive capacity for being faithful in love," faithful past death.[67] This passionate steadfastness is finally the foremost mark of Fleur's seeming otherness to the present, the irreducible signifier of her singularity in an age of sex-without-commitment and a hasty, linear time

38. A romantic triangulation is suggested by recurring three-shots in *Rouge*:
the two journalists become smitten with the ghost.

where promises of meeting in the afterlife would make no sense. This of
course, in subdued form, resembles *Haplos*'s uncanny ménage à trois; in
that film, as in *Rouge*, the mortal female becoming enamored with the anti-
quated woman's idealized but confining femininity underscores the sometimes troubling sexual politics of nostalgia.

Even more than in *Haplos*, narrative focalization through the ghost in
Rouge is rhymed by cinematography and editing. *Rouge* sees the city of
Hong Kong through a sentimental specter's eyes. The film's affective stance
toward noncontemporaneous times and places literally colors the mise-
en-scène with nostalgia: the film gives us flashbacks in which the past,
rendered in lush red and gold tones, looks far more captivating than the
present, which is almost always filmed in clinical blues and whites. This
use of color complements the other cinematic device for figuring recollection in *Rouge*, the superimposition of memory images, as in the Cantonese
opera performance from decades past reflected in a present-day shop window (see figs. 34 and 35).

Rouge suggests that Hong Kong is a city so in flux, so traversed by immiscibility, that "even ghosts cannot recognize it."[68] When Fleur looks at
the streets of Hong Kong, her disjointed view of the city—half recognition,
half estrangement—is conveyed through a striking reinvention of point-

39. In *Rouge*, point-of-view editing articulates spectral space and time, prefiguring recollection with a shot of Fleur's wistful face.

of-view editing. In a discontinuous editing strategy that recurs throughout the film, we see a shot of the journalist and Fleur looking at the cityscape; we then cut from a close-up of Fleur's wistful face to a point-of-view shot of a façade she remembers from 1930s Hong Kong; this image fades to black, followed by a reaction shot of Fleur's melancholy face; and finally, we are given a shot of the 1980s building that has replaced the place Fleur remembers (fig. 39).

Such scenes frustrate the viewer's expectation of a spatial whole experienced in a single present, instead enabling a discontinuous traversal of space and time. Fades between shots are a cinematic convention for a brief temporal ellipsis. In *Rouge*, however, when one image of built space fades into another, the elapsed time is both much longer (a half-century) and, crucially, part of a past that, rather than subsiding, persists, rising to our notice through a specter's glance.

By looking *with* a ghost, *Rouge* visualizes temporal critique in splintering the homogeneous time and space of cinema's continuity editing system. As is well known, point-of-view editing's conventional grammar relies on eyeline matches and the directional quality of the gaze to suture a shot of someone looking with an adjacent shot of what she is looking at, hiding the cut and inviting spectators to infer a whole, homogeneous space.[69] But space in the ghost film, as I have argued, is profoundly heterogeneous in a Bergsonian sense: a continuity composed of both change and permanence, where the appearance of stasis and solidity gives way to the awareness of an ever-humming, ceaselessly moving, temporally discrepant world. Abbas provides one of the most acute descriptions of spectral spectatorship in *Rouge*: "the films of the new Hong Kong cinema . . . define for us the spatial conditions of viewing and of filmmaking, where the act of looking itself has become problematic: the more you try to make the world hold still in a reflective gaze, the more it moves under you."[70] Thus *Rouge* undermines not only the assumption of a homogeneous space but also the comforting fiction of a static reality easily grasped by vision.

For Bergson, our "visual perception of a motionless external object" confirms that, in reality, spectatorship is never changeless or still. Even in the example of an apparently immobile object and a correspondingly immobile spectator, change, movement, and transition are unceasing because of time:

> The object may remain the same, [and] I may look at it from the same side, at the same angle, in the same light; nevertheless the vision I now have of it differs from that which I have just had, even if only because the one is an instant older than the other. My memory is there, which conveys something of the past into the present. My mental state, as it advances on the road of time, is continually swelling with the duration which it accumulates: it goes on increasing—rolling upon itself, as a snowball on the snow.[71]

In Bergsonism, spectatorship, like all forms of perception and consciousness, is itself a form of enduring, one interlaced with remembrance, a reservoir of the ever-accreting past. Thus in Bergson we find two diametrically opposed perspectives toward spectatorship. First, in *Time and Free Will* spectatorship is a form of false simultaneity (a syncing up of my authentic duration with the homogeneous, spatialized time of the clock I am watching). Second, in *Creative Evolution* spectatorship is authentically durative (despite the seeming stillness of my gaze and of the object I am looking at, I and the object both endure, time and memory are passing and accumulating, each passing moment renews my gaze). If we "change without ceasing," then the act of looking is possessed of as much temporal multiplicity as the rest of being, though we often fail to notice this.[72] Fleur, the revenant-flâneur who wanders through the spatial palimpsest of Hong Kong, is manifestly a spectator, and her bruising look, a surrogate for our

40. An allusion to scholar-courtesan romances in *Rouge*.

own, is fully temporalized, colored by duration and memory. *Rouge* is nostalgic not only for Fleur but for her ways of seeing.

Rouge makes special demands on its audience; the film's allusive resonance is best appreciated by viewers who recognize that this nostalgic allegory of Hong Kong's conflicted, hybridized cultural identity in the late 1980s takes as its vehicle a protagonist who is three things at once: specter, prostitute, and woman. Fleur is not just a prostitute lost in time but a ghost-courtesan who hails from the pleasure houses of what the film nostalgically envisions as a more romantic, gracious age. These three aspects of Fleur coalesce so powerfully in *Rouge*'s evocation of cultural and historical loss because the film deftly alludes to older Chinese intertexts around ghost and courtesan as deeply symbolic feminine figures. As Chow compellingly demonstrates, *Rouge* is rife with allusion to traditional scholar-courtesan romances. Chow writes that, in Fleur's first meeting with Twelfth Master (fig. 40), she sings a song familiar to Cantonese audiences, "A melancholy autumn away from home" [Ke tu qui hen]:

> The words of "Ke tu qui hen" tell of the love of a scholar and a courtesan-songstress. . . . For audiences who do not recognize the tune, this opening scene is by itself a beautiful capturing of the elusive romantic encounter of a prostitute and a dandy; but for those who do, the preordained and thus nostalgic nature of the encounter is remarkable. This encounter signifies how the "spontaneous" love between Ruhua and Shier Shao [Twelfth Master]—the

"original" story from the 1930s—is itself already a modern (re)enactment, a nostalgic (re)play of older tales, legends, and romances.[73]

That a spectator who recognizes the tune can perceive several encounters where others see only one confirms that allegory is quintessentially a hieroglyph, a public secret that proffers its meaning with seemingly open hands (hence its general comprehensibility on some levels) while other semantic strata are available only to those privy to its system of encryption.[74] "What the allegory reveals at the same time it hides, since the more visible and audible it is to ordinary eyes and ears, the more accommodated it is to limited vision, and therefore the less directly representative of the secrets it would tell," writes J. Hillis Miller.[75] *Rouge* is a ghost film whose nuanced invocation of older texts and cultural discourses is directed toward just such a "limited vision," its coded references selectively constituting and addressing a particular audience. This makes allegory an especially rich vehicle for culturally specific expression, because its second layer of allusions is utilized to selectively constitute and address a particular audience.

The dual-tiered, allegorical address to a cultural insider deployed by *Rouge* has much in common with the practice of "enigmatization" conceptualized by Linda Chiu-han Lai in reference to 1990s Hong Kong films. For Lai, enigmatization is a bifurcated textual address that makes certain aspects of a given film enigmatic or indecipherable to "outsiders" while rewarding local audiences with a layer of allusion legible only to those who possess "a shared history of popular culture." An enigmatic textual design, then, knowingly relies on durative spectatorship, a spectatorship actualized in viewing and remembering. What I find particularly significant about Lai's argument is that it acutely counterweights New Hong Kong Cinema's success with international audiences with enigmatic enjoyments reserved for the cultural insider: "Many Hong Kong films, starting for the most part in the early 1990s, are carefully designed to harbor multiple layers of meanings, so that they produce messages coded in ways that the local audience alone can interpret but that remain comprehensible to an international audience on a more general level."[76] All too often the question of localism in Hong Kong cinema is raised as a diegetic, representational element, when it can also be conceived as a horizon of reception, legibility, and resonance, as Lai does. A dual-tiered textual address demarcates and preserves—against an account that flattens Hong Kong cinema as an absolutely self-deracinating set of films—a bulwark against global cosmopolitanisms that empty out the particularities of culture-specific (and place-specific) audiences.

For an audience of cultural insiders able to see more than meets the eye, *Fleur* recalls and revises two figures from traditional Chinese ghost literature: the "avenging ghost," a "perturbed spirit" who aims to redress a grievance inflicted by someone she trusted; and the "amorous ghost," who seeks to overcome the "impeded path of love" by rejoining a lost lover.[77] That the ghostly Fleur should arouse sympathy rather than horror might have something to do with the film's similarity to late imperial ghost literature, in which the allure of ghostly women corresponds to "the widespread fascination with the death of beautiful, talented women in the sentimental culture of th[e] period."[78] In classical Chinese literature, the female specter merely underscores an existing affinity between ghosts and the feminine: positioned as pure yin in relation to "man as the fullest flowering of yang," the ghost is a foil to human, as woman is to man. The female ghost thus incarnates the perceived resemblance between ghostliness and femininity and (regrettably) affirms the corollary, that masculinity is equivalent to humanity.[79]

The figure of the ghost courtesan is not unusual in Chinese classical discourses of the strange (*zhiguai*) and marvelous (*chuanqi*); indeed, the sentimental fascination with the death of talented women segues easily into late imperial literature's nostalgia for the courtesan, an alluring woman of great talent whose passing reminded Ming and Qing literati of the lost splendor of an earlier age.[80] Since the mid-nineteenth century, the late Ming courtesan was collocated with "the sense of an ending," be it "personal loss, the end of a dynasty, [or] the destruction of a culture."[81]

In *Rouge*, a nostalgic enchantment with Fleur infuses the film with a sentimental longing for the brothel as a privileged place for love in courtesan culture. One critic remarks the "uniqueness of the courtesan world as a meeting ground for men and women" in late imperial China, which, "in contrast to the rigid segregation of men and women in gentry society," opened a space for men and women to interact in a context where women were valued for their "comparable talents" and shared artistic and intellectual concerns with men.[82] In counterpoint to the casual pragmatism informing the journalists' relationship are Fleur's glamorous affair with Twelfth Master in the 1930s and the film's implicit celebration of her economic and sexual power over her clients. This upholds courtesan culture as a privileged social space, a meeting ground for men and women where desires could be played out and affections formed between partners of equal talent. In addition to being nostalgic for "superhuman lovers" like Fleur, then, the film could also be said to be nostalgic for the brothel as a social space in which women were allowed a relatively greater degree of autonomy in love as opposed to the strict confines of an arranged marriage.

Rouge's historical allegory is focalized through a woman who is both ghost and courtesan, two intensely feminized positions. In this the film rehearses a long tradition in Chinese literature of seeing ghostly return, or a courtesan's decline, as a sentimental allegory for the passing of an era. For an audience alert to the allusions of this ghost allegory, then, Fleur is deeply coded by literary tradition as a profoundly eloquent figure for history. The spectral female courtesan's capacity to evoke the "sense of an ending" (though as a revenant she also evokes a sense of perpetuity) is exploited to intense effect in *Rouge*, grafting the phantom's literary antecedents to New Hong Kong Cinema's concerns over the "handover" to mainland China in July 1997. Ghostly temporality, already heavy with references to more times than one, is powerfully combined with the figure of the courtesan specter, an affective structure in Chinese classical literature for contemplating the passing of an age.

When the two journalists in *Rouge* rummage through antique stores for news of events that transpired half a century ago, they do so not only because Fleur is prominently entangled in the tabloid gossip of the 1930s but because they suddenly find that they themselves have a stake in "old news" too. In this scene at the antique shop, the student who claims to have "failed" history thus reclaims a spectral version of it as his own. At first, Fleur's commitment to holding her lover to his original promise puzzles the two journalists, who chide her about her obsession with the failed promises of the past. Yet as the story unfolds, Fleur's obsession with finding her lover becomes a catalyst for the other characters and the spectator to reflect on the idea that possesses Fleur—the question of the past's claims on the present, of whether history can be addressed/redressed or whether, as Fleur's missed encounters suggest, it is ever entirely eclipsed.

Allegory as a redemption of a vanishing past is evident in *Rouge* and *Haplos* inasmuch as both love stories encourage us to see a foregrounded encounter filtered through nearly forgotten events so that we perceive the echoes of "old" romances in "new" ones. Yet this is not the only level of signification that allegory demarcates. In *Haplos*, skirmishes in the forest and the townspeople's chancing upon a local spirit caution against a nation's propensity toward historical amnesia. The same is true for *Rouge*, in which the journalists first come to terms with their having failed history and later, with empathy and compassion, renew their historical consciousness in an enchanted, profoundly meaningful, way. In both films, the modern couple's nostalgic romances with old-fashioned ghosts confiscate the conventional motif of the love triangle, reinscribing it with the vicissitudes of sexual-historical entanglements. Indeed, several scenes in both *Haplos* and *Rouge*—the forest denouement, Fleur and Twelfth Master's duet—exemplify allegory's capacity to "condense" the palimpsest of disparate incidences in such a way that a "vertical reading of allegorical correspondences" comes sharply into view.[83]

Spectral Justice

The spectral heroines of *Haplos* and *Rouge* direct our gaze not only to our accountability to the nearly forgotten past but also to its unrealized vision of the future. The motif of the broken promise, as instantiated in Fleur's attempt to hold her forgetful lover to his word, speaks of the present's failure to fulfill the expectations of the past, while Auring's tragic romance with Al reminds us that past wrongs have yet to be redressed in the future, as ongoing controversies concerning "comfort women" and overseas Filipino/a workers since the 1990s attest.[84]

The ghost calls us to a radicalized conception of historical justice. Derrida defines justice as being accountable to ghosts, to those who are no longer with us yet still are:

> It is necessary to speak *of the* ghost, indeed *to the* ghost and *with* it. . . . No justice . . . seems possible or thinkable without the principle of some *responsibility*, beyond all living present, within that which disjoins the living present, before the ghosts of those who are not born or who are already dead, be they victims of wars, political or other kinds of violence. . . . Without *this non-contemporaneity with itself of the living present*, without that which secretly unhinges it, without this responsibility and this respect for justice concerning those who *are not there*, of those who are no longer or who are not yet *present and living*, what sense would there be to ask the question, "where?" "where tomorrow?" "whither?"[85]

Here Derrida asserts that the capacity to be with specters is at the core of ethical politics. Historical accountability is a matter of being responsible, not merely to the past but also to noncontemporaneity, to the ghosts who perturb the present with their simultaneous presence and absence, making a simple fenced-in present impossible.

This ethics of historical accountability recalls Benjamin's "now-time" (*Jetztzeit*), a shock that bursts open the homogeneity of a historicist conception of time. Now-time is an "emphatic renewal" of a consciousness that sees the possibilities inherent in every moment (the messianic), espousing a "radical orientation toward the past." Benjamin's "now-time signifies a time," writes Ernst Bloch, "when what is long past suddenly becomes a now. . . . What is long past touches itself in an odd, enveloping, circular motion. . . . In short: the continuum was exploded, so that the suddenly raw citation rises before our eyes."[86] Benjamin is arguing against modernity's complacency toward the past, that is, the way that a "future-oriented" present understands the past only insofar as it serves the aims of the future. Conversely, remembering a "suppressed" and "oppressed past" can radicalize our orientation toward the future. Whereas the idea of progress had "close[d] off the future as a *source* of disruption with the aid of teleological constructions of history," the orientation to the past that Benjamin argues for is not oriented toward confirming the ways in which the future has fulfilled its promise to the past; rather, he bids us remember the ways it has precisely failed to do so.[87] This renewed historical consciousness is awake to the future's betrayal of its responsibility to the past—in neglecting to address its injustices and in failing to fulfill its horizon of expectations. Benjamin thus calls us to distance ourselves from our own anticipated future in order to take stock of the past's "unfulfilled future." Habermas elaborates:

> Benjamin proposes a drastic reversal of horizon of expectation and space of experience. To all past epochs he ascribes a horizon of unfulfilled expectations, and to the future-oriented present he assigns the task of experiencing a corresponding past through remembering, in such a way that we can fulfill its expectations with our weak messianic power. In accordance with this reversal . . . each respective present generation bears responsibility not only for the fate of future generations but also for the innocently suffered fate of past generations. . . . The pressure of the future is multiplied by that of the past (and unfulfilled) future.[88]

Thus, in opposition to the modern view that the present's expectations of the future determine its appropriation of the past, Benjamin advocates a reversal of conventional historical consciousness so that the past is not merely appropriated for the interests of the future; instead, the past's horizon of expectation is one to which our present and our future are acutely responsible. He writes, "Every image of the past that is not recognized by the present as one of its own concerns threatens to disappear irretrievably." Seen in this light, haunting as a recognition of commonalities between those who are and those who are no longer "blast[s] . . . a specific era out of the homogeneous course of history."[89] Benjamin importunes us "to fight on behalf of previous generations, the dead . . . [for] if this struggle fails, the dead may be said to die a second death."[90] In this call to accountability, Derrida's disjointed time with specters and Benjamin's now-time, mindful of the dead, coincide. The nostalgic allegory of ghost films like *Rouge* and *Haplos* undermines modernity's homogeneous time, fomenting instead a radicalized accountability to those who are no longer with us, a solidarity with specters made possible by remembering.

Gendering National Time: The Sexual Politics of Nostalgia

Despite its ability to unsettle the homogeneous time of historical progress, the ghost film's nostalgia for anachronistic, spectral women is not without disturbing aspects. It is as though the insight into immiscible times, achieved by focalizing the story through the ghost and encouraging a nostalgic affection for her, ends up undermining that radical temporal view by limiting it to a fascination with "old-fashioned" femininity, compensating for the breach of homogeneous time by idealizing patriarchal gender roles. Anderson, as well as other scholars, has pointed out the temporal paradox of the nation: the "newness" of the nation as a political form contrasts starkly with its felt "antiquity," its "immemorial" reach.[91] As Anne McClintock has compellingly argued, the "gendering of national time" is an attempt to resolve the temporal contradiction posed by the claim that the nation is both recently invented and eternal. Such contradictions of national time are dissembled through the logic of gender. The sexualization of national-historical time does several things at once: naturalize social hierarchy under a heteronormative division of labor and familial asymmetries of power; metaphorize teleological development under the "evolutionary family of man"; and, finally, sexualize archaic, traditional aspects of the nation as feminine, while its progressive tendencies are masculinized. She writes, "nationalism's anomalous relation to time is thus managed as a natural relation to gender."[92] In light of McClintock's argument, the sexual politics of nostalgia in *Haplos* and *Rouge*, both of which engage conflicted national-postcolonial histories, can be seen as attempts to domesticate spectral time by gendering the purported temporal continuities of tradition and cultural authenticity as "anachronistically" feminine.

In a different but suggestively analogous context, Dai Jinhua notes that nostalgia became ubiquitous in mainland Chinese cities of the 1990s, when the Chinese, "who could hardly wait to burst through gateway 2000, [were] suddenly seized by a nostalgic languor," deliberately fashioning themselves into a "mesmerizing mirror of the West while at the same time relentlessly fabricating Oriental mythology in front of this magical mirror."[93] This evocative mirror metaphor is reminiscent of both *Rouge* and *Haplos*, in which Asian film industries caught up in the successful mirroring of global hegemonic culture forge their own nostalgically pictured spectacle of (what is felt to be a diminishing) cultural difference. This spectacularizing of cultural difference as *feminine* is visible in these films' enframing: in the longing backward look at Fleur's coy glamour in *Rouge* and in the wistful portrait of Auring's gracious living, reflective of Spanish colonial influences, in *Haplos* (fig. 41).

Costume, setting, and all the resources of mise-en-scène are marshaled in service of the sexual politics of nostalgia: in *Rouge*, Fleur applies lip color the old-fashioned way, from an eponymous rouge locket in the film's opening scene; and in *Haplos*, Auring entertains Al with delicate cups of chocolate in wood-paneled rooms hung with lace curtains made by hand. The occult disruption of progressive national time is managed via gender, personifying "traditional" cultural difference via the femininity of anachronistic women.

Hong Kong and the National Cinema Effect

Rouge's old-fashioned ghost-heroine and her fantastic transgression of limits (of time, logical categories, and mortality) have been read as a figuration of collective anxieties over the 1997 handover of Hong Kong. Schol-

41. Nostalgia and the spectacularizing of cultural difference in the mise-en-scène is evident in *Haplos*'s wistful portrait of the ghost's colonial-era lifestyle. Photograph courtesy of Ricardo Lee.

ars of the New Hong Kong Cinema put *Rouge* in the context of a cinema of "wandering spooks," in which elegiac or ghostly elements betray a pre-occupation with a vanishing history—a cultural identity specific to pre-1997 Hong Kong—which these films inscribe in response to fears that the handover from Britain to mainland China augured the disappearance of that identity.[94] As 1997 drew nearer, this allegorical language of history as a specter—and of Hong Kong denizens themselves as ghosts "crossing over" between the boundaries of the living and the dead or, figuratively speaking, Chinese tradition and Western modernity—attained the status of a critical commonplace. "We have a situation," the critic Sek Kei declared, "where ghosts become modernized and modern men grow superstitious."[95] Fleur, the "abandoned harlot" who has a "missed encounter" with her past, was seen as personifying Hong Kong's own historical trajectory (its future "reunion" with its past roots in China), as well as its cultural hybridity (an amalgam of Chinese and British elements).[96]

In hindsight, Chow notes that the 1997 handover resulted in a curious rhetorical reversal among the international media's "China-watchers." Whereas commentators had previously disparaged Hong Kong's materialistic emphasis on prosperity as producing a culture of political apathy, in the years leading up to the change of governance, a sudden fear that Hong Kong's economic prosperity would be imperiled by mainland rule led to a rhetorical backflip: economic wealth was now seen to enable political democracy.[97] This supports Abbas's claim that, at a decisive moment, market freedom and political sovereignty were conflated.[98] What Chow incisively identifies as a temporally frozen fantasy apropos of 1997 ("the collective wish that Hong Kong 'remain the same' after being returned to China") depended on an "ideological impasse" whereby British colonialism was now to be thanked for having nourished a thriving capitalist economy that—inequity and exploitation notwithstanding—guaranteed political democracy. The frequently voiced concerns over ideological differences between the United Kingdom, the United States, and the People's Republic of China, and the imperiled fate of democracy in Hong Kong in the immediate aftermath of 1997, masked a convergence of geopolitical interests in the era of global capital: the mutual "wish" that Hong Kong remain, but never be more than, "the capital of freewheeling capital."[99]

This wish belongs, to a certain extent, to what Blanche Chu dubs a "status quo imaginary," a self-understanding embedded in a linear narrative of Hong Kong's achievement of progress.[100] The concept of historical progress structures the search for cultural identification in much nostalgic cinema, whose affection for the past veils a presentist disposition: "in relation to history, the status-quo imaginary sets the foundation of viewing the golden present always as the emergence of prosperity and stability from past poverty and chaos." Like many other scholars writing on Hong Kong's "nostalgia films" (a trend first inaugurated by *Rouge*), Chu is highly critical of cinematic nostalgia for cynically using the past merely to confirm the ascendancy of the present. In a cultural climate that values the current economic situation and fears its possible loss, nostalgia has a particular function: it is not deployed in order to articulate a historical identity that challenges British colonialism. Rather, in nostalgic comedies like *He Ain't Heavy, He's My Father* (Peter Chan, 1993) "nostalgia is about the making use of a less 'desirable,' i.e., less modernized and advanced, past as an antithetical counterpart to reaffirm the 'prosperous and stable' present."[101]

The nostalgia that Chu and others detect in 1990s Hong Kong cinema, a nostalgia in the service of the present, is, I would argue, the antipode of nostalgic allegory in *Rouge*. In Kwan's film, the present lives of the modern journalists are listless and uncommitted by comparison to the far more vibrant, if sometimes deceived and misguided, energies and passions of the old-timers. In fact, the modern couple only become passionate (about life and one another) when they become immersed in the past, when they fall for Fleur, who fascinates and repels them by turns, but who, in the end, emerges as their heroine as well as ours. More important, *Rouge* frustrates the ideological fantasy that a prosperous, pre-1997 Hong Kong can remain perpetually unchanged after the handover, frozen in time. Fleur's return to a city that is no longer the same city, incapable of stasis, always vibrating under her gaze, speaks unforgettably of changes that cannot be anticipated, a space and time that both becomes and remains.

For some time, 1997 was the touchstone of all criticism on contemporary Hong Kong cinema. Yet its descent (or ascent) into scholarly convention should not diminish the singularity of a cultural situation in which temporal immiscibility and spatial heterogeneity were vociferously registered across a host of media forms and in everyday life. Hong Kong's fateful return to mainland Chinese governance refused three truisms of decolonization: first, an ethnic return to the motherland; second, a nationalist return to sovereignty; and finally, the linear chronology and calendrical transparency of historical events. The handover refuted the linear temporal expectations that attribute progress to the colonizer and regression to the colonized. "When sovereignty reverts to China," Abbas dryly remarked, "we may expect a situation that is quasi-colonial, but with an important historical twist: the colonized state, while politically subordinate, is in many other crucial respects not in a dependent subaltern position but is in fact more advanced—in terms of education, technology, access to international networks, and so forth—than the colonizing state."[102] The agreed-upon date of Hong Kong's reunification with China notwithstanding, it was clear that cultural consequences had long preceded the political rendezvous itself. That is, the "aftermath" of July 1, 1997, had been keenly felt since the 1980s, more than a decade in advance of the appointed calendar date for the historical event. As Abbas puts it, "the eventualities have arrived before the event."[103] This latency of historical experience, the non-coincidence of historical event with a calendrical index, forcefully attests to a temporality that exceeds linear ordering.

Departing from the recognizable template of decolonization, the end of British colonialism in Hong Kong was not viewed as the beginning of independence but as "Chinese nationalist/nativist repossession." In the years leading up to Hong Kong's historic "return" to the "motherland," Chow famously characterized Hong Kong as caught "between two colonizers," foreign domination on the one hand, and the imperialism of a hegemonic "native" culture on the other. Chow's memorable articulation of this historic bind, "the struggle between the dominant and subdominant within the 'native' culture itself" and her call "to combat from the inside the totalizing nativist vision of the Chinese folk," signals the need to be wary of recent film scholarship that enfolds Hong Kong cinema too quickly into "quasi-national" status under the culture of the motherland.[104] To label Hong Kong quasi-national runs the risk of eliding asymmetries of power with regard to Tibet, Taiwan, and Hong Kong—that is, "China's relation to those whom it deems politically and culturally subordinate."[105]

In her recent book, for example, Yingchi Chu offers several arguments for viewing Hong Kong as a "quasi nation," most important of which are the "triangular relationship between the [British] colonizer, the motherland, and Hong Kong itself," and Hong Kong's sense of being "part of the Chinese national community," via a "dual cultural identity—that of Hong Kong and China." Claims such as the following seem plausible enough: "Every year, thousands of Hong Kong people cross the Chinese border to celebrate various traditional festivals with their families, and to renew their ethnic cultural links with China. . . . The shared ethnic cultural tradition with the Mainland has encouraged Hong Kong to view China as its motherland, despite the latter being under Communist government."[106] But the problem with this argument is its conflation of ethnicity with nation, commonsensically assuming their synonymy.

As Allen Chun has demonstrated, however, the substantive content of "Chinese ethnic tradition," a Sinocentric cultural core that Chinese living elsewhere must journey to the mainland in order to fully experience, does not have the verifiable givenness presumed by the logic of such statements. The fairly recent yoking of nation to ethnicity (a discursive and institutional coupling specific to the needs of a new Chinese republic under Sun Yat-sen) undermines claims to an immemorial Chineseness embodied by a nation-state.[107] The significance of Chun's argument lies in his challenge to think Chineseness, not so much as a substantive identitarian content but as a rhetorical-institutional form, namely, the *form of an invocation*:

"The factual substance of culture is, in this regard, less important than the rhetorical forms it takes. That is to say, behind the message itself, it is more important to know who is really speaking, how statements are produced and disseminated, how they relate to other discourses, and, finally, how they become systematized and institutionalized, if at all."[108] The performative invocation of Chineseness, then, is a political-institutional act that, in the context of the modern nation's imagined homogeneity and boundedness, takes on the quality of unambiguousness, as in the invocation of a Chinese motherland.

Notions of a Chinese motherland end by obfuscating the well-documented, profoundly meaningful ambivalence of Hong Kong residents toward the change of governance in the decade leading up to 1997. July 1, 1997, was celebrated by Chinese the world over as a long-awaited denouement to the Opium Wars of the prior century; at the same time, Hong Kong's return to China could not be an unproblematic reunion with a homeland. Instead, it pointed to resistance against nativist governmentality, to imperialism within a nation's realm. Moments when Chineseness is invoked or the powerful tug of ethnic affiliations is felt, then, cannot be read at face value as a mere compliance toward the hailing of a bounded, homogeneous nation.

More useful is Yingchi Chu's articulation of a paradox: though Hong Kong is not a nation, since the 1970s Hong Kong cinema has functioned and been regarded as something very much like a national cinema.[109] This produces, in effect, the anomalous case of a seeming national cinema in the absence of a formally instituted or internationally recognized nation. A crucial site for the discursive constitution of Hong Kong film as a national cinema is what Hector Rodriguez terms a "film culture field," a historically circumscribed cinephilic public sphere (composed of critical practice and social institutions like film publications, clubs and student groups, film festivals, university programs, and cultural centers) crucial to the emergence of the Hong Kong New Wave.[110] The film culture field established linguistic, aesthetic, and cultural distinctions between Hong Kong and Shanghai film; erected a reflectionist model for reading Hong Kong cinema as expressive of social realities; and, in championing a "New Wave," also inaugurated a comparativist structure in which Hong Kong films and filmmakers were likened or contrasted to the works and auteurs of other national film movements.

According to Esther M. K. Cheung and Chu Yiu-wai, most critics regard national cinema as "antithetical" to Hong Kong cinema, preferring a transnational approach. Hong Kong cinema "exposes the imperfections and inadequacies of 'national cinema' as an analytical category" for several reasons: Hong Kong, though possessed of a certain geopolitical unity, "has never been a nation state per se." The growing body of academic writing on Hong Kong cinema (special journal issues, book anthologies, and monographs) shifted critical perspectives steadily away from "the tripartite model of the PRC, Taiwan and Hong Kong," the "greater China model" that had animated earlier English-language scholarship on Hong Kong cinema. Ironically, the intense scholarly focus on Hong Kong cinema discounted the validity of the national cinema paradigm, on the one hand, while elevating Hong Kong cinema to a scholarly status previously reserved only for canonized national cinemas, on the other.[111]

A national cinema paradigm rooted in the auteurist model of the postwar European new waves remains poorly suited to Hong Kong cinema, whose own new wave was not an art cinema but an innovative form of commercial filmmaking that viewed Hollywood less as an object of critique than a partner and rival to Hong Kong cinema. The national cinema model typically works on a contrastive principle of difference from Hollywood, but in the case of Hong Kong cinema, the prominent other against which to demarcate cultural and stylistic distinction is not Hollywood but other Chinese cinemas.[112] Despite its intransigence to national cinema paradigms, however, Hong Kong cinema as an object of cinephilia and critical study has produced a *national cinema effect* that makes it possible, for example, to consider Hong Kong and Philippine ghost films side by side, as I have done here.

Haplos vivifies the historical past only to wreak havoc on linear notions of national progress, calling the future to responsibility for its unfulfilled promises to an oppressed past. *Rouge* exceeds (but invites consideration within) the confines of national cinema studies. New Hong Kong Cinema, which exudes a pronounced national cinema effect in the absence of a nation, teaches us that, to paraphrase Chris Berry, it is not nations that make movies but movies that help to make nations.[113] The rise of Hong Kong cinema to national cinema status in the absence of an originating nation coincided with the profound recognition, in the 1980s and 1990s, that Hong Kong could neither claim national status nor be properly understood within prior narratives of decolonization.

Hong Kong's "society of migrants, immigrants, and urban nomads" does not provide a unified category of "the people" on which to anchor a national cinema or invocations of national identity. Abbas has noted that "Hong Kong cinema is not at all seduced by the epic mode, i.e., by narratives of nation-building."[114] Not specifically epic, then, but broadly generic—New Hong Kong Cinema has used genre conventions as enabling constraints that prompt, rather than repress, historical inscription.

As I mentioned in my introduction, an important through-line in this book is the way in which temporal translation is obliged to work within the parameters of genre. The Filipino and Hong Kong ghost films considered in this chapter represent moments when the new cinemas' attempts to grapple with historical trauma take the form of a play with genre, a play that is not parody but fruitful innovation and transformation. Abbas writes that New Hong Kong Cinema "begins by working within the conventions of a specific genre, only to depart quite radically from them. Even more important is the fact that the formal innovation points to a historical situation that can only be felt in some new and original way."[115] I am making the same point with a slightly different emphasis: faced with historical singularity (*Rouge*), or with the challenge of vivifying a betrayed past (*Haplos*), the New Cinema movements in Hong Kong and the Philippines resorted to generic repetition. This, then, is another modality of temporal critique: the familiar, centuries-old genre of the ghost story pushed to articulate startlingly urgent forms of historical consciousness.

CHAPTER 4

The Ghostliness of Genre

Global Hollywood Remakes the "Asian Horror Film"

The preceding chapter on ghost films explored the ways in which spectral women can provoke a sense of historical accountability, vivifying pasts nearly effaced from memory. In this final chapter, I examine not the allegorical singularity of cinematic ghosts but their *generic* quality — the iterability of the specter as a stock figure of the horror film — in order to suggest, in quite another light, the ghostliness of genre itself.

Perhaps the quintessential embodiment of the fantastic narrative, the ghost is above all a revenant, a figure of return. Genre, likewise, is a formal, social, and industrial contract to repeat and to return and, as such, is always temporally diverse, involving the unmooring and entanglement of the "old" with the "new" and with versions yet to come. Bergson's idea of a heterogeneous past condensed, contracted into, and coextant with the present, with neither moment signifying a chronological unicity, holds for genre, as does his insistence that exact repetition and perfect recurrence are impossibilities.[1] A hint of genre's temporal plurality emerges when Gledhill, writing about the cyclical nature of genres, brackets the notion of the old: "'old' films circulate among us still, enabling film and critical production to hook back into the past and dust off apparently worn-out formulae for present uses and possible renaming." For Gledhill, "the life of a genre is cyclical, coming round again in corkscrew fashion, never quite in the same place. Thus the cultural historian lacks any fixed point from which to survey the generic panorama."[2] Her consideration of the cyclical temporality of genre emphasizes decline and reemergence, keying us to persistence, return, reinvention, and movement rather than stasis. Thus the musical, after several decades, might bob its head up again but not in the same guise as before. Similarly, the heterogeneous range of screen texts we refer to under the banner of the horror film has undergone, with dizzying speed in the past few decades alone, a series of deaths, returns, and transmutations: as B film, high concept, indie, slasher, splatter, gore, and ghost film, and in the first decade of the new millennium, in the guise of Asian specters furiously retooled by Hollywood studios.

The preceding chapters drew on postcolonial, historical, and ontological modes of temporal critique to unseat the ascendancy of homogeneous time: positing plural times, refusing anachronism, and discerning untranslatable, immiscible temporalities. Thus far, this book has used genre—the fantastic conceptualized as a mode of temporal translation—as a means of focalizing cinema's capacity to intimate nonchronological time. This concluding chapter shifts the methodological gears of temporal critique, while retaining the triangulation between genre, temporality, and translation. Genre is conceived of not only transhistorically but also *cross-nationally* and *industrially*; temporality is explored along the axes of *generic repetition and the speed of film-industrial appropriation*; and finally, translation refers us to the work of *deracination and refamiliarization* in global Hollywood's remakes of screen rivals from Asian film industries.[3]

As discussed in my introduction, Jameson's modal approach conceptualizes genre as a range of formal and semantic possibilities not confined to a single historical period. Each work borrows, retools, and renews these modal possibilities in relation to a historically specific combinatoire, those horizons of emergence, reception, and intertextuality that function as limiting conditions of possibility for the individual text.[4] Yet the modal consideration of genre pursued thus far in this book, as linked to time and translation, can take still another form. Gledhill emphasizes that mode is not only transhistorical but cross-national, a means of tracking generic influence and exchange *between* film industries and audiences on national, regional, and global scales:

> The notion of modality, like register in socio-linguistics, defines a specific mode of aesthetic articulation adaptable across a range of genres, across decades, and across national cultures. It provides the genre system with a mechanism of

"double articulation," capable of generating specific and distinctively different generic formulae in particular historical conjunctures, while also providing a medium of interchange and overlap between genres. . . . In such permeability lies the flexibility of the system necessary to the forming of a mass-produced "popular culture" for a broadening society, drawing into public view a diversity of audiences, sometimes dividing but working more generally to unite them, while at the same time facilitating international exchange.[5]

Adopting Gledhill's modal view of genre—across decades and national-popular cultures—we might conceive of the "productivity of genre" in terms of the "international exchange" between national cinemas, domestic and overseas audiences, cult aficionados, film producers, studio distributors, critics, and promoters.[6] If genres "serve diverse groups diversely," as Rick Altman puts it, then no player on the generic field is a monolith. What critics call—as a form of shorthand—global Hollywood, Asian cinema, popular audiences, cult devotees, and so on, are variegated cultural agents who do different things with the "same" genre film. As Altman points out, genres "have multiple conflicting audiences" and "Hollywood itself harbors many divergent interests."[7]

Genre itself provides the best justification for adopting Altman's "pragmatic approach," one attuned to the different uses to which cultural products are put by contending, disparate interests.[8] As this book has attempted to show, genre is a powerful analytic lens for the film theorist and historian; at the same time, it is an invaluable category around which a host of synergistic film-industrial practices — story development and film production, optioning and financing, marketing and distribution, and the pitch to global audiences in diverse locales — are organized. For all the productivity of the fantastic as a generic lens for temporal critique, the fantastic—in extradiegetic terms—is not a broadly legible category for film production or distribution; horror is. Though many of the horror films mentioned in this chapter may come under the definitional arch of the fantastic, the two terms are not coextensive, testifying to what Altman and Gledhill have identified as the very ground of genre scholarship: the "*inevitable* mismatch between industrial and critical histories."[9]

To the four temporal problems explored in preceding chapters—first, Bergson's time of the cinematic apparatus; second, the times of reception, remediation, and reinscription of the aswang as a media-convergent event; third, the affective temporality of the ghost film's nostalgic allegory; and fourth, the occulting of a national meanwhile—this final chapter adds a fifth: the temporality of transnational generic appropriation and exchange, centering on global Hollywood remakes of genre films that originate in Asian film industries and are marketed in a regionalist-globalist vein. In the ensuing analysis of what I call the new "Asian horror film," genre refers not only to horror but also to a generic practice: the remake.

Repetition is the engine of genre. But, given Bergson's reminder that ceaseless change makes exact repetition impossible, I would add that generic repetition inevitably encodes difference or novelty. Generic repetition is always inexact, never a precise iteration. Accordingly, the pleasures of genre's iterative temporality are ones to which genre scholarship must always return: what are the pleasures of variance-in-repetition? What new pressures to be like-but-different confront a genre film that repeats but cannot stage a precise rehearsal of its successful predecessors?

This chapter considers the multiple temporal rhythms of a transnational generic practice—Hollywood's global remaking of "Asian" genre cinemas—and deracinating cultural translations that homogenize difference in an attempt to achieve maximum palatability across multiple domestic and overseas markets. These dynamics of deracinative translation are considered in relation to Takashi Shimizu's *Ju-on: The Grudge* (2003), remade by the same director for Paramount and released the following year as *The Grudge*. Generic exchange, repetition, and transformation across national, regional, and global film industries, involving diverse cultural actors, audiences, and markets, are at once popular cultural phenomena and economic transactions.

For the film scholar, remakes and sequels have always thrown the financial considerations underwriting film as industry into stark relief. Several distinct but intertwined temporal rhythms are at work in the generic practice of remaking a precursor text: the temporality of perception or consumption of an individual text; the repetitive, cyclical temporality of genre; the durative aspect of a precursor's cultural survival and continued influence; the temporally discrepant character of intertextuality, which cautions against conceiving of the time of remakes and sequels as a chronological "afterward"; and finally, the speed of global Hollywood's transnational appropriation of the cinematic signatures of its overseas rivals. These layered, noncoinciding temporalities coalesce in a case study that closes the chapter, Kim Jee-woon's South Korean ghost film, *A Tale of Two Sisters* (2003).

Remaking the New "Asian Horror Film"

Starting around 2002, trade publications and mainstream journalism began to take note of a brief but furious burst of transnational exchange between Hollywood and what has been dubbed the "Asian horror film"—a new regionalist appellation less inclusive than it sounds, since it consists chiefly of a limited slate of Japanese, South Korean, Hong Kong, and Thai horror films. In 2003 *Variety* quipped, "In the Hollywood remake kitchen, French is no longer the *cuisine du jour*, Italian has lost some of its flavor, Latin dishes may be starting to tickle taste buds, and Asian fusion is so hot it's smoking."[10] A year earlier, one reviewer wrote that Hideo Nakata's *Ringu* (1998), Takashi Miike's *The Audition* (1999), and the Pang Brothers' *The Eye* all "confir[m] Asia's position at the vanguard of modern horror cinema."[11] Rights to *The Eye* (dir. Oxide Pang Chun and Danny Pang, 2002) were bought by Tom Cruise and Paula Wagner for a remake at Paramount, released in 2008. The Pang Brothers' *The Eye* was among several "original Asian horror films" that American studios saw as "reviving" the "creatively dead" Hollywood horror film, whose own slasher film sequels had run out of steam. One reporter wrote, "Hollywood's horror industry is running scared. The formulas and franchises have been squeezed dry. And now Hollywood is turning to Asia to restock the cupboard."[12] Nakata's 1998 *Ringu*, a filmic adaptation of the 1991 novel by Suzuki Koji, is often positioned as the progenitor of the Asian horror remake trend, sparking generic repetition across Asian and Hollywood film industries, a regional-international cycle replete with its own conventional iconography: "girls with long hair hiding their malevolent faces, dotty old ladies, child zombies caked in white—all of which you can expect to see in the Hollywood remakes."[13] Beginning around 2001, and continuing for about five years, Hollywood was caught in the grip of an Asian horror remake frenzy. Witness DreamWorks' remakes of the *Ringu* cycle (*The Ring* [2002] and *The Ring 2* [2005]), Senator International and Paramount's remake of Takashi Shimizu's *Ju-on: The Grudge* (2003) as *The Grudge* (2004), and Disney-based Pandemonium's remake of Nakata's *Dark Water* (2005), to name only a few.[14] By 2003, at least eighteen remakes of films from South Korea, Japan, and Hong Kong were either completed or in the works at various studios: DreamWorks, Paramount, Miramax, Warner Bros., United Artists, Fox, Universal, and MGM among them;[15] and in 2004, with the cycle's momentum still unchecked, one writer noted, "The list of remake options seems to get longer by the week."[16]

Hollywood's recent crop of remakes is certainly not confined to Asian horror alone; nor is the current preponderance of horror on studio slates surprising. In 1999, with *The Blair Witch Project* and *The Sixth Sense*, Hollywood horror films turned a profitable corner, away from previously exhausted genre trends (1980s slasher films and their ironized 1990s counterparts, e.g., *Scream* [1996]).[17] By 2002, *Variety* was reporting a wave of new and upcoming Hollywood horror releases.[18] In 2003, *Sight and Sound* remarked the popularity of remakes and sequelizations of 1970s Hollywood horror classics. Like 1980s horror films that revisited 1950s movies, remakes such as *The Texas Chainsaw Massacre* (2003), "a hallmark 1970s horror product cunningly rebranded for a jaded 21st-century audience," testify to what has been called horror cinema's "regurgitative" impulse, an "enthusiasm for devouring and regurgitating its own entrails."[19]

The genre film is cannibalistic: "implicitly, each new genre film ingests every previous film."[20] The centrality of intertextual repetition in genre films is particularly pronounced in the cannibalism of a remake, which even more emphatically "ingests" its precursors. The names for intertextuality and generic exchange are many: *remake*, *sequel*, *allusion*, and *influence* retain, to greater or lesser degree, the more pejorative cast of *rip off*, *steal*, and *copy*. Their shared semantic horizon, of course, is repetition: a repetition often faulted both for lack of originality and for imitation found wanting. David Wills offers an incisive definition of the remake, writing that "what distinguishes the remake is not the fact of its being a repetition, rather the fact of its being *a precise institutional form of the structure of repetition*, what I am calling the 'quotation effect' or 'citation effection,' the citationality or iterability, that exists in and for every film."[21] As a precise institutional structure of repetition, the remake, like the sequel, has long stood accused as "an exploitative device, a cynical ploy to sell an inevitably inferior new text on the basis of an earlier work's success."[22] Faced with such dismissals, it is helpful to bear in mind that the remake, which has also been productively defined as an intensified, hypervisible form of intertextuality, announcing and foregrounding its citational, allusive structure, actually "problematizes the notion of originality."[23] For instance, the supposed inferiority of the imitative text in relation to a prior original is a difficult accusation to sustain in the wake of concentric influences that are transhistorical as well as transcultural. One of the blurbs on the DVD release of the U.S. Verbinski version of *The Ring* calls this remake "the best scary movie since *The Sixth Sense*" (fig. 42).

42. Global intertextuality: a blurb on the U.S. DVD release of Gore Verbinski's remake *The Ring* (2002) promises "The Best Scary Movie Since *The Sixth Sense*."

This line condenses the dense and dizzying tissue of global intertextuality subtending the film. *The Ring*, being a remake, quotes the Japanese *Ringu*; but the quotation doesn't end there. This film about children who personify occult forces also references the far-from-original *The Sixth Sense* (1999), which is itself indebted to a venerable Hollywood genealogy of the monstrous child from the late 1960s to the 1980s: to wit, *Rosemary's Baby* (1968), *The Exorcist* (1973), *The Omen* (1976), and *The Shining* (1980).[24] This lineage is made explicit in several print advertisements for the 2002 theatrical release that prominently feature one reviewer's intertextual endorsement: "Not since 'The Exorcist' or 'Rosemary's Baby' has a movie been so truly frightening."[25]

Why horror? Why the remake? What accounts for the new conspicuousness of a genre (horror) and a generic practice (the remake) in transnational generic exchange between Hollywood and regional Asian cinemas? The answers to these questions are both generic and economic: first, the "value proposition" of playing in the "genre space" of the midpriced horror film. "Horror films are often cheap to make, they are not usually star-driven, don't need a lot of expensive special effects and can be made in a tight locale."[26] Senator International, one of the companies involved in the *Ju-on* remake, sees itself as playing in the "genre space" of horror and comedy, a "robust" clearing in the international film market for moderately priced fare (productions between US$10 and $40 million, at a time when production and marketing costs for Hollywood releases averaged around US$90 million).[27] Second, remakes and sequels are at base financially conservative studio strategies, considered a "foolproof," inexpensive, alternative form of development, since the screenplay has already been proven market-worthy. In addition to being defined as an institutional structure of repetition, the remake can also be usefully considered as an alternative form of studio development. A Fox executive quips that remakes constitute "a different kind of development—not necessarily easier or harder." The hope, nonetheless, is that the remake delivers a "foolproof idea": by tinkering with a script that has already proven successful, studios can avoid lengthy and costly development.[28] In addition, the remake names a labor practice: in the context of globalized Hollywood production and distribution, the labor market has also become transnational. Christina Klein writes that when Hollywood studios purchase remake options for South Korean films, "in effect, they are buying the labor of South Korean screenwriters, which is much cheaper than that of American writers."[29]

As scholars have pointed out, classical Hollywood horror was characterized by sequels. In the 1960s, sequelization was part of the conservatism of New Hollywood marketing.[30] Horror film remakes and sequels, then, are truly nothing new; nonetheless, the preponderance of Hollywood remakes of commercial Asian fare is a striking recent phenomenon. Of course, there have long been horror films produced in Asia. But what I am calling the new Asian horror film refers to the pronounced role played by horror, among other commercial genre fare, in the convergence of regional, "pan-Asian" cinema with global Hollywood initiatives from about 2001 onward.

Part of this story is already the stuff of recent American film-industrial legend. The *New Yorker* describes Roy Lee as the "remake man" who "brings Asia to Hollywood." By 2003, Lee, a Korean-American film producer working in a white-ruled industry, had sold Hollywood studios remake rights to eighteen Asian films, including *Ringu* and *Ju-on*. Test market studies for Hollywood films often come too late (after the film has already been financed and completed) and are frequently inaccurate (relying on small, unrepresentative audience samples). In this light, Lee's opportunistic pitch—telling Hollywood executives to regard an Asian movie as "a script that someone had taken the trouble to film, and that happened to have been tested and proved as a hit in its own country"—is extremely appealing to studios uncertain about market tastes.[31]

My analysis of generic-economic factors in Hollywood's remaking of the new Asian horror film as a regionalist-globalist phenomenon is confirmed by Roy Lee's own responses in an interview with Gary Xu. In *Sinascape: Contemporary Chinese Cinema*, Xu writes:

> Why has remaking East Asian films become such a popular trend at the turn of the millennium? Conversations with Roy Lee yielded several interesting clues. . . . First of all, Lee mentioned several times that he did not have a particular interest in Asian horror films. All he saw was market potentials. If East Asian remakes become no longer profitable, he would easily switch to other venues for his film productions. Second, Lee emphasized repeatedly how cheap it was to make films in East Asia. East Asian filmmakers were all happy to sell the remake rights to Hollywood, for the fee paid by Hollywood studios (albeit a small portion of the cost of remaking the pictures) would most likely recoup what they originally spent on making the films. Third, Lee did not need to search hard for profitable East Asian films. The films came to him: filmmakers sent him videos, and they even asked him to read their scripts before their films went into production. It is thus not exaggerating to say that many East Asian films aiming at commercial success now have a built-in "remaking mentality" that self-consciously measures themselves against the Hollywood standard. Fourth, all of the originals of Lee's films had been tested well in the East Asian cinema markets: *The Ring*, *The Grudge*, *My Sassy Girl*, and *Infernal Affairs* were megahits in East Asia. Lee's trust in the testing effect of East Asian markets reveals an assumption that North America and East Asia share the same patterns of consumption.[32]

Together with generic and economic factors (the demonstrable market success of a relatively inexpensive foreign film, on the one hand, and the attractiveness of Hollywood's purchasing price for remake rights to Asian film producers, on the other), a deracinating, globalist pitch unites both players. As Xu notes, Asian filmmakers have begun to make films with an eye toward Hollywood uptake in remake form, a "remake mindset" among local filmmakers that represents an amplification and internalization of Hollywood as a global norm, an institutionalized set of standards and ex-

pectations. Meanwhile, Hollywood players like Lee, who function as bro-
ker and liaison between international film industries and markets, also
presume a deracinated, globalist horizon of reception, or, as Xu puts it,
an assumption that what works in Asian markets will work in American
ones.

I first began to work on Hollywood's spate of Asian horror remakes when
it was gathering momentum; at this writing, the cycle appears to have run
its course, with market exhaustion setting in for audiences inundated by a
string of horror releases (not all of them remakes of foreign antecedents).
Genre cycles always spiral toward decline: one journalist quips, "J-horror
is dead. J-horror has never been bigger." This observation points to fears
that Hollywood remakes are bound to "kill" or betray their source, even
as the status of J-horror films declines, going from cult standing among
cinephiles to "cash cow" once the remakes become high-grossing hits
with mainstream U.S. audiences.[33] Cult aficionados of Asian horror, early
adopters ahead of the studios' mainstreaming curve, have closely scruti-
nized Hollywood's remake cycle. English-language fan reviews I have come
across, whether in print sources or online, sound an unmistakable note
of exasperation—ranging from skepticism to outright resistance—in relation to Hollywood remakes of beloved works drawn from the corpus of
what has been called Asia's "dark cinema."[34]

In June 2007 the *Los Angeles Times* noted wryly, "The chill is gone," adding: "Call it a market correction. Call it a slump. Call it audience fatigue with
a subpar rash of crazed killers, wanton vampires and jiggling coeds, but
horror, one of Hollywood's enduring staples, is tanking." Forty-some horror films were released in 2007, more than doubling the numbers for the
year before. It had been three years, however, since a horror film earned
more than $100 million in domestic box office receipts in the United States.
That film was a remake of a Japanese thriller cycle with origins in video: *The
Grudge*.[35]

Deracinating Genres: From Hong Kong Action
to Asian Horror Cinema

Any notion of the distinctiveness of national cinema (whether formal, cultural, economic, or historical) must contend with Hollywood's voracious
capacity to *deracinate*—that is, uproot, efface, and delocalize—such forms

of distinction. Historically, Hollywood's deracination of "Asian cinema" has taken aim at the genre film: first, "Hong Kong action film style" from the 1990s on; and second, the appropriation of "pan-Asian" horror cinema in the following decade. The recent emergence of a generic practice, the remake, as a vehicle for Hollywood's globalist deracination of Asian genre films points to the recruitment of generic intertextuality for flexible accumulation. Generic repetition and influence are here a function of the *speed* with which film industries respond to their rivals by mimicking and deracinating their local, cultural, or national signatures onscreen. The recently minted "Asian horror film" represents the convergence of both regionalist discourses on the "pan-Asian film" and globalist profiteering of Asian commercial cinema as at once culturally specific and culturally neutral, hence immensely appealing to audiences worldwide.

Hollywood's once-furious remaking of Asian horror films was composed of two moments: a first moment of triumph for local Asian film industries, whose inexpensive genre films outdid high-dollar Hollywood productions domestically; and a second, bleaker, moment, when Hollywood remade these modes of resistance into global profits, outperforming domestic productions once again by retooling the Asian horror film as a cultural key to enticing Asian markets.

In an article first published in 1999, Cindy Wong writes presciently of the "sinister globalism" that subtends Hollywood's interest in Hong Kong cinema. "By taking over Hong Kong," she warns, "Hollywood ultimately denatures and denies it. . . . Hong Kong films may be different from Hollywood, but as Hollywood analyzes what sells in Hong Kong film, it finds that it can appropriate these features and sell them better." That year and the following, *The Matrix* (1999) and *Charlie's Angels* (2000), two films that notably did not feature Hong Kong stars or directors, premiered. With the help of two prominent Hong Kong action choreographers, the brothers Yuen Woo-ping and Yuen Cheung-yan, both films arguably found "what sells in Hong Kong film" and "sold them better" to audiences the world over, fulfilling Wong's prediction that "the general audience may see a Hollywood movie with or without knowledge of its Hong Kong connections at all."[36] Such films did not originate in the Hong Kong film industry but brandished a set of cinematic strategies (editing, action choreography, cinematography) formerly identifiable as stylistic signatures of particular Hong Kong action film genres.

Through *The Matrix*, *Charlie's Angels*, and a host of others in their wake, including the global blockbuster/art film coproduction *Crouching Tiger, Hidden Dragon* (2000), global Hollywood has invoked, with great success, a deracinated understanding of "Hong Kong cinema" as a style, an aesthetic, a mark of polish in certain high-concept action films. This makes it possible for "Hong Kong cinema" to be in the room, so to speak, in a film starring Cameron Diaz, even for an audience unaware of action choreographer Yuen Woo-ping's lineage in Hong Kong martial arts film production nor his status as Hollywood filmmaker-émigré. (Nonetheless, in a dual-tiered mode of address, publicity around both *The Matrix* and *Charlie's Angels* was poised to draw the interest of knowing Hong Kong film buffs as well.) The appropriation of Hong Kong action films by Hollywood productions is not new, nor is it the first time that Chinese martial arts genres have been absorbed into American action films in the service of American stardom.[37]

An unmistakable aspect of this earlier moment of deracination was its generic stamp, its reductive caricature of Hong Kong cinema as "action film style." Stephen Teo calls the international misrecognition of Hong Kong cinema as action film the "supreme irony in the history of Chinese cinema," given that martial arts films were on the wane for domestic Hong Kong audiences at the time of Hollywood's infatuation with the genre in the 1990s.[38] Critical ambivalence toward the *wuxia* or martial arts genre has long structured debates on the "quality film," first in mainland China in the late 1920s and early 1930s, then in Hong Kong via Shanghai expatriate filmmakers in the 1930s.[39] The deracination of Hong Kong action cinema was a "prequel," so to speak, for the current deracination of Hong Kong genre movies under the banner of the Asian horror film. In hindsight, what is most striking about Hollywood's deracination-and-appropriation of Hong Kong genre cinema (and soon after, of "Asian" genre cinema) is the speed with which it was accomplished. In 1996, *Time* magazine asked: "Will Hollywood Ever Make a Place for Hong Kong Cinema?" The question referred to the hesitant overtures of Hong Kong film luminaries John Woo and Jackie Chan to the U.S. film market. At that time, a Hong Kong genre, the action film, was also being touted as Hollywood's much-needed "shot of adrenaline," echoing more recent rhetoric hailing the new Asian horror film as a tonic for another depleted Hollywood genre.[40]

Hollywood's uptake of Japanese and South Korean genre films happened quickly as well. To take the example of South Korean commercial films:

in 2001, when Miramax paid $950,000 for remake rights to *My Wife Is a Gangster*, trade journalists were still regretting that "South Korea's movie miracle"—powerful domestic box-office successes that outshone Hollywood summer blockbusters—"largely remains a secret reserved for its 45 million people." Said *Variety*, "The irony is that all this success, which mirrors other celluloid renaissances in Thailand and Hong Kong, is little appreciated beyond home turf." While "Korea Fever" for popular music, television, and film ran strong in the region (especially in South Korea's most lucrative entertainment market, Japan), the window of opportunity to Western audiences appeared narrow owing to the lack of a clearly identifiable generic trend and Hollywood's limited slots for Asian films: "With the West able to absorb only a handful of Asian pics every year, Korean cinema still lacks a popular hook in audience's minds. Chinese cinema is martial arts extravaganzas and arty peasant dramas, Wong Kar-wai and Zhang Yimou. But Korean? Even upscale Western auds would be hardpressed to name a single director, let alone a popular genre, that identifies Korean cinema."[41]

Hence, for *Variety* in 2001, the "global breakout" "eyed" by Korean cinema still seemed to be a question of gaining international legibility through a single signature genre or via globally recognized stars and/or directors. Yet by the end of the decade, South Korean cinema emerged at the forefront of the Hollywood remake fever: Universal is at work on a retooling of Park Chan-wook's *Oldboy* (2003),[42] and *The Uninvited*, DreamWorks' remake of *A Tale of Two Sisters* was released in 2009.[43]

Cinephilia and Difference

Avid DVD collectors and self-proclaimed connoisseurs of Asian cult cinema in the United States occupy a contradictory or equivocal position in this picture. Asian genre film buffs in English-language markets outside Asia are often regarded as a kind of taste-making vanguard whose prior adoption of foreign films signals a growing market proximity carefully eyed and cultivated by studios and distributors. (The rhetoric of teleological temporality here is not accidental: taste-making trends across commodity culture are deeply enmeshed in a capitalist temporality privileging firstness, since subcultural distinction derives from novel, trendsetting "discoveries" yet unknown to the imagined mainstream other. Cult aesthetes often regard the subsequent popular embrace of trends they pioneered as a loss of rarefication crucial to subcultural capital.)[44] Most fan sentiments in print and online film reviews are strongly critical of Hollywood appropriation, even though a certain degree of mainstreaming—American or international distribution of foreign genre titles—is the enabling possibility for their cinephilia. In the absence of first-run theatrical releases for films like *Ringu, Ju-on,* or *A Tale of Two Sisters* in the United States, readily available, English-subtitled commercial releases on DVD are key, and these DVDs become the focus of fan practices of collection and critique. One shared concern for cult devotees is that Hollywood remakes, which are usually high-dollar productions in comparison to the Asian originals, entail a homogenization and oversimplification—via narrative linearity, glossy production values, and a sanitizing of grisly scenarios—of films whose disturbing qualities or narrative ambiguity were prized by aficionados as a source of pleasure.

A 2007 thread in the online Snowblood Apple Forums, a self-described "discussion forum for East Asian movies, primarily, with an emphasis on horror and cult cinema," exemplifies the cult fan's understandable skepticism toward the DreamWorks remake of Kim Jee-woon's formally accomplished and perceptually difficult ghost film, *A Tale of Two Sisters.* In a thread begun in June 2007, one member responds to the planned Hollywood remake as follows: "If it ain't broke, don't fix it. What the hell is wrong with Hollywood? Their scriptwriters running out of ideas?" A subsequent post replies that the logic of "If it ain't broke don't fix it" is in actuality "the opposite of Hollywood studio thinking. 'If it ain't broke, cash in on it.' The struggle we constantly have here is not knowing if we are going to get art, or corporate crap. Sometimes we are pleasantly surprised. Too often we get what we expected." While one film buff continues the thread by remarking that he or she is trying not to be "depressed by all the money-grubbing remakes," another states quite explicitly that higher Hollywood production budgets do not guarantee cinematic quality: "If Hollywood insists on a remake, I hope it is a decent remake. All that budget and still they always border on crap. I think the big budget tends to kill these remakes. It's the dingy, grimy film quality that gives many horror films that desolate, disturbing atmosphere. Sometimes, less is more."[45]

The Asian horror film buff's typical skepticism with regard to Hollywood remakes conforms closely to J. P. Telotte's account of the selective pleasures of cult audiences and their general suspicion of the profit-driven conservatism of franchises, remakes, and sequels. Whereas the cult film "seems to speak meaningfully (or *lovingly*) to a select group," Telotte writes that Hollywood films

> are generally targeted at and marketed for the broadest possible audience, as production companies, distributors, and theater owners all try to capture as great a share of the viewing dollar as possible. As a result, most films still take the most conservative path, following a classical narrative pattern that reiterates far from disturbing truisms about the moviegoers' culture. Controversial topics tend to disappear—or to dissolve in the most simplistic imaginary formulations. So there is nothing to truly offend, nothing to hate, but by the same token often little *to love*. At its extreme, this practice leads to the current sequel mania, as almost every film that demonstrates a certain earning power quickly generates a slightly modified sequel, prequel, or third cousin—so we get, and perhaps as a culture well deserve, a *Friday the 13th, Part n*.
>
> Against this backdrop, the conjunction of a *limited* audience and a limited, even unconventionally measured success becomes significant. For it underscores how that "love" aspect of the cult film functions: it works in a realm of *difference*—from normal film viewing practices and from marketing customs.[46]

Cult cinephilia's emphasis on difference is a useful reminder that studio attempts to unify heterogeneous transnational audiences via a global smash hit may meet with pronounced resistance in certain subcultural quarters. But at the same time, such filmgoers exemplify the market proximity of Japanese, Korean, Hong Kong, and Thai films to various national-popular audiences elsewhere in Asia, in the United States, and in the United Kingdom, a market proximity on which the new regionalist and globalist Asian horror films overtly rely. Likewise, the emphasis on difference can sometimes reveal troubling inflections. In *Asia Shock*, for example, a compilation of film reviews intended for consumption by other fans of "Dark Cinema" or "Asian Extreme Cinema," Patrick Galloway writes: "when you really sit down and dig into dark Asian cinema, comparing what's on the menu with Western fare, there's no escaping the conclusion that the Asian stuff is far more intense. *Asia Shock* is a celebration of this filmic fact, imbued as it is with a general theme of *vive la difference!*"[47] The rest of that work reveals a peculiar strain of culturalism, one that purportedly upholds "Asian" cultural difference against Hollywood homogeneity, paying lip service to the film historical differences between the various film industries included in the survey (those of Japan, South Korea, Hong Kong, and Thailand) while simultaneously homogenizing Asian cinema, collapsing cultural differences between various national cinemas and markets. Galloway's allusions to the intrinsically Asian quality of the films reviewed seem rooted in a regional logic that may ultimately be less a culturalist argument than a racialized one.

Generic Ghosts and Refamiliarizing Translations: *Ju-on* and *The Grudge*

The ghost film's core conceit, visualized in its mise-en-scène, is that *space has a memory*. Fractious times permeate a no-less-heterogeneous space, in which the past, to use a Bergsonian figure, presses against the half-open door of consciousness.[48] The mise-en-scène of haunted domestic spaces suffused with traumatic recollection recurs frequently in the Asian horror films recently retooled by Hollywood. Space as immersed in a profoundly vengeful memory emerges in the enormously popular *Ju-on* cycle, which began, as one writer puts it, with a "straight-to-video cheapie" made in 2000. Several glowing reviews on a cinephile's Web site—specializing in DVD reviews of "horror films and fantasy from Japan, South Korea and Europe," "cult movies from the 1960s and 1970s," and "unusual anime, giant monsters, and rarities still not on DVD"—attest to the strong cult standing of the *Ju-on* cycle. According to those reviews, *Ju-on* characters were first featured in two short episodes shot on video by Takashi Shimizu for a television series, *Gakko no kaidan G* (School Ghost Stories G) in 1998; in 2000, two full-length films by the same director, commonly referred to as *Ju-on: The Curse* and *Ju-on: The Curse 2*, were theatrically released, though shot on video.[49]

Taka Ichise, the producer of the Japanese *Ringu* and *Ju-on* cycles, espoused a low budget, no-stars aesthetic when he came back to Japan in 1997 after working in Hollywood. The Asia edition of *Time International* notes, "He discovered a clique of talented young directors, including *Ringu*'s Hideo Nakata and *Ju-on*'s Takashi Shimizu, absorbed with making straight-to-video ghost stories. Working with budgets of about $10,000 per one-hour segment forced Asian horror's avant-gardists to rely on suspense instead of special effects."[50] The low-budget video release *Ju-on: The Curse* and subsequent iterations directed by Shimizu were remade as *The Grudge* in 2004, earning $110 million in the U.S. domestic market.[51] In his November 2004 article for *Variety*, David Cohen noted that *The Grudge* was "the year's highest grossing horror pic, at 89 million" in domestic box-office returns after four weeks in release. In a table detailing the domestic box-office grosses of *The Grudge* relative to other profitable horror films from recent years, Cohen's article extrapolated that *The Grudge*'s earnings would reach an estimated US$110 million by year's end. Cohen noted that the profitability of *The Grudge* would not likely be confined to its box-office earnings alone; the horror genre is distinguished by its "leggy DVD profit potential," that is, an extended "afterlife" of a decade or more in video and DVD sales and rentals, a "long-term playability" *The Grudge* was also expected to enjoy.[52]

The theatrical and video profitability of *The Grudge* is owing in no small measure to the material reworked by Shimizu's precursor text, the *Ju-on* cycle that moved from brief television segments in 1998 to further iterations in video and film. For Alvin Lu, successful straight-to-video J-horror "subverts cinema by suggesting how modest homegrown entertainments like Japanese horror must morph like a virus through different media in order to survive Hollywood's onslaught. No more potent work of J-horror exists than the straight-to-video, shot-on-video *Juon*."[53]

Shimizu's third reworking of the *Ju-on* cycle is *Ju-on: The Grudge* (hereafter referred to as simply *Ju-on*). Shot on film, the 2003 Japanese theatrical release made the most of its larger budget in comparison to the prior video versions. The opening intertitles of *Ju-on* apprise spectators of the narrative premise: "Ju-on: the curse of one who dies in the grip of a powerful rage." This epigraph is reproduced almost exactly at the beginning of the Hollywood remake, *The Grudge* (2004), whose intertitles continue as follows: "The curse gathers in that place of death. Those who encounter it will be consumed by its fury." Such opening lines do more than explain the supernatural blight that destroys a string of hapless protagonists; they also link death to memory, emotion, and place, highlighting *Ju-on*'s reinvention of the conventional haunted house motif.

In ghost films, *space remembers*. The haunted house refers to a space of recollection charged with affect: alternately fearsome, thrilling, or tragic.

The haunted house is a shape-shifter, never static or frozen because completely temporalized. To grasp such a space, one cannot resort to quantitative schema: units of measure are irrelevant to the "Terrible Place" of horror, which can capriciously reveal a different aspect of the macabre to each protagonist it encounters. Carol Clover notes that "the Terrible Place, most often a house or tunnel in which the victims sooner or later find themselves, is a venerable element of horror." Though for Clover what defines the terrible place are "the terrible families—murderous, incestuous, cannibalistic—that occupy them," her discussion of the conventions of slasher-horror also implicitly acknowledges the durative character of the terrible place. Past events abide there, drawing present-day characters into their destructive ambit: "Into such houses unwitting victims wander in film after film, and it is the conventional task of the genre to register in close detail those victims' dawning understanding . . . of the human crimes and perversions that have *transpired there*. That perception leads directly to the perception of their own immediate peril."[54]

Ju-on is notable for reworking the durative, traumatic space of the haunted house through the motif of transposable contagion. In years past, a jealous husband, Saeki Takeo, killed his wife, Kayako; his son, Toshio; and, finally, himself in their family home. Though other families subsequently move into the former Saeki residence, they find, to their fatal misfortune, that the original owners have never really departed. The temporal and spatial reach of the terrible place in *Ju-on* is enormous in comparison to conventional haunted house narratives, where evil befalls protagonists only on the house's premises. In contrast, the curse of *Ju-on* is place-rooted but peripatetic, able to snuff out several lives that come only indirectly into its compass, its malevolence reaching victims who seemed to have been spared, only to consume them many years later, in other locales. The retooling of the haunted house convention into a motif of transposable contagion is made explicit in the highly expository dialogue of the investigating detective in *The Grudge*: "It is said in Japan that when a person dies in extreme sorrow or rage, the emotion remains, becoming a stain upon that place. The memory of what happens repeats itself there. Death becomes a part of that place, killing everything it touches. Once you have become a part of it, it will never let you go." The logic of the terrible place in *Ju-on* is not so much repetitive as incorporative: the narrative traces the ways in which the spectral house ruins several lives, among them a woman

43. A visuality of suspense in *Ju-on: The Grudge* (dir. Takashi Shimizu, 2003): Staging in depth across multiple planes allows spectators to glimpse a ghost-child who appears on every floor, behind a character's shoulders, as an elevator ascends.

whose death-by-haunting becomes incorporated into the curse narrative, written into the house's gruesome script.

Ju-on's low production costs were an enabling constraint, spurring the filmmakers to make fresh use of cinematic devices while eschewing costly special effects. The film's ingenious sound design depends on incongruous sound mixing, so that a boy opens his mouth and emits a cat's piercing screech, while mobile phones emit macabre groans. Atmospheric horror hinges on mise-en-scène. Instead of relying on special effects, the house in a state of messy dereliction becomes metonymic of haunting, as opposed to the relative orderliness of the house when humans try to bring it under their (ever-eroding) control.

Ju-on adapts deep focus and deep space to the constraints of small apartments and tight shooting spaces: over the characters' shoulders, only four or five feet away, the ghost-child Toshio walks unseen or watches the living from just beyond their line of sight. Staging in deep space is reinvented as staging in relative depth across multiple planes in tiny living spaces, giving spectators a glimpse of what moves unseen behind the characters, unnoticed in glass-door reflections, or what waits on every floor as a terrified young woman leans with her back to an elevator door (fig. 43). The dynamic of seen and unseen in such sequences guarantees that attentive spectators will know more than the characters, constituting a visuality of suspense.[55]

Ju-on unfolds through an episodic narrative. Six plot segments are named for a corresponding number of characters, all of whom are victimized by the supernatural curse that lingers in the house where Takeo murdered his family. The film's episodic structure enables it to follow the silken threads of capture constituting the house's web of death. The first episode, "Rika," details the eponymous female protagonist's first visit to the cursed house, but this opening situation is already emplotted in the middle of the fatal web. A volunteer at a social welfare center, Rika has to substitute for a caregiver assigned to look after an elderly woman who lives in the Saekis' former home. The plot opens on the day that the caregiver fails to show up for work (spectators later infer Rika's predecessor has also died by supernatural means). When Rika arrives at the house, no one answers the door, so she lets herself in. The house is in an advanced state of disarray, trash strewn everywhere, furniture awry. Rika discovers the old lady in a badly neglected state, uncommunicative and despondent. An odd noise draws Rika to a taped-up closet, where she is horrified to find that a bruised little boy named Toshio has been shut in the closet with a black cat. Rika's conversation with Toshio is interrupted by another strange sound. Going to investigate, Rika witnesses the old woman's death at the hands of Kayako, the murdered ghost-wife.

The rest of the temporally disjoint plot unfolds through various characters. In the next episode, "Katsuya," which takes place a day or so earlier than Rika's visit, spectators learn that the elderly woman's son and daughter-in-law, who were living with her in the same house, also succumbed to the curse prior to Rika's arrival. The third episode, named after the elderly woman's daughter, "Hitomi," jumps forward in chronological time and returns to the evening of Rika's first visit to the house but follows events elsewhere: Hitomi is stalked by Kayako's ghost as she leaves her office building at the end of a workday; the specter follows her home to her apartment and kills her there.

The viewer's perception of a near-simultaneity between the old woman's death in the house, witnessed by Rika, and Hitomi's attack in her high-rise apartment, is fostered by a "meanwhile effect" that links the first episode, "Rika," with the third, "Hitomi." This meanwhile effect is realized through a single incident—Hitomi phoning her brother's house and leaving a message—that is repeated in the two nonadjacent plot segments. In the first episode Rika, in the haunted house, lets the answering machine pick up and listens as Hitomi's phone call to her brother and sister-in-law is recorded. The third episode restages this event from the other end of the telephone line, as Hitomi calls from her office building and leaves the message Rika overhears. This simultaneity provides a tenuous temporal anchorage for a narrative whose disjunctive, episodic plot repeatedly leaps forward and backward in story time. Once it is understood that Rika's visit and Hitomi's death happen on the "same day," the sequential order of story events can be roughly pieced together by the spectator, though the inferred temporal coordinates of most events remain inexact.

The fourth episode, "Toyama," unfolds later in the same day, as the old woman's death is reported by Rika's boss, and police find the corpses of her son and daughter-in-law hidden in the attic. A traumatized Rika is confined to the hospital, where she is visited by the officer in charge of the recent murders. Expository conversations between Rika and the police reveal that since Takeo killed his wife five years ago, all subsequent families who have moved into that house have died or disappeared. Soon after, the police request the assistance of an ex-cop, Toyama, the only surviving officer involved in the Saeki case. Late that night, Toyama attempts to set fire to the cursed house, but a nonsynchronous encounter with the future, not the past, stops him in his tracks. In the yellow-orange light of the afternoon (a first index of nonsynchrony: night had fallen by the time Toyama arrived at the house), an adolescent schoolgirl is running out of the house, terrified. Offscreen, we hear her classmates jeering at her for believing rumors that the place is haunted. Viewers are expected to infer that the tall teenager is Izumi, Toyama's daughter, who was just depicted as a prepubescent child in a prior scene. Chronological time falls away as Toyama in the "present" (a few days after Rika's first visit to the Saeki house) locks eyes with his grown-up daughter in years to come (years after Toyama's death, we learn, and a few days after Rika's own grisly end). Both doomed but still alive in nonidentical times, Toyama and his daughter, Izumi, do not inhabit the same calendrical now, but in this terrible place, homogeneous time shatters as those shrouded in the house's fatal residue meet in an immiscible, momentarily dovetailing meanwhile.

That space is ontologically possessed of memory is the enabling condition for the encounter of nonsynchronous temporalities in a haunted place:

it is because space is a palimpsest of multifarious times that the already-dead and the soon-to-die can meet in a fractured locale whose awful past persists. Such a space is not the neutral container imagined by notions of empty homogeneous time-as-space, a space evacuated of any time but the present. As explored in the previous chapter, ghost films insist that spaces endure and often outlive us; in enduring, they function as repositories of time whose immiscible temporalities are often nonsynchronously encountered by unnerved protagonists.

In the fifth episode, "Izumi," the plot jumps several years ahead, detailing Izumi's own death shortly after her nonsynchronous encounter with her father in the haunted house that classmates dared her to enter. On the afternoon before ghosts claim Izumi, a news reporter announces Rika's death on television. This passing sound bite is the barest clue for spectators seeking to reconstruct the sequence of story events in chronological order. Though "Izumi" is not the final episode in the plot, it occurs last of all depicted narrative events in story time: the hapless schoolgirl is, in sequential story terms, the final victim we see claimed by the vengeful curse.

The concluding episode, "Kayako," which takes place shortly before Izumi's death, follows the tragic end of Rika, the protagonist whose visit to the house several years earlier opened the plot. Having failed to save her best friend, Mariko, from the terrible place, Rika is also beset by ghosts, but, before dying, she looks in a mirror and perceives herself to be the murdered ghost-wife's double (figs. 44 and 45).

This, of course, is calendrically impossible: Rika, a young woman victimized by ghosts perhaps a decade after the Saeki murders, cannot all along have been Kayako, the wife killed by her jealous husband. But in ghost films, doublings that contravene homogeneous time are feasible. As the nonsynchronous encounters between Toyama and Izumi and the impossible doubling between Rika and Kayako illustrate, *Ju-on* pays mere lip service to the chronological meanwhile that only nominally anchors story and plot. Spectators and critics alike have repeatedly remarked the temporally disorienting quality of *Ju-on*, but the film's disjointed episodic structure is no accidental shortcoming. The unsewing of chronology is wholly consistent with the spatial heterogeneity of the terrible place at the center of the narrative and the ghost film's riotous times. It is difficult to piece together the shards of *Ju-on*'s temporal puzzle because the world of ghosts defies calendar time.

44, 45. On the threshold of her own death in *Ju-on*, Rika looks in a mirror and relives past events, seeing herself as the double of Takeo's murdered wife, Kayako.

In the derelict house, the face Rika sees in the mirror is not her own but Kayako's. In a morbid revisionist vignette (a montage of prior set pieces in which Rika is shown in Kayako's place), she relives the latter's terrible fate and sees herself as always-already written into the house's death-script, both murdered and murderer, victim and monster. This narrative climax suggests that repetitive violence in the ominous house bears a disturbing resemblance to the equivalizing logic of serial killing. Indeed, the house in *Ju-on* might be understood as both serial killer and bloody chamber, both the agent and the stage setting for a Bluebeard-like sequential murder of a string of hapless wives. Rika's vision of doubleness as Kayako, at the threshold of the former's demise, allows one to speculate that all the other women Takeo haunted and killed are placeholders for the wife he first murdered on suspicion of adultery. Rika recognizes not only her likeness to Kayako but the equivalizing fate that lies in store for her (Kayako's horrible death in the past is the selfsame future that awaits Rika). One awful effect of serial murder's logic of repetition is a deliberate erasure of differences between women.

The temporality of sexualized serial murder is an issue I have considered elsewhere;[56] here I want only to underscore the nonsynchronous temporality of serial killing. The mirror into which Rika peers in the bloody chamber reveals at least two times: the prior downfall of her predecessor, Kayako, and her own impending demise. The linear past, present, and future assumed by homogeneous time gives way to an inexorable, fatal circularity, the "repetition of a fate that is both not yet and always and already hers." Rika, the heroine trapped in a malign house with a murderous patriarch out to punish his wife, stands on the threshold of Kayako's prior fate: "seriality always implies a rendezvous with fate, the heroine's providential meeting with and becoming her double."[57] Rika is entangled in a nonsynchronous temporality that is fatally foreclosed.

This macabre doubling is brought home by two montage sequences dominated by a graphic-thematic motif: a face whose eyes, widened in terror, are only partially obscured by a pair of hands. In the first montage that follows Rika's confrontation with her own spectral reflection as Kayako, staccato editing juxtaposes images of people half-peering at ghosts: the old woman whose death Rika witnessed (fig. 46), a geriatric patient playing peekaboo with a spectral child at the welfare center (fig. 47), and Rika's own face, terrified eyes half-shielded by her fingers, wanting and not wanting to see what horrifies her (fig. 48).

The second montage is dominated by the same motif but shifts to a revisionist remembrance of various set pieces in the film that show Kayako to have been Rika all along. In both sequences, the peekaboo motif literalizes what scholars of horror and the fantastic have identified as "an aesthetic of pleasurable fear." Didier T. Jaén writes that "the effect of the literature of fear is fascination; instead of fleeing from it we are strongly attracted by it; we are repulsed and fascinated at the same time."[58] *Ju-on* closes on a temporally discordant note and self-reflexively demonstrates that a spectatorship founded on fascinated repulsion, not chronological consistency, is one of the narrative's most vital concerns.

Andrew Horton and Stuart Y. McDougal have cogently formulated the

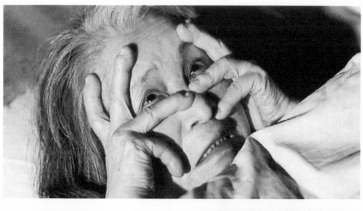

46–48. An aesthetic of fascinated revulsion: characters half-covering their eyes on seeing a ghost in *Ju-on*.

spectatorial dynamic at work in remakes: "By announcing by title and/or narrative its indebtedness to a previous film, the remake invites the viewer to enjoy the *differences* that have been worked consciously and sometimes unconsciously, between the texts. . . . They provoke a double pleasure in that they offer what we have known previously, but with novel or at least different interpretations, representations, twists, developments, resolutions."[59] The point of looking critically at remakes, then, is not to ask the question of fidelity to a supposed original but instead to ask the question of transformation. What is significant about what the remake retains from the precursor text vis-à-vis what it transforms?

Hollywood's remakes of the two most profitable J-horror cycles — *The Ring* and *Ju-on* — represent a departure from usual Hollywood practices in that the original Japanese directors (Nakata for *Ring 2* and Shimizu for *The Grudge*) signed on to remake their own films.[60] Repetitive authorship grounds these films in a horizon of similitude, but the expectation of difference in a remake is no less at work. *The Grudge* corresponds to several categories in Robert Eberwein's "preliminary taxonomy" of remakes: a remake of a foreign film; "a remake that changes the cultural setting of a film"; "a remake that switches the gender of the main characters"; and a "remake that changes the race of the main characters."[61] Such a remake — involving racial, cultural, and gendered conversions — is a *refamiliarizing translation.*[62] *The Grudge* pitches the cultural specificity of the Japanese ghost narrative in the internationally legible vocabulary of Hollywood conventions, hoping to avoid the difficulties posed by a foreign screen text by making it seem already-known and familiar: dispensing with the need for English subtitles, changing the race and ethnicity of the main protagonists, and replacing the same-sex friendships between women (Rika and Mariko in *Ju-on*) with a heterosexual romance (Karen and Doug in *The Grudge*), while retaining the Japanese setting.[63]

Writing about a U.S. remake of a French film, one critic has characterized the Hollywood remake as motivated by an attempt to erase the foreign film's subtitles. Subtitles are always evidence of "the process of being transposed, translated, exported," of the labor of repeating and recontextualizing a film, of the need to render a foreign utterance in a local tongue. Subtitles also disrupt the seamlessness of sound and image through the obviousness of the need to work at legibility. The remake seeks to efface the sign of cross-cultural negotiation in order to deliver the foreign as already domesticated and familiar.[64] In this light, Hollywood's feverish spate of Asian horror remakes can be recognized as deracinating acts of cultural appropriation.

Deracinative appropriation contrasts starkly with the kind of translation that delights in "idiomatic singularity." Derrida writes that such a translation "approach[es] as closely as possible while refusing at the last moment to threaten or to reduce, to consume or to consummate, leaving the other body intact but not without causing the other to appear."[65] Its antipode is a deracinating translation, which transposes to another register the other that it erases. In this sense the remake, construed as an avoidance of subtitles, could be understood as an attempt to circumvent the idiomaticity of the precursor text and to efface the sign of the work of cultural translation.

Interestingly, erasure and deracination as characteristic gestures in Hollywood remaking emerge even in titling practices. Xu writes:

> The title of *Ringu* is indicative of the gains and losses of remaking as outsourcing. Originally named *The Ring*, this original must yield the "original" title to the remake and is forced to use the Japanese transliteration of "ring" as its "authentic" title. The Japanese film industry might have gained recognition and a small share of the remake's profit, but the gain for the "native," symbolized by the letter "u" added to "ring," is precisely what has been lost: the original ethnicity, the "aura," the intellectual property, and the identity and history of the entire national film industry.[66]

The Grudge is a deracinating remake but one in which the selvedges of the refamiliarizing translation are conspicuous and begin to unravel. The narrative attempts to motivate the use of the same locale and mise-en-scène that proved so effective in *Ju-on* while providing a culturalist explanation for the supernatural. (The idea of a cursed place is now named a "Japanese" belief in expository dialogue: "It is said in Japan . . ."). Alongside this bracketing of the supernatural as foreign belief, the remake strives to make *Ju-on*'s narrative more palatable to Hollywood audiences, blurring the hard edges of that very foreignness by putting Hollywood stars at the center of a Japanese ghost story. The "cultural novelty" of a Japanese curse merges with the globally familiar generic conventions of the Hollywood slasher film, embodied in an instantly recognizable star of the genre on both film and television—Sarah Michelle Gellar—who, in this light, becomes the very figure of transnational generic exchange. Heroine of Hollywood slasher/teen film revivals and icon of occult television in the prior decade, Gellar finds her new overseas horror home as the investigative "Final Girl" in Japan: the "Terrible Place" of the horror film has unmistakably gone global.[67] In addition, the casting of Gellar, star of the 1990s television series *Buffy the Vampire Slayer*, is an attempt to harness what trade publications dub the "Buffy effect": using female horror protagonists to lure young girls to the movies, since exit polls show that the new breed of horror films, including Hollywood remakes of Asian popular fare, are attracting disproportionately young, female audiences.[68]

The unwitting effect of this deracinative translation is fascinating. Remaking *Ju-on* as the story of American exchange students literally scared to death in Japan links horror to insurmountable and alienating cultural differences. Karen, an exchange student, must navigate Tokyo's subway system and street names in an unmastered foreign language, finding locals less than willing to help her make sense of a bewildering new city. Jennifer, the American housewife who grudgingly moved to Japan (and into the cursed house) when her husband took a new job there, likewise alludes to spatial disorientation as an index of cultural dislocation: "I went for a walk yesterday, just to explore. And I got so lost. I couldn't find anyone who spoke English who could help me." Reassured by her husband that "we're going back to the States" if things don't get easier for her, Jennifer ventures out to the supermarket, only to be confronted by unrecognizable food options in the aisles. Surreptitiously puncturing a sealed package of instant soup, she takes a sniff of the foreign fare in order to decide whether she finds it edible. Such small scenes of culture contact speak volumes for the limits encountered by the deracinating, refamiliarizing translation. The Hollywood remake's attempt to erase or at least neutralize foreignness as a barrier to global popular-cultural entertainment is belied by a narrative that thematizes cultural differences that cannot be entirely overcome. The title word, *grudge*, describes not only the trauma-stained house but also the resentment the American expatriate harbors toward a foreign social space that, for its part, destroys rather than accommodates her. As opposed to the well-worn narrative of the American in Paris, a story that belongs to the buoyant, carefree world of the classical Hollywood musical, the story of the American in Japan, *The Grudge* suggests, is that of an afflicted cultural and racial outsider, the foreigner beset and finally ruined by local ghosts.

In contrast to the multiple-character narrative of *Ju-on*, the remake centers on a single protagonist—Karen, the investigative heroine and near–Final Girl played by Gellar. The prior film was never solely focalized through Rika; weblike, it explored various threads of acquaintance and encounter, however brief or attenuated, that bound characters to each other and to the place of the grudge. Though *The Grudge* lifts several set pieces and the answering machine motif from *Ju-on*, using the latter as a temporal anchor for the narration and the spectator, its use of the repeated phone message, like its plot structure, reveals important departures from the prior film. In *Ju-on*, the answering machine message that recurs in two distinct episodes is a nominal temporal yardstick, providing a barebones chronology to a narrative otherwise overwhelmed by achrony. In contrast, *The Grudge* dilutes the temporal immiscibilities thematized in *Ju-on*. First, the answering machine message as played back by the police in *The Grudge* provides a precise temporal index: "Thursday, 8:27 p.m.," the machine announces. This enables most narrative events to be unambiguously reconstructed in a chronological story line. Karen visits the old lady on Thursday and beholds the latter's horrible death on Thursday night. Later that same evening, Susan, the woman's daughter, dies in Kayako's clutches. In *The Grudge*, episodes are no longer named for various characters; they are organized instead along Karen's investigation. The house and the curse slowly reveal their secrets to her; she becomes the central agent for the audience's growing knowledge. The narrative structure is also far more expository, concerned with explicitly briefing the spectator on the intricacies of character motivations and the backstory presumed by the plot. For example, unlike *Ju-on*, where the death of Rika's predecessor was never shown, *The Grudge* depicts Yoko's demise on Wednesday, the day before Karen's visit. The nonsynchronous encounter between a cop and his grown-up daughter in the future is dispensed with in favor of fleshing out the circumstances that provoked Takeo's deadly jealousy in the past. No such details were ever given in *Ju-on*. In *The Grudge*, Karen has a nonsynchronous encounter with the American professor with whom Kayako was romantically obsessed. Kayako's unrequited infatuation, discovered by her jealous husband, led to the latter's murderous rampage. This meeting between a present-day Karen and the professor Kayako stalked three years earlier has the effect of reducing nonsynchronous temporality to a mere pretext for an expository flashback that spells out the killer's motives in the first series of murders. In *The Grudge*, the cause of narrative clarity is advanced, thereby reducing the spectator's labor of sense-making, since narrative temporality and causal chains are precisely clarified. But clarity, explicitness, and the viewer's ease of use are won at a price: *The Grudge* forgoes the temporally unwieldy idiom of its precursor.

Remake Time

As horror cycles wear on, ghosts grow ever more generic. This paradox is encapsulated in the Derridean understanding of the ghost, explored in the prior chapter, as "repetition *and* first time."[69] We are faced, on the one hand, with the force of singularity: the singularity of the jolt, of the first time one sees a ghost or screams at a terrifying turn in a movie. On the other hand, we encounter formulaic repetition: one sees the same ruse again and again. A scream gives way to a chuckle; the horror film fails to horrify, losing the affective charge for which the genre was named. The ghost becomes generic, the very figure of genre. Through singularity and repetition, the ghost figures both the force and depletion of return.

From a Todorovian perspective, the recurrence of set pieces in a horror remake and in the precursor text, as well as the very familiarity of the previously encountered narrative, presents certain challenges to the fantastic. If Bergson visualizes temporality, Todorov temporalizes the fantastic around the duration of affect, the "duration of uncertainty."[70] For Todorov, the fantastic borrows its temporality from the audience's unique experience of a first-time encounter with the text. The affective charge of the fantastic—the reader's hesitation in the face of a seemingly supernatural event—can only be provoked by a first encounter with the work. Thus the Todorovian fantastic, premised on the emphatically "irreversible" time of perception—the fantastic begs to be consumed from start to finish, respecting the temporal order in which the plot's events unfold—points up the contradictions of genre itself.[71] The possibly corrosive effects of repetition on the spectator's affective responses to fantastic narratives are heightened by a remake. Watching *Ju-on* and *The Grudge* one after the other, for example, makes repeated set pieces and staging conspicuous. Recognizable repetition means that the audience, to a certain degree, can see the scares coming; the spectator becomes better equipped to anticipate and perhaps defuse the shocks that lie ahead. Despite this degree of familiarity, however, audiences, as Horton notes, watch remakes to discover other novelties, the play of sameness and difference within an explicitly comparatist viewing scheme.

But even when the genre film is neither sequel nor remake, it still runs into problems vis-à-vis Todorov's insistence that the emotional and aesthetic potency of a fantastic narrative depends on a first-time reading. Fantastic narratives, even on an initial encounter, are already somewhat familiar to most audiences, inasmuch as they are rehearsals of generic conventions. The affective charge of the fantastic narrative—whether hesitation, fear, disquiet, or nostalgia—depends on the singularity of the supernatural anomaly, but this singularity is inevitably bound to its antithesis: generic repetition. Even if one has not encountered this particular ghost film before, one has encountered ghost narratives like it before.

The repetitive temporality of genre films has several implications, as Altman points out. Genre films look past the finitude of each screening (for example, a particular movie's denouement), operating instead on the "cumulative" effect of the repetition of motifs, images, and narratives across other similar films. The foregrounding of intertextual repetition, apart from resulting in the "predictability" of genre films, also makes for a different kind of audience pleasure for aficionados of the genre: however much the horror-film lover hopes to find newness, innovation, difference, and surprise, this desire for novelty and difference is always enfolded within the already-known. As Altman puts it, "the pleasure of genre film spectatorship thus derives more from reaffirmation than from novelty."[72] Yet at the same time, remakes, like sequels, frustrate "an audience's desire to re-experience in some way a memorable story," because such reworkings arise from "inevitably changed conditions which make it impossible to achieve a precise repetition."[73]

In addition to the temporal rhythms of perception and generic repetition, the remake attests to the cultural longevity of texts, their intertextual survival, calling into question the presumed closure of the original and bringing it to new audiences.[74] Hence, the specific contours of transnational generic exchange undermine the temporality conventionally attributed to sequels and remakes. These are usually differentiated from other forms of generic repetition via their temporality, which might be dubbed the time of afterward: the sequel or remake is thought to always follow from a precursor text. Yet this "post"-temporality, as with the premise of originality, proves upon closer view to be illusory. The time of afterward starts to come apart the closer one looks at things, since intertextuality is itself always temporally discrepant: in contrast to the linear temporality underpinning the assumption that the remake "comes after" and is thus obliged to be faithful to its antecedent, intertextuality is radically nonsynchronous, a juxtaposition of discourses from diverse eras. Mikhail Bakhtin writes that language is "heteroglot from top to bottom," embodying "the co-existence of socio-ideological contradictions between the present and the past, between differing epochs of the past."[75] So perhaps remakes and sequels are not only afterward but also a *refusal of the time of afterward*. What do we make of the spectator who comes to Nakata's "original" *Ringu* second, having first seen Gore Verbinski's remake, *The Ring*? In this case the remake becomes the ground for the reception of the precursor text, introducing instability into the very terms *original*, *copy*, *precursor*, *remake*, and *sequel*—in short, to questions of priority and cultural value in genre studies.

In addition to the abovementioned temporal rhythms of transnational remaking and exchange—the times of consumption, cyclical repetition, cultural survival, temporally discrepant intertextuality, and the remake's eschewal of a chronological afterward—I turn to a last temporal rhythm: the speed of global Hollywood's appropriation of profitable foreign films.

Speed: Intertextuality and Flexible Accumulation

Every genre film presents us with "a mosaic of quotations." As Julia Kristeva puts it, "any text is the absorption and transformation of another."[76] However original a horror film may appear, that seeming originality is always qualified by its debts to narrative formulas and conventions, by the way it intersects with other films, consciously or unconsciously. The remake intensifies the repetition and intertextuality, the cannibalism inherent in all genre films.

As this chapter demonstrates, intertextuality can also serve the ends of capital. In the case of Hollywood's Asian remake cycles, the ability to seize on, to trope (whether by allusion, imitation, or transformation) a prior commodity's most marketable signature, and to do it with enough speed to exploit the currency of always-presentist audience demands, must be understood as a form of flexible accumulation.

A cogent discussion of flexible accumulation, though not one that is spe-cific to film industries, is offered by Aihwa Ong. In contrast to a moderniza-tion model of capitalism, which anticipated an increase in mass-assembly production and the decline of third world cottage industries, flexible accu-mulation names the actual industrial patterns of late capitalism globally since 1970. It is characterized by Free Trade Zones, subcontracting firms, family labor (including women and children in informal economies and sweatshops) and by strategies (such as outsourcing to cheap overseas labor) that flexibly bypass high production costs, labor militancy, and en-vironmental concerns at home.[77]

In the usage of film scholars Yeh Yueh-Yu and Darrell William Davis, flexible accumulation refers to the ways in which both Hong Kong and Hollywood film industries operate on a "decentralized workshop model," in contrast to large, vertically integrated, slow-moving film factories. From their discussion it becomes clear that flexible accumulation is a tempo-ral category. It means above all the rapid appropriation and containment of a competitor's market innovations: "Flexible accumulation means that producers have one eye on the competition, ready at all times to borrow elements embraced by audiences."[78] The flexible accumulation typified by Hong Kong's workshop model accounts for the speed with which the in-dustry is able to respond to and appropriate the strengths of foreign com-petitors, thus accelerating each cycle's movement from novelty to exhaus-tion in generic exchange. Flexible accumulation means that "when a genre or fad proves popular in Hong Kong, it swiftly blazes out of control. This exemplifies a flexible system of production because it depends on a very quick turn around between the popular embrace of a Japanese television drama, for instance, and a Hong Kong reworking of its motifs. The chal-lenge in Hong Kong is to produce a recognizable knockoff or parody before the shelf life of the source has expired."[79]

This attempt to capitalize on the aficionado's knowledge and interest in transnational genre trends before their shelf life has expired is not unique to Hong Kong: as I have shown, flexible accumulation is at work on a greater scale in Hollywood's deracination of Hong Kong cinema's (once) signature action cinema.

Clearly, several processes are at work in Hollywood's deracination of Asian genre cinemas: on the one hand, a signature (a mark of innovation, of originality, of newness or novelty greeted by vigorous, profitable audience demand) is being transformed into a formula (no longer a mark of local, national, or cultural singularity but a sign of deracinated iterability). This deracinative process is evident in the terrifying speed of Hollywood's own capacity—whether by way of homage, by hiring émigré talent, through distributor pickups of foreign films, or by funding transnational productions—to neutralize national or regional cinemas that have acquired cult U.S. audiences and have proven able box-office adversaries abroad. This is intertextuality as flexible accumulation, in the service of capital and deracination. All of a sudden, Hollywood action blockbusters look just like Hong Kong martial arts flicks, and the distinctions between J-horror and Hollywood horror become less acute. This aspect of flexible accumulation, in another film-industrial context (Hong Kong media producers' ability to imitate profitable Japanese products), has been described by Yeh and Davis as the "softening of contrast."[80] The softening of contrast, the quickly accomplished reduction of the distance between generic innovation and generic repetition, is the very sign of intertextuality in the service of late capitalism, literalized by the operation of genre: commodity distinction made iterable, rapidly repackaged and redistributed for market gain before its popularity runs dry. With startling celerity, an infusion of freshness, a break in generic formulae, becomes a trend that runs high risks of exhaustion.

The Play of Globalism and Regionalism

The discourse of exceptionalism that underwrites most Hollywood studio rhetoric on the Asian horror remake cycle is caught between two moves, emphasizing the *cultural specificity* of the Asian horror film while imputing a *cultural neutrality* that guarantees its appeal to global audiences. Exceptionalist claims regarding the superiority of Asian horror films constitute one pole of journalistic commentary, a counterpart to the opposite claim that such films are nothing but poor Hollywood copies.[81] A Miramax executive explains the Asian remake fever in universalizing terms: "These stories can work in any culture."[82] Similarly, an American distributor of Asian horror films states that these films succeed because they boast strong, "cerebral" writing and because the "Asian mythologies" behind these monsters "are new to us and make the terror feel more rooted, less arbitrary." This rhetoric is at once exceptionalist, regionalist, and globalist: Asian horror, in this account, is exceptionally well-written, rooted in mythology, and different from all other generic fare. At the same time, it is exceptionally rootless, deracinated, globalist. "What does it tell us," one reviewer asks, "that Asians are turning out stories that can be transplanted, that embody a form of postpunk youth culture as meaningful to kids in London and L.A., as those in Tokyo and Seoul?"[83]

Naming is never neutral. The recently conspicuous, spectacularly lucrative "Asian horror film" is not only a film cycle but also a complex generative act of naming, a discursive formation, regionalist and globalist in character, that allows an array of movies to become coherent and marketable in particular ways. Why call the naming of the new Asian horror film regionalist and globalist? The regional rather than national appellation (Asian, rather than simply Korean, Japanese, Hong Kong, or Thai) establishes a horizon of reception for Asian horror across the board for Hollywood studios, producers, distributors, exhibitors, critics, and audiences. Regionalist framing encourages spectators and critics to downplay the differences between Hideo Nakata and the Pang brothers, directing us instead to make sense of them as part of the same phenomenon. In effect, to global (read Americanist) audiences, the coinage "Asian horror film" affords an abstracted measure of cultural distinction. The films are culturally distinguished as Asian; yet their cultural distinction has been blunted by both regionalism and generic familiarity, by all the ways in which these horror films are new yet readily recognizable. This rhetoric betrays a play with cultural and regional identity that, in the same breath, discounts cultural specificity, claiming a universal, culture-neutral appeal.

Regionalist-globalist discourse on Hong Kong genre films like *The Eye* does not stem from U.S. distributors alone. Regionalist rhetoric hawking a commercial Asian cinema to global audiences is articulated by Asian film producers themselves. Made under the mantle of Applause Pictures and Singapore's Raintree Pictures, *The Eye* is an instructive example in this regard. Applause Pictures is one of many Hong Kong companies—Media Asia, Emperor Movie Group (EMG), and Filmko Pictures among them—aiming to fashion a pan-Asian cinema palatable to global, Americanist tastes.[84] Peter Ho-Sun Chan, the Hong Kong director and producer who cofounded Applause Pictures in 1999, articulates the gist of this deracinated battle plan: "The people who are portrayed in the movies that strike

Americans as very Chinese, such as martial arts films, are not real people. . . . The truth is we are alike. America's way of life has become the world's way of life."[85]

In an interview, he enjoins Hong Kong to "take the lead in Asia to organize other industries . . . to produce an Asian cinema. The trend is towards non-local development." Chan envisions an "Asian Cinema" (as opposed to a "Hong Kong cinema") in which distinguishing between Japanese, Taiwanese, Korean, and Chinese cultural traits would become difficult, if not impossible.[86]

Peter Chan is among the mini-exodus of Hong Kong film personalities who worked in Hollywood in the 1990s.[87] Many of them have since returned to Hong Kong while maintaining a regionalist-globalist filmmaking purview. These filmmaker émigrés belong to globalization's new breed of "transnational design professionals," "cultural specialists and intermediaries working in the film, television, music, advertising, fashion, and consumer culture industries," who, though based in different "quarters" of various "world cities," exhibit a "degree of homogenization in [their] procedures, working practices, and organizational cultures." Jetting back and forth between Hong Kong, Los Angeles, and New York, these mediators of "intercultural communication"[88] can only work in the global film industry by speaking its lingua franca (English) and mastering and personifying the latter's transnational protocol, which they constantly exhort their local film industry to take up in the interests of staying competitive or becoming more efficient. One senses in these émigré filmmakers' 1990s interviews a kind of euphoria at being newly initiated into these ranks, as well as the stresses of having had to prove their mettle in a Hollywood that is far from leaving orientalist prejudices behind. Once vetted, they remain well aware of gatekeeping at the doors of global cultural regimes but decide this is well worth the cost. In return, they are granted access to better financial compensation, global audiences, positioning in the world's filmmaking capital, and the power to shape global culture as transnational media professionals.

Audiences and Transnational Generic Exchange

Toby Miller writes: "We live in an international age that by its very formulation decrees that we are also in a national one."[89] Miller et al. characterize "the paradigmatic nature of the national in an era of global companies" as "the requirement to reference the local in a form that is obliged to do something with cultural-economic meeting-grounds."[90] This paradox is internal to Hollywood's hailing of world audiences. The internationalization of the Asian horror film prompts the question: How does the genre film manage to craft "a version of the 'popular' capable of producing recognition for a range of audiences from different classes, localities, and national groupings?"[91] Put another way, how do audiences exert local ownership over cross-cultural texts? The role of transnational, heterogeneous audience formation here is vital. The globalist genre film, pitched at audiences all over the world, strives to unify the proliferation and differentiation of a genre's diverse users in search of a worldwide hit.

The Eye (2002) exemplifies the pan-Asian cinema model, harnessing talent from various countries in the region in order to hail regional audiences. The careers of the film's Thailand- and Hong Kong–based directors, Oxide and Danny Pang, are themselves indebted to the renaissance of the Thai film industry in 1997, which allowed the brothers to collaborate on Oxide's directorial debut feature, with Danny editing. Tony Rayns further credits the Pang brothers' Hong Kong–Thai background with their insights into genre innovation: "Anyone who has worked in the faltering Hong Kong and Thai film industries in the past decade must have learned to doubt the market potential of by-the-numbers genre film-making." Casting for *The Eye*, which drew actors from Hong Kong, Taiwan, Singapore, and Thailand, for a film set in both Hong Kong and Thailand, was calculated to allow "maximum reach" across regional audiences.[92]

Applause Pictures' *Three* (2002), an omnibus horror anthology by three directors, encapsulates the regionalist-globalist aspiration of the new Asian horror film perhaps even more forcefully than *The Eye*. In *Three*, each director's name functions as shorthand for a local cinematic renaissance. Alongside Hong Kong's Peter Chan, the other two directors are Thailand's Nonzee Nimibutr, whose box-office successes spearheaded the newfound vigor of the Thai film industry since the late 1990s,[93] and South Korea's Kim Jee-woon, whose film *A Tale of Two Sisters* performed vigorously in Korea, ousting *The Matrix Reloaded* from first place in the domestic box office in June 2003.[94]

All of this underscores the value of looking beyond what Yeh and Davis call "the blinkered perspective of cross-cultural criticism that deals with cultural flow solely on the East-West or Hong Kong–Hollywood axis."[95] Faced with the regionalist-globalist character of the new Asian horror film, film and media scholars are required to look closely at cultural traffic between other coordinates, the way in which call and response in transnational genre cinema of late answers as much to interregional sensibilities as to Hollywood's long shadow.

Films like *The Eye* and *Three* are couched to address a "pan-Asian film-going culture." Critics using this terminology usually refer to Hong Kong, Japan, and Korea, but it is clear that regional networks are also extending to Thailand, Malaysia, Singapore, Taiwan, the Philippines, and beyond. According to Yeh and Davis, "What this pattern reveals is the gradual tightening of Asian regional connections, the result of finer, improved feedback networks between entertainment and audiences, producers and their multiple publics."[96] The perceived collocation and synonymy of Asian horror films from various nations is precisely the effect cultivated by regionalist coproduction, distribution, marketing, and critical and popular audience reception.[97]

I have learned a great deal from Yeh's and Davis's analysis of "the ubiquity of Japanese media" in Hong Kong and from their discussion of Hong Kong pan-Asian production companies like Media Asia. Media Asia is cued to what they call, variously, "a regional, transpacific youth culture" and "inter-Asian transnational entertainment," a kind of pan-Asian popular culture that encompasses the production and circulation of film and television among nations, as well as the heightened cultural competencies of audiences grown familiar with such inter-Asian commodities. What is key in their discussion of pop cultural flows between Japan and Hong Kong, which I would extend to the pan-Asian character of the horror films under discussion, are their notions of "instantaneity" and "market proximity" in the consumption of film and television in Asia (in the past few years, for example, journalistic coverage shows that Koreans, Filipinos, Singaporeans, and Malaysians alike have all thrilled to the Japanese *Ringu* and *Ju-on* cycles). The term *market proximity* refers to a close familiarity between one national-popular audience and another nation's screen texts. Yeh and Davis suggest that in some cases, the market proximity of regional cultural products might be able to counterbalance Hollywood dominance in domestic Asian film and television markets.[98]

Hollywood remakes of Asian horror are premised on the relatively new market proximity of Asian cinemas as a whole. In 2004, *Variety* noted a "sea change" at that year's Cannes Film Festival. In a reversal of prior years, art films by "elite auteurs" were the exception, while the "popular cinemas of East Asia . . . attract[ed] the most attention on the world stage."[99] How did this come about? Clearly, many rivers fed this current: the cult love of Asian cinema by overseas audiences; the triumph of Asian auteurist cinema over the past two decades; the mainstream audiences drawn to deracinated, high-dollar Hollywood films made with émigré Asian talent; and the critical and popular success of foreign-language, subtitled global Hollywood productions (e.g., *Crouching Tiger, Hidden Dragon*). Like Hong Kong action cinema before it, the growing audience for Asian horror films in the United States emerges in part from the mainstreaming of subcultural cult fandom. The example of one New York–based Asian cult-fan-turned-festival-programmer is instructive: as cult film tastes in Asian horror dovetail with enormous profits, small cinephilic Asian film festivals run by avid fans, early adopters many years ahead of the Hollywood curve, become financially imperiled.[100] The mainstreaming of subcultural spectatorial sensibilities might also be seen as part of the complex dynamic between the various social actors involved in genre-making and unmaking. "Marginal reception" practices become widespread as new genre trends are first "poached"; once established, these are "raided" in turn.[101]

Within the last fifteen years, from the prominence of auteurist art cinema from China, Taiwan, Hong Kong, Japan, and Korea in the early 1990s to the mainstreaming of cult tastes in Asian genre films (primarily from Hong Kong and Japan) by the end of the decade, Asian cinema has been an increasingly familiar regional presence on the horizon for moviegoers in the United States. The legibility of Asian genre cinema to American audiences today makes the early difficulties encountered by Jackie Chan in his attempts to break into the U.S. market seem dated by contrast,[102] attesting once again to the speed with which the market proximity of Asian cinema in regionalist-globalist terms has been accomplished. In the United States, this market proximity is orchestrated by theatrical, broadcast, and video distribution, film festivals, the mainstreaming of Asian cult cinephilia, promotional discourse, and critical acclaim. In this light, transnational generic exchange must be understood not only in intertextual-aesthetic terms of influence, the debt of one genre film to all others, but also in terms of the regional and global legibility of genre cycles, in particular, the perceived interchangeability and synonymy of a genre film from one industry with that of another (Hong Kong and Korean horror films become collocated with J-horror). If genre films address an ideal spectator, an insider-aficionado whose familiarity is born of long spectatorship in the genre, then transnational generic exchange presupposes a transnational aficionado familiar not only with *Carrie* (1976) and *The Exorcist* (1973) but with *Ringu* and *Memento Mori* (1999) as well.

At the same time, I would hesitate to overstate such proximity. Whereas in Asia, various national-popular audiences might have firsthand familiarity with Asian sources for Hollywood horror remakes, certain American viewers may not always know that these films are remakes in the first place, since promotional materials for films like DreamWorks' version of *The Ring* are characteristically silent on this score. Even where some American spectators may know that they are watching a remake, they may not have seen the Asian "original" prior to the Hollywood version, in which case the question of firstness in remakes and sequels requires greater nuance, as I have argued above.

From National Cinemas to Asian Markets

In retrospect, the brief, feverish transnational circulation of a generic practice characterized in simultaneously globalist and regionalist terms (Hollywood remaking the "Asian horror film") challenges film scholars to rethink prevailing paradigms for national cinema and its imbrication with genre scholarship in the discipline of film and media studies. Given that popular film cycles from Hong Kong, Japan, and South Korea are increasingly framed via discursive slippage as "Asian horror films," how do globalist-regionalist remaking and generic exchange force a reconsideration of the truisms of genre studies and national cinema?

The global, cross-cultural dimensions of the film industry pressure conventional notions of national cinema. Writing in 1989, Andrew Higson already understood the problems posed by Hollywood to the issue of national cinema. To begin with, any essentialist understanding of national cinema that seeks to define it in terms of an absolute difference from Hollywood films is bound to fail, not least because, as Klein points out, "the globalization of production means much more than just shooting studio films in Asia. . . . Hollywood today is going into the business of producing and distributing 'foreign' movies" through special overseas divisions and corporate partnerships.[103] Hollywood has also profoundly infused what counts as national-popular throughout the world, beating domestically produced films in their own backyard. To take seriously the question of what national-popular film audiences are actually watching, the paradigm of national cinema must acknowledge the existence of the Hollywood other within. Thus a model of national cinema that seeks to work contrastively, via a rhetoric of singularity or exceptionalism, runs aground vis-à-vis the suffusive reach of Hollywood. Higson writes that the attempt to define a national cinema in terms of national differences in cultural production

> becomes increasingly problematic as cinema develops in an economy charac-
> terised by the international ownership and circulation of images and sounds. It
> is therefore necessary to examine the overdetermination of Hollywood in the
> international arena. By Hollywood, I mean *the international institutionalization
> of certain standards and values of cinema, in terms of both audience expectations,
> professional ideologies and practices and the establishment of infrastructures of
> production, distribution, exhibition, and marketing, to accommodate, regulate, and
> reproduce these standards and values.* . . .
>
> Hollywood never functions as simply one term within a system of equally
> weighted differences. Hollywood is not only the most internationally powerful
> cinema — it has also, of course, for many years been an integral and naturalised
> part of the national culture, or the popular imagination, of most countries in
> which cinema is an established entertainment form. In other words, Holly-
> wood has become one of those cultural traditions which feed into the so-called
> national cinemas of, for instance, the western European nations.[104]

Higson's definition of Hollywood as the internationalization and institutionalization of filmic standards and values — affecting audiences, film
professionals, production, distribution, exhibition, and marketing strategies — has great analytical force. Nonetheless, his discussion of the traffic
between Hollywood and national cinemas remains regrettably one-sided.
His argument emphasizes Hollywood's contributions to national cinema,
especially national-popular cinema, but he fails to mention the converse:
Hollywood's debts to other national cinemas, its founding reliance on émigré talent, its appropriation of aesthetic hallmarks, its practices of borrowing and remaking, and its eye on foreign markets.

How, then, does global Hollywood—defined not only as a geographically situated film industry, but as the *internationalization* of filmic standards, values, professional ideologies, industrial practices, marketing strategies, labor markets, and audience expectations—require a more nuanced conceptualization of national cinema? First, as Higson points out, national cinema cannot be defined via absolute difference from Hollywood; second, the economic reality is such that, to survive, national cinemas must play in the key of this juggernaut's standards:

> Part of the problem, of course, is the paradox that for a cinema to be nationally popular it must also be international in scope. That is to say, it must achieve the international (Hollywood) standard. For, by and large, it is the films of the major American distributors which achieve national box-office success, so that filmmakers who aspire to this same level of box-office popularity must attempt to reproduce the standards, which in practice means colluding with Hollywood's systems of funding, production control, distribution and marketing. Any alternative means of achieving national popular success must, if it is to be economically viable, be conceived on an international scale.[105]

The regionalist-globalist thrust of the new Asian horror film and its uptake in Hollywood underscores Higson's argument that to be national-popular is to be international. Framing the question of transnational generic exchange between "Asian horror" and Hollywood remakes in light of such vexed issues regarding national cinema brings several issues into view: first, as I have argued, the limits of a naive insistence on the exceptionalism of the "Asian horror film" that claims hard-and-fast distinctions from Hollywood analogues. Second, against Higson's image of Hollywood radiating a one-way stream of influences to the rest of the world, it is clear that Hollywood, too, pillages from its rivals, a conspicuous instance of national-regional counterflows, in which the center imitates its cinematic elsewheres, lest we forget that film is truly global. Finally, there is the complicated question of what is really being mimicked here: not just genre, but globalized film culture writ large, the internationalization of film standards, and the imbrication of this internationalization/standardization with the national-popular.

Here Higson's observations appear to be borne out, since the new Asian horror films prove to be nationally popular (achieving strong domestic box office able to equal or better Hollywood competitors), while also meeting the "international standard," yielding the familiar, globally recognized pleasures of the "well-made film" (engaging narrative conceits, visual élan, effective set pieces). Speaking the internationally legible language of the generic standard with culturally specific flair, such films do well, first nationally, then regionally, then, at the farthest remove, globally, especially in the mouths of their new Hollywood versions.

But the so-called Asianization of Hollywood requires critics to look further than the national cinema–Hollywood nexus to assess the impact of regionalist-globalist rhetoric on national cinema markets in an internationalized frame. Studies on the "Asianization of Hollywood" and the corollary "Hollywoodization of Asia" point to the globalization of film production and distribution, cultural labor, and film markets. Christine Klein puts it this way: "Hollywood is becoming an export industry, making movies primarily for people who live outside the U.S." At present, overseas earnings account for more than half of a Hollywood film's revenue. Over the last two decades, Asian film markets in particular have taken center stage: "Today, Hollywood movies take about 96% of the box office receipts in Taiwan, about 78% in Thailand, and about 65% in Japan, which has become Hollywood's single most profitable export market." The Asian film market has been described as "Hollywood's fastest growing regional market," with Hollywood keen to fully tap the vast audiences of China and India. As noted earlier, Klein points out that the remake phenomenon must be seen in the context of the globalization of labor, since Hollywood studios are purchasing "the labor of South Korean screenwriters, which is much cheaper than that of American writers." I disagree, however, with Klein's assessment that "far from weakening the South Korean industry by extracting talent from it, the studios are strengthening it by providing it with a new source of revenue."[106] This is true only in the short run; over the long haul, Hollywood appropriations of Asian filmmaking (whether in terms of talent, film markets, or the distribution or cofinancing of "local" productions) are poised to extract revenue from their internationalizing of Asian cinemas.

The recent box-office triumphs of J-horror (such as the overwhelmingly cheap and successful *Ring* and *Ju-on* movies) are a concrete example of how small Asian B films can outperform, in domestic and regional markets, high-dollar Hollywood products that are exponentially better financed and more aggressively marketed by comparison. At least prior to their ingestion by Los Angeles studios, Asia's recent spate of audience-grabbing, low-rent, not-by-Hollywood horror films did seem to confirm the observation that "the absolute significance of story over cost for audiences goes against classical economics' standard assumptions about the role of price in balancing supply and demand."[107]

The other half of the story is darker, though. Remakes of Asian commercial films allow Hollywood to more effectively penetrate foreign markets with borrowed force, outdoing the originals in their own home markets and beyond. Nakata's *Ringu* cost US$1.2 million in production and reaped US$6.6 million in Japan. The Verbinski remake *The Ring* cost US$40 million and brought in US$8.3 million in Japan in its opening weeks alone. Globally the Japanese *Ringu* reaped US$20 million, its sequel earning twice that amount; Hollywood's remake, meanwhile, is reported to have grossed US$230 million worldwide.[108]

This disturbing pattern is not confined to J-horror. In 2004, *Variety* reported that the Korean horror film's domestic success story closed on a less sure-footed note that summer, when Hollywood films dominated the protectionist Korean film market more powerfully than at any time in the prior twenty-two months. While Hollywood studios were gearing up for global profits on remakes of successful Korean films, Korea was hard pressed to produce new hits of its own. This downturn was attributed to Hollywood competition and generic exhaustion.[109] This sobering reversal recalls Hollywood's appropriation of the Hong Kong action film from the late 1990s onward, which coincided with Hong Kong cinema's losing ground in local and overseas Asian markets, its historical bailiwicks.[110]

The Hollywood appropriation of pan-Asian signatures in the horror genre is particularly unsettling considering that not too long ago it was precisely this kind of regional intertextual borrowing that scholars hailed as a form of resistance to Hollywood, "a potential breakwater for the powerful onslaught of Hollywood," enabling national cinemas to "catch their breath in the fight to win back audiences."[111]

As one correspondent dryly points out, remakes are not necessarily a triumph for the Asian national cinemas from which they are sourced: the recent slew of Hollywood remakes are "unlikely to stimulate much interest in Korea or Korean cinema. . . . It's probably more meaningful to have a Korean film gross $1M in the US than to have a remake gross $100M."[112] Noting Hollywood's enormous appetite for "remake rights, distribution deals, and talent relationships" in the wake of successful South Korean films, one observer puns, "Hollywood is searching for its creative Seoul." The fact that South Korea has emerged as a major Asian film market, second only to Japan, has resulted in mixed, highly charged responses on the part of both South Korean and Hollywood players. In 2006, the South Korean government pledged more than US$500 million to the goal of "doubling" Korea's share of the international film market by 2011. Key Korean entrepreneurs are poised to respond as well. In 1998, Samsung's Miky Lee, an early investor in DreamWorks SKG, opened the first state-of-the-art multiplexes in South Korean cities (via her company, CJ Entertainment). CJ Entertainment has also announced ambitious plans to cultivate a broad U.S.-based market for South Korean films, beginning with plans for a multiplex in Los Angeles' Koreatown. Meanwhile, Hollywood is eyeing not only remake rights to Korean movie hits but, more important, further penetration of Hollywood product into the carefully protected South Korean film industry. According to the *Los Angeles Times*, in 2006 the Korean government yielded to pressure from both the United States and local filmmakers and cut South Korean screen quotas by half, allowing increased entry of Hollywood product. As Korean films try to make headway in the U.S. market and Hollywood presses for trade liberalization so as to control more screens across South Korea, the ways in which these high-stakes transnational gambles will play themselves out remain to be seen.[113]

The Asianization of Hollywood has been touted as an end to Eurocentrism or as financially advantageous to domestic Asian film industries, but in the long run the converse is true.[114] Culture, whether operating as difference or resonance, "is simultaneously the key to international textual trade and one of its limiting factors,"[115] at once enabling and constraining the transnational and cross-cultural lives of commodities. Hollywood's remakes of Asian horror films might be seen as one attempt to forge a cultural key to open the door to Asian markets.

If remakes as a whole are a "precise institutional structure of repetition," then Hollywood remakes of "Asian horror," in particular, are refamiliarizing forms of cultural translation, merging the temporal rhythms of generic repetition to the velocity of flexible accumulation, as well as deracinating, among other things, culturally specific reservoirs of the fantastic and innovations originating in rival national cinemas. In its bid to dominate promising and increasingly important Asian markets, Hollywood swiftly embraces homogenizing cultural translation in generic guise.

More Times Than One: *A Tale of Two Sisters*

The fantastic poses the question of a temporal translation that is obliged to contend with the productive constraints of generic conventions. Throughout this book, I have argued that the fantastic film is a genre in which forked worlds — split by secularism and supernaturalism and by disjointed, immiscible times — are made visible in the mise-en-scène. Kim Jee-woon's achingly beautiful horror film, *A Tale of Two Sisters*, reveals the potency of a cinema of specters that pushes against the limits of genre, of genre as a limiting situation that is not repressive but productive of temporal critique.

In interviews, both the film director and the art director forthrightly address the question of a formal newness that must negotiate generic familiarity. Kim Jee-woon relates:

> The film is giving a new feeling. It's showing new things that haven't been shown in Korean horror films. Style, mise-en-scène, emotion. I wanted to show real people in a horror movie. I wanted to show the real fear and sadness of people. I wanted the audience to feel this. That was my starting point. I never thought of making a movie outside the genre. I change things within the genre. I tried to overcome certain restraints. I tried to give pleasure to people through the use of genre conventions, rules, and tools to present an interesting movie. That was the idea.[116]

That newness, mediated by the well-worn conventions of the ghost film, produces a psychological depth whose narrative rationalizations never quite erase the lessons of a traumatized heroine who must learn to live with ghosts. More than a mere figure for guilt and traumatic memory, the ghost also insists on the concrete irreducibility of the vivid dead. The collaboration between Kim Jee-woon and the film's art director, Jo Geun-hyeon, results in a meticulous production design governed by three principles: horror, sadness, and beauty.[117] The elegant formal unity of mise-en-scène, sound, and narration in *A Tale of Two Sisters* results in the film's visual and aural beauty and its ability to elicit both terror and melancholy in the audience, a complex affective response that mirrors the dualisms of the film's overall mood: both pretty and grim, both deeply sad and surprisingly scary. A string and piano leitmotif composed by Lee Byeong-woo infuses the thrilling set pieces of horror and the perceptual ambiguity of the fantastic with melancholy. In the context of the film's spare sound design, the recurrence of Lee's leitmotif, "A Tale of Two Sisters," becomes quite pronounced. The leitmotif unifies conflicting versions of the central traumatic event: different retellings of Su-yeon and the wardrobe and of characters arriving at the house on the fateful day of Su-yeon's death. The repetition-in-variance of the leitmotif becomes an auditory analogue for traumatic repetition, which is likened to the painful beauty of a haunting melody.[118] In a genre piece that tries to overcome, from within, certain conventional restraints, a multiplicity of temporalities — the speed of transnational re-making, as well as temporalities of extradiegetic spectatorship and diegetic spectrality — brings home the ways in which even a single film cannot be said to adhere to only one time.

In *A Tale of Two Sisters*, a young girl, Su-mi, comes home after having been institutionalized for mental illness. On her return, she notices that the pendulum clock on her bedroom wall has stopped. Viewers familiar with the plot's many secrets may come to read this detail, which happens early in the film, as a literalization of traumatic memory's unbidden return. A young girl, Su-mi's sister, once died in the house, a loss so deep that, to the devastated Su-mi, it seems to have stopped all the world's clocks. But when she reinitiates the pendulum's movement, the clock, in this ghost film, no longer tells a homogeneous time. Hours and minutes purportedly tick away, but the house proves to be inhabited by times immiscible to chronometry.

A Tale of Two Sisters, the story of a haunted girl in a house full of memories, is itself a retelling of a Korean folktale of the same name, "Janghwa, Hongryeon" (Rose Flower, Red Lotus). The folktale, like the film, centers on a family in which a recently widowed father remarries. His two daughters become locked in a deadly rivalry with their new stepmother. The corrosive antagonism between the sisters and the father's new lover is an echo of the romantic rivalry between the father's two wives, living and dead, and the sisters are tragically caught in the crossfire of this conflict.[119] The film departs from the folktale, however, in one crucial way: the accidental death of the younger sister, Su-yeon, is no longer the result of the stepmother's wickedness. The film points instead to the shared culpability of the father, the stepmother, and the elder sister, Su-mi, whose common, fatal error is not one of active abuse but of inaction. While Su-yeon suffocates under a fallen wardrobe upstairs in her bedroom, parallel editing juxtaposes three lateral tracking shots of the other family members, who all fail to grasp the meaning of the ominous offscreen thud and who all consequently fail to save her. In underscoring shared culpability and fatal inaction over malicious intent, the film implicitly advances a critique of the wicked stepmother motif, what Marina Warner calls the "women against women" structure of the old wives' tale.[120]

Edward Branigan has explained that narration is "intermittent," since story information is only gradually conveyed to spectators, exploiting "disparities of knowledge" by carefully withholding and revealing aspects of a narrative's causal chain.[121] *A Tale of Two Sisters* employs exceedingly frugal narration, heightening ambiguity by exploiting the discrepancy between story and plot. For most of the film, the plot misdirects viewers into believing that both sisters are alive in the house while their stepmother mercilessly torments them. This narrational misdirection, which increases the spectator's perceptual labor in terms of decrypting the narrative puzzle, is accomplished in several ways.

First, the death of Su-yeon, which is chronologically earliest in story time, is shown last in the plot. Su-yeon, whose quiet, buoyant presence lends the film much of its charm, is revealed to have been already dead when the film opens, so that most of the scenes we watch are actually delusions on the part of the guilt-ridden sister who survives her. Second, much of what is depicted in the plot consists of delusions on the part of Su-mi, who has been driven mad by her failure to save her sister. Most of the film is focalized through Su-mi, who inhabits a complex delusion in which the girls' mother is dead (diegetically true) while her sister, Su-yeon, is alive (diegetically untrue). In retrospect, the spectator gathers, the only scenes that carry straightforward, clearly expository value (instead of being ambiguous or colored by Su-mi's delusions) are those at the very beginning and end of the plot: the opening scene in which a psychiatrist asks an institutionalized Su-mi to recall the events of "that day," the day on which both her mother and her sister perished; and the final scene, in which Su-mi, along with other characters, particularly the nurse-stepmother and the father, are shown to be partly culpable for the accidental death of Su-yeon.

The circumstances of Su-yeon's death, linked to that of her mother, are the final secrets of a film built on "layers of secrets."[122] These "secrets" are crucial bits of story information withheld from spectators for most of the film. The most important of these secrets are that Su-yeon, for much of the film, is already dead (she is only really "there" at the very end of the film, on the day of her death as belatedly related by the plot); and second, that Su-yeon's death could have been averted but for the inaction of those around her. A fateful, tragic confluence of events leads up to Su-yeon's death-by-negligence. On the day that her father brings home his wife's nurse to live with his children and their sick mother, the sisters Su-mi and Su-yeon respond acridly toward the nurse, believing her to be their father's mistress. Later that same day, the mother hangs herself in the green wardrobe in Su-yeon's room (in protest or despair at the father's infidelity, viewers infer). On discovering and attempting to untie her mother's corpse from the wardrobe, Su-yeon inadvertently causes the cabinet to tip over. As a result, she dies of suffocation. The deaths of both Su-yeon and her mother thus take place in or under the green wardrobe, which becomes the single most important prop motif in the film, as signaled earlier in the film by enigmatic references to the wardrobe in conversations between Su-mi, her father, and her sister. In addition to this prop motif, color motifs also provide clues that allow spectators (in hindsight, and through repeated screenings) to piece together story events from a deliberately disorienting plot. In a predominantly jewel-toned film, emerald green always adverts to Su-yeon and her terrible end under the wardrobe on the day of her mother's suicide. Green is the color of Su-yeon's bedroom, of the wardrobe, of a dress Su-yeon is wearing in a framed photograph that falls and cracks when her mother dies. The same dress is worn by a spectral girl who sits in the deep space of the dining room and lurks under the kitchen sink in some of the film's most terrifying set pieces. In turn, red recalls Su-mi's guilt at her sister's death, her unshakable sense of culpability. On the day that Su-yeon dies, the only day depicted in the plot in which she is alive and actually present in the house, her sister, Su-mi, is wearing a mustard-yellow coat. Thereafter, and for much of the film, Su-mi wears a red cardigan, a visual cue that marks certain scenes as delusions, cueing attentive viewers to the fact that such events are taking place after Su-yeon's death. Red flowers frame Su-yeon's face in an early scene, depicting the first day that Su-mi and Su-yeon return to the house after a long absence; a red wardrobe dominates the frame in Su-mi's bedroom; and Su-mi wears the red cardigan in two shots by the wharf that bookend the film and for a good deal of the narrative action. In Su-mi's delusion, the nurse-stepmother appears as a polished, beautiful, cruel witch with a deep red mouth, often dressed in shimmering scarlet, as in the party scene in which the crazed stepmother, in hindsight, plays the part of Su-mi's delusional double.

The intermittent character of the film's narration, heightened by parsimonious, eleventh-hour disclosures of story information, involves what Branigan calls a process of "revising and forgetting" on the part of spectators.[123] In making sense of the gradually unfolding narrative, viewers constantly adjust their interpretations, weighing story probabilities and plausible interpretations, reworking and discarding different understandings of how story events are connected and how the narrative will finally end. By demanding a high degree of perceptual labor on the part of spectators, *A Tale of Two Sisters* calls attention to this perceptual process of revising and forgetting. The film seems, at the beginning, to be a haunted house film, but the growing cruelty of the stepmother leads one to suspect a nonsupernatural story of child abuse. Further ambiguities encourage hesitation as to whether Su-mi, the stepmother, or both, are mentally unstable, but the final, highly expository scene unveils a truth more horrible than occult malice. On the day the father brought home his new mistress, Su-yeon accidentally suffocated to death while Su-mi and her stepmother-to-be traded barbs in a catfight rather than acting decisively to save her. Such an ending profoundly changes the viewer's understanding of the narrative to this point, forcing a revision of all interpretations of the film thus far. All along, there have only been two people in the house, Su-mi and her father. Scenes in which the stepmother viciously abuses Su-yeon never actually happened but are instead sequences in which Su-mi has projected her self-reproach at her sister's death onto an imaginary stepmother. On rescreening, the tone of the film becomes strongly ironic. Su-mi has for the most part been alone in the house, feverishly haunted by a morbid self-reproach. Confrontations with her evil stepmother are, in retrospect, really encounters with her own hated self.[124]

If spectatorship is an act of ceaseless revision, then it follows that a first screening of any given film cannot be replicated, confirming Todorov's argument that the temporality of perception is unique and irreversible: we cannot really ever watch the same film twice. Yet in *A Tale of Two Sisters*, the irretrievable experience of a first-time encounter with this "puzzle film" is replaced by the new pleasures of repetitive viewing, a repeated rescreening that the film's meticulous crafting—in an age in which fans often revisit films multiple times on DVD—both expects and invites.[125]

The multiple temporalities—diegetic and extradiegetic—of this ghost film resonate with the Bergsonian understanding of existence as characterized by both permanence and change, a world that both moves and remains. That exact repetition is impossible when all aspects of the spectatorial situation have duratively altered—the same spectator is no longer really the same spectator; the same film is no longer really the same film—belongs to one side of this Bergsonian paradox, to time as ceaseless succession and movement. On the other hand, the complementary Bergsonian thematics of permanence, of the undeniable survival of a past that remains, biting into the future, presiding over the present, and prompting one to see through the illusion of a pure calendrical contemporaneity, also constitute explicit concerns of the diegesis.

In a scene that prefigures the film's complex denouement, the weird stepmother provides a terrifying answer to her own question, spoken to a trembling stepdaughter: what is really scary is the inability to forget. Haunted by memory, Su-mi feels keenly her responsibility toward her spectral sister, who seems at once still-alive and already-dead. When her impatient father forces Su-mi to acknowledge that Su-yeon is gone, their tense exchange is framed as a three-shot (fig. 49). On learning that she is already dead, Su-yeon, the young ghost, screams. With wrenching pathos, the film solicits compassion for a child who had forgotten she was dead.

In *A Tale of Two Sisters*, setting is so vital that one reviewer considers the house to be practically another character.[126] Staging in deep space and conspicuous color motifs of emerald and scarlet suffuse the house with the conflicted temporalities embraced by the narration: not only past and present, but never-was and might-have-been. Though the story unfolds in the present, Jo Geun-hyeon's set design consciously strove to replicate the style of a late nineteenth-century Korean mansion, when, according to Jo, accoutrements of Western "stand-up living culture" were first introduced to Korea. The costuming of the two sisters, strongly coordinated to setting, is likewise period-influenced, as in the delicate cotton lacework of their Victorian nightdresses.

A key aspect of the mise-en-scène is the floral motif that envelops the house, a design element that is given special prominence in the film's title sequence. The art director's stated intent was to use pervasive floral designs in the costume and setting in order to literalize both the Korean title of the film and the names of the two eponymous sisters, Rose and Lotus. The sisters' rooms are accordingly emblazoned with flowers, but the rest

49. In this three-shot from *A Tale of Two Sisters* (dir. Kim Jee-woon, 2003), the ghost (center) is horrified to learn that she is dead.

of the house is also covered in somewhat more abstract or subdued floral and botanical designs.[127] This means that the house, immersed in visual motifs that advert to the two girls, living and dead, externalizes in physical space the interior life of the two heroines, a fully temporalized space inhabited by ghosts and those who survive them. The house is a heterogeneous place in which past and present coexist and in which being is a question of memory.

In *The Fantastic*, Todorov identifies the literary devices that achieve fantastic ambiguity:

> Ambiguity also results from the use of two stylistic devices which suffuse the entire text: imperfect tense and modalization. . . . The latter consists, let us note, in using certain introductory locutions which, without changing the meaning of the sentence, modify the relation between the speaker and his utterance. For example, the two sentences "It is raining outside" and "Perhaps it is raining outside" refer to the same fact; but the second also indicates the speaker's uncertainty as to the truth of the sentence he utters. The imperfect has a similar effect. If I say "I used to love Aurelia," I do not specify whether I still love her now; the continuity is *possible*, but as a general rule *unlikely*.[128]

Todorov's discussion of literary devices for producing ambiguity in fantastic texts prompts the following question for those who work on fantastic film: what are the means for achieving such heightened effects of uncertainty or equivocation in cinematic narration? In *A Tale of Two Sisters*, the richly suggestive use of the two-shot, the film's most prominent means of enframing the dual protagonists, together with a temporally disorienting narration, are cinematic analogues for the literary-linguistic devices (modalization and the imperfect tense) that Todorov identified as formal means of effecting ambiguity in fantastic literature. During a spectator's first viewing of *A Tale of Two Sisters*, two-shots establish the deep bonds between the sisters, their constant togetherness and their solidarity in the face of a vicious adversary. But on learning the secrets of the narrative, one looks at these two-shots in light of the realization that Su-yeon is not actually there. The two-shot not only visualizes Su-mi's delusional disavowal but also quite painfully conveys her actual solitude. Though predominantly depicted with Su-yeon, Su-mi is in actuality alone. This is the secret of the graphically matched shots that bookend the film: in a repeated composition, Su-mi sits at the wharf with her sister; the film ends with a variant of this same shot, in which Su-yeon is no longer there (figs. 50 and 51). Though enframed in solitude, the sheer force of memory guarantees that Su-mi is not by herself, just as the present is never self-grounding. The seeming solitude of the present is disjoined by the survival of the past, by the vivid, unbidden memories of others. Su-mi is alone with a spectral other, alone in the company of ghosts.

Cinematic ambiguity is also accomplished via temporal confusion: because the chronological positions of flashbacks are not clearly demarcated, spectators are unsure of the temporal register of depicted events. This results in a dilation of the duration of spectatorial hesitation as to narrated events that persists almost to the film's end. The film opens in medias res, with Su-mi in a sanitarium. Such an opening calls into question the veridical status of flashbacks that follow the doctor's question, "Can you tell me about that day?" The use of the two-shot and temporal confusion, alongside color, prop, and costume motifs, and an emphatic gap between story and plot, are all cinematic means of accomplishing fantastic ambiguity in this film.

Kim Jee-woon's *A Tale of Two Sisters* remakes a folktale that has been adapted to film several times before; this tissue of adaptations is itself overlaid by another Hollywood remake. The multifarious times embraced within the diegesis, and without, are often at odds with one another. As I have tried to show, the spectral times of the narration also require another,

50, 51. In *A Tale of Two Sisters*, a two-shot of the sisters on the wharf from early in the film is graphically rhymed in the film's last shot, which reveals the final secret: Su-mi has always been alone.

answering temporality, that of repetitive spectatorship. Film reviewers have commented that *A Tale of Two Sisters* demands and rewards a second screening, as the film slowly unfurls its secrets, yielding narrative clues and formal motifs whose significances are only apprehended on repeated viewing. In the DreamWorks remake, *A Tale of Two Sisters* is sifted through another repeated rescreening, one in which the director reportedly declined involvement.[129] As this film's slowly paced, deliberate narration becomes entangled with the speed of deracinative transnational generic exchange, the Hollywood iteration attempts to interpellate a global audience through the cinematic equivalent of a common, homogenizing denominator.[130] But studio executives are not the only audiences, nor can they ever truly anticipate each spectator's mercurial pleasures with profit-driven fantasies of foolproof generic formulas. The pragmatics of spectatorship, whether obeisant or resistant, are themselves caught up in Bergsonism's unforeseeable becoming.

Writing within Time's Compass

From Epistemologies to Ontologies

The modes of temporal critique pursued in this study have uncovered several analytical problems in relation to cinema and the fantastic. The first chapter considered the time of cinema as apparatus, as well as the historical moment when Bergsonism's mental cinema—film as an analogue for habitual mechanisms of thought—becomes possible. The second chapter explored the noncontemporaneous times of reception, remediation, and reinscription of the *aswang* as event: eventfulness here names the continuing effectuality of the extraordinarily durative aswang. The so-called aswang complex is not so much a set of beliefs as an eventful congeries of rival translations that are experienced, refuted, and remade by various publics, spoken by competing interests across histories of circulation and articulation. The affective temporality of the ghost film's generic worlds was the focus of the third chapter. The affective charge of nostalgic allegory is wedded, in *Haplos* and *Rouge*, to a mise-en-scène that concretely envisions the spectrality of these films' fantastic worlds: in the forest ruin or in urban built space, spatiotemporal palimpsests reveal the fraying of homogeneous space and time. Both ghost films and the media-convergent aswang event accomplish a splitting of national time, an occulting of the national meanwhile that binds the imagined community of the nation in the fantasy of a shared calendrical present. Despite attempts to nationalize the aswang or to manage the contradictions of national time by recourse to a sexual politics of nostalgia, ghosts and viscera-suckers exceed the fiction of calendrical coincidence that underwrites the presumed cultural homogeneity of the nation.

Haplos and *Rouge* both belong to the celebrated New Cinema movements of film industries often analyzed under the rubric of "national cinema." Yet in both cases, the ghost film proves to be contrarian to cultural, historical, and national homogenization, partly unraveling the culture-binding function of auteurist film movements by foregrounding spatiotemporal discrepancy. As the occult splitting of national time in ghost and aswang films demonstrates, a consideration of the fantastic attentive to temporal translation puts a certain pressure on national cinema as a category of analysis. This is because, first, the fantastic tends to undo the nation-binding presumption of a shared, homogeneous, modern time and because, second, to track generic exchange in an age of media convergence and globalized popular cultures is to recognize that genres are borrowed and reworked in ways that cross national borders and muddle the presumed purity of national cultural traditions. Accordingly, the fourth chapter considered the ways in which the analytic of national cinema, while indisputably salient, must be reformulated in relation to the temporalities of transnational generic appropriation and exchange, the speed of global Hollywood's deracinating forms of cultural translation.

Bergson, for whom the question of freedom is bound to time, readily acknowledges that he writes from within the grip not merely of language but of the practical requirements of everyday life, ruled by time-discipline and routine. He recounts the manner in which his usual workday begins. "In the morning, when the hour strikes at which I am accustomed to rise," Bergson finds himself impelled by "the idea of rising and attending to my usual occupations." The critique of automatism, which permeates so much of Bergson's writing, makes its appearance here: "In this instance I am a conscious automaton, and I am so because I have everything to gain by being so."[1] For Bergson, our compliant acquiescence toward homogeneous, spatialized time is a social survival mechanism. Homogeneous time alienates us from ourselves but, ironically, "answer[s] better the requirements of social life,"[2] the necessity of syncing up, at some cost to ourselves, with the external time of social convention.

The illusion of spatialized, homogeneous time is not, for Bergson, a simple mistake but rather, as Deleuze puts it, "an illusion that belongs to the true," that is, to the necessary: a *necessary illusion*.[3] (Here Deleuze's exegesis of Bergson recalls certain gestures crucial to postcolonial critique: Chakrabarty's "inadequate but indispensable" and Spivak's "critique of something we cannot do without." The shared critical element for all these thinkers is a rigorous consideration, rather than a mere repudiation, of practical and theoretical necessities.)[4] Homogeneous time as a necessary illusion is, then, no mere error, rooted as it is in the abstractions of our speech, the operative utility of our science, the pragmatism of socially objectivated time, and the usefulness of regarding the future as calculable and the past as long dead. Bergsonism thus suggests that homogeneous time—as a necessary, but no less pernicious, illusion—can be exposed but never entirely dissipated.

In *Time and Free Will*, Bergson registers a moment in which his refutation of clock time is itself interrupted by the tolling of a clock: "Whilst I am writing these lines, the hour strikes on a neighbouring clock, but my inattentive ear does not perceive it until several strokes have made themselves heard."[5] I am arrested by this moment in his writing, when Bergson's attempt to contest homogeneous time is disrupted by the very clock time he endeavors to unseat. It is an admission that all critical writing or thinking about homogeneous time takes place, nevertheless, within its grip. Scholarly critiques of time-discipline or modern time consciousness are written from within its realm, within hearing distance, in Bergson's case, of the range of the clock tower's sounding of the hours. Similarly, any scholar writing on time-discipline or modern time consciousness writes within its temporal frame—the workday or workweek, the academic calendar, the publication deadline—straining against, but never completely outside, its temporal regime, attempting to find a mode of temporal critique from within the range of the tolling of the clock, the compass of modern time. Critics of habituated time consciousness know that homogeneous time "answers the requirements of social life," yet they still seek to strip off its invisibility, to parry its dominance.

Unfashionable though they may be, ontological claims underpin not only Bergson's philosophy of temporalized freedom but also the trenchant postcolonial and historical critiques of homogeneous time and temporal containment from which this study has drawn. Fabian, for example, in his justly celebrated critique of allochronism in anthropology, writes that "intersubjectivity . . . is inconceivable without assuming that the participants involved are coeval, i.e., share the same Time. In fact, further conclusions can be drawn from this basic postulate to the point of realizing that for human communication to occur, coevalness has to be *created*. Communication is, ultimately, about creating shared Time."[6]

Shared time is the prerequisite for intersubjectivity, which is why, for Fabian, "field research as the fundamental source of anthropological knowledge" is a "powerful practical corrective" to temporal distancing.[7] Two linked points are especially significant in Fabian's bold claim that a shared, processual, constantly created coevalness is the ontological precondition for intersubjectivity. First is its implication that empty homogeneous time has never been the a priori condition for intersubjectivity, communication, or encountering the other. Fabian's notion of shared time points to something else, not that modern notion of time as a uniform, quantifiable, world-historical development in which difference can only be temporally repositioned as backwardness, obsolescence, or primitivism. The homogeneity of modern time consciousness is achieved by a posture of cultural neutrality, masking a potent intolerance toward intractable differences that are contained by being allochronized. Modern time consciousness pretends to universality, but the real ontological ground of intersubjectivity, of being with others, lies elsewhere (elsewhen) than this imposition of sameness. Second, the complex ontological ground of shared time is not granted or already given beforehand: it is always in the making. Moreover, Fabian's insistence on the shared involvement of creative participants — the tension between similitude/singularity and plurality/difference in "shared Time" — suggests that the temporal ground of intersubjectivity, of being with the other, is not a single shared time. (I meet others not only on my times but also on theirs. Their times differ from but dovetail, in our meeting, with mine; this is why shared time is both the prerequisite of our meeting and also the becoming that our encounter creates.)

Does shared time — that time of coevalness, encounter, and intersubjective exchange — presuppose only one time? Can multiple temporalities be shared? This question is posed and answered, I think, in Chakrabarty's discussion of the differences between "minority histories" and "subaltern pasts." Minority history is Chakrabarty's term for the well-meaning inclusive or incorporative gesture of historiographies that try to give voice to the un- or underrepresented but keep the fundamental premises of historical writing and historical time intact: "The expression 'minority histories' has come to refer to all those pasts on whose behalf democratically minded historians have fought the exclusions and omissions of mainstream narratives of the nation. . . . [They] in part express the struggles for inclusion and representation that are characteristic of liberal and representative democracies. Minority histories as such do not have to raise any fundamental questions about the discipline of history."[8] In contrast, subaltern pasts "represent moments or points at which the archive that the historian mines develops a degree of intractability with respect to the aims of professional history. In other words, these are pasts that resist historicization."[9] The concrete example of a subaltern past resistant to the disciplinary aims of modern historiography that Chakrabarty explores is drawn from Ranajit Guha's work on the Santals, "a tribal group in Bengal and Bihar who rebelled against both British and nonlocal Indians in 1855." The archive becomes refractory to historicizing when political agency is not regarded as disenchanted: "Santal leaders explained the rebellion in supernatural terms, as an act carried out at the behest of the Santal god Thakur." Chakrabarty notes that such moments are problematic for the historian because, "in his own telling, the subaltern is not necessarily the subject of his or her own history." The Santal's own account is in tension with the sympathetic, democratically inclined historian's desire to portray the subaltern as a self-driven historical agent.[10] Because the historian cannot, within the modern understanding of historical time as disenchanted and homogeneous, accept that God was the motive force in the rebellion, "the Santal's statement that God was the main instigator of the rebellion has to be anthropologized (that is, *converted into somebody's belief* or made into an object of anthropological analysis) before it finds a place in the historian's narrative." Objectifying profound differences in understandings of time and agency as *belief* allows historians to both distance themselves from the peasant's perspective as valid (you see things differently, which I respect) while portraying that perspective as alienated with reference to the real (your version of the past is itself a historical object, a "signifier of other times and societies"). Chakrabarty proposes that the subject-object relationship that characterizes the historian's distancing of peasant worlds can be avoided by asking a different question: "the Santal with his statement 'I did as my god told me to do' also faces us as a way of being in this world, and we could ask ourselves: Is that way of being a possibility for our own lives and for what we define as our present? Does the Santal help us to understand a principle by which we also live in certain instances?" The two modes — one that historicizes the peasant and keeps historical time intact, another that acknowledges another possibility of life in the present, thereby opening to an unsettled conception of the now — must be held in tension with each another, since they constitute the vital double-gesture that allows the historian encountering subaltern pasts to "stay with heterogeneities without seeking to reduce them to any overarching principle that speaks for an already given whole."[11]

Chakrabarty ends his discussion of these points by adverting to a plural temporal ontological ground for intersubjectivity that recalls and sharpens Fabian's implicit claim regarding the multiply-shared time that anchors intersubjectivity: "But the nineteenth-century Santal — and indeed, if my argument is right, humans from any other period and region — are always in some sense our contemporaries: that would have to be the condition under which we can even begin to treat them as intelligible to us. Thus the writing of history must implicitly assume a plurality of times existing together, a disjuncture of the present with itself. Making visible this disjuncture is what subaltern pasts allow us to do."[12]

To grope for a different ontology, in Fabian and Chakrabarty's work, is to conceive time precisely as a *relation: a profoundly plural relation with difference*. What I have tried to sketch in the pages of this study belongs to a similar hope of descrying or imagining, dimly, the contours of a temporal coexistence with otherness that is both prior to every encounter but not pregiven or foreclosed (Fabian's notion of a shared time assumed by intersubjectivity but also created contingently by participants); a shared time around which we ford differences, when the very fording — not overcoming, but precisely wading through, otherness — discloses the variegation of the present (Chakrabarty's plural, coextant times, a present disjointed from itself).

I noted earlier that ontological claims are unfashionable, and by this I mean that they have for some time been viewed with an understandable degree of suspicion. Historically, ontological claims have been bound up with the legitimizing ruses and apparatuses of power (upholding, for example, the normative, unchanging, universal subject of history and knowledge), ruses that feminist, antiracist, working-class, postcolonial, and queer political interventions have contested and exposed. Temporal critique, however, provokes, as Elizabeth Grosz puts it, a "reconstituted ontology" that has a vital role to play in cultural, social, and political work. Grosz elaborates:

> The forgotten debt that epistemologies, images, and representations of various kinds owe to ontology, to the force of the real, to that which is larger than and beyond the control of the knowing subject, needs to be acknowledged if new kinds of knowledges and different kinds of relations to the real—beyond and within knowledges—are to be developed.
>
> In restoring ontology to its rightful place at the center of knowledges and social practices, the ways in which ontology has been previously conceptualized—as static, fixed, composed of universal principles or ideals, indifferent to history, particularity, or change—require transformation and revitalization. "The real," "being," "materiality," "nature," those terms usually associated with the unchanging, must themselves be opened to their immaterial or extra-material virtualities or becomings, to the temporal forces of endless change, in other words, to history, biology, culture, sexuality. In this reconfigured form, ontology is no longer too broad, unchanging or abstract to be relevant to political struggles of various kinds; instead it is (in part, and most indirectly) what is fundamentally at stake in such struggles.[13]

Where this study is concerned, the epistemological vector of the argument (the fantastic as a temporal translation that renders supernaturalisms in the language of homogeneous time) expresses and entails a political-ontological commitment to radical temporal heterogeneity. The epistemological argument about translation is undergirded by the ontological conviction that there is no such thing as a single, empty, homogeneous time (the undeniable modern ascendancy and practical utility of the latter notwithstanding). Immiscible times—the temporal disquietude provoked by supernaturalisms that are never entirely enfolded or assimilated into the ever-accelerating, preemptive forward push of chronology and capital—are indexical signs of strain, stress-fissures in homogenizing, deracinating translations. They point to an ontological condition of temporal multiplicity that confounds the modern truism that obsolescent enchantments have been dispelled. Like modern time consciousness itself, fantastic cinema is preoccupied with enchantment, beset by differences that beckon beyond and before chronology.

NOTES

Introduction

1. The Bergsonian notion of the contemporaneousness of past and present in a nonchronological, nonspatialized time is developed by Deleuze in *Cinema 2: The Time-Image*, especially in relation to the concept of the crystalline image. There is doubtless a shared ground between the project of this book (which pursues the implications of the Bergsonian survival of the past for a postcolonial understanding of the fantastic narrative) and facets of Deleuze's discussion of the time-image (a splitting present or forking time, multiple temporal coexistence, and strata of memory). I am less interested, however, in Deleuzian concepts of the actual and virtual, of the shot as intermediate image and as a mobile section of duration, and in the taxonomic and auteurist impulses of Deleuze's discussion of movement-images and time-images. Deleuzian virtuality treats the past as preserved but no longer acting, or acting only indirectly. In contrast, I argue that in the fantastic the survival of the past is, in Deleuzian terms, far more actual than it is virtual. The Bergsonian concept of the survival of the past elaborated in this book is that of an *abiding, actual, and acting past*, as in the following quote from Bergson's *Creative Evolution*: "Like the universe as a whole, like each conscious being taken separately, the organism which lives is a thing that *endures*. Its past, in its entirety, is prolonged into its present, and abides there, actual and acting" (15).

Thus, my engagement with Deleuze centers on the crucial insights his Bergsonian commentaries shed on Bergson's philosophy of time rather than pursuing Deleuze's own departures from and transformations of Bergsonism. Certainly some scholars have chosen not to distinguish between Bergsonian and Deleuzian positions, with productive results (see, e.g., Elizabeth Grosz's discussion of virtuality in *Time Travels* [esp. 94]). In this book, I have largely maintained the distinctions between these two thinkers for the reasons cited above. I refer readers interested in Deleuze's own creative transfiguration of Bergsonian ideas of time, memory, and the cinema to David N. Rodowick's excellent discussion in *Gilles Deleuze's Time Machine*.

2. Bergson, *Matter and Memory*, 75–77.

3. Ileto's book opens with a discussion of the violent suppression of the Lapiang Malaya in 1967. Led by Valentin de los Santos, an eighty-six-year-old charismatic peasant leader who sought to overthrow incumbent Philippine president Ferdinand Marcos, hundreds of adherents confronted the Philippine Constabulary's automatic rifles with sacred *bolos* (knives), *anting-anting* (talismans), charmed vests, and *oraciones* (prayers). Ileto writes:

> The Lapiang Malaya affair is not an isolated event in Philippine history. It is not an aberration in an otherwise comprehensible past. We should be able to find meaning in it, not resorting to convenient explanations like "fanaticism," "nativism," and "millenarianism," which only alienate us further from the *kapatid* who lived through it. . . . The meaning of the revolution to the masses — the largely rural and uneducated Filipinos who constituted the revolution's mass base — remains problematic for us. We cannot assume that their views and aspirations were formless, inchoate, and meaningless apart from their articulation in *ilustrado* thought. . . . This leads to the foregone conclusion that early popular movements were largely failures, and continued to be so until they turned more "rational" and "secular." (Ileto, *Pasyon and Revolution*, 2, 4–5)

4. Mike de Leon is among the major directors of the Philippine New Cinema, or what has been called the "Second Golden Age" of Filipino filmmaking. In 1975, at the very beginning of the New Cinema movement, de Leon was executive producer and cinematographer of Lino Brocka's *Maynila: Sa kuko ng liwanag* [Manila: In the Claws of Neon]. *Maynila* ushered in a film movement characterized by creative accomplishment in a Marcos-era context of political repression. In the closing years of the Second Golden Age, de Leon directed *Sister Stella L* (1984), though most of his films in the intervening years are also considered major accomplishments of the period. *Itim* is Mike de Leon's multiawarded first film, named Best Picture at the 1978 Asian Film Festival. It received the Urian Award for Best Cinematography, Music, Editing, and Sound (conferred by the Philippine Film Critics' Circle, or the Manunuri ng Pelikulang Pilipino), and won the local film industry's FAMAS awards for cinematography, sound, and production design. See David, "A Second Golden Age (an Informal History)."

5. The provincial elite who own and lend the saintly images for Catholic rites underwrite the costs of the santo's upkeep, traditionally derived from the *lupa ng santo*, or saint's land, a portion of rice land owned by the family. The feudal structuring of santo-ownership is perpetuated by the inheritance of respective social obligations: the original santo owners were primarily landowners, while those who

carried the processional floats aloft were their tenants. See Venida, "The Santo and the Rural Aristocracy," 503–6.

6. Mike de Leon remarked in a 1983 interview: "In fact it has always been my dream to do a film about the upper class, maybe a thriller, and then there is an investigation and through it you see all these relationships, perversions, insanity, which was rampant in my family, and the values. . . . There was something interesting about our family because *ganyan*, landed gentry, *pumasok pa sa pelikula* [they were landed gentry who got involved with filmmaking], [a] very surreal combination" (Caagusan, "Interview with Mike de Leon," 48–50). To my mind, the goals de Leon articulates here, of portraying an elite family's relationship to cinema (understood broadly to also be a relationship with photography) in the form of an investigative thriller critical of class foibles, had already been realized in *Itim*. Shot on location at the ancestral house of de Leon's grandmother, LVN film studio matriarch Narcisa "Doña Sisang" de Leon in San Miguel, Bulacan, *Itim* literalizes by way of its mise-en-scène the social world de Leon knew well.

7. Ileto, *Pasyon and Revolution*, 14, 42, 65.

8. Bergson, *Creative Evolution*, 4–5.

9. Barthes writes: "For me the Photographer's organ is not his eye (which terrifies me) but his finger: what is linked to the trigger of the lens, to the metallic shifting of the plates (when the camera still had such things). I love these mechanical sounds in an almost voluptuous way. . . . For me the noise of Time is not sad: I love bells, clocks, watches — and I recall that at first photographic implements were related to techniques of cabinetmaking and the machinery of precision: cameras, in short, were clocks for seeing, and perhaps in me someone very old still hears in the photographic mechanism the living sound of the wood" (Barthes, *Camera Lucida*, 15).

10. Note, however, that Walter Benjamin distinguishes between the calendar and the empty, homogeneous time of the clock. His revaluation of calendar time as opening to something other than linear progression centers on holidays, which contravene empty homogeneous time with the kind of "remembrance" that makes each holiday a "historical time-lapse camera." Despite the calendar's instrumentality to homogeneous time, I agree that holidays — which have also been a contested issue in struggles over labor time — do disrupt the pure forward progression posited by homogeneous time. See Benjamin, "Theses on the Philosophy of History," 261–62.

11. For one of the most influential accounts of time-discipline see Thompson, "Time, Work-Discipline, and Industrial Capitalism." An important reference point for modern regimes of time discipline, of the stopwatch as an apparatus for the surveillance and disciplining of workers, was the emergence of the scientific management of labor time, begun in 1883 by Frederick W. Taylor and continued by his disciple Frank B. Gilbreth. See the discussions of Taylor and Gilbreth in Kern, *The*

Culture of Time and Space, 115–16; and Doane, *The Emergence of Cinematic Time*, 5–6. On the "speed of life" in capitalist society, see Neary and Rikowsky, "Time and Speed in the Social Universe of Capital," 53–59.

12. Benjamin, "Theses on the Philosophy of History," 261.

13. I borrow the phrase "indispensable but inadequate" from Dipesh Chakrabarty, who uses it to refer to the legacy of European political modernity in general, and modern historical time consciousness in particular, as providing necessary tools for postcolonial critique. At the same time, his work points up the limits of modern historical time for the writing of subaltern histories. See Chakrabarty, *Provincializing Europe*, 3–8. In addition, the concept of the necessary illusion is from Deleuze's discussion of the notion of "false problems" in Bergson's method: "an illusion that carries us along, or in which we are immersed, inseparable from our condition" (Deleuze, *Bergsonism*, 20–21). For the concept of "socially objectivated time," which I discuss more fully in chapter 1, see Luckmann, "The Constitution of Human Life in Time," 154–59.

14. According to historian Gerhard Dohrn-van Rossum, the decisive emergence of the mechanical clock occurred in the late thirteenth or early fourteenth century. The mechanical clock is thought to have originated in European monasteries, possibly in response to Chinese or Islamic influences. Its development hinged on the perfection of a clock escapement, a regulating mechanism capable of uniform, repetitive movement. The first public clocks of the fourteenth century appeared in Italian cities; others soon followed. By the fifteenth century, the public mechanical clock was an "index of urban modernization," marking not only the high standing of a given city but coming to define the medieval experience of city life itself as a mode of living by the clock. Dohrn-van Rossum claims that the emergence of the mechanical clock was crucial to "the fundamental change in time consciousness that occurred with the transition from an agrarian to an industrial society that began in the Middle Ages." Though our modern understanding of time has, to some degree, inherited notions of temporalized self-discipline, order, regularity, and punctuality from medieval monastic life, Dohrn-van Rossum cautions against characterizing the latter as mechanistic. As opposed to the modern temporal regime introduced by the mechanical clock, the monastic idea of punctuality, to take one example, was not pinned to abstract time but allowed for a certain amount of leeway. The Church's hour-reckoning prior to the appearance of the mechanical clock was flexible rather than unvarying. Though time was regulated and apportioned, this did not correspond, as modern schedules do, to definite, standard intervals (e.g., sixty minutes in every hour). In the Middle Ages, the canonical hours were adjusted in response to practical considerations and shifts in the length of the solar day. Medieval *hora* were modes of "rationing and rationalizing" time, but they were not modes of time measurement and time-discipline linked to precise, uniform, ab-

stract periods. See Dohrn-van Rossum, *History of the Hour*, 2, 29–31, 35–38, 46–47, 104, 113–18, 126, 272.

15. As Dohrn-van Rossum succinctly puts it, "Work time has been one of the great themes of social conflict since the beginning of industrialization" (Dohrn-van Rossum, *History of the Hour*, 289).

16. See Chakrabarty, *Provincializing Europe*, 93–95. For Bergson's concept of multiple temporal rhythms see Bergson, *Matter and Memory*, 268–69, 272–76.

17. As Deleuze points out, in Bergson's later works, *Creative Evolution* and *Duration and Simultaneity*, Bergson would fall back on the idea of a limited temporal pluralism (time is a multiplicity that is one; the multiplicity of durational rhythms belong only to a "single time, one, universal, and impersonal"). But in *Matter and Memory*, as Deleuze notes, Bergson "goes furthest in the affirmation of a radical plurality of durations: The universe is made up of modifications, disturbances, changes of tension and energy, and nothing else. Bergson does indeed speak of a plurality of rhythms of duration; but in this context he makes it clear—in relation to durations that are more or less slow or fast—that each duration is an absolute, and that each rhythm is itself a duration" (Deleuze, *Bergsonism*, 76–78). It is this earlier Bergsonian notion of radical temporal multiplicity, rather than limited temporal pluralism, that I draw on to argue for an ontological multiplicity of times.

18. Bergson, *Creative Evolution*, 37–39, 45.

19. Ibid., 37.

20. Luciana Parisi and Steve Goodman argue that contemporary crises of national and global security in relation to bioterrorism link affect to temporality, as fear and futurity are collapsed: "From the mass modulation of mood via affective epidemics, to the release of viral spores into oblivious populations, fear or apprehension, as the future lurking in the present, becomes a starting point for a discussion of cybernetic control and becoming. These affective syndromes, dread, or ominous anticipation, are modes of sensitized contact with bodies not yet actualized. . . . Control no longer attempts merely to stop an unwanted future from happening, but switches towards the rule of the pre-emptive strike whose very intervention, in a strange paradoxical feedback, activates the future at every turn" (Parisi and Goodman, "The Affect of Nanoterror," n.p.).

Drawing on Parisi's and Goodman's account of the shift away from deterrence toward preemptive power in contemporary control societies, Patricia Ticineto Clough et al. describe preemptive power as the "dream" of contemporary capitalism, the dream of foreclosing, that is, anticipating and thereby controlling, the disruptiveness of the future: "We will propose that governance is now a matter of pre-emption, but not only to anticipate and control the emergent but rather to precipitate emergence and thereby act on a future that has not yet and may not ever arrive" (Clough et al., "Notes Towards a Theory of Affect-Itself," 63, 70–71).

21. McClintock, *Imperial Leather*, 5, 30, 40.

22. Chakrabarty, *Provincializing Europe*, 3–23.

23. In a related vein, Susan Buck-Morss writes of Benjamin's commitment to unseating a developmental image of historical progress in the unfinished *Passagen-Werk* (1927–40): "Benjamin was most persistent in his attack against the myth of automatic historical progress. In his lifetime, at the very brink of the nuclear age and the twilight of technological innocence, this myth was still largely unshaken, and Benjamin considered it to be the greatest political danger. . . . The earliest notes describe the project's aim: 'to drive out any trace of "development" from the image of history'; to overcome 'the ideology of progress . . . in all its aspects'" (Buck-Morss, *The Dialectics of Seeing*, 79).

24. Bergson writes, "The doctrine of teleology, in its extreme form, as we find it in Leibniz for example, implies that things and beings merely realize a programme previously arranged. But if there is nothing unforeseen, no invention or creation in the universe, time is useless again." See Bergson's critique of mechanism and determinism in *Creative Evolution*, 37–39, 45.

25. Bergson, *Creative Evolution*, 4–5.

26. Bergson, *Time and Free Will*, 152.

27. Deleuze, *Bergsonism*, 55.

28. Ibid., 59.

29. Ibid., 57. In his Fourth Commentary on Bergson, Deleuze writes: "Memory is not in us; it is we who move in a Being-memory, a world-memory. In short, the past appears as the most general form of an already-there, a pre-existence in general, which our recollections presuppose" (Deleuze, *Cinema 2*, 98).

30. Fabian, *Time and the Other*, 31. The notion of the "ethnographiable" subject (supposedly anachronistic peoples on whom visual anthropology trained its gaze) is developed in Fatimah Tobing Rony's critique of ethnographic cinema: "The people depicted in an 'ethnographic film' are meant to be seen as exotic, as people who until only too recently were categorized by science as Savage and Primitive, of an earlier evolutionary stage in the overall history of humankind: people without history, without writing, without civilization, without technology, without archives. In other words, people considered '*ethnographiable*,' in the bipolar schema articulated by Claude Lévi-Strauss, as opposed to people classified as '*historifiable*,' the posited audience of the ethnographic film, those considered to have written archives and thus a history proper" (Rony, *The Third Eye*, 7).

31. Rafael, *Contracting Colonialism*, 111–14.

32. "Beyond the decisive turn" is a phrase Deleuze quotes from Bergson's *Matter and Memory*; for Deleuze, it exemplifies the Bergsonian method of going beyond experience to seek the conditions of that experience. See Deleuze, *Bergsonism*, 29.

33. Bergson, *Time and Free Will*, 122.

34. Ibid., 133.

35. Ibid., 165.

36. Ibid., 221.

37. Ibid., 181–82.

38. Ibid., 122, 131–32.

39. Chakrabarty, "The Time of History and the Times of Gods," 36.

40. Chakrabarty writes, "If a language, as has been said, is but a dialect backed up by an army, the same could be said of the narratives of 'modernity' that, almost universally today, point to a certain 'Europe' as the primary habitus of the modern" (Chakrabarty, *Provincializing Europe*, 43).

41. Chakrabarty writes of "an ideal of objectivity entertained by Newtonian science where translation between different languages is mediated by the higher language of science itself. Thus *pani* in Hindi and *water* in English can both be mediated by H_2O. Needless to say, it is only the higher language that is capable of appreciating, if not expressing, the capacities of "*the* human mind." I would suggest that the idea of a godless, continuous, empty, and homogeneous time that history shares with the other social sciences and modern political philosophy as a basic building block belongs to this model of a higher, overarching language — a structure of generality, an aspiration toward the scientific — which is built into conversations that take the modern historical consciousness for granted." See Chakrabarty, *Provincializing Europe*, 73–76.

42. Chakrabarty, *Provincializing Europe*, 93.

43. Ibid., 88–89. Chakrabarty's discussion of translational tensions in the term "precapital" — which, he emphasizes, names something more than a mere antecedent to capital — leads to a very different view of temporal difference than one sees in thinkers like Harry Harootunian. For Harootunian, the problem of "divided or mixed temporalities" (in industrial Euroamerican heartlands and non-Western peripheries alike) is still *explained by*, rather than *disruptive of*, the Marxian account of subsumption and what Harootunian calls "the production and reproduction of unevenness" characterized by notions of "arrest," "lag," and "delay." See Harootunian, "Remembering the Historical Present," especially 473–75.

44. Ibid., 3, 72, 89.

45. Ibid., 89.

46. Ibid., 12–13.

47. Ibid., 238.

48. Ibid., 16.

49. Weber, "Science as a Vocation," 13–14.

50. Michel, "Differentiation vs. Disenchantment," 348.

51. The most famous "Hottentot Venus" is Saartje Bartman, a South African woman who was very popularly and controversially exhibited in London in 1810.

(Her Dutch name was Anglicized to Sarah Bartmann; her original name is not known.) On her death in 1816 she was, like several other women of color in the nineteenth century, the subject of comparative anatomical studies conducted by European scientists. Anne Fausto-Sterling and Sander Gilman explore the ways in which Bartman epitomized nineteenth-century science's pronounced fascination with the supposedly deviant anatomical features of so-called Hottentots. Fausto-Sterling points out that calling Bartman a "Hottentot" was already a misnomer since, by Bartman's lifetime, the Khoikhoi—the people dubbed Hottentots by their Dutch colonizers—were already extinct. As Fausto-Sterling notes, "Within sixty years after the Dutch settlement [at the Cape of Good Hope in 1652], the Khoikhoi, as an organized, independent culture, were extinct, ravaged by smallpox and the encroachment of the Dutch. . . . Nevertheless, nineteenth-century European scientists wrote about Hottentots, even though the racial group that late-20th-century anthropologists believe to merit that name had been extinct for at least three-quarters of a century" (Fausto-Sterling, "Gender, Race, and Nation," 22). See also Gilman, "The Hottentot and the Prostitute."

52. Daston and Park, *Wonders and the Order of Nature*, 172.

53. Kenseth, "The Age of the Marvelous," 25, 27–30.

54. Ibid., 36.

55. Daston and Park, *Wonders and the Order of Nature*, 329.

56. Ibid., 342.

57. Ibid., 350.

58. Ibid., 360–68. For disenchantment tropes of cultural childhood and adulthood (corresponding to primitive and modern humanity, respectively) applied to the fantastic, see Sandor, "Myths and the Fantastic," 350–54.

59. Glynn, "Challenging Disenchantment," 437–38. Glynn's examples are drawn from U.S. television programming in the late 1990s: *Buffy the Vampire Slayer*, *The X-Files*, and *Charmed*, among others. *The X-Files* slogan, "the truth is out there," has been read by Glynn as a pun. Rather than a statement of faith in the discoverability of a truth that is out there, waiting to be revealed, the slogan is for Glynn almost an expletive—the truth is "out there"—an assertion of the outlandish, disruptive quality of the truth being invoked.

In my view, *The X-Files* can be read as a reification of the binary that flanks the fragile border of the Todorovian fantastic: in the early seasons, Mulder represented a willingness to believe in the supernatural (Todorov's marvelous), whereas Scully stood for scientific investigation and rational explanation (Todorov's uncanny). The very premise of the series is the notion of a contentious process of checks and balances, with Scully appointed to the X-Files to keep Mulder within rational bounds. The categories of the Todorovian fantastic were mapped onto the romantic comedy's convention of the well-matched couple, adversaries who incessantly battle and are thus inevitably drawn to one another. In this television series, the eroticization of the Todorovian dynamic (the push and pull of the marvelous and the uncanny, generating an eroticized frisson of the fantastic) consistently tended to corroborate the marvelous.

60. Chakrabarty, *Provincializing Europe*, 86.

61. Ibid., 88.

62. I borrow the phrase "contained alterity" from Gayatri Spivak's discussion of the experience of otherness in translation. See Spivak, "The Politics of Translation," 181.

63. Chakrabarty, *Provincializing Europe*, 95.

64. Jameson, "Magical Narratives," 135.

65. Scholes, "Foreword," viii.

66. Prawer, *Caligari's Children*, 110.

67. This has been demonstrated persuasively by Jeffrey Sconce in his book *Haunted Media*, a cultural history of the occult horizons of reception that greeted the "electronic presence" of emerging telecommunications media: telegraphy, telephony, wireless, and television.

68. Jameson, "Magical Narratives," 136–37.

69. Todorov, 24–40.

70. Jameson, "Magical Narratives," 136–37. This semantic or modal approach can also be limiting; Jameson cautions against abstract personifications such as the comic or tragic "spirit." In film studies, however, there are several works in which semantic criticism has been rigorously pursued: Jane Feuer has incisively characterized the exuberant, spontaneous world of the self-reflexive musical; a semantic approach is also at work in Altman's insightful reading of "supra-diegetic" music in American film musicals as belonging to a transcendent, timeless, and ideal world. See Feuer, "The Self-Reflective Musical and the Myth of Entertainment," 32; and Altman, *The American Film Musical*, 66–67.

71. Gledhill, "Rethinking Genre," 235.

72. Jameson, "Magical Narratives," 141–42.

73. Heidegger, *Being and Time*, 50, 61.

74. Blitz, *Heidegger's* Being and Time *and the Possibility of Political Philosophy*, 48–52.

75. Jameson, "Magical Narratives," 141–42. My repeated references to the musical film are not accidental; the being-in-the-world or generic verisimilitude of the musical, like that of the fantastic, is emphatically antiquotidian. See Altman, *The American Film Musical*; and Feuer, "The Self-Reflective Musical and the Myth of Entertainment."

76. Jameson, *The Political Unconscious*, 111.

77. Gledhill speaks of "a specific mode of aesthetic articulation adaptable across a range of genres, across decades, and across national cultures," enabling articula-

tions at "particular historical junctures, while also providing a medium of inter-change and overlap between genres" (Gledhill, "Rethinking Genre," 230). Gledhill's notion of mode as cross-national and cross-generic is considered closely in chapter 4 of this study.

78. The centrality of time to a postcolonial theory of the fantastic is evident in Chris Morash's work on the supernatural narrative in Irish literature. According to Morash, anachrony or disjointed time is not merely a narrational device deployed on the level of plot (*sjuzet*) but is the characteristic temporality of the supernatural tale's diegetic world (*fabula*). Morash never explicitly mentions temporal translation in his analysis of Celticism in nineteenth-century vampire tales; nonetheless, I read his account of the willful and conflicted conversion of Celtist cultural anachrony into an ascendant modern present as a fascinating instance of temporal translation in the Irish fantastic. See Chris Morash, "The Time is Out of Joint (O Cursèd Spite!)," especially 131–39.

79. Jameson, "Magical Narratives," 142.

80. The reader's hesitation is for Todorov the defining attribute of the fantastic. See Todorov, *The Fantastic*, 25–32.

81. For Todorov the inexplicable event is able to provoke the reader's hesitation only insofar as it is taken literally, which means that the pure fantastic can only exist in the absence of poetic and allegorical interpretations. Todorov, *The Fantastic*, 24–25, 32–33.

82. Ibid., 44.

83. Ibid., 42.

84. Ibid., 41.

85. Gledhill, "Rethinking Genre," 221–22.

86. Jameson, *The Political Unconscious*, 130–31.

87. Gledhill, "Rethinking Genre," 221.

88. For Rafael, the universalizing posture is claimed by Castilian in relation to Tagalog and other Philippine languages, which, through the encounter with Spanish evangelical imperialism from the late sixteenth century on, were constituted after the fact as local vernaculars (Rafael, *Contracting Colonialism*, xiii). For Chakrabarty the universal position is assumed by the homogeneous time of secular historiography in relation to contemporaneous peasant lifeworlds that admit of supernatural agency (Chakrabarty, *Provincializing Europe*, 76).

89. Spivak, "The Politics of Translation," 183.

90. Ibid., 181, 183.

91. Lippit, *Atomic Light (Shadow Optics)*, 111.

92. Chakrabarty, *Provincializing Europe*, 93–94.

93. Spivak, "The Politics of Translation," 180.

94. Skepticism toward the supernatural as the guarantor of modernity is the

approach espoused, for example, by Margaret Carter: "In the typical fantastic situation, the character whose beliefs about the nature of reality differ from the majority view suffers the doubts of others (whose skepticism represents, within the fiction, the presumed skepticism of the reader) and possibly self-doubt. We may note that such fiction could not have been written in earlier periods, when the existence of the supernatural was universally accepted. The modern ghost story is addressed to a reader skeptical about ghosts" (Carter, *Specter or Delusion?* 1). Carter's account relies on a fully realized, world-historical process of disenchantment, which I critique here and in chapter 2.

95. Higson, "The Concept of National Cinema," 36–46.

96. Benedict Anderson writes, "If nation-states are widely conceded to be 'new' and 'historical,' the nations to which they give political expression always loom out of an immemorial past, and, still more important, glide into a limitless future" (Anderson, *Imagined Communities*, 11–12).

97. Altman, *Film/Genre*, 13–14.

98. See the segment "Horror and Ideology" in Carroll, *The Philosophy of Horror* (195–206). Carroll speculates on the possible objections of political criticism to the "universal and general theories of horror" he advances in his book. But in anticipating such objections, he reduces political genre criticism to a mere adjudication of the supposedly subversive or reactionary ideology espoused by a text:

> A politically minded critic, however, might balk at this way of dealing with the persistence of the horror genre. He might complain that its bias is too individualistic, whereas a truly effective explanation of the existence of the horror genre should highlight the pertinent socio-political factors that give rise to it. In this case, emphasis would, nowadays, be likely to be placed on the ideological role that horror fictions play. The argument would be that horror exists because it is always in the service of the status quo; that is, horror is invariably an agent of the established order. It continues to be produced because horror is in the interest of the established order. This presupposes that the creations of the horror genre are always politically repressive, thereby contradicting the (equally incorrect) view, discussed earlier, that horror fictions are always emancipatory (i.e., politically subversive). (Carroll, *The Philosophy of Horror*, 196)

99. Jameson, "Magical Narratives," 157–58.

100. Stephen King has remarked that "horror fiction is really as Republican as a banker in a three-piece suit" and that "monstrosity fascinates because it appeals to the conservative Republican in a three-piece suit who resides in all of us." King's thoughts on the conservatism of horror are quoted in Carroll, *The Philosophy of Horror*, 199.

In this book, I argue that the kernel of the fantastic is its temporalized translation of supernaturalism, whereas most influential definitions of horror in film studies center on monstrosity and the solicitation of audience affect (terror or horror, for which the genre is named). See Carroll, *The Philosophy of Horror*; and Wood, "The American Nightmare," 70–86.

101. As Caroline S. Hau eloquently argues, the relationship of truth to error is not one of antinomy but of "ineluctable intimacy." To take error seriously means to "shift the debate about the status of error away from a consideration of error *per se* (which often bogs down into an examination of the injurious consequences of false beliefs and bad analysis) to a consideration of the *uses* of error." One of the uses of error, one learns from Hau's work, is political-ontological:

> The risk of error inherent in political struggle impels rather than suspends or terminates the theoretical task of the intellectual because we learn about ourselves and about the world *in the course* of our social practices in and our active theorizing about the world. . . . Far from rendering intellectual work useless, the possibility of error demands and impels the ordeal and responsibility of the intellectual task, in the same way that it demands that we do something about the situation we find ourselves in. It is, in one sense, the condition of possibility of truth, of any form of political inquiry and struggle, of history itself. Liberation struggles are, indeed, "the best schools of good sense" because they deepen our understanding not only of what is involved in the fight for radical change, but also of what is involved in the principled study of reality. (Hau, "On Representing Others," 20–23)

Chapter 1. Two Modes of Temporal Critique

1. Lynne Kirby has argued for the privileged historical, perceptual, and social relationships between train and cinema in the early decades of the medium's emergence. The birth of cinema, Kirby observes, coincides with railway travel's golden age. The railroad introduces and bequeaths a new mode of spectatorship, panoramic perception, to the cinema. Kirby posits a relationship of doubling, or mirroring, between trains and early cinema: "Like film's illusion of movement, the experience of the railroad is based on a fundamental paradox: simultaneous motion and stillness. In both cases, passengers sit still as they rush through space and time, whether physically and visually, as on the train, or merely visually, as in the cinema. The train would then be cinema's mirror image in the sequential unfolding of a chain of essentially still images and the rapid shifts of point of view that the train and cinema experiences entail" (Kirby, *Parallel Tracks*, 2).

2. Rodowick's framing of Deleuze's project in the *Cinema* books is extremely helpful for clarifying this concept. As he demonstrates, cinema for Deleuze furnishes a

historically specific "image of thought." Every era thinks through certain concrete practices, and in the case of cinema, shifts in cinematic signification after the Second World War inaugurated a new semiotic regime (the time-image as opposed to an earlier era's movement-image). Rodowick writes: "Deleuze depicts image practices as social and technological automata where each era thinks itself by producing its particular image of thought. . . . For Deleuze this is the most compelling gambit of writing a history of 'cinematic' philosophy: to take an era's strategies of thinking-through, represented aesthetically in the nature of its images and signs, and render them in the form of philosophical concepts. But also for philosophy to understand how the possibilities of thought are renewed in aesthetic practices" (Rodowick, *Gilles Deleuze's Time Machine*, 5–7).

3. For Johannes Fabian "allochronic discourse" consists of "devices of temporal distancing" that effect a *"denial of coevalness,"* that is, *"a persistent and systematic tendency to place the referent of anthropology in a Time other than the present of the producer of anthropological discourse"* (Fabian, *Time and the Other*, 31, 37–39).

4. Bergson, *Time and Free Will*, 98, 100–101.

5. Deleuze, *Bergsonism*, 21–23, 27. "Pure duration" and "pure heterogeneity" are phrases that occur in Bergson, *Time and Free Will*, 104.

6. Deleuze, *Bergsonism*, 22.

7. F. L. Pogson writes: "The idea of a homogeneous and measurable time is shown to be an artificial concept, formed by the intrusion of the idea of space into the realm of pure duration" (Pogson, "Translator's Preface," vii).

8. Bergson, *Time and Free Will*, 94–95.

9. Bergson, *Creative Evolution*, 4–6, 272.

10. Deleuze writes: "Bergson evolved, in a certain sense, from the beginning to the end of his work. The two major aspects of his evolution are the following: Duration seemed to him to be less and less reducible to a psychological experience and became instead the variable essence of things, providing the theme of a complex ontology. But, simultaneously, space seemed to him to be less and less reducible to a fiction separating us from this psychological reality; rather, it was itself grounded in being and expressed one of its two slopes, one of its two directions" (Deleuze, *Bergsonism*, 34–35; see also 49).

11. Ibid., 31.

12. Bergson, *Creative Evolution*, 46–48.

13. Grosz, *The Nick of Time*, 156–57. Deleuze makes a similar point: "If we recall Bergson's profound desire to produce a philosophy which would be that of modern science (not in the sense of a reflection on that science, that is an epistemology, but on the contrary in the sense of an invention of autonomous concepts capable of corresponding with the new symbols of science), we can understand that Bergson's confrontation with Einstein was inevitable" (Deleuze, *Cinema 1*, 60).

14. Bergson, *Time and Free Will*, 96–97.

15. The Bergsonian concept of subjectivity that emerges in his discussion of temporalized freedom is both self-knowing ("the existence of which we are most assured and which we know best is unquestionably our own") and yet self-blind or unknowing ("we close our eyes to the unceasing variation of every psychical state"). Becoming aware of true duration would mean moving from self-blindness to the freedom of self-creation: "we are, to a certain extent, what we do . . . and we are creating ourselves continually. This creation of self by self is the more complete, the more one reasons on what one does" (Bergson, *Creative Evolution*, 1–2, 7).

16. Bergson, *Time and Free Will*, 193, 199–201, 218; *Creative Evolution*, 10–11.

17. Bergson, *Time and Free Will*, 90–91.

18. Ibid., 101–2.

19. Ibid., 76.

20. Ibid., 106–7.

21. Kern, *The Culture of Time and Space*, 22.

22. Ibid., 18–19.

23. As D. N. Rodowick points out, the Newtonian universe is orderly, homogeneous, and static. Mathematical constants, like the value for gravity, would be the same regardless of time or space; the laws of celestial mechanics would hold for all eternity, anywhere in the universe. Thus, ideally, to a suprahuman intelligence, everything could be knowable, calculable, and foreseeable, since the laws of nature are constant, even though our grasp of them is still in progress. It is this static, timeless, homogeneous view that Bergson challenges with his notion of duration as becoming, time as inventiveness, and the future as open and absolutely unforeseeable, impossible to extrapolate from laws or constants derived from the evidence of the past, since the passage of time is not mere repetition. See Rodowick, *Gilles Deleuze's Time Machine*, 19–20.

24. Bergson, *Time and Free Will*, 77.

25. Ibid., 79.

26. Ibid., 101. In his critique of science and common sense in *Creative Evolution*, Bergson likens the spatialized all-at-onceness of chronological time to a number line: "Therefore the flow of time might assume an infinite rapidity, the entire past, present and future of material objects or of isolated systems might be spread out all at once in space, without there being anything to change either in the formulae of the scientist or even in the language of common sense. The number t would always stand for the same things; it would still count the same number of correspondences between the states of the objects or systems and the points of the line, ready drawn, which would be then the 'course of time'" (Bergson, *Creative Evolution*, 9).

27. Bergson, *Time and Free Will*, 107–8.

28. Bergson, *Creative Evolution*, 11.

29. Bergson, *Time and Free Will*, 108–9.

30. Bergson's presumptive masculine subject is evident, for instance, in his discussion of free will as a self-authoring act, described in masculine terms as a kind of autopaternity: "In a word, if it is agreed to call every act free which springs from the self and from the self alone, the act which bears the mark of our personality is truly free, for our self alone will lay claim to its paternity" (Bergson, *Time and Free Will*, 172–73).

31. Ibid., 110.

32. "Although the positions occupied by the moving body vary with the different moments of duration, though it even creates distinct moments by the mere fact of occupying different positions, duration properly so called has no moments which are identical or external to one another, being essentially heterogeneous, continuous, and with no analogy to number" (Bergson, *Time and Free Will*, 120); and also: "What duration is there existing outside us? The present only, or, if we prefer the expression, simultaneity" (ibid., 227).

33. Ibid., 116 (Bergson's emphasis).

34. Bergson, *Creative Evolution*, 9. The Bergsonian motif of the devaluation of the interval in spatialized homogeneous time has a corollary in Wolfgang Schivelbusch's account of the epochal shift in space-time consciousness ushered in by late eighteenth-century industrialization. By the nineteenth century, railroad travel had introduced a sense of space as comprising nodes of departure and arrival, devaluing the interval between points of origin and destination, the interval or duration of the journey itself:

> On the one hand, the railroad opens up new spaces that were not as easily accessible before; on the other, it does so by destroying space, namely, the space between points. That in-between space, or travel space, which it was possible to "savor" while using the slow, work-intensive eotechnical form of transport, disappears on the railroads. The railroad knows only points of departure and destination.... As the space between the points—the traveling space—is destroyed, those points move into each other's immediate vicinity: one might say that they collide. They lose their old sense of local identity, which used to be determined by the spaces between them. (Schivelbusch, *The Railway Journey*, 44–45)

35. Bergson, *Creative Evolution*, 21–23.

36. Ibid., 8.

37. Bergson, *Time and Free Will*, 110–12, 114–16.

38. Ibid., 234.

39. Bergson, *Creative Evolution*, 272–73.

40. Ronald Bogue points out that "Bergson's insistence that there are no static, irreducibly solid, impermeable things (the corpuscular view of matter consonant

with an atomistic view of time) but rather a universe composed of movement, inter-penetration, and flux—a vibrational universe—anticipated later developments in physics" (Bogue, *Deleuze on Cinema*, 16–17).

41. Bergson, *Creative Evolution*, 302 (my emphasis).

42. Ibid., 304.

43. Braun, *Picturing Time*, xv, xvii.

44. Ibid., xviii.

45. For a fascinating comparative analysis of Marey's and Muybridge's motion studies, in particular the latter's emphasis on reconstituting the illusion of movement in a narrative, fictionalized form, see ibid., chapter 6.

46. Ibid., xv–xix.

47. Alfred A. Blaker writes: "The history of science is full of examples of parallel invention, for when the underlying facts become known there will always be many fertile minds working simultaneously on the development of fundamentally new processes. The beginnings of photography are typical of this effect" (Blaker, *Photography*, 5).

48. Brown, *Picturing Time*, 150–51, 156, 183, 193.

49. Bergson, *Creative Evolution*, 305–6 (Bergson's emphasis).

50. Barsam, *Looking at Movies*, 24–25.

51. See Metz, *The Imaginary Signifier*.

52. Bruckner writes: "As such, the film image does not simply appear; its movement appears by disappearing into those unphotographed moments, or intervals, between successive photographic instants. The image disappears in order to appear, pushing the logic of appearance beyond its logical limits. To see movement in the film image is to see the failure of a certain vision's rationale: an image that gains visibility only by slipping perpetually out of sight, into the dark. . . . Those 'empty' intervals between frames, far from empty, carry all of the film's movement" (Bruckner, "The Instant and the Dark," 22).

53. Bergson, *Creative Evolution*, 311.

54. Deleuze, *Cinema 1*, 1.

55. Bergson, *Creative Evolution*, 313.

56. Ibid., 30.

57. Baudry, in "asking the cinema about the wish it expresses," concludes that the cinema responds to the desire for a machine that mimics not the real but the spectator's own psychic structure: "This wish is remarkably precise, and consists in obtaining from reality a position, a condition in which what is perceived would no longer be distinguished from representations. It can be assumed that it is this wish which prepares the long history of cinema: the wish to construct a simulation machine capable of offering the subject perceptions which are really representations mistaken for perceptions" (Baudry, "The Apparatus," 697, 705).

58. Bergson, *Creative Evolution*, 329.

59. Ibid., 315–16.

60. Ibid., 330.

61. Ibid., 330.

62. Ibid., 221.

63. Ibid., 332.

64. Bergson's position in this regard resembles one articulated nearly a century later by Italo Calvino: "the 'mental cinema' of the imagination has a function no less important than that of the actual creation of the sequences as they will be recorded by the camera and then put together on the moviola. This mental cinema is always at work in each one of us, and it always has been, even before the invention of the cinema. Nor does it ever stop projecting images before our mind's eye" (Calvino, *Six Memos for the Next Millennium*, 83).

65. Deleuze, *Cinema 1*, 7–8.

66. Ibid., 1.

67. Ibid., 2.

68. Ibid., 3.

69. Bergson, *Creative Evolution*, 48.

70. D. N. Rodowick glosses Deleuze's Bergsonian commentary on movement and the cinematograph as follows: "Writing before 1907 in a scientific context, Bergson probably had little knowledge of the newly emerging narrative cinema. At the same time, the scientific uses of cinematography for motion analysis, including the time/motion studies advocated by Frederick Winslow Taylor, were well advanced. In this sense, Bergson's characterization of reified movement and mechanized time as 'cinematographic' is perhaps well deserved" (Rodowick, *Gilles Deleuze's Time Machine*, 21).

71. Doane incisively identifies three strands of cinematic time that are frequently conflated with one another: the distinct temporalities of apparatus, diegesis, and reception. As Doane astutely notes, "the developing classical cinema attempts to fuse [the temporality of reception] as tightly as possible to that of the apparatus, conferring upon it the same linear predictability and irreversibility" (Doane, *The Emergence of Cinematic Time*, 30). In light of Doane's argument, Bergson's suspicion of the cinema as inevitably bound to the logic of homogeneous time can be understood as collapsing the time of reception onto the mechanical temporality of the cinematographic apparatus. Though dominant forms of filmmaking (the classical cinema) and practices of exhibition have historically endeavored to suture the plural temporalities of spectatorship onto that of the apparatus, these two forms of cinematic time remain extricable from one another: the temporality of reception, Doane reminds us, cannot always be foreclosed or systematized by the apparatus.

72. See Bergson, *Matter and Memory*, 26, 28–32, 34, 57–58.

73. Deleuze, *Cinema 1*, 59.

74. My thanks to Akira Lippit for raising the question of whether Bergsonism would have been possible without the cinema.

75. Sobchack, "Bringing It All Back Home," 147–48.

76. Musser, *The Emergence of Cinema*, 2–5.

77. Ibid., 329.

78. Abel, *The Ciné Goes to Town*, 9.

79. Ibid., 10.

80. Musser, *The Emergence of Cinema*, 2.

81. The period immediately following the publication of *Creative Evolution* has been called the "transitional era" in U.S. filmmaking; the years 1908 to 1917 were marked by vigorous changes in industrial practice (production companies cohere around Los Angeles; the studio system, trade publications, and the star system arise and become standardized). In addition, there were transformations in film form with far-reaching consequences for world cinema (after 1913, the shift from single-reel to multiple-reel feature films; the evolution of linear continuity editing, spatial, temporal, and narrative coherence; and, as Tom Gunning has shown, the working out of an overall stylistic system stressing narrative integration). See Keil and Stamp, introduction, 1–3; see also Gunning, *D. W. Griffith and the Origins of American Narrative Film*.

82. Abel, *The Ciné Goes to Town*, 25, 30, 53.

83. Ibid., xiii, 23–24.

84. Ibid., 9–10.

85. Ibid., 36–37.

86. Musser, *The Emergence of Cinema*, 432–33.

87. Bergson, *Matter and Memory*, 273.

88. Ibid., 276.

89. Bergson, *Creative Evolution*, 9–10 (Bergson's emphasis).

90. Deleuze, *Cinema 1*, 7.

91. Bergson, *Creative Evolution*, 4–6.

92. Deleuze, *Cinema 1*, 9–10.

93. Deleuze, *Bergsonism*, 32.

94. Bergson, *Matter and Memory*, 24.

95. Ibid., 24–25.

96. Ibid., 70.

97. Ibid., 71.

98. Ibid., 296–97.

99. Rodowick, *Gilles Deleuze's Time Machine*, xv.

100. Bergson, *Creative Evolution*, 7.

101. Luckmann, "The Constitution of Human Life in Time," 154–59.

102. Marx, *Capital*, 5–6.

103. Ibid., 12, 46.

104. Neary and Rikowski, "Time and Speed in the Social Universe of Capital," 53.

105. Doane, *The Emergence of Cinematic Time*, 4.

106. Neary and Rikowski, "Time and Speed in the Social Universe of Capital," 55–57 (Neary's and Rikowski's emphasis).

107. See Thompson, "Time, Work-Discipline, and Industrial Capitalism"; Adorno, "Free Time"; and Baudrillard, "The Drama of Leisure or the Impossibility of Wasting One's Time." Key to these analyses is the degree to which workers have internalized time-discipline and commodified temporality. These thinkers suggest that we are increasingly unable to live free time under conditions of unfreedom.

108. Lukács, "Reification and the Consciousness of the Proletariat," 83–84.

109. Marx, *The Poverty of Philosophy*, n.d., quoted in Lukács, "Reification and the Consciousness of the Proletariat," 89.

110. See Doane, *The Emergence of Cinematic Time*, 20. In this historical light, Doane reads Bergson's work as a symptomatic philosophical response to the modern capitalist imperative to quantify and subdivide time: "The rationalization of time ruptures the continuum par excellence and generates epistemological and philosophical anxieties exemplified by the work of Henri Bergson, in his adamant reassertion of temporal continuity in the concept of durée . . . The intense debates around continuity and discontinuity at the turn of the century . . . are a symptom of the ideological stress accompanying rationalization and abstraction" (Doane, *The Emergence of Cinematic Time*, 9–10).

111. O'Malley, *Keeping Watch*, 55–59.

112. Ibid., 58, 64.

113. Ibid., 59–60.

114. Schivelbusch, *The Railway Journey*, 10, 12.

115. Ibid., 12–13.

116. Ibid., 41–43.

117. Ibid., 23–24.

118. O'Malley, *Keeping Watch*, 59–60, 63.

119. Kern, *The Culture of Time and Space*, 12.

120. O'Malley, *Keeping Watch*, 65, 73–74.

121. Ibid., 66–67, 72.

122. Ibid., 111, 115, 116.

123. Ibid., 130, 133, 140–44. For a description of resistance to standard time in various U.S. states see ibid., 126–44.

124. Ibid., 108–9; Kern, *The Culture of Time and Space*, 12–13.

125. Kern, *The Culture of Time and Space*, 13–14.

126. Anderson, *Imagined Communities*, 24.

127. Kern, *The Culture of Time and Space*, 65–68.

128. For a detailed account of these critiques of homogeneous space see ibid., 132–36.

129. Ibid., 212–18.

130. This spatialized nostalgia prompted the establishment of national parks like Yellowstone in 1872 to protect the vanishing wilderness. See ibid., 164–66.

131. See Koselleck, "Time and History," 112–13; and Koselleck, "The Eighteenth Century as the Beginning of Modernity," 160–61.

132. Koselleck, "'Neuzeit,'" 241.

133. Koselleck, "Concepts of Historical Time and Social History," 120; Habermas, *The Philosophical Discourse of Modernity*, 6–7.

134. Koselleck, "The Eighteenth Century as the Beginning of Modernity," 156–57, 162.

135. Ibid., 161.

136. "The composite concept *Neuzeit*, according to Grimm, was first used by Freiligrath in 1870. . . . The concise concept *Neuzeit* became established about four centuries after the beginning of the period it was to typify as a unity. It penetrated the lexica only during the last quarter of the previous century" (Koselleck, "'Neuzeit,'" 233).

137. Koselleck, "'Progress' and 'Decline,'" 228–29.

138. Ibid., 229–30.

139. Koselleck, "The Eighteenth Century as the Beginning of Modernity," 162.

140. Koselleck, "Concepts of Historical Time," 127–28.

141. Koselleck, "Time and History," 112–13.

142. I am referring to Deleuze's argument regarding Bergson's insight into the modernity of the cinema as the latter's discovery of the "any-instant-whatever." See Deleuze, *Cinema 1*, 3–4, 6.

143. Koselleck, "Time And History," 10.

144. Koselleck, "'Neuzeit,'" 232.

145. See Dipesh Chakrabarty's discussion in *Provincializing Europe*:

Marxist intellectuals of the West and their followers elsewhere have developed a diverse set of sophisticated strategies that allow them to acknowledge the evidence of "incompleteness" of capitalist transformation in Europe and other places while retaining the idea of a general historical movement from a premodern stage to that of modernity. These strategies include, first, the old and now discredited evolutionist paradigms of the nineteenth century—the language of "survivals" and "remnants"—sometimes found in Marx's own prose. But there are other strategies as well, and they are all variations on the theme of "uneven development"—itself derived, as Neil Smith shows, from Marx's use of the idea of "uneven rates of development" in his *Critique of Political Economy* (1859) and from Lenin's and Trotsky's later use of the concept. The point is, whether they speak of "uneven development," or Ernst Bloch's "synchronicity of the non-synchronous," or Althusserian "structural causality," these strategies all retain elements of historicism in the direction of their thought (in spite of Althusser's explicit opposition to historicism). They all ascribe at least an underlying structural unity (if not an expressive totality) to historical process and time that makes it possible to identify certain elements in the present as "anachronistic." The thesis of "uneven development" . . . goes "hand in hand" with the date grid of an homogeneous, empty time. (Chakrabarty, *Provincializing Europe*, 12)

"Field of differences" is a phrase I borrow from Chakrabarty's discussion (see *Provincializing Europe*, 76).

146. Koselleck, "'Neuzeit,'" 247–48, 256 (my emphasis).

147. Koselleck, "Time and History," 114.

148. Mignolo, "The Enduring Enchantment," 928.

149. Koselleck, "'Neuzeit,'" 249.

150. Quoted in O'Malley, *Keeping Watch*, 78.

151. Chakrabarty writes:

Historicism enabled European domination of the world in the nineteenth century. Crudely, one might say that it was one important form that the ideology of progress or "development" took from the nineteenth century on. Historicism is what made modernity or capitalism look not simply global but rather as something that became global over time, by originating in one place (Europe) and then spreading outside it. This "first in Europe, then elsewhere" structure of global historical time was historicist . . . posit[ing] historical time as a measure of the cultural distance (at least in institutional development) that was assumed to exist in the West and the non-West. (Chakrabarty, *Provincializing Europe*, 7)

152. Dussel, "Beyond Eurocentrism," 3–5 (my emphasis).

153. Fabian, *Time and the Other*, 11–12, 31.

154. Ibid., 143, 146.

155. Ibid., xi. "The history of our discipline reveals that such use of time almost invariably is made for the purpose of distancing those who are observed from the time of the observer" (ibid., 25).

156. Ibid., 17.

157. Koselleck, "'Neuzeit,'" 247.

158. Fabian writes: "A discourse employing terms such as primitive, savage (but

also tribal, traditional, Third World, or whatever euphemism is current) does not think, or observe, or critically study, the "primitive"; it thinks, observes, studies in terms of the primitive. Primitive being essentially a temporal concept, is a category, not an object, of Western thought" (Fabian, *Time and the Other*, 17–18).

159. Rony, *The Third Eye*, 6–8.

160. Ibid., 16, 133. Rony reads *King Kong* as popular cinema's reflexive literalization of the ethnographic imaginary: "The lineage of *King Kong* should be obvious: the filming, capture, exhibition, photographing, and finally murder of Kong takes its cue from the historic exploitation of native peoples as freakish "ethnographic" specimens by science, cinema, and popular culture. Critics have consistently passed lightly over the fact that, in the 1920s, Cooper and Schoedsack were well-known ethnographic filmmakers, producing and directing both *Grass* (1925) and *Chang* (1927). *King Kong*, moreover, begins with an expedition, fully equipped with film camera, to a remote tropical island: *King Kong* is literally a film about the making of an ethnographic film" (Rony, 159).

161. Ibid., 9.

162. Ibid., 46.

163. Ibid., 101.

164. Ibid., 126, 141.

165. Ibid., 91.

166. Habermas, *The Philosophical Discourse of Modernity*, 6–7.

167. Chakrabarty, *Provincializing Europe*, 244.

168. Ibid., 95.

169. Ibid., 238.

170. Ibid., 239.

171. See Todorov, *The Fantastic*, 24–40.

172. *On Cannibalism* [video recording], written, directed, and edited by Fatimah Tobing Rony (New York: Women Make Movies, 1994), 8 minutes, color.

173. Rony makes similar points in her book *The Third Eye*. Indeed, her experimental video *On Cannibalism* and her book's scholarly interruption of the ethnographic episteme are companion pieces that demand to be read and seen together. See Rony, *The Third Eye*, 3–17, 157–91.

174. McClintock, *Imperial Leather*, 27.

175. According to Esther Shub, "the intention was not so much to provide the facts, but to evaluate them from the standpoint of the revolutionary class. This is what made my films revolutionary and agitational—although they were composed of counter-revolutionary material" (quoted in Vlada Petric, "Esther Shub," 24).

176. I am using oppositional spectatorship here in the sense of bell hooks's pioneering conceptualization of the oppositional gaze. See bell hooks, "The Oppositional Gaze," 307–20.

177. Rony, *The Third Eye*, 4.

178. Ibid., 49.

179. See Fausto-Sterling, "Gender, Race, and Nation," 19–49. See also McClintock's discussion of scientific racism and the monogenetic/polygenetic debates, McClintock, *Imperial Leather*, 49–52.

180. *King Kong* has spawned a host of remakes, the most recent directed by Peter Jackson in 2005.

Chapter 2. The Fantastic as Temporal Translation

1. The orthography of the term *aswang* varies; *asuwang* and *asuang* are also used by other writers. I am adopting the usage of anthropologists and folklorists F. Landa Jocano, Richard Lieban, and Maximo Ramos, who note that *aswang* is a term used by the Visayans of Panay, the Cebuanos of Negros Oriental, the Waray of Samar and Eastern Leyte, and the Tagalogs of Luzon.

2. Pastor, "Manananggal Tales Bring Spine-Chilling Diversion from Polls," 10.

3. Ramos, *The Aswang Complex in Philippine Folklore*, xv–xvi.

4. Loarca, "Relación de las Islas Filipinas," 135; Vaño, "Folk Religion and Revolts in the Eastern Visayas," 40–41. Vaño writes of the Spanish motives for the colonial annexation of the Philippines: "She had three objectives: to have a base of operations for the conversion of China and Japan, to break the Portuguese monopoly of the lucrative spice trade, and to convert the natives to Christianity for employment as laborers or soldiers."

5. Ortiz, *Práctica del ministerio que siguen los religiosos del orden de N.S. Agustín en Filipinas*, 193. For comparison, the Blair and Robertson translation of Ortiz's text reads as follows: "That being ['the sorcerer called *usang*'] takes its position on the roof of the neighboring house and thence extends its tongue in the form of a thread, which it inserts through the anus of the child, and by that means sucks out its entrails and kills it" (Ortiz, "Superstitions and Beliefs of the Filipinos," 108).

6. According to Maximo Ramos, the Tagalog term *manananggal* is of Malay extraction: "fr. Malay *tanggal*, 'to detach,' plus a particle meaning 'one who is in the habit of or is expert at'" (Ramos, *The Aswang Complex in Philippine Folklore*, xviii–xix). In various folkloric and anthropological sources, other forms of the self-segmenting viscera sucker do not detach at the waist but at the neck (in Caticugan, Siquijor) or at the knees (in Atimonan, Quezon).

7. Todorov, *The Fantastic*, 82.

8. Cartwright, "Film and the Digital in Visual Studies," 7–8.

9. The full quote reads:

When history separated itself from story, it started indulging in accumulation and facts. Or it thought it could. . . . Story-writing becomes history-writing, and history quickly sets itself apart, consigning story to the realm of tale, legend, myth, fiction, literature. Then, since fictional and factual have come to a point where they mutually exclude each other, fiction, not infrequently, means lies, and fact, truth. . . . Literature and history once were / still are stories: this does not necessarily mean that the space they form is undifferentiated, but that this space can articulate on a different set of principles, one which may be said to stand outside the hierarchical realm of facts. (Trinh, *Woman, Native, Other*, 119–21)

10. Deleuze, *Bergsonism*, 16. Deleuze writes: "True freedom lies in a power to decide, to constitute problems themselves. . . . The truth is that in philosophy and even elsewhere it is a question of finding the problem and consequently of positing it, even more than of solving it. For a speculative problem is solved as soon as it is properly stated. By that I mean that its solution exists then, although it may remain hidden and, so to speak, covered up: The only thing left to do is to uncover it. But stating the problem is not simply uncovering, it is inventing" (*Bergsonism*, 15).

11. See Greenblatt, *Marvelous Possessions*, 6.

12. One example of a confusion between the fantastic and fantasy is found in Hume, *Fantasy and Mimesis*. Hume considers fantasy an impulse "as significant as the mimetic impulse" in the production of literature and defines *fantasy* as "any departure from consensus reality, an impulse native to literature and manifested in innumerable variations, from monster to metaphor." Hume's argument rests on dubious truisms about "human nature," but her central claim, which defines fantasy in relation to its other, reality, is typical of a critical tradition on the fantastic that views fiction and reality as unproblematically separable spheres. See Hume, *Fantasy and Mimesis*, xii, 21.

13. Cornwell identifies three understandings of fantasy that have been confused with the fantastic—fantasy as a wide, transgeneric quality, impulse, or mode; as relating to dreams; and as a type of "unambiguously supernatural" narrative, corresponding to Todorov's marvelous. He is particularly critical of the work of the following writers: Rosemary Jackson, who, in *Fantasy: The Literature of Subversion*, fails to distinguish between "fantasy" and the "fantastic as a mode"; Linda Hutcheon, who, in *Narcissistic Narrative*, writes that Todorov is talking about "fantasy literature"; and Kathryn Hume, who, in *Fantasy and Mimesis*, "seems to regard 'fantastic'" as the "adjectival form of 'fantasy' and as the opposite of 'real,'" and who "read[s] what are theories of 'the fantastic' (as a genre) as though they were in fact, or intention, theories of the concept of fantasy (as a whole)." See Cornwell, *The Literary Fantastic*, esp. 29–30.

14. Todorov's *The Fantastic: A Structural Approach to a Literary Genre* was completed in 1968 and first published in French in 1970. As Amy Ransom shows,

Todorov's formulation is "firmly rooted in the French tradition of confusion and uncertainty." Pierre-Georges Castex described the fantastic as a "brutal intrusion of mystery into the setting of real life," while for Roger Caillois it is "a bizarre, almost unbearable, eruption into the real world." For Louis Vax, "the fantastic is a moment of crisis" that interrupts "the reassuring world of everyday certainties." See Ransom, *The Feminine as Fantastic in the Conte fantastique*, 9–12.

15. Todorov, *The Fantastic*, 168, 175.

16. Jameson, *The Prison-House of Language*, 203, 216.

17. Ibid., 195, 200.

18. Monleón, *A Specter Is Haunting Europe*, 4.

19. Todorov's formulation of the fantastic is not the only account that relies on the notion of an implied reader. In *The Fantastic in Literature*, Eric Rabkin defines the fantastic as an "aesthetic shock" occasioned by an event that contradicts the ground rules of the narrative world. The reader Rabkin has in mind is a purely textual function: the "source of the fantastic depends not at all on the reader's perspectives on the world, but rather on the reader's willing participation in the text. . . . The fantastic can exist wholly within the world of language." Rabkin's implied reader possesses a competency that coincides perfectly with that of the actual reader. This competency is what Rabkin calls a grapholect: the textual signals of the fantastic "can be properly interpreted only by reference to the ground rules of the narrative world, ground rules that are foisted upon the reader in large part by his whole life's training in the reading of literature and its many grapholects" (Rabkin, *The Fantastic in Literature*, 6–12, 23–25).

Rabkin conceptualizes the reader's engagement solely as an application of the proper grapholect so as to decipher a meaning that is imputedly immanent to the text. Rabkin's theory attempts to exclude misreadings of the fantastic by a reader who lacks what Rabkin considers proper training; to do so, Rabkin's argument must rely on a self-enclosed notion of the text. Yet Rabkin undermines his own argument by referring to the training necessary for a correct reading of a grapholect. Such a requirement confounds any attempt to close the text off from the horizon of social history; a historical reader actualizes a contingent set of dispositions toward reading that are forged by lived experience.

20. Todorov, *The Fantastic*, 31.

21. Morash, "The Time is Out of Joint (O Cursèd Spite!)," 124.

22. Jameson, *The Prison-House of Language*, 26.

23. Todorov, *The Fantastic*, 20.

24. Jauss, *Toward an Aesthetic of Reception*, 18–19.

25. Jameson, "Magical Narratives," 135.

26. Carroll, *The Philosophy of Horror*, 12–42.

27. Jameson, "Magical Narratives," 136.

28. Altman, *Film/Genre*, 209.

29. Todorov, *The Fantastic*, 25, 46.

30. Ibid., 82.

31. Morash, "The Time is Out of Joint (O Cursèd Spite!)," 128.

32. Sandor, "Myths and the Fantastic," 343. For Tobin Siebers, the limits of Todorov's account are inherent to the structuralist approach: "Structuralist criticism in general circumvents the problem of supernaturalism, perhaps the most important question of nineteenth-century social science. Claude Lévi-Strauss, the founder of structuralism, ignores the question of the sacred in favor of relational analysis. . . . When Todorov expels the supernatural from the fantastic in favor of narrative codes, he is following the same structuralist tradition" (Siebers, *The Romantic Fantastic*, 36).

33. Monleón, *A Specter Is Haunting Europe*, 5.

34. Todorov, *The Fantastic*, 24.

35. Milton, "The Origin and Development of the Concept of Laws of Nature," 174–91.

36. Ibid., 195.

37. Daston, "The Nature of Nature in Early Modern Europe," 154. As Raymond Williams has pointed out, culture as a name for an abstract civilizing process comes into use only in the mid-eighteenth to nineteenth centuries. See Williams, "Culture," 87–88.

38. Daston and Park, *Wonders and the Order of Nature*, 192.

39. Daston, "The Nature of Nature in Early Modern Europe," 154.

40. Daston and Park, *Wonders and the Order of Nature*, 120–21.

41. Daston, "The Nature of Nature in Early Modern Europe," 154–58.

42. Daston and Park, *Wonders and the Order of Nature*, 14.

43. Ibid., 350–54.

44. In his modal analysis of medieval romance, Jameson identifies the key semantic codes of magical narratives as the opposition between good and evil. For the purposes of this study of the fantastic, I rework that proposition into a temporal binary of familiarity (homogeneous time) and otherness (immiscible times). See Jameson, "Magical Narratives," 139.

45. Siebers, *The Romantic Fantastic*, 33.

46. For example, the Italian Russianist Vittorio Strada calls the fantastic "a poetic reason born in the post-mythic age, an age in which the model of knowledge and of truth is constituted from an empirical and positive science, from the viewpoint of which myth, deprived of its symbolic significance, turns into pure superstition, or a primitive stage of knowledge — imperfect and superseded. . . . The fantastic is a poetic mythology of a disenchanted and demythologized world" (trans. and quoted in Cornwell, *The Literary Fantastic*, 20–21). In a similar vein, Mircea Eliade sees the

fantastic as a species of "mythic survival" in which magical thinking attempts to construct a meaningful world that shields humanity from the "terror of history." See Kleiner, "Mircea Eliade's Theory of the Fantastic," 13.

47. Freud, "The Uncanny," 247–48.

48. Chakrabarty, "The Time of History and the Times of Gods," 48–50.

49. Todorov, *The Fantastic*, 166, 160–61. The quote continues: "There is no need today to resort to the devil in order to speak of an excessive sexual desire, nor to resort to vampires in order to designate the attraction exerted by corpses: psychoanalysis, and the literature which is directly or indirectly inspired by it, deal with these matters in undisguised terms. The themes of fantastic literature have become, literally, the very themes of the psychological investigations of the last fifty years."

50. Ibid., 157–58.

51. Ibid., 158, 159.

52. Gayatri Spivak uses the phrase "contained alterity" in her discussion of uncanny translation. See Spivak, "The Politics of Translation," 181.

53. Sicam, "'Manananggal' Season," 31.

54. Tejero, "'Dugo! Dugo!' The Manananggal of Tondo," 4.

55. Sicam, "'Manananggal' Season," 31.

56. The temporal logic espoused by this journalist in 1992 is nearly identical to that employed by Maximo Ramos in the American scholarly journal *Western Folklore* in 1968. Ramos's article, "Belief in Ghouls in Contemporary Philippine Society," is caught in a conflicted temporal gesture: though Ramos begins by noting the persistence and contemporaneousness of such practices, his essay continually deploys historicist vocabulary. He writes, "Today, vestiges and variations of these beliefs and practices still exist." Such a statement skirts the tension between the current and the archaic, the denial of coevalness that happens between the two words of his opening phrase, the contemporaneity of "today" and the allochronism of "vestiges." See Ramos, "Belief in Ghouls in Contemporary Philippine Society," 189.

57. Two recent films in the franchise, *Shake, Rattle and Roll 2k5* (2005) and *Shake, Rattle and Roll 8* (2006), are by other directorial teams, but both featured aswang and vampires.

58. A writer for the *Sunday Inquirer*, for example, remarks: "Strange things happened, various sightings were seen, and for weeks now the people have been agog over this latest addition to Tondo's assorted malefactors. The tabloids are making a killing." Tejero, "'Dugo! Dugo!' The Manananggal of Tondo," 4.

59. Ibid., 7.

60. Previous misunderstandings of Méliès's *trucage* or cinematic trickery have been corrected: the stop-trick Méliès is famous for, once considered an in-camera practice of switching the camera on and off to effect a "magical" transformation

when film is projected (the girl turns into a bus) has been revealed as a substitution splice, that is, as a specifically cinematic manipulation. The belated recognition of the substitution splice points to Méliès's role as an important pioneer in the development of invisibility editing: for all the disruption and amazement caused by the substitution splice (an image turns into a living woman), this trickery operated against a ground of seamlessness. The surprising aspects of the trick were achieved through a smooth, technical polish that was the result of laborious editing and careful enframing (the unicity of the mise-en-scène). As Richard Abel and Elizabeth Ezra note, the double spectacle of the Méliès film is that which operates between the visible magician and the invisible apparatus. See Abel, *The Ciné Goes to Town*, 63; and Ezra, *Georges Méliès*, 27–29.

Méliès's films belong to what Tom Gunning calls the cinema of attractions. The attributes of the cinema of attractions—the direct solicitation of spectatorial engagement and, above all, the notion of the cinema as itself an attraction, in contradistinction to a voyeuristic spectator's diegetic absorption in a hermetically sealed world—come through with particular force in Méliès films, for two reasons: first, because of the recurring character of the magician or showman. Méliès as filmmaker-character is an exhibitionist of the first degree, an onscreen circus barker hawking his own wares. The second reason is because his films above all *display* the cinema: and it is this display of the newly discovered virtuosic capacities of the medium that takes center stage, before and above the scantily clad women, whether flying, vanishing, or freshly conjured in his films, and before and above the wondrous antics of the anthropomorphized celestial bodies, that winking moon for which he is best remembered. See Gunning, "The Cinema of Attractions," 57–58.

61. See "An Aswang Who Lured a College Student," told by a student from San Jose, Antique, in Ramos, *The Aswang Complex in Philippine Folklore*, 113. Tejero recounts a similar narrative from Iloilo: "Another case is the prewar tale of Tinyente Gemo, a *teniente del barrio* of Dueñas, Iloilo, who prepared to slaughter three sleeping female guests on the eve of the fiesta, but by mistake dropped his own daughter into the cauldron of boiling water" (Tejero, "'Dugo! Dugo!' The Manananggal of Tondo," 4, 6).

62. Lim, "The Politics of Horror," 84.

63. Aswang are not often associated with nuns, though Pertierra cites a similar account originating in Caticugan, in the Visayan province of Siquijor. During a typhoid epidemic, an aswang in the form of a headless nun preyed on the barrio. Pertierra cites the case as an example of the extraordinary adaptability of the aswang complex to diverse circumstances. Presumably, Pertierra is arguing that the aswang complex records the presence of religious orders dispensing medication during the typhoid epidemic; on the other hand, in view of Pertierra's argument that the aswang complex is a social idiom, the account could perhaps be read as

articulating a submerged suspicion of and resistance to Catholic missionary presence. See Pertierra, "Viscera-Suckers and Female Sociality," 329.

64. Sicam, "'Manananggal' Season," 31.

65. Fojas, "Manananggal," 35–36.

66. See Sobchack, "'Lounge Time.'"

67. Tejero, "'Dugo! Dugo!' The Manananggal of Tondo," 3.

68. Sicam, "'Manananggal' Season," 34.

69. Tejero writes: "And soon the creature went town hopping all over Metro Manila. Sightings have also been reported in Quezon City, Kalookan, Valenzuela, Mandaluyong, Marikina, Antipolo, Pasay" (Tejero, "'Dugo! Dugo!' The Manananggal of Tondo," 4).

70. Elliott Stein, "Manila's Angels," 50. For Joel David, *Maynila: Sa kuko ng liwanag* signals the emergence of what he dubs the "Second Golden Age" of Philippine cinema. See David, "A Second Golden Age (an Informal History)," 5.

71. Associated Press, "'Manananggal' Terrorizes Tondo Folks," 10.

72. Anderson, *Imagined Communities*, 35.

73. Ibid., 33.

74. Sicam, "'Manananggal' Season," 31.

75. Pastor, "Manananggal Tales Bring Spine-Chilling Diversion from Polls."

76. Zeitlin, *Historian of the Strange*, 46.

77. Dube, "Presence of Europe," 862–63.

78. Rolando B. Tolentino points out that Reynes was frequently cast as the "*probinsyana* (provincial)" who, "fresh out of the boat or bus . . . steps out of her transit vehicle in Manila—the city, site of urban cosmopolitanism and also the site of the national movie industry . . . When at the height of her fame, she was named "Star of the 90s," [and] her ethnic figure proliferated on the screen as the heroine in horror flicks; and later on, when her career was dwindling, as the *katulong* ([domestic] helper) with a thick Cebuana accent. Her ethnicity would become one of the reasons for being the abject figure in horror films" (Tolentino, "Media and Ethnicity," iii). Tolentino's analysis of Reynes as an ethnically-marked figure in popular Philippine cinema emphasizes abjection, an interpretation that is certainly borne out by several of Reynes's horror film roles. In *Aswang*, however, Reynes's Veron is upheld as the virtuous, imperiled, and finally, triumphant heroine whose devotion to the child under her care saves the latter from malevolent forces in both city and province.

79. Tejero, "'Dugo! Dugo!' The Manananggal of Tondo," 4; also in Sicam, "'Manananggal' Season," 31, 34.

80. Pertierra, "Viscera-Suckers and Female Sociality," 333–34.

81. F. Landa Jocano, interviewed in Tejero, "'Dugo! Dugo!' The Manananggal of Tondo," 6–7.

82. Balce, "Manananggal," 42–44.

83. Ibid., 44.

84. Lynch, "An Mga Asuwang," 184. Lynch was an American Jesuit priest who in 1960 founded the Ateneo de Manila's Department of Sociology and Anthropology and the Institute of Philippine Culture at the same university.

85. Ibid., 198–99.

86. According to Jocano, "One of the underlying principles in child training and adult orientation to the norms of Malitbog society is the development of individuals who are easily controlled. . . . [Supernatural agents] cause illness and misfortune to those who do not observe the rules of conduct; they reward those who are obedient and faithful. . . . The pattern of social life is fixed because it is part of the general order of the universe, and even if this were hardly understood and regarded as mysterious, it is nevertheless accepted as invariant and regular" (Jocano, *Growing Up in a Philippine Barrio*, 104, 109).

87. Pertierra, "Viscera-Suckers and Female Sociality," 319–20, 323.

88. Sicam, "'Manananggal' Season," 34.

89. Trinh, *Woman, Native, Other*, 119–21.

90. In an earlier article on the aswang, I had espoused just such a secular, disenchanted view of aswang as a form of mystification: "If occult figures like the aswang gain currency in the cinema because of a peripheral protest articulated in magical idiom against projections of the dominant, does this challenge to domination not lapse into alienation as well? . . . Penetrating the obfuscatory representation of modernity as separate from magic and the privileged metropolitan elite as benefactors of the excluded masses, the aswang figure dissolves mystificatory borders but involves a half-forgetfulness of the relation of its critique to the real" (Lim, "The Politics of Horror," 97).

91. Comaroff and Comaroff, "Alien-Nation," 782, 787.

92. Ibid., 780–81, 783, 785, 793–94.

93. Ibid., 782, 785.

94. Ibid., 782, 792.

95. Ibid., 784, 787–88.

96. Ibid., 797–99.

97. Chakrabarty, *Provincializing Europe*, 62–64, 69.

98. Loarca, "Relación de las Islas Filipinas," 129–35.

99. Ramos, "Belief in Ghouls in Contemporary Philippine Society," 184–87. Ramos is referring to *The Robertson Translation of the Pavon Manuscripts of 1838–1839* (Chicago, 1957), transcript no. 5-d, p. 34. Quoted in Ramos, 186.

100. Meñez, "The Viscera-Sucker and the Politics of Gender." In pursuing this line of interpretation, Meñez explicitly challenges Pertierra's structuralist reading of viscera suckers as expressive of the gendered spheres of public and private in Filipino societies. For Pertierra, the aswang complex derives from the patriarchal

ordering of public social life as the domain of men and the domestic sphere as the realm of women; the aswang articulates the fear of what women might accomplish covertly, in private (e.g., causing the death of children or spouses). Pertierra, "Viscera-Suckers and Female Sociality," 330–35. According to Meñez, however, Pertierra does not consider that the gendered dichotomy of public and private was not inherent to indigenous societies, in which native priestesses or *baylanes* wielded significant religious, political, and sexual power. The gendered dichotomy Pertierra presumes may be, in part, a historical consequence of Spanish evangelists' struggle to stamp out indigenous resistance.

101. Meñez, "The Viscera-Sucker and the Politics of Gender," 87, 90–94.

102. Ibid., 93. Historical accounts of baylan-led revolts against the Spanish in Cebu support Meñez's claims. Manolo Vaño writes that uprisings in 1621 in Bohol and 1622 in Leyte were led by male baylanes (Vaño, "Folk Religion and Revolts in the Eastern Visayas," 48). According to Mario Bolasco, "Following Spanish cooptation of datu leadership, a significant recomposition of the babaylan took place; previously predominantly female, men took over religious leadership. All the babaylan revolt leaders [in the Visayas] were male, indicating that these movements may have recreated the magical datu war leader from the elements of a once coherent magical world view" (Bolasco, *Points of Departure*, 222).

103. Meñez, "The Viscera-Sucker and the Politics of Gender," 87.

104. Plasencia, "Los costumbres de los Tagalogs," 192–96.

105. Greenblatt, *Marvelous Possessions*, 8, 12–13, 15.

106. Early missionary accounts of the Philippines exemplified what Walter D. Mignolo calls the "ethnoracial foundation" of sixteenth-century to eighteenth-century writing that represented the colonies as enchanted in relation to the imperial center: "In 'modern space,' epistemology was first Christian and then White. In 'enchanted places,' wisdom, and not epistemology, was first non-Christian (and this was one of the reasons why Christianity remained complicit with its critics, the secular philosophers) and later on, of color" (Mignolo, "The Enduring Enchantment," 934–35).

107. Greenblatt, *Marvelous Possessions*, 6.

108. Ibid.

109. See Nashel, *Edward Lansdale's Cold War*, 25–48.

110. I discuss the Huks in more detail in chapter 3.

111. Nashel, *Edward Lansdale's Cold War*, 3, 38, 44.

112. Ibid., 39–41. See also Lansdale's autobiographical account of his "asuang psywar" campaign against the Huks (Lansdale, *In the Midst of Wars*, 72–73).

113. Sicam, "'Manananggal' Season," 31; see also Tejero, "'Dugo! Dugo!' The Manananggal of Tondo," 4.

114. Ramos, *Creatures of Philippine Lower Mythology*, 116.

115. Clavel, "Philippine Revolution in Capiz," 26.

116. Anderson, *Imagined Communities*, 5–7, 24.

117. Ibid., 33.

118. Because "few states contain coherent historically stable communities of shared descent," a form of "symbolic maintenance" on the part of the state is necessary, imposing coherence not only spatially (on "territorial space") but also temporally (via "historical narratives"). See Shapiro, "National Times and Other Times," 79–80.

119. Anderson, *Imagined Communities*, 166.

120. Ibid., 175.

121. The national premise was a serious limitation of Pertierra's approach to the gender politics of the viscera sucker. Pertierra assumes the equivalence of ethnos and nation in order to claim that the Philippines presents a homogeneous cultural field that makes it a fit object for ethnological study. In contrast, Meñez seriously engages the implications of the fact that aswang and baylan "predate" the nation and that these figures might have been seriously transformed by responses to colonial rule. See Pertierra, "Viscera-Suckers and Female Sociality," 319.

122. Jauss, *Toward an Aesthetic of Reception*, 20–21.

123. Cartwright, "Film and the Digital in Visual Studies," 7–8.

124. Ibid., 16–22.

125. I am using Jauss's notion of the literary event—"a literary event can continue to have an effect only if those who come after it still or once again respond to it—if there are readers who again appropriate the past work or authors who want to imitate, outdo, or refute it"—with the caveat that the eventfulness of the aswang is not solely literary. Jauss, *Toward an Aesthetic of Reception*, 22.

126. Dube, "Presence of Europe," 863.

127. Ibid., 862.

Chapter 3. Spectral Time, Heterogeneous Space

1. In an earlier version of this article (see Lim, "Spectral Times: The Ghost Film as Historical Allegory"), I wrote about my desire to retool or radicalize Bloch's concept of nonsynchronism, defined in his 1932 essay as "unsurmounted remnants of older economic being and consciousness," a concept derived from Marx's idea of "unequal rates of development" (Bloch, "Nonsynchronism and the Obligation to Its Dialectics," 22). In my earlier work I asked, "Is it possible or even viable to rescue the concept of noncontemporaneity from its kinship with the notion of progress in order to forge a different conception of history? Can we redeem the insights of nonsynchronism from the elitism of modernity's consciousness of time?" Yet in reconsidering my earlier argument, it now seems to me that the concept of nonsynchronism would be difficult to radicalize, being too much of a piece with the

various forms of temporal exclusions (anachronism, historicism, noncontempo-raneousness, and the denial of coevalness) that Koselleck, Chakrabarty, and Fabian call attention to. Hence, in this book I advocate a different means of pursuing the critique of homogeneous time: not via the radicalization of Bloch's concept of non-synchronism but by conceptualizing fantastic cinema as a mode of temporal trans-lation that points up the untranslatability of the immiscible temporalities at its core. See Lim, "Spectral Times," 297.

2. Fabian, *Time and the Other*, 34.

3. Important critical definitions and descriptions of the New Hong Kong Cinema and the Hong Kong New Wave include Abbas, *Hong Kong*; Law Kar, "An Overview of Hong Kong's New Wave Cinema"; Teo, *Hong Kong Cinema*; and Li Cheuk-to, Sek Kei, and Law Wai-ming, "Three Critics Sum up the Hong Kong New Wave."

4. The script for *Haplos* was one of four prizewinners written by Lee in the first ECP script writing contest in 1981, along with *Himala* [Miracle], *Bulag* [Blind], and *Bukas may pangarap* [Tomorrow There Is Hope]. *Himala* (directed by Ishmael Bernal, 1982) was produced by the ECP, while *Haplos* garnered partial funding. For an account of cultural policy in the ECP see David, "A Cultural Policy Experience in Philippine Cinema."

5. See David, "A Second Golden Age (an Informal History)"; and David, *Fields of Vision*.

6. Of justice as a matter of *being-with* specters, Derrida writes: "The time of the 'learning to live,' a time without tutelary present, would amount to this . . . : to learn to live *with* ghosts, in the upkeep, the conversation, the company, or the companionship, in the commerce without commerce of ghosts. To live otherwise, and better. No, not better, but more justly. But *with them*. No *being-with* the other, no *socius* without this *with* that makes *being-with* in general more enigmatic than ever for us. And this being-with specters would also be, not only but also, a *politics* of memory, of inheritance, and of generations" (Derrida, *Specters of Marx*, xviii–xix; Derrida's emphasis).

According to Benjamin, "the past carries with it a temporal index by which it is referred to redemption. . . . Like every generation that preceded us, we have been endowed with a *weak* Messianic power, a power to which the past has a claim. That claim cannot be settled cheaply. Historical materialists are aware of that" (Benjamin, "Theses on the Philosophy of History," 254).

7. Chakrabarty, *Provincializing Europe*, 73.

8. Derrida, *Specters of Marx*, 11.

9. Ibid., xviii–xix.

10. Ibid., 17–18.

11. Ibid., xx.

12. Jameson, "Marx's Purloined Letter," 38.

13. Bergson, *Time and Free Will*, 76–79, 90–91.

14. Ibid., 98–99.

15. Ibid., 231.

16. Ibid., 95–97.

17. Bergson, *Matter and Memory*, 280.

18. Ibid., 241–44.

19. Ibid., 280–82.

20. Bergson, *Time and Free Will*, 97.

21. "Every clear idea of number implies a visual image in space" (Bergson, *Time and Free Will*, 79).

22. Bergson, *Matter and Memory*, 259–60.

23. See ibid., 289–93.

24. Bogue, *Deleuze on Cinema*, 16.

25. Bergson, *Matter and Memory*, 264–65.

26. For Abbas, the port city that is Hong Kong is a space marked by "a weakening of the sense of chronology, of historical sequentiality, so that old and new are easily contemporaneous and continuities and discontinuities exist side by side . . . [in a] kind of spatial palimpsest" (Abbas, "Building on Disappearance," 448).

27. Owens, "The Allegorical Impulse," 68–69.

28. Abbas, "Building on Disappearance," 452.

29. Benjamin, *The Origin of German Tragic Drama*, 177–79.

30. Ibid., 182.

31. Jameson, *The Political Unconscious*, 29–30. For Benjamin's views on allegory's temporality see Buck-Morss, *The Dialectics of Seeing*, 165–68.

32. The term was coined by Alsatian Johannes Hofer in a medical thesis written in 1688. See Vromen, "The Ambiguity of Nostalgia," 70–71.

33. Steinwand, "The Future of Nostalgia in Friedrich Schlegel's Gender Theory," 9–10.

34. Appadurai, "Consumption, Duration, and History," 36.

35. Benjamin, "Theses on the Philosophy of History," 261.

36. Benjamin, *The Origin of German Tragic Drama*, 166.

37. In *The Origin of German Tragic Drama*, as translated by Buck-Morss, Benjamin writes: "The greater the meaning, the greater the subjection to death, because death digs out most deeply the jagged line of demarcation between physical nature and meaning" (Buck-Morss, *The Dialectics of Seeing*, 161). Samuel Weber writes:

> The allegorist picks up where death leaves off, with a nature that is historical in passing away, and natural in its endurance and recurrence. Death is at work in allegory however not just as decline and decay, but more intimately, as that which separates each thing from itself: from its essence and from its significance. . . . [Benjamin writes:] "If the object becomes allegorical when submitted to the

glance of melancholy, which drains the life from it, if it remains dead, albeit assured for all eternity, it is all the more at the mercy of the allegorist. . . . It acquires the significance that the allegorist gives it. He lays it into and lays into it: this must be understood not psychologically, but ontologically. In his hand the thing becomes something else. (Weber, "Genealogy of Modernity," 496–97)

38. See Chow's discussion of the relationships between death, temporality, and the filmic image in the writing of Pier Paolo Pasolini. Chow, *Primitive Passions*, 32 and 41.

39. Rey Chow writes that Fleur in *Rouge* espouses a "cyclical" view of time, in contrast to the contemporary journalists' "linear," "uni-directional," and "irreversible" view of time: "Ruhua alludes to her past and future as if the meaning of her life, rather than beginning and ending at any one point, was repeating and recurring continually. A feeling of cyclical time . . . in which the debts of the past may be paid in the present, and in which unfinished events of the present may be completed in the future, accompanies Ruhua's endeavor of returning from the dead." Conversely, the journalists are "bound to their time . . . acutely conscious of time as a limit" (Chow, "A Souvenir of Love," 66).

40. Vera, "Butch Perez: Portrait of the Director as a Perfect Gentleman."

41. Bliss Cua Lim, telephone interview with Antonio "Butch" Perez, April 1, 2008.

42. According to the director, the fictional town of Buendia was a "composite" of four or five towns in the Quezon-Laguna area of the southern Tagalog region, where *Haplos* was filmed. The church scenes were shot in Pakil; river scenes, with Mt. Banahaw (a mountain sacred to various Rizalista cults) prominent in the background, were shot on the Pagsanjan River; lastly, scenes in Auring's enchanted forest house were shot in an ancestral house by the national highway in Candelaria, Quezon (Lim, telephone interview with Antonio "Butch" Perez, April 1, 2008). In another interview, Perez relates that the town of Buendia was named for the Buendia family in Gabriel Garcia Marquez's novel *One Hundred Years of Solitude* (Bliss Cua Lim, personal interview with Antonio "Butch" Perez, April 4, 2008).

43. *Pagbabalik*, or "return," which in *Haplos* is also used to describe the phantom Auring ("isang gabi, siya'y nagbalik"), is closely associated with the nearest rendering for "nostalgia" in Tagalog: *pag-asam* (longing), as in "pag-asam na makabalik sa sariling bayan" [the longing to return to one's homeland] (Fr. Leo James English's example in his *English-Tagalog Dictionary* [1977]).

44. I borrow this line from Dai Jinhua's characterization of nostalgia in a story by Wang Shuo. See Dai, "Imagined Nostalgia," 145.

45. When Cristy tells Al about her work with the population commission, Al notes that she is still a committed leftist, but she demurs (since she is working for government now), though she says she is still socially committed. Her move from

the student left to population-control work would have been seen by some Philippine leftists as suspect, since population control is considered to deflect an analysis of poverty onto state regulation of sexuality, blaming social inequities on numbers rather than the inequitable distribution of resources. On the other hand, Cristy's work could also be viewed as women-positive to a certain extent and subversive of the dictates of the Catholic Church, which discourages any birth control options other than structured abstinence.

46. The point of Al's dark witticisms — "brain drain" (the best minds of the Philippines leaving to work in other countries) and "Filipinos for export" (shorthand for the immense profits [dollar remittances] generated by overseas labor, at the cost of making Filipinos themselves an export commodity) — is that economically motivated migration to other countries might be the most effective way of thinning the Philippine population.

47. The director relates that he and the production designer of *Haplos*, Laida Lim Perez, deliberately costumed Auring's character in the garb of the *cofradias* (female members of lay religious groups prominent in the late nineteenth century and early twentieth) in her introductory scene. The white dress, blue sash, and corsage all call to mind the appearance of devout Catholic Filipinas in earlier times (Lim, personal interview with Antonio "Butch" Perez, April 4, 2008).

48. In a telephone interview, the director relates that the possession ending belongs to the television broadcast version of *Haplos*, the version I screened for this chapter. Several alternative endings, though, were conceived (see Lee's remarks on the final scene in the following note). Perez intended the film to close not with Al and Cristy's final embrace but with the townspeople finding their corpses in the aftermath of a storm: as Perez puts it, "the river claimed them." The producers objected to this ending, which would have killed off characters played by the film's two box-office superstars, Vilma Santos and Christopher de Leon. For this reason, the theatrical release version ends with what Perez calls the "effluvial funeral" of Mang Ilyong, Auring's wartime sweetheart, who perished in the scene's climactic parallel editing scene, a funeral attended by Cristy and Al. The narrative closures of both versions make prominent use of the river, which Perez sees as a "character in itself." He expects spectators familiar with Philippine folklore to have understood that both versions of the final scene (in which death, the river, and other water motifs are prominent) imply that Auring, as *diwata* (a beautiful fairy maiden) of both river and forest, had claimed the living (Lim, telephone interview with Antonio "Butch" Perez, April 1, 2008). Perez also added that Ilyong's drowning was the occasion for the director's own cameo, in keeping with Alfred Hitchcock's well-known practice of appearing briefly in his own films. When Ilyong drowns in *Haplos*, his arm extended for help, it is Perez's arm we see, not that of actor Eddie Infante, who played Ilyong in the film (Lim, personal interview with Antonio "Butch" Perez, April 4, 2008).

49. Ricardo Lee, the script writer of *Haplos*, has remarked that the ending in which Cristy takes on Auring's persona is consistent with an earlier version of the script. In that version, Cristy is not a population commission worker but a young theater student, an actress for whom "there is no boundary between the imagination and physical reality," so that allowing Auring to inhabit her person was just an extension of what she was trained to do as an actress. Lee originally envisioned a young actress, Amy Austria, for the role of Cristy. When Vilma Santos was cast instead, Cristy's character was rewritten for a somewhat older woman. Lee had also envisioned the ending as an explicit ménage à trois in which Cristy and Al, who reconcile by sleeping together, are joined by the ghost, but this ending was also rewritten in keeping with Vilma Santos's star persona. Ghost possession, then, can be said to veil the overtly sexual intention of Lee's earlier draft (Joel David and Bliss Cua Lim, telephone interview with Ricardo Lee, September 12, 1999).

50. Hollywood examples of this genre include Robert Altman's *Nashville* (1975) and *Short Cuts* (1994). See David, "The Multiple-Character Format."

51. In later years, shifts in Filipino/a labor migration trends would see an increase in female overseas workers destined for employment in Hong Kong, Japan, and Singapore, while male migrant workers continued to seek work in the Middle East. In both cases the Philippine government, which benefited crucially from the dollar remittances of Filipino/a labor-for-export, failed to systematically protect the rights of these vulnerable workers in foreign nations. See Margold, "Narratives of Masculinity and Transnational Migration," 275–76, 284–88.

52. Margold writes: "In the Ilocos (and elsewhere in Southeast Asia), male status had long derived not from the sexual division of labor but from the cosmopolitan knowledge that men gleaned from their regional and international journeys. Remarkably, male migrants to the Middle East had hardly spoken publicly of their trips. Even wives were often surprised to hear the details that emerged during my interviews with the men. . . . By remaining silent about the humiliations they had endured overseas, the men could trade upon the cultural notion that foreign travel had imbued them with new social and political skills" (Margold, "Narratives of Masculinity and Transnational Migration," 292).

53. In addition, the director, as noted above, has spoken of Auring as a kind of *diwata* of both the river and the woods. The diwata's place-bound aspect and her feminine beauty are shared attributes with the ingkanto or ingkantada. In an interview, Perez called attention to an establishing shot of a local store named "Diwatas" in *Haplos*, which underscores the diwata motif. Perez also stated that he considers the notion of "ingkanto" or "ingkantada" to be a later, near-synonymous variant of the precolonial "diwata" (Lim, personal interview with Antonio "Butch" Perez, April 4, 2008).

54. Meñez, "Mythology and the 'Ingkanto' Syndrome," 65–66.

55. In the contest of wills with an ingkanto, it is thought that if the mortal suc-

cumbs to the spirit's seduction, his or her consciousness becomes captive (*nabi-hag na dungan*), and the mortal is lost to the human realm. The process of healing and rescuing the victim from the grip of the specter involves delivering his or her consciousness from this otherworldly control, and propitiating the spirit for the welfare of the victim. See Meñez, "Mythology and the 'Ingkanto' Syndrome," 66, 71–72.

56. Saulo, *Communism in the Philippines*, 29–31.

57. See Kerkvliet, *The Huk Rebellion*, 61–118.

58. I am indebted to Joel David for pointing out the resonances of the term *hapon* years ago, when I first began to write about *Haplos*. The director has also pointed out the same linguistic slippage of *hapon* as standing for the PC in NPA parlance, indicating that the multitiered significations of this term were known to the filmmakers (Lim, personal interview with Antonio "Butch" Perez, April 4, 2008).

59. Joel David and Bliss Cua Lim, telephone interview with Ricardo Lee, September 12, 1999.

60. Lim, personal interview with Antonio "Butch" Perez, April 4, 2008.

61. Joel David and Bliss Cua Lim, telephone interview with Ricardo Lee, September 12, 1999.

62. Recall Gerard Genette's idea of tense as composed of order (sequence of events), duration (length of events), and frequency (singular or iterative mention of events) in the time of the narrative discourse as compared to the temporality of the story told. In film studies, Genette's postulates concerning narrative have been applied by Tom Gunning to an analysis of what the latter calls the "narrator system" of the classical Hollywood text. The emphasis Genette and Roland Barthes place on temporality and spatial orientation in the linear trajectory of narrative discourse and diegesis corresponds in Gunning's schema to editing, which he defines as the filmic equivalent of tense in verbal language, while focalization (the perspective that orients the narration) translates as point-of-view editing. See Genette, *Narrative Discourse*; Gunning, *D. W. Griffith and the Origins of American Narrative Film*, 10–30; and Barthes, *S/Z*.

63. Barthes, *Camera Lucida*, 96–97.

64. Derrida, *Specters of Marx*, 10.

65. Benjamin, "Theses on the Philosophy of History," 263.

66. My thoughts on the film are greatly indebted to Chow's discussion of the film and the novella on which it was based, *Yanzhi kou*, by Li Bihua. Chow has pointed out that the romance at the heart of *Rouge* is very much in keeping with the plot of early twentieth-century Mandarin Duck and Butterfly novels (*Rouge* adopts the following conventions of the said novels: the love story between a courtesan and a well-bred young man, the faithfulness of the heroine, the tragic result). See Chow, "A Souvenir of Love," 65–67.

67. Ibid., 65.

68. Teo, *Hong Kong Cinema*, 190.

69. Bordwell and Thompson, *Film Art*, 234–40.

70. Abbas, *Hong Kong*, 26.

71. Bergson, *Creative Evolution*, 2–3.

72. Ibid., 2.

73. Chow, "A Souvenir of Love," 71–72.

74. Benjamin, *The Origin of German Tragic Drama*, 174–75. On allegory as a public secret see Miller, "The Two Allegories," 356–57. In a similar vein, Angus Fletcher argues that the presence of allegory does not depend on whether or not every reader can recognize its doubled meaning:

> The whole point of allegory is that it does not need to be read exegetically; it often has a literal level that makes good enough sense all by itself. But somehow this literal surface suggests a peculiar doubleness of intention. . . . We must avoid the notion that all people must see the double meaning for the work to be rightly called allegory. At least one branch of allegory, the ironic *aenigma*, serves political and social purposes by the very fact that a reigning authority (as in a police state) does not see the secondary meaning of the "Aesop language." But someone does see that meaning, and, once seen, it is felt strongly to be the final intention behind the primary meaning. (Fletcher, *Allegory*, 7–8)

75. Miller, "The Two Allegories," 358.

76. Lai defines enigmatization as follows: "the selection and reorganization of existing images from popular culture in order to distinctly select the local audience as a privileged hermeneutic community, thus facilitating a state of internal dialogue, distinguishing those within from the 'outsiders' by marking who partakes in a shared history of popular culture." Lai's argument refers specifically to Hong Kong cinema's 1990s nostalgia films and the nonsense comedies of Stephen Chiau. See Lai, "Film and Enigmatization," 232.

77. Yu, "'Rest, Rest, Perturbed Spirit!'" 415–16, 423.

78. Judith T. Zeitlin cites *The Peony Pavilion or the Soul's Return* (1598) as emblematic of this trend. See Zeitlin, "Embodying the Disembodied," 242.

79. Ibid., 243–44.

80. Ropp, "Ambiguous Images of Courtesan Culture in Late Imperial China," 25–31.

81. Wai-yee Li, "The Late Ming Courtesan," 47.

82. See Ropp, "Ambiguous Images of Courtesan Culture in Late Imperial China," 21.

83. Owens, "The Allegorical Impulse," 76.

84. Auring's wartime violation in the forest evokes the victimization of "comfort

women" in Southeast Asian countries occupied by the Japanese Imperial Army in World War II. This issue reemerged explosively in the late 1990s as Taiwan, South Korea, and the Philippines demanded that Japan make reparations for these wartime atrocities against comfort women and correct distortions in Japanese schoolbook accounts of the war. Similarly, Al's feminization as a migrant worker in the Gulf in the early 1980s foreshadows the subsequent economic and sexual abuse of female overseas Filipino workers (OFWs) in neighboring Asian countries. In later years the numbers of female OFWs would far outpace those of male migrant workers, as the Philippines became the second largest exporter of human labor in the world and as Filipinas themselves became the nation's main export commodity. See Tigno, "Ties That Bind," 1–6.

85. Derrida, *Specters of Marx*, xix.

86. Quoted in Fritzman, "The Future of Nostalgia and the Time of the Sublime," 170.

87. See Habermas, *The Philosophical Discourse of Modernity*, 11–13.

88. Ibid., 13–16.

89. Benjamin, "Theses on the Philosophy of History," 255, 263.

90. Fritzman, "The Future of Nostalgia and the Time of the Sublime," 186. This is Fritzman's gloss on Benjamin's pronouncement, in "Theses on the Philosophy of History," that the working class must not "forget both its hatred and its spirit of sacrifice, for both are nourished by the image of enslaved ancestors rather than that of liberated grandchildren" (Benjamin, "Theses on the Philosophy of History," 260).

91. Anderson, *Imagined Communities*, 5, 11.

92. McClintock, "'No Longer in a Future Heaven,'" 89–92.

93. Dai, "Imagined Nostalgia," 145.

94. See Sek Kei, "The Wandering Spook," 13–16.

95. Sek Kei writes, "If martial arts films [were] the Hong Kong cinema's flesh and blood in the seventies, then Horror films have occupied its soul in the eighties. . . . [Hong Kong] people have suddenly realized that a spectre is haunting their city — the spectre of 1997, the year when the city's sovereignty returns to Communist China" (Sek Kei, "The Wandering Spook," 13–15).

96. Eng, "Love at Last Site," 76, 94–95. Similarly, Abbas sees the ghost story deployed in *Rouge* as a narrative device that allows divergent times and spaces in Hong Kong's history to coalesce in a "historical montage." See Abbas, "The New Hong Kong Cinema and the Deja Disparu," 75. An allegorical interpretation of transmigration and reincarnation in *Rouge* also emerges in Audrey Yue's reading of the film. For Yue, "Buddhist themes of transmigration" are a figuration of "the passage of Hong Kong-in-transition, where the narrative of the homeless female ghost becomes a narrative about the quest for home," staging Hong Kong's "dilemma of homelessness" (Yue, "Preposterous Hong Kong Horror," 366–67).

97. Chow, "King Kong in Hong Kong," 102–103.

98. Abbas writes:

By the same logic, the only form of political idealism that has a chance is that which can go together with economic self-interest, when "freedom," for example, could be made synonymous with the "free market." This is, I believe, how one can understand the unprecedented mass demonstrations over the Tiananmen Massacre by the hundreds of thousands of the middle class who had never before marched in the streets. June 1989 in Hong Kong was a rare moment when economic self-interest could so easily misrecognize itself as political idealism. There was certainly genuine emotion and outrage, which does not preclude the possibility that many of the marchers were moved by how much they were moved. (*Hong Kong*, 5)

99. Chow, "King Kong in Hong Kong," 103, 105.

100. "In relation to history, the status-quo imaginary hence pre-conditions a collective understanding of history as a linear development which is marked by visible temporal divides with each phase of deprivation and impoverishment (as in the 60s), the replacement of anxiety and despair (as in the 80s) by 'progress' achieved in the present" (Chu, "The Ambivalence of History," 333).

101. Ibid., 332–34. Linda Lai makes a similar point about another Peter Chan nostalgia film, *Comrades, Almost a Love Story*, which Lai reads as an allegory of the Hong Kong citizen's path to "economic progress, the most widely perpetuated 'Hong Kong story' in all public dominant discourses," rehearsing tropes of Hong Kong's myth of personal success as economic progress: "the integral components of the typical Hong Kong legend, such as overnight success, overnight downfall, economic opportunities for all, flexibility in crisis management, and so on" (Lai, "Film and Enigmatization," 241–42).

102. Abbas, *Hong Kong*, 6–7.

103. Abbas, "Hong Kong: Other Histories," 285. Also see Yau, "The Full Emptiness of the Decolonization Event," for Esther Yau's reading of the handover and the inherent latency and protracted nature of the historical event.

104. Chow, "Between Colonizers," 153–56, 158.

105. Chow, "Can One Say No to China?" 151.

106. Chu, *Hong Kong Cinema*, 49.

107. Chun, "Fuck Chineseness," 111, 114, 117.

108. Ibid., 115.

109. Chu, *Hong Kong Cinema*, 58–59. Other scholars have made similar arguments with regard to Hong Kong's singularity as a nonnational entity. Marchetti, for example, points out that Hong Kong is plugged into the global without ever having been national: "This part of the project of modernity is missing from Hong Kong's history. It has never been a nation or an independent state with a uniquely defined

precolonial past. Perhaps this is what makes the city postmodern: It easily bypasses the national and has always, already been part of the global in terms of economic relationships and cultural formations" (Marchetti, "Buying American, Consuming Hong Kong," 302).

110. As many commentators have pointed out, the Hong Kong New Wave was not an organized film movement in which directors explicitly articulated and adhered to a common filmic vision. The various filmmakers did share a mutual experiential horizon (their background in television), and audiences responded to their treatment of contemporary Hong Kong concerns (a critical localism). Yet beyond this, the Hong Kong New Wave was crucially shaped by a cinephilic critical public sphere that began to take form in the 1960s and 1970s. The Hong Kong New Wave was as much a corpus of important works by key filmmakers as a horizon of critical practice and interpretation that had its own set of interrelated axioms: first, the critical preference for art cinema over commercial mainstream film; second, auteurism fashioned after Euro-American antecedents; and third, a reflectionist preference for localism rooted in the critics' ethical commitment to a socially responsible cinema. But this emphasis on localist realism was accompanied by a preference for cosmopolitan auteurs. The critical emphasis on art cinema vis-à-vis the New Wave directors led to a fourth critical trope: "widespread disappointment with its eventual evolution" as a result of the New Wave filmmakers' perceived "failure to break away from the traditions of Hong Kong commercialism." Hence the New Wave is, for these critics, exceedingly short-lived (a four- or five-year period beginning in 1979). From an alternate perspective, however, I would suggest that the brevity of this film movement represents a conspicuous example of the lack of fit between critical and film-industrial practice. The critical constitution of the Hong Kong New Wave appears, in retrospect, to itself be cloaked in nostalgia, as the earliest years of the New Wave represent a short-lived "golden age" when traits much valorized by the film culture field found fleeting expression onscreen. See Rodriguez, "The Emergence of the Hong Kong New Wave," 54–64, 67.

111. Cheung and Chu, "Introduction: Between Home and World," xix–xxii.

112. Ibid., xxiii–xxv.

113. Berry writes: "The variety of such significations itself belies their frequent significations of 'China' as singular, essential, and naturalized, revealing instead not that 'China' is a nonexistent fiction but that it is a discursively produced and socially and historically contingent collective entity. In this sense, it is not so much China that makes movies but movies that help to make China" (Berry, "If China Can Say No, Can China Make Movies?" 160).

114. Abbas, "Hong Kong: Other Histories," 284.

115. Abbas, *Hong Kong*, 33.

Chapter 4. The Ghostliness of Genre

1. For Bergson, heterogeneous duration means that exact repetition is impossible and that the future is completely unforeseeable. Because our personality "changes without ceasing," this nonidenticality of self to self "prevents any state, although superficially identical with another, from ever repeating in its very depth." The same thing could not happen twice because it could not happen to the same person or in the same universe, since everything changes incessantly. See Bergson, *Creative Evolution*, 4–6.

2. Gledhill, "Rethinking Genre," 226–27.

3. Toby Miller et al.'s influential analysis of "global Hollywood" develops several key themes: the accelerating speed of American popular culture's dissemination and dominance throughout the world, resulting in the homogenization of cultural products and practices as well as the ownership and control of media conglomerates. Miller et al. write: "The source of Hollywood's power extends far beyond the history of cinema, to the cultural-communications complex that has been an integral component of capitalist exchange since the end of the nineteenth century. In the second half of the twentieth century . . . that complex [was referred to] as cultural imperialism. By the late twentieth century, it became fashionable to think of this power in terms of globalisation." Miller et al. also link Hollywood to the velocity and spatial mobility of globalization. "Hollywood both animates and is animated by globalisation. And what distinguishes Hollywood from other industries in the present stage of capitalist expansion, but also makes the organisation of film and television crucial signs of the future, is the industry's command of the New International Division of Cultural Labour . . . through its control over cultural labour markets, international co-production, intellectual property, marketing, distribution and exhibition." (Miller et al., *Global Hollywood 2*, 50–52). For a concise explication of these themes, see also Miller, "Hollywood and the World." Global Hollywood as a critical rubric also refers to the understanding that Hollywood does not merely refer to a geographically-circumscribed American film industry, situated in Los Angeles, comparable to any other national film industry in the world. Hollywood's historical dominance on world screens and the emphatically transnational character of all its operations, from financing and production to distribution and exhibition, ensure that it is much more than the national cinema of the United States; instead, it helps secure the Americanist cast of popular culture throughout the world. Global Hollywood's dominance permeates and influences what counts as the national-popular in other countries, as Andrew Higson's work, discussed later in this chapter, underscores, while also aggressively recruiting film labor and appropriating formal innovations from rival film industries in order to better penetrate foreign film markets. In particular, critics like Christina Klein

note the "growing ties between Asian and American film industries—ties which are leading to the Asianization of Hollywood and the Hollywoodization of Asia." See Higson, "The Concept of National Cinema," 38–43, and Klein, "The Asia Factor in Global Hollywood," n.p.

4. Jameson, "Magical Narratives," 157–58.

5. Gledhill, "Rethinking Genre," 229–30.

6. I borrow the phrase "productivity of genre" from ibid., 226.

7. Altman, *Film/Genre*, 208.

8. See ibid., 208–10.

9. Gledhill, "Rethinking Genre," 226. Altman makes the same point as Gledhill in *Film/Genre*: "Multiple genre practitioners use genres and generic terminology in differing and potentially contradictory ways" (208).

10. Rooney, "Remake Wranglers Mine Asia, South America," 14.

11. Richards, "*The Eye*," 80.

12. Rose, "Nightmare Scenario," 11.

13. Corliss, "Horror," 76.

14. Some accounts date the beginning of this trend to DreamWorks' purchase of remake rights to Hideo Nakata's 1998 Japanese horror film *Ringu* in 2001, others to Miramax's acquisition of remake rights to Jo Jing-yu's South Korean action-comedy *My Wife Is a Gangster* in the same year. See Friend, "Remake Man," 43–44; and Chute, "Spotlight," C1.

15. What follows is a partial list of Asian films—not confined to horror films alone—whose remake rights have been optioned by Hollywood studios. The list is organized by studio. DreamWorks: *Ringu* (Japan, 1998), *Ringu 2* (Japan, 1999), *My Sassy Girl* (South Korea, 2001), and *A Tale of Two Sisters* (South Korea, 2003); Miramax: *My Wife Is a Gangster* (South Korea, 2001) and *Shall We Dance?* (Japan, 1996); Dimension: *Teacher Mister Kim* (South Korea, 2003) and *Jail Breakers* (South Korea, 2003); Warner Bros.: *Infernal Affairs* (Hong Kong, 2002), *Il Mare* (South Korea, 2000), *Marrying the Mafia* (South Korea, 2002), and *Akira* (Japan, 1988); United Artists: *The Cure* (Japan, 1997); Universal: *Chaos* (Japan, 1999); Radar Pictures: *Turn* (Japan, 2001); Paramount: *The Eye* (Hong Kong, 2002), (with Sam Raimi and Senator International) *Ju-on* (Japan, 2000), and *Ikiru* (Japan, 1952); MGM: *Hi Dharma* (South Korea, 2001); Fox: *Afterlife* (Japan, 1998) and *Tell Me Something* (South Korea, 1999).

16. Chute, "East Goes West," 10.

17. Lyman, "The Chills! The Thrills! The Profits!" 1.

18. See Dunkley, "H'wood's Fright-Geist." Dunkley mentions the following releases: *They* (2002); *Ghost Ship* (2002); *Van Helsing* (2004); *Darkness Falls* (2003); *The Exorcist: The Beginning* (2004); *Dreamcatcher* (2003); *Jeepers Creepers 2* (2001);

Gothika (2003); *Freddy vs. Jason* (2003); *Final Destination 2* (2003); *Highwaymen* (2003); and remakes of *The Texas Chainsaw Massacre* (2003) and *Willard* (2003).

19. See Kermode, "What a Carve Up!" The films Kermode mentions include recent remakes (*The Texas Chainsaw Massacre*; *Dawn of the Dead* [2004]; *Amityville Horror* [2005]); rereleases (*Alien: The Director's Cut* [2003]; *The Exorcist: The Version You've Never Seen* [2000]); sequelizations of 1970s horror classics (*Land of the Dead* [2005]); and 1980s remakes of 1950s horror (*The Fly* [1986]; *The Thing* [1982]).

20. Altman, *Film/Genre*, 26.

21. Wills, "The French Remark," 148 (my emphasis).

22. Budra and Schellenberg, "Introduction," 3–4.

23. Horton and McDougal, "Introduction," 3.

24. See Sobchack, "Bringing It All Back Home," for Vivian Sobchack's astute reading of the monstrous child as a figure of generic exchange.

25. The quote is attributed to WWOR reporter Pat Collins and ran as a blurb in U.S. newspaper advertisements for the film in 2002.

26. Dunkley, "H'wood's Fright-Geist," 1.

27. Dunkley and Swart, "Cannes Preview," B1; see also Klein, "The Asia Factor in Global Hollywood."

28. McNary, "Remakes Need a Makeover."

29. Klein, "The Asia Factor in Global Hollywood."

30. Harris, "You Can't Kill the Boogeyman," 98–99.

31. Friend, "Remake Man," 41–44.

32. Xu, *Sinascape*, 155.

33. Derakhshani, "Hollywood Not Scared Off by Talk of J-Horror's Death," E7.

34. This term is used by Patrick Galloway (see Galloway, *Asia Shock*).

35. "Consider the numbers. Last year, the studios released 23 horror movies. This year the tally will be 42, nearly double, and too often, the take at the box office has been anemic, leaving studios and distributors with lots of red ink gushing through the bottom line. . . . 'The Grudge,' released in 2004, is the last horror film to break $100 million at the domestic box office. Horror has been faring even worse in the international market, which for typical studio films constitutes 60% of horror box office grosses" (Abramowitz and Crabtree, "Hollywood Horror Films Suffer Box Office Anemia," A1).

36. Wong, "Cities, Cultures and Cassettes," 102–4.

37. David Desser writes that when the kung fu craze spearheaded by Bruce Lee movies subsided, a deracinated martial arts genre continued to be popular in late 1970s American Vietnam War films. According to Desser, such films saw "the rise of white male martial arts stars who, in a sense, co-opt Asian martial arts for the American action hero, for the American movie star, for the American man." See Desser, "The Kung Fu Craze," 39.

38. "Ironically, when *Iron Monkey* came out in Hong Kong, that film style was going down," says the film's star Donnie Yen. "But Woo-ping's fight standards are so high" ("Hollywood Embraces Three Legendary Hong Kong Film Directors").

39. Teo argues that this reduction of Hong Kong cinema to *wuxia* overlooks achievements in other genres, especially the *wenyi* [realistic, socially conscious] melodrama acclaimed by local critics. Subsequently banned by the Guomindang government of pre–Second World War China, the wuxia was revived in postwar Hong Kong, where it soon became a generic staple. See Teo, "Hong Kong's Electric Shadow Show," 19, 24. For more on Hollywood's "selective uptake" of Hong Kong cinema see Cheung, "Hong Kong Filmmakers in Hollywood: Terence Chang," 130–31. According to Cheung, "When Hong Kong cinema was in fashion in Hollywood, many directors made their U.S. debuts; and stars like Chow Yun-fat and Michelle Yeoh were cast as leads in Hollywood A productions. The Hong Kong style of action has been adopted in the hugely popular *The Matrix*, choreographed by Yuen Woo-ping, setting off a new 'kung fu craze.' However, this by no means shows that Hollywood has accepted Asians and Chinese language films; only that it is being very selective about certain elements of Hong Kong cinema."

40. Corliss, "Go West, Hong Kong," 67.

41. Elley, "South Korea," 20, 25.

42. James, "Cinematic Seoul," 42–43.

43. According to *Han Cinema: The Korean Movie and Drama Database*, the screenplay was adapted by Craig Rosenberg (whose other writing credits include *Jurassic Park 3*), and the film marked the directorial feature debut of the British brothers Tom and Charlie Guard. Remake rights were purchased in 2003 by DreamWorks for 1 million U.S. dollars. See "A Tale of Two Sisters," at *Han Cinema: The Korean Movie and Drama Database*, www.hancinema.net (accessed January 29, 2007).

44. For a discussion of taste-making trends deeply imbricated in teleological temporality, see Gladwell, "The Coolhunt." For a conceptualization of subcultural capital and a critique of subcultural communities' demonization of an imagined mainstream other, see Thornton, *Club Cultures*. The classic account of cultural capital as linked to rarefication, as well as class stratification, is Bourdieu, *Distinction*. See in particular Bourdieu's argument that the rarer the aesthetic disposition, the greater the symbolic profits reaped. Popularization can begin to devalue works perceived to be legitimate objects for the judgment of taste (Bourdieu, *Distinction*, 228–29).

45. See www.mandiapple.com/forum/showthread.php?t=3692 (accessed Dec. 6, 2007).

46. Telotte, "Beyond All Reason," 7.

47. Galloway, *Asia Shock*, 11.

48. Bergson, *Creative Evolution*, 233–34.

49. Hodgson, "Black Hole DVD Reviews."

50. Garger, "Selling Screams."

51. Hagiwara, "Shimizu So Successful It's Scary," 13.

52. Cohen, "Afterlife Spawns Horror Boutiques."

53. Lu, "Horror Japanese-Style," 38.

54. Clover, *Men, Women, and Chain Saws*, 30–31 (my emphasis).

55. Edward Branigan argues that film narration creates "hierarchies of knowledge" that crucially determine spectatorial response. When spectators know more than onscreen characters, suspense results; when spectators and characters share parity of knowledge, this generates a sense of mystery; and when spectators know less than the characters, the outcome is surprise. See Branigan, *Narrative Comprehension and Film*, 75.

56. See Lim, "Serial Time."

57. Ibid., 172.

58. Jaén, "Mysticism, Esoterism, and Fantastic Literature," 108. Also, in her study of Gothic horror, Judith Halberstam writes: "Producing and consuming monsters and monstrous fictions, we might say, adds up to what Eve Sedgwick has called, in her study of Gothic conventions, 'an aesthetic of pleasurable fear.' The Gothic, in other words, inspires fear and desire at the same time—fear of and desire for the other, fear of and desire for the possibly latent perversity lurking within the reader herself" (Halberstam, *Skin Shows*, 13).

59. Horton and McDougal, "Introduction," 6.

60. Corliss, "Horror," 76.

61. See Eberwein, "Remakes and Cultural Studies," 28–30.

62. I owe this insight to the undergraduate students in my Fantastic Cinema course. In class discussions, several students responded to Andrew Horton and Stuart McDougal's discussion of the defamiliarization effect in remakes by talking about remakes as a tactic for *refamiliarization*. See Horton and McDougal, "Introduction," 1–11.

63. Xu makes a similar point about Hollywood's recent Asian remake frenzy: "What has been remade is not only the story but also ethnicity. While the originals are ethnically specific, albeit Hollywoodized, representations, the remakes are completely severed from the original ethnic soil and become solely the product of Hollywood. The remakes, therefore, have nothing to do with the supernatural aura, the long development of East Asian cinemas, or the peculiarly 'Asian' aesthetic based on cultural and ethnic specifics" (Xu, *Sinascape*, 155).

64. Wills, "The French Remark," 148–49.

65. Derrida, "What Is a 'Relevant' Translation?" 175.

66. Xu, *Sinascape*, 155.

67. See Carol Clover's pioneering discussion of the slasher film's conventions. One of those conventions is a heroine or "Final Girl," who survives to vanquish the monster. Clover, *Men, Women, and Chain Saws*, 21–64.

68. See Snyder, "'Buffy' Effect," 6–7; and Stanley, "Like Jason, Horror Flicks Don't Stay Dead and Buried, but Keep on Rising," 4.

69. Derrida, *Specters of Marx*, 10.

70. Todorov, *The Fantastic*, 25.

71. Ibid., 89–90.

72. Altman, *Film/Genre*, 25.

73. Budra and Schellenberg, "Introduction," 5–7.

74. See Eberwein, "Remakes and Cultural Studies," 15.

75. Bakhtin, "Discourse in the Novel," 291.

76. Kristeva, "Word, Dialogue and Novel," 36–37.

77. Ong, "The Gender and Labor Politics of Postmodernity," 61–66.

78. Yeh and Davis, "Japan Hongscreen," 61–62.

79. Ibid., 61–65.

80. Ibid., 66.

81. For an example of such exceptionalist rhetoric see Rafferty, "Why Asian Ghost Stories Are the Best," 13. Renee Graham, reviewing *A Tale of Two Sisters*, writes: "There's a reason why Hollywood has been so busy in recent years remaking Asian horror movies. Scare for scare, they're generally better, relying more on things-that-go-bump-in-the-night suspense than the blood-splattered gorefests that overwhelm so many contemporary American films" (Graham, "'Two Sisters' Truly Frightens, without the Gore," D5). See also Ong, "Horrifying Thoughts."

82. Chute, "Spotlight," C1, C3.

83. Chute, "East Goes West," 10.

84. Kan, "Reconstruction Project," A1, A4.

85. Quoted in Chute, "East Goes West," 10.

86. Cheung, "Hong Kong Filmmakers in Hollywood: Peter Chan Ho-Sun," 134–35, 137.

87. Other personalities include John Woo, Tsui Hark, Ringo Lam, and Stanley Tong (directors); Jackie Chan and Chow Yun-fat (actors); Terence Chang (producer); and Yuen Woo-ping, Corey Yuen, and Yuen Cheung-yan (action choreographers). See Cheung, "Hong Kong Filmmakers in Hollywood: Peter Chan Ho-Sun," 129.

88. Featherstone, "Localism, Globalism, and Cultural Identity," 60–61.

89. Miller, "Screening the Nation," 94.

90. Miller et al., *Global Hollywood 2*, 80.

91. Gledhill, "Rethinking Genre," 230.

92. Rayns, "*The Eye*," 43–44.

93. Rithdee, "Bangkok Journal," 12–13.

94. Elley, "*A Tale of Two Sisters*," 24–25.

95. Yeh and Davis, "Japan Hongscreen," 67.

96. Ibid., 78.

97. Reviews suggest that such films, regardless of national origin, are received within a shared generic field. A Malaysian film critic writes, "If you liked *The Eye*, you'd definitely like *Dark Water*. Language barriers don't matter when you're gripping the sides of your chair with knuckles turned white." The same writer also plays down language differences by recourse to the shared horizon of affect: "Though the movie is Japanese, the English subtitles will take you through the story effectively. And besides, most of the eerie bits take place when no one is speaking" (Omar, "*Dark Water*," 6).

98. Yeh and Davis, "Japan Hongscreen," 63–78.

99. Chute, "East Goes West," 10.

100. See the *New Yorker*'s profile of Grady Hendrix, a cofounder of the New York Asian Film Festival. "J-horror has become more and more mainstream, with several big-budget Hollywood remakes scheduled to open this year, which may well spell the end of Hendrix's film series, since he will no longer be able to wrest festival rights from the studios" (Agger, "The Pictures," 37–38).

101. Altman, *Film/Genre*, 211.

102. See Fore, "Jackie Chan and the Cultural Dynamics of Global Entertainment."

103. Klein, "The Asia Factor in Global Hollywood," n.p.

104. Higson, "The Concept of National Cinema," 38–39 (my emphasis).

105. Ibid., 41.

106. Klein, "The Asia Factor in Global Hollywood," n.p.

107. Miller, "Hollywood and the World," 371.

108. Garger, "Selling Screams," 49.

109. Kim, "Biz Pines for Summer Horror Hits," 14.

110. Plagued by rampant piracy, regional economic crisis, a sharp decline in local movie attendance, and the defeat of Hong Kong films by Hollywood fare in its own backyard, the Hong Kong film industry in the late 1990s was in dire straits, a circumstance aggravated by the migration of its brightest talents. Whereas there used to be two hundred local films screened a year in Hong Kong, in 1997 and 1998 this dropped to about ninety, so the film industry went from dominating 80 percent of the local film market to less than half that amount. The unemployment rate in the film industry soared to 70 percent at its worst, but in 2001 the *South China Morning Post* announced that the industry was on its way to recovery, with local films screened rising to 150 and several new government services and funds established to help the ailing industry. See Lo, "Transnationalization of the Local in Hong Kong Cinema of the 1990s," 262, 265. See also Lee, "Scene Set for Reel Recovery," 15; and Leung, "SAR Film-Makers Prepare for Boom Year as Budgets Rise," 1.

111. Yeh and Davis, "Japan Hongscreen," 75–77.

112. James, "Cinematic Seoul."

113. Munoz and Friedman, "Coming Attractions," 1.

114. See Fore, "Home, Migration, Identity," 130; and Klein, "The Asia Factor in Global Hollywood," n.p.

115. Miller et al., *Global Hollywood 2*, 79.

116. "Behind the Scenes," *A Tale of Two Sisters* DVD, Tartan Asia Extreme Special Two-Disc Set (U.S. version), 2005.

117. "Production Design Featurette," *A Tale of Two Sisters* DVD, Tartan Asia Extreme Special Two-Disc Set (U.S. version), 2005.

118. In an interview included on the U.S. DVD release of *A Tale of Two Sisters*, the film's sound designer and composer, Lee Byeong-woo, comments that sadness and beauty were expressed through the leitmotif (nondiegetic film music) while aspects of terror/scariness were conveyed by nondiegetic film sound (synthesizers, sounds of radio waves or murmuring voices). "Music Score Featurette," *A Tale of Two Sisters* DVD, Tartan Asia Extreme Special Two-Disc Set (U.S. version), 2005.

119. The film departs significantly from the folktale, which has been adapted for the screen several times before. But allusions to the tale remain in buried motifs: the macabre water in which the carefree girls dip their feet at the beginning of the film (no harm comes to them, but the viewer expects something monstrous to happen) is filmed ominously enough to recall that, in the folktale, both girls die by drowning in a forest lake. A deleted scene includes a set piece involving rats; a dead rat was crucial to the stepmother's defamation of the older sister in the folktale.

120. Warner, "Women against Women in the Old Wives' Tale." In a conversation with the director, the filmmaker Im Pil-Sung remarks on the same point: "Your film shows the sadness or the tragedy between women." "An Explanation by the Director," *A Tale of Two Sisters* DVD, Tartan Asia Extreme Special Two-Disc Set (U.S. version), 2005.

121. Branigan, *Narrative Comprehension and Film*, 62–85, 114–24.

122. Kim, the film's director and screenwriter, remarks: "In the structure and the story of the film, there are layers of secrets within the family. "Deleted Scenes: Secrets," *A Tale of Two Sisters* DVD, Tartan Asia Extreme Special Two-Disc Set (U.S. version), 2005.

123. Branigan writes:

As a spectator engages the procedures which yield a story world, something extraordinary occurs: his or her memory of the actual images, words, and sounds is erased by the acts of comprehension that they require. Comprehension proceeds by canceling and discarding data that is actually present, by revising and remaking what is given. A new representation is created which is not a copy of the original stimuli nor an imperfect memory of it. In comprehending a narrative, the spectator routinely sees what is not present and overlooks what is present. . . .

. . . When we watch a narrative film we are actually watching four films: a celluloid strip of material; a projected image with recorded sound; a coherent event in three-dimensional space; and finally a story we remember (i.e., the film we think we have seen). There are perceptual "gaps" between each of these four films in which certain facts are concealed and "forgotten" about one film in order to perceive another. (Branigan, *Narrative Comprehension and Film*, 83–84)

124. The director, Kim Jee-woon, has explained that his decision to portray a multiple personality disorder using different, rather than the same, actors is meant to further the thematic of self-duality and self-othering: "An imaginary adversary haunts her. It's so ironic. She realizes the enemy was herself. She cannot escape from this" (Kim interview in "Behind the Scenes," *A Tale of Two Sisters* DVD, Tartan Asia Extreme Special Two-Disc Set [U.S. version], 2005).

In addition, a small plot point about Su-yeon, Su-mi, and the nurse-stepmother all menstruating on the same day underscores the veiled insight that all three women are the same girl.

125. David Bordwell and Kristin Thompson note that media convergence, in particular, the distribution and exhibition of films on video, results in discernable changes in cinematic form and spectatorship. "Video distribution and exhibition have created new choices in the realm of storytelling. Until the 1980s, people couldn't rewatch a movie whenever they wished. With videotape, and especially DVD, viewers can pore over a film. Bonus materials encourage them to rerun the movie to spot things they missed. Some filmmakers have taken advantage of this opportunity by creating *puzzle* films . . . which fans scrutinize for clues to plot enigmas" (Bordwell and Thompson, *Film Art*, 42).

126. Elley, "*A Tale of Two Sisters*," 24–25. See also Munoz and Friedman, "Coming Attractions," 1.

127. "Production Design Featurette," *A Tale of Two Sisters* DVD, Tartan Asia Extreme Special Two-Disc Set (U.S. version), 2005.

128. Todorov, *The Fantastic*, 38.

129. An online review of the Tartan Asia Extreme DVD UK release of *A Tale of Two Sisters* refers to a twenty-eight-minute "UK Exclusive Director Interview by Billy Chainsaw." According to the August 9, 2004, review, "Kim Jee-woon discusses the (far simpler) original Korean folk tale, his interest in all genres besides romantic comedy, and his refusal to be involved in the Hollywood remake" (www.movie-gazette.com/cinereviews/897).

130. At a public lecture, Roy Lee was asked whether he hired cultural consultants to address cultural differences (in gender norms and storytelling conventions) be-

tween the Asian source films and their Hollywood remakes. Lee responded that cultural consultants were unnecessary because only American cultural perceptions were relevant for adapting Asian films for Hollywood audiences. Later in the same talk, Lee recalled that the screenwriter's pitch for *The Uninvited* (2009) was based only upon having watched the trailer—not the entire source film—beforehand. According to Lee, this explains why *A Tale of Two Sisters* and its Hollywood remake differ strongly in the second half of the films. Roy Lee, "Korean Cinema and Hollywood Remakes."

Epilogue

1. Bergson, *Time and Free Will*, 168.

2. Ibid., 139.

3. Deleuze, *Bergsonism*, 20–21, 34.

4. "Deconstruction, whatever it may be, is not most valuably an exposure of error, certainly not other people's error, other people's essentialism. The most serious critique in deconstruction is the critique of things that are extremely useful, things without which we cannot live on" (Spivak, "'In a Word,'" 359).

5. Bergson, *Time and Free Will*, 127.

6. Fabian, *Time and the Other*, 30–31.

7. Ibid., 33.

8. Chakrabarty, *Provincializing Europe*, 97.

9. Ibid., 101.

10. Ibid., 102–3.

11. Ibid., 105 (my emphasis), 107–8.

12. Ibid., 109.

13. Grosz, *Time Travels*, 5.

BIBLIOGRAPHY

Abbas, Ackbar. "Building on Disappearance." *Public Culture* 6 (1994): 441–59.

———. *Hong Kong: Culture and the Politics of Disappearance*. Minneapolis: University of Minnesota Press, 1997.

———. "Hong Kong: Other Histories, Other Politics." In Cheung and Chu, *Between Home and World*, 273–96.

———. "The New Hong Kong Cinema and the Deja Disparu." *Discourse* 16, no. 3 (1994): 65–77.

Abel, Richard. *The Ciné Goes to Town: French Cinema, 1896–1914*. Berkeley: University of California Press, 1994.

Abramowitz, Rachel, and Sheigh Crabtree. "Hollywood Horror Films Suffer Box Office Anemia." *Los Angeles Times*, June 9, 2007, A1.

Adorno, Theodor W. "Free Time." In *The Culture Industry: Selected Essays on Mass Culture*, 162–70. London: Routledge, 1991.

Agger, Michael. "The Pictures: Gross and Grosser." *New Yorker*, June 28, 2004, 37–38.

Altman, Rick. *The American Film Musical*. Bloomington: Indiana University Press, 1987.

———. *Film/Genre*. London: British Film Institute, 1999.

Anderson, Benedict. *Imagined Communities: Reflections on the Origin and Spread of Nationalism*. London: Verso, 1991.

Appadurai, Arjun. "Consumption, Duration, and History." In *Streams of Cultural Capital: Transnational Cultural Studies*, ed. David Palumbo-Liu and Hans Ulrich Gumbrecht, 23–45. Stanford: Stanford University Press, 1997.

Associated Press. "'Manananggal' Terrorizes Tondo Folks." *Philippine Daily Inquirer*, May 9, 1992, 10.

Bakhtin, Mikhail. "Discourse in the Novel." In *The Dialogic Imagination: Four Essays by M. M. Bakhtin*. Ed. Michael Holquist. Trans. Caryl Emerson and Michael Holquist. 259–422. Austin: University of Texas Press, 1981.

Balce, Nerissa S. "Manananggal." *Philippines Free Press*, Nov. 21, 1992, 42–44.

Barsam, Richard. *Looking at Movies: An Introduction to Film*. New York: Norton, 2004.

Barthes, Roland. *Camera Lucida: Reflections on Photography*. Trans. Richard Howard. New York: Hill and Wang, 1981.

———. *S/Z*. New York: Hill and Wang, 1974.

Baudrillard, Jean. "The Drama of Leisure or the Impossibility of Wasting One's Time." In *Consumer Society: Myths and Structures*, 151–58. London: Sage, 1998.

Baudry, Jean-Louis. "The Apparatus: Metaphysical Approaches to the Impression of Reality in the Cinema." In *Film Theory and Criticism: Introductory Readings*, ed. Gerald Mast, Marshall Cohen, and Leo Braudy. 4th ed., 690–707. New York: Oxford University Press, 1992.

Benjamin, Walter. *The Origin of German Tragic Drama*. Trans. John Osborne. London: Verso, 1998.

———. "Theses on the Philosophy of History." In *Illuminations*. Ed. Hannah Arendt. Trans. Harry Zohn. 253–64. New York: Schocken Books, 1968.

Bergson, Henri. *Creative Evolution*. Trans. Arthur Mitchell. New York: Henry Holt, 1911.

———. *Matter and Memory*. Trans. Nancy Margaret Paul and W. Scott Palmer. London: George Allen and Unwin, 1911.

———. *Time and Free Will: An Essay on the Immediate Data of Consciousness*. 1889. Trans. F. L. Pogson. Mineola, N.Y.: Dover, 2001.

Berry, Chris. "If China Can Say No, Can China Make Movies? Or, Do Movies Make China?" In *Modern Chinese Literary and Cultural Studies in the Age of Theory: Reimagining a Field*, ed. Rey Chow, 159–80. Durham, N.C.: Duke University Press, 2000.

Blaker, Alfred A. *Photography: Art and Technique*. 2nd ed. Boston: Focal, 1988.

Blitz, Mark. *Heidegger's* Being and Time *and the Possibility of Political Philosophy*. Ithaca, N.Y.: Cornell University Press, 1981.

Bloch, Ernst. "Nonsynchronism and the Obligation to Its Dialectics (1932)." *New German Critique* 11 (1977): 22–38.

———. "Recollections of Walter Benjamin." Trans. Michael W. J. Jennings. In *On Walter Benjamin: Critical Essays and Recollections*, ed. Gary Smith, 339–45. Cambridge: MIT Press, 1988.

Bogue, Ronald. *Deleuze on Cinema*. New York: Routledge, 2003.

Bolasco, Mario V. *Points of Departure: Essays on Christianity, Power, and Social Change*. Manila: St. Scholastica's College, 1994.

Bolter, Jay David, and Richard Grusin. *Remediation: Understanding New Media*. Cambridge: MIT Press, 1999.

Bordwell, David, and Kristin Thompson. *Film Art: An Introduction*. 8th ed. New York: McGraw Hill, 2008.

Bourdieu, Pierre. *Distinction: A Social Critique of the Judgment of Taste*. Trans. Richard Nice. Cambridge: Harvard University Press, 1984.

Branigan, Edward. *Narrative Comprehension and Film*. London: Routledge, 1992.

Braun, Marta. *Picturing Time: The Work of Etienne-Jules Marey*. Chicago: University of Chicago Press, 1992.

Bruckner, Rene Thoreau. "The Instant and the Dark: Cinema's Momentum." *Octopus* 2 (2006): 21–36.

Buck-Morss, Susan. *The Dialectics of Seeing: Walter Benjamin and the Arcades Project*. Cambridge: MIT Press, 1989.

Budra, Paul, and Betty A. Schellenberg. "Introduction." In *Part Two: Reflections on the Sequel*, ed. Paul Budra and Betty A. Schellenberg, 3–18. Toronto: University of Toronto Press, 1998.

Caagusan, Flor. "Interview with Mike de Leon." *Diliman Review* 31, no. 5 (Sept.–Oct. 1983): 44–56.

Calvino, Italo. *Six Memos for the Next Millennium*. Trans. Patrick Creagh. London: Jonathan Cape, 1992.

Carroll, Noël. *The Philosophy of Horror, or, Paradoxes of the Heart*. New York: Routledge, 1990.

Carter, Margaret. *Specter or Delusion? The Supernatural in Gothic Fiction*. London: UMI Research Press, 1987.

Cartwright, Lisa. "Film and the Digital in Visual Studies: Film Studies in the Era of Convergence." *Journal of Visual Culture* 1, no. 1 (2002): 7–23.

Chakrabarty, Dipesh. *Provincializing Europe: Postcolonial Thought and Historical Difference*. Princeton, N.J.: Princeton University Press, 2000.

———. "The Time of History and the Times of Gods." In *The Politics of Culture in the Shadow of Capital*, ed. Lisa Lowe and David Lloyd, 35–60. Durham, N.C.: Duke University Press, 1997.

Cheung, Esther M. K., and Chu Yiu-wai, eds. *Between Home and World: A Reader in Hong Kong Cinema*. Hong Kong: Oxford University Press, 2004.

———. "Introduction: Between Home and World." In Cheung and Chu, *Between Home and World*, xii–xxxv.

Cheung Suk-yee. "Hong Kong Filmmakers in Hollywood: Peter Chan Ho-Sun." Trans. Stephen Teo. In Law, *Fifty Years of Electric Shadows*, 134–37.

———. "Hong Kong Filmmakers in Hollywood: Terence Chang." Trans. Bede Chang. In Law, *Fifty Years of Electric Shadows*, 130–33.

Chow, Rey. "Between Colonizers: Hong Kong's Postcolonial Self-Writing in the 1990s." *Diaspora* 2, no. 2 (1992): 151–70.

———. "Can One Say No to China?" *New Literary History* 28, no. 1 (1997): 147–51.

———. "Introduction: On Chineseness as a Theoretical Problem." *boundary 2* 25, no. 3 (1998): 1–24.

———. "King Kong in Hong Kong: Watching the 'Handover' from the U.S.A." *Social Text* 55 (1998): 93–108.

———. *Primitive Passions: Visuality, Sexuality, Ethnography, and Contemporary Chinese Cinema*. New York: Columbia University Press, 1995.

———. "A Souvenir of Love." *Modern Chinese Literature* 7 (1993): 59–76.

Chu, Blanche W. K. "The Ambivalence of History: Nostalgia Films as Meta-Narratives in the Post-Colonial Context." In Cheung and Chu, *Between Home and World*, 331–51.

Chu Yingchi. *Hong Kong Cinema: Coloniser, Motherland, and Self*. London: Routledge-Curzon, 2003.

Chun, Allen. "Fuck Chineseness: On the Ambiguities of Ethnicity as Culture as Identity." *boundary 2* 23, no. 2 (1996): 111–38.

Chute, David. "East Goes West." *Variety*, May 10–16, 2004, 10.

———. "Spotlight: Pusan Film Festival: Hollywood Catches Case of Remake Fever." *Variety*, Sept. 29–Oct. 5, 2003, C1, C3.

Clavel, Leothiny. "Philippine Revolution in Capiz." *Diliman Review* 43, nos. 3–4 (1995): 25–37.

Clough, Patricia Ticineto, Greg Goldberg, Rachel Schiff, Aaron Weeks, and Craig Willse. "Notes Towards a Theory of Affect-Itself." *Ephemera* 7, no. 1 (2007): 60–77; available at www.ephemeraweb.org (accessed March 16, 2008).

Clover, Carol. *Men, Women, and Chain Saws: Gender in the Modern Horror Film*. Princeton, N.J.: Princeton University Press, 1992.

Cohen, David S. "Afterlife Spawns Horror Boutiques: Rash of New Companies Rushes to Cash in on the Genre's Leggy DVD Profit Potential." *Variety*, Nov. 15–21, 2004, 9–10.

Comaroff, Jean, and John Comaroff. "Alien-Nation: Zombies, Immigrants, and Millennial Capitalism." *South Atlantic Quarterly* 101, no. 4 (2002): 779–805.

Corliss, Richard. "Go West, Hong Kong: John Woo and Jackie Chan Meet Hollywood." *Time*, Feb. 26, 1996, 67.

———. "Horror: Made in Japan." *Time*, Aug. 2, 2004, 76.

Cornwell, Neil. *The Literary Fantastic: From Gothic to Postmodern*. New York: Harvester Wheatsheaf, 1990.

Dai Jinhua. "Imagined Nostalgia." Trans. Judy T. H. Chen. *boundary 2* 24, no. 3 (fall 1997): 143–61.

Daston, Lorraine. "The Nature of Nature in Early Modern Europe." *Configurations* 6, no. 2 (1998): 149–72.

Daston, Lorraine, and Katharine Park. *Wonders and the Order of Nature, 1150–1750*. New York: Zone Books, 1998.

David, Joel. "A Cultural Policy Experience in Philippine Cinema." In *Wages of Cinema: Film in Philippine Perspective*, 48–61. Diliman, Quezon City: University of the Philippines Press, 1998.

———. *Fields of Vision: Critical Applications in Recent Philippine Cinema*. Quezon City: Ateneo de Manila University Press, 1995.

————. "The Multiple-Character Format." In *Wages of Cinema: Film in Philippine Perspective*, 14–25. Diliman, Quezon City: University of the Philippines Press, 1998.

————. "A Second Golden Age (an Informal History)." In *The National Pastime: Contemporary Philippine Cinema*, 1–17. Pasig, Metro Manila: Anvil, 1990.

Deleuze, Gilles. *Bergsonism*. Trans. Hugh Tomlinson and Barbara Habberjam. New York: Zone Books, 1991.

————. *Cinema 1: The Movement-Image*. Trans. Hugh Tomlinson and Barbara Habberjam. Minneapolis: University of Minnesota Press, 1986.

————. *Cinema 2: The Time-Image*. Trans. Hugh Tomlinson and Robert Galeta. Minneapolis: University of Minnesota Press, 1989.

Deleuze, Gilles, and Claire Parnet. *Dialogues*. Trans. Hugh Tomlinson and Barbara Habberjam. London: Athlone, 1987.

Derakhshani, Tirdad. "Hollywood Not Scared Off by Talk of J-Horror's Death; Sixteen Remakes on Tap—but Some Say Creepy Asian Films Have Taken Last Breath." *Seattle Times*, June 19, 2006, 4th ed., Northwest Life sec., E7.

Derrida, Jacques. *Specters of Marx: The State of the Debt, the Work of Mourning, and the New International*. Trans. Peggy Kamuf. New York: Routledge, 1994.

————. "What Is a 'Relevant' Translation?" *Critical Inquiry* 27, no. 2 (winter 2001): 174–200.

Desser, David. "The Kung Fu Craze: Hong Kong Cinema's First American Reception." In *The Cinema of Hong Kong: History, Arts, Identity*, ed. Poshek Fu and David Desser, 19–43. Cambridge: Cambridge University Press, 2000.

Doane, Mary Ann. *The Emergence of Cinematic Time: Modernity, Contingency, the Archive*. Cambridge: Harvard University Press, 2002.

Dohrn-van Rossum, Gerhard. *History of the Hour: Clocks and Modern Temporal Orders*. Chicago: University of Chicago Press, 1996.

Dube, Saurabh. "Presence of Europe: An Interview with Dipesh Chakrabarty." *South Atlantic Quarterly* 101, no. 4 (2002): 859–68.

Dunkley, Cathy. "H'wood's Fright-Geist: Studios Add New Twists to Their Scare Tactics." *Variety*, Nov. 4–10, 2002, 1–3.

Dunkley, Cathy, and Sharon Swart. "Cannes Preview: Beachy Keen." *Variety*, May 3–9, 2004, B1.

Dussel, Enrique. "Beyond Eurocentrism: The World-System and the Limits of Modernity." In *The Cultures of Globalization*, ed. Fredric Jameson and Masao Miyoshi, 3–31. Durham, N.C.: Duke University Press, 1998.

Eberwein, Robert. "Remakes and Cultural Studies." In Horton and McDougal, *Play It Again, Sam*, 15–33.

Elley, Derek. "South Korea: Local Hitmakers Eye Global Breakouts." *Variety*, Dec. 3–9, 2001, 20, 25.

————. "A Tale of Two Sisters." *Variety*, July 14–20, 2003, 24–25.

Eng, David L. "Love at Last Site: Waiting for Oedipus in Stanley Kwan's *Rouge*." *Camera Obscura* 32 (1993–94): 75–101.

Ezra, Elizabeth. *Georges Méliès: The Birth of the Auteur*. Manchester: Manchester University Press, 2000.

Fabian, Johannes. *Time and the Other: How Anthropology Makes Its Object*. New York: Columbia University Press, 1983.

Fausto-Sterling, Anne. "Gender, Race, and Nation: The Comparative Anatomy of 'Hottentot' Women in Europe, 1815–1817." In *Deviant Bodies: Critical Perspectives on Difference in Science and Popular Culture*, ed. Jennifer Terry and Jacqueline Urla, 19–49. Bloomington: Indiana University Press, 1995.

Featherstone, Mike. "Localism, Globalism, and Cultural Identity." In *Global/Local: Cultural Production and the Transnational Imaginary*, ed. Rob Wilson and Wimal Dissanayake, 46–77. Durham, N.C.: Duke University Press, 1996.

Feuer, Jane. "The Self-Reflective Musical and the Myth of Entertainment." In *Hollywood Musicals: The Film Reader*, ed. Steven Cohan, 31–40. London: Routledge, 2002.

Fletcher, Angus. *Allegory: Theory of a Symbolic Mode*. Ithaca, N.Y.: Cornell University Press, 1964.

Fojas, Felix. "Manananggal." *Philippines Free Press*, Oct. 30, 1993, 35–36.

Fore, Steve. "Home, Migration, Identity: Hong Kong Film Workers Join the Diaspora." In Law, *Fifty Years of Electric Shadows*, 130–35.

———. "Jackie Chan and the Cultural Dynamics of Global Entertainment." In *Transnational Chinese Cinemas*, ed. Sheldon Hsiao-peng Lu, 239–62. Honolulu: University of Hawaii Press, 1997.

Freud, Sigmund. "The Uncanny." In *The Standard Edition of the Complete Psychological Works of Sigmund Freud*. Ed. James Strachey and Anna Freud. 17:218–52. London: Hogarth, 1955.

Friend, Tad. "Remake Man." *New Yorker*, June 2, 2003, 40–47.

Fritzman, J. M. "The Future of Nostalgia and the Time of the Sublime." *Clio* 23, no. 2 (1994): 167–90.

Galloway, Patrick. *Asia Shock: Horror and Dark Cinema from Japan, Korea, Hong Kong, and Thailand*. Berkeley: Stone Bridge, 2006.

Garger, Ilya. "Selling Screams: A New Generation of Filmmakers Is Turning Once Lowly Asian Horror into a Hot Global Commodity." *Time International* (Asia edition), Nov. 29, 2004, 49.

Genette, Gérard. *Narrative Discourse: An Essay in Method*. Trans. Jane E. Lewin. Ithaca, N.Y.: Cornell University Press, 1980.

Gilman, Sander L. "The Hottentot and the Prostitute: Toward an Iconography of Female Sexuality." In *Difference and Pathology: Stereotypes of Sexuality, Race, and Madness*, 76–108. Ithaca, N.Y.: Cornell University Press, 1985.

Gladwell, Malcolm. "The Coolhunt." In *The Consumer Society Reader*, ed. Juliet B. Schor and Douglas B. Holt, 360–74. New York: New Press, 2000.

Gledhill, Christine. "Rethinking Genre." In *Reinventing Film Studies*, ed. Christine Gledhill and Linda Williams, 221–43. London: Arnold, 2000.

Glynn, Kevin. "Challenging Disenchantment: The Discreet Charm of Occult TV." *Comparative American Studies* 1, no. 4 (2003): 421–47.

Graham, Renee. "'Two Sisters' Truly Frightens, without the Gore." *Boston Globe*, Feb. 25, 2005, D5.

Greenblatt, Stephen. *Marvelous Possessions: The Wonder of the New World*. Chicago: University of Chicago Press, 1991.

Grosz, Elizabeth. *The Nick of Time: Politics, Evolution, and the Untimely*. Durham, N.C.: Duke University Press, 2004.

———. *Time Travels: Feminism, Nature, Power*. Durham, N.C.: Duke University Press, 2005.

Gunning, Tom. "The Cinema of Attractions: Early Film, Its Spectator and the Avant-Garde." In *Early Cinema: Space, Frame, Narrative*, ed. Thomas Elsaesser and Adam Barker, 56–62. London: British Film Institute, 1990.

———. *D. W. Griffith and the Origins of American Narrative Film: The Early Years at Biograph*. Urbana: University of Illinois Press, 1991.

Habermas, Jürgen. *The Philosophical Discourse of Modernity: Twelve Lectures*. Trans. Frederick Lawrence. Cambridge: MIT Press, 1993.

Hagiwara Shogo. "Shimizu So Successful It's Scary." *Daily Yomiuri*, Feb. 17, 2005, 13.

Halberstam, Judith. *Skin Shows: Gothic Horror and the Technology of Monsters*. Durham, N.C.: Duke University Press, 1995.

Harootunian, Harry. "Remembering the Historical Present." *Critical Inquiry* 3, no. 33 (spring 2007): 471–94.

Harris, Martin. "You Can't Kill the Boogeyman." *Journal of Popular Film and Television* 32, no. 3 (2004): 98–109.

Hau, Caroline S. "On Representing Others: Intellectuals, Pedagogy, and the Uses of Error." *Journal of English Studies and Comparative Literature* [Department of English and Comparative Literature, University of the Philippines] 1, no. 2 (Jan. 1998): 3–36.

Heidegger, Martin. *Being and Time: A Translation of* Sein und Zeit. Trans. Joan Stambaugh. Albany: State University of New York Press, 1996.

Higson, Andrew. "The Concept of National Cinema." *Screen* 30, no. 4 (1989): 36–46.

Hodgson, Mark. Black Hole DVD Reviews. "Ju-on The Curse 1 and 2 (2000) The first Grudge movies" (Aug. 28, 2006); and "Ju-on: The Grudge (Japan, 2003), the curse continues" (Sept. 8, 2006); available at http://blackholereviews.blogspot.com (accessed April 9, 2008).

"Hollywood Embraces Three Legendary Hong Kong Film Directors." *China Daily*, Oct. 25, 2001; available at www.china.org.cn (accessed Nov. 8, 2005).

hooks, bell. "The Oppositional Gaze: Black Female Spectators." In *Feminist Film*

Theory: A Reader, ed. Sue Thornham, 307–20. New York: New York University Press, 1999.

Horton, Andrew, and Stuart Y. McDougal. "Introduction." In Horton and McDougal, *Play It Again, Sam*, 1–11.

———, eds. *Play It Again, Sam: Retakes on Remakes*. Berkeley: University of California Press, 1998.

Hume, Kathryn. *Fantasy and Mimesis: Responses to Reality in Western Literature*. New York: Methuen, 1984.

Hutcheon, Linda. *Narcissistic Narrative: The Metafictional Paradox*. Ontario: Wilfred Laurier University Press, 1980.

Ileto, Reynaldo Clemena. *Pasyon and Revolution: Popular Movements in the Philippines, 1840–1910*. Quezon City: Ateneo de Manila University Press, 1979.

Jackson, Rosemary. *Fantasy: The Literature of Subversion*. London: Methuen, 1981.

Jaén, Didier T. "Mysticism, Esoterism, and Fantastic Literature." In *The Scope of the Fantastic — Theory, Technique, Major Authors: Selected Essays from the First International Conference on the Fantastic in Literature and Film*, ed. Robert A. Collins and Howard D. Pearce, 105–11. Westport, Conn.: Greenwood, 1985.

James, Victoria. "Cinematic Seoul: World Film — Forget *Crouching Tiger* and *Spirited Away* — Asia's Best New Movies Are South Korean." *New Statesman*, Jan. 16, 2006, 42–43.

Jameson, Fredric. "Magical Narratives: Romance as Genre." *New Literary History* 7, no. 1 (autumn 1975): 135–63.

———. "Marx's Purloined Letter." In *Ghostly Demarcations: A Symposium on Jacques Derrida's* Specters of Marx, ed. Michael Sprinker, 26–67. London: Verso, 1999.

———. *The Political Unconscious: Narrative as a Socially Symbolic Act*. Ithaca, N.Y.: Cornell University Press, 1981.

———. *The Prison-House of Language: A Critical Account of Structuralism and Russian Formalism*. Princeton, N.J.: Princeton University Press, 1972.

"Janghwa, Hongryeon (2003)." Review of Tartan's 2-disc DVD release of *Janghwa, Hongryeon*, dir. Kim Jee-woon. Movie Gazette, Aug. 9, 2004; available at www.movie-gazette.com (accessed Dec. 7, 2007).

Jauss, Hans-Robert. *Toward an Aesthetic of Reception*. Minneapolis: University of Minnesota Press, 1982.

Jocano, F. Landa. *Growing Up in a Philippine Barrio*. New York: Holt, Rinehart and Winston, 1969.

Kan, Wendy. "Reconstruction Project: Filmmakers Focus on Revamping Biz." *Variety*, April 29–May 5, 2002, A1, A4.

Keil, Charlie, and Shelley Stamp. Introduction to *American Cinema's Transitional Era: Audiences, Institutions, Practices*, ed. Charlie Keil and Shelley Stamp, 1–11. Berkeley: University of California Press, 2004.

Kenseth, Joy. "The Age of the Marvelous: An Introduction." In *The Age of the Mar-*

velous, ed. Joy Kenseth, 25–60. Hanover, N.H.: Hood Museum of Art / University of Chicago Press, 1991.

Kerkvliet, Benedict. *The Huk Rebellion: A Study of Peasant Revolt in the Philippines.* Quezon City: New Day, 1979.

Kermode, Mark. "What a Carve Up!" *Sight and Sound*, Dec. 2003, 12–16.

Kern, Stephen. *The Culture of Time and Space, 1880–1918.* Cambridge: Harvard University Press, 1983.

Kim Jin. "Biz Pines for Summer Horror Hits." *Variety*, Sept. 6–12, 2004, 14.

Kirby, Lynne. *Parallel Tracks: The Railroad and Silent Cinema.* Durham, N.C.: Duke University Press, 1997.

Klein, Christina. "The Asia Factor in Global Hollywood." YaleGlobal Online, March 25, 2003; available at http://yaleglobal.yale.edu (accessed Aug. 16, 2005).

Kleiner, Elaine L. "Mircea Eliade's Theory of the Fantastic." In *Visions of the Fantastic: Selected Essays from the Fifteenth International Conference on the Fantastic in the Arts*, ed. Allienne R. Becker, 13–18. Westport, Conn.: Greenwood, 1996.

Koselleck, Reinhart. "Concepts of Historical Time and Social History." Trans. Adelheis Baker. In *The Practice of Conceptual History: Timing History, Spacing Concepts*, trans. Todd Samuel Presner et al., 115–30. Stanford: Stanford University Press, 2002.

———. "The Eighteenth Century as the Beginning of Modernity." Trans. Todd Samuel Presner. In *The Practice of Conceptual History: Timing History, Spacing Concepts*, trans. Todd Samuel Presner et al., 154–69. Stanford: Stanford University Press, 2002.

———. "'Neuzeit': Remarks on the Semantics of the Modern Concepts of Movement." In *Futures Past: On the Semantics of Historical Time*, trans. Keith Tribe, 231–66. Cambridge: MIT Press, 1985.

———. "'Progress' and 'Decline': An Appendix to the History of Two Concepts." Trans. Todd Samuel Presner. In *The Practice of Conceptual History: Timing History, Spacing Concepts*, trans. Todd Samuel Presner et al., 218–35. Stanford: Stanford University Press, 2002.

———. "Time and History." Trans. Kertin Behnke. In *The Practice of Conceptual History: Timing History, Spacing Concepts*, trans. Todd Samuel Presner et al., 100–114. Stanford: Stanford University Press, 2002.

Kristeva, Julia. "Word, Dialogue and Novel." Trans. Alice Jardine, Thomas Gora, and Leon S. Roudiez. In *The Kristeva Reader*, ed. Toril Moi, 34–61. New York: Columbia University Press, 1986.

Lai, Linda Chiu-han. "Film and Enigmatization: Nostalgia, Nonsense, and Remembering." In Yau, *At Full Speed*, 231–50.

Lansdale, Edward Geary. *In the Midst of Wars: An American's Mission to Southeast Asia.* New York: Harper and Row, 1972.

Law Kar, ed. *Fifty Years of Electric Shadows: Proceedings of the 21st Hong Kong International Film Festival.* Kowloon, Hong Kong: Urban Council, 1997.

————. "Introduction." In *Hong Kong New Wave: Twenty Years After. The 23rd Hong Kong International Film Festival, March 31 to April 15, 1999*. Hong Kong: Provisional Urban Council of Hong Kong, 1999.

————. "An Overview of Hong Kong's New Wave Cinema." In Yau, *At Full Speed*, 31–52.

Lee, Ella. "Scene Set for Reel Recovery." *South China Morning Post*, Feb. 15, 2001, 15.

Lee, Roy. "Korean Cinema and Hollywood Remakes." Public lecture delivered at the University of California, Irvine, March 2, 2009.

Leung, Loretta. "SAR Film-Makers Prepare for Boom Year as Budgets Rise." *South China Morning Post*, Jan. 7, 2002, 1.

Leung Ping-kwan. "Urban Cinema and the Cultural Identity of Hong Kong." In Cheung and Chu, *Between Home and World*, 369–98.

Li Cheuk-to. "The Return of the Father: Hong Kong New Wave and Its Chinese Context in the 1980s." In *New Chinese Cinemas: Forms, Identities, Politics*, ed. Nick Browne, Paul G. Pickowicz, Vivian Sobchack, and Esther Yau, 160–79. Cambridge: Cambridge University Press, 1994.

————, Sek Kei, and Law Wai-ming. "Three Critics Sum up the Hong Kong New Wave." In *Hong Kong New Wave: Twenty Years After. The 23rd Hong Kong International Film Festival, March 31 to April 15, 1999*, 118–22. Hong Kong: Provisional Urban Council of Hong Kong, 1999.

Lieban, Richard W. *Cebuano Sorcery: Malign Magic in the Philippines*. Berkeley: University of California Press, 1967.

Lim, Bliss Cua. "Generic Ghosts: Remaking the New 'Asian Horror Film.'" In *Hong Kong Film, Hollywood and the New Global Cinema*, ed. Gina Marchetti and Tan See Kam, 109–25, 244–49. London: Routledge, 2007.

————. [as Lim, Felicidad] "The Politics of Horror: The Aswang in Film." *Asian Cinema* 9, no. 1 (fall 1997): 81–98.

————. "Serial Time: Bluebeard in Stepford." In *Literature and Film: A Guide to the Theory and Practice of Film Adaptation*, ed. Robert Stam, 163–90. Oxford: Blackwell, 2005.

————. "Spectral Times: The Ghost Film as Historical Allegory." *positions: east asia cultures critique* 9, no. 2 (2001): 287–329.

Lippit, Akira Mizuta. *Atomic Light (Shadow Optics)*. Minneapolis: University of Minnesota Press, 2005.

Loarca, Miguel de. "Relación de las Islas Filipinas." In *The Philippine Islands, 1493–1898*, ed. Emma Helen Blair and James Alexander Robertson. Vol. 5, 35–187. Cleveland, Ohio: A. H. Clark, 1903–9.

Lo Kwai-cheung. "Double Negations: Hong Kong Cultural Identity in Hollywood's Transnational Representations." In Cheung and Chu, *Between Home and World*, 59–84.

———. "Transnationalization of the Local in Hong Kong Cinema of the 1990s." In Yau, *At Full Speed*, 261–76.

Lu, Alvin. "Horror Japanese-Style." *Film Comment*, Jan.–Feb. 2002, 38.

Luckmann, Thomas. "The Constitution of Human Life in Time." In *Chronotypes: The Construction of Time*, ed. John Bender and David E. Wellbery, 151–66. Stanford: Stanford University Press, 1991.

Lukács, Georg. "Reification and the Consciousness of the Proletariat." In *History and Class Consciousness: Studies in Marxist Dialectics*, trans. Rodney Livingstone, 83–222. Cambridge: MIT Press, 1968.

Lyman, Rick. "The Chills! The Thrills! The Profits!" *New York Times*, Aug. 31, 1999, 1.

Lynch, Francis X. "An Mga Asuwang: A Bicol Belief." In *Philippine Society and the Individual: Selected Essays of Frank Lynch, 1949–1976*, ed. Aram A. Yengoyan and Perla Q. Makil, 184–206. Quezon City: Institute of Philippine Culture, Ateneo de Manila University, 2004.

Marchetti, Gina. "Buying American, Consuming Hong Kong: Cultural Commerce, Fantasies of Identity, and the Cinema." In *The Cinema of Hong Kong: History, Arts, Identity*, ed. Poshek Fu and David Desser, 289–313. Cambridge: Cambridge University Press, 2000.

Margold, Jane A. "Narratives of Masculinity and Transnational Migration: Filipino Workers in the Middle East." In *Bewitching Women, Pious Men: Gender and Body Politics in Southeast Asia*, ed. Aihwa Ong and Michael G. Peletz, 274–98. Berkeley: University of California Press, 1995.

Marx, Karl. *Capital*. Vol. 1, *A Critical Analysis of Capitalist Production*. Trans. Samuel Moore and Edward Aveling. Ed. Frederick Engels. New York: International Publishers, 1947.

———. *The Poverty of Philosophy*. Moscow: Foreign Languages Publishing House, n.d.

McClintock, Anne. *Imperial Leather: Race, Gender, and Sexuality in the Colonial Contest*. New York: Routledge, 1995.

———. "'No Longer in a Future Heaven': Gender, Race, and Nationalism." In *Dangerous Liaisons: Gender, Nation, and Postcolonial Perspectives*, ed. Anne McClintock, Aamir Mufti, and Ella Shohat, 183–209. Minneapolis: University of Minnesota Press, 1997.

McNary, Dave. "Remakes Need a Makeover: H'wood Steps Up Its Updates, but Idea Is Far from Surefire." *Variety*, July 21–27, 2003, 9–10.

Meñez, Herminia. "Mythology and the 'Ingkanto' Syndrome." In *Explorations in Philippine Folklore*, 61–76. Quezon City: Ateneo de Manila University Press, 1996.

———. "The Viscera-Sucker and the Politics of Gender." In *Explorations in Philippine Folklore*, 86–94. Quezon City: Ateneo de Manila University Press, 1996.

Metz, Christian. *The Imaginary Signifier: Psychoanalysis and the Cinema.* Trans. Celia Britton, Annwyl Williams, Ben Brewster, and Alfred Guzzetti. Bloomington: Indiana University Press, 1982.

Michel, Andreas. "Differentiation vs. Disenchantment: The Persistence of Modernity from Max Weber to Jean-François Lyotard." *German Studies Review* 20, no. 3 (Oct. 1997): 343–70.

Mignolo, Walter D. "The Enduring Enchantment (or the Epistemic Privilege of Modernity and Where to Go from Here)." *South Atlantic Quarterly* 101, no. 4 (fall 2002): 927–54.

Miller, J. Hillis. "The Two Allegories." In *Allegory, Myth, and Symbol*, ed. Morton W. Bloomfield, 355–70. Cambridge: Harvard University Press, 1981.

Miller, Toby. "Hollywood and the World." In *The Oxford Guide to Film Studies*, ed. John Hill and Pamela Church Gibson, 371–81. Oxford: Oxford University Press, 1998.

————. "Screening the Nation: Rethinking Options." *Cinema Journal* 38, no. 4 (1999): 93–97.

Miller, Toby, Nitin Govil, John McMurria, Richard Maxwell, and Ting Wang. *Global Hollywood 2.* London: BFI, 2005.

Millington, W. H., and Berton L. Maxfield. "Philippine (Visayan) Superstitions." *Journal of American Folklore* 19, no. 74 (1906): 205–11.

Milton, John R. "The Origin and Development of the Concept of Laws of Nature." *Archives européennes de sociologie* 22 (1981): 173–95.

Monleón, Jose B. *A Specter Is Haunting Europe.* Princeton, N.J.: Princeton University Press, 1990.

Morash, Chris. "The Time Is Out of Joint (O Cursèd Spite!): Towards a Definition of Supernatural Narrative." In *That Other World: The Supernatural and the Fantastic in Irish Literature and Its Contexts*, ed. Bruce Stewart, 123–42. Gerrards Cross, Buckinghamshire: Colin Smythe, 1998.

Munoz, Lorenza, and Josh Friedman. "Coming Attractions: As Its Filmmakers and Moviegoers Gain Hollywood's Attention, South Korea Aims to Broaden Its Share of the World's Cinema Market." *Los Angeles Times*, Nov. 5, 2006, Home ed., Business sec., 1.

Musser, Charles. *The Emergence of Cinema: The American Screen to 1907.* Berkeley: University of California Press, 1990.

Nashel, Jonathan. *Edward Lansdale's Cold War.* Amherst: University of Massachusetts Press, 2005.

Neary, Michael, and Glenn Rikowski. "Time and Speed in the Social Universe of Capital." In *Social Conceptions of Time: Structure and Process in Work and Everyday Life*, ed. Graham Crow and Sue Heath, 53–65. Houndmills, Basingstoke, Hampshire: Palgrave Macmillan, 2002.

O'Malley, Michael. *Keeping Watch: A History of American Time.* New York: Viking, 1990.

Omar, Rina. "*Dark Water*." *New Straits Times*, Sept. 13, 2002, 6.

Ong, Aihwa. "The Gender and Labor Politics of Postmodernity." In *The Politics of Culture in the Shadow of Capital*, ed. Lisa Lowe and David Lloyd, 61–97. Durham, N.C.: Duke University Press, 1997.

Ong, Soh Chin. "Horrifying Thoughts; Asian Horror Films Resonate Because They Are Closer to Home and Acknowledge Cultural Myths and Folklore." *Straits Times*, Nov. 27, 2004, Life sec.

Ortiz, Tomás. *Práctica del ministerio que siguen los religiosos del orden de N.S. Agustín en Filipinas*. Manila: Convento de Nuestra Señora de los Ángeles, 1731. Translated in Fletcher Gardner, "Philippine (Tagalog) Superstitions," *Journal of American Folklore* 19, no. 74 (1906): 191–193.

———. "Superstitions and Beliefs of the Filipinos." In *The Philippine Islands, 1493–1898*, ed. Emma Helen Blair and James Alexander Robertson. Vol. 18, 103–12. Cleveland, Ohio: A. H. Clark, 1906.

Owens, Craig. "The Allegorical Impulse: Toward a Theory of Postmodernism." *October* 12 (1980): 67–86.

Parisi, Luciana, and Steve Goodman. "The Affect of Nanoterror." *Culture Machine* 7 (2005): http://culturemachine.tees.ac.uk/frm_f1.htm (accessed March 25, 2008).

Pastor, Rene. "Manananggal Tales Bring Spine-Chilling Diversion from Polls." *Malaya*, May 11, 1992, 10.

Pertierra, Raul. "Viscera-Suckers and Female Sociality: The Philippine Asuang." *Philippine Studies* 31 (1983): 319–37.

Petric, Vlada. "Esther Shub: Film as a Historical Discourse." In *Show Us Life: Toward a History and Aesthetics of the Committed Documentary*, ed. Thomas Waugh, 21–46. Metuchen, N.J.: Scarecrow, 1984.

Plasencia, Juan de. "Los costumbres de los Tagalogs." In *The Philippine Islands, 1493–1898*, ed. Emma Helen Blair and James Alexander Robertson. Vol. 7, 173–98. Cleveland, Ohio: A. H. Clark, 1903.

Pogson, F. L. "Translator's Preface." In Bergson, *Time and Free Will*, v–viii.

Prawer, S. S. *Caligari's Children: The Film as Tale of Terror*. New York: Da Capo, 1988.

Rabkin, Eric S. *The Fantastic in Literature*. Princeton, N.J.: Princeton University Press, 1976.

Rafael, Vicente L. *Contracting Colonialism: Translation and Christian Conversion in Tagalog Society under Early Spanish Rule*. Durham, N.C.: Duke University Press, 1993.

Rafferty, Terrence. "Why Asian Ghost Stories Are the Best." *New York Times*, June 8, 2003, 13.

Ramos, Maximo. *The Aswang Complex in Philippine Folklore*. 1969. Quezon City: Phoenix Publishing House, 1990.

―――. "Belief in Ghouls in Contemporary Philippine Society." *Western Folklore* 27, no. 3 (1968): 184–90.

―――. *Creatures of Philippine Lower Mythology*. Quezon City: Phoenix Publishing House, 1990.

Ransom, Amy J. *The Feminine as Fantastic in the Conte fantastique: Visions of the Other*. New York: Peter Lang, 1995.

Rayns, Tony. "*The Eye*." *Sight and Sound*, Nov. 2002, 43–44.

Richards, Andy. "*The Eye*." *Time Out*, Sept. 25, 2002, 80.

Rithdee, Kong. "Bangkok Journal: Kong Rithdee on Cinematic Renewal in Thailand." *Film Comment*, Sept.–Oct. 2002, 12–13.

Rodowick, D. N. *Gilles Deleuze's Time Machine*. Durham, N.C.: Duke University Press, 1997.

Rodriguez, Hector. "The Emergence of the Hong Kong New Wave." In Yau, *At Full Speed*, 53–69.

Rony, Fatimah Tobing. *The Third Eye: Race, Cinema, and Ethnographic Spectacle*. Durham, N.C.: Duke University Press, 1996.

Rooney, David. "Remake Wranglers Mine Asia, South America." *Variety*, July 21–27, 2003, 14.

Ropp, Paul S. "Ambiguous Images of Courtesan Culture in Late Imperial China." In Widmer and Chang, *Writing Women in Late Imperial China*, 17–45.

Rose, Steve. "Nightmare Scenario: Hollywood Horror Is Creatively Dead but Asian Films Are Reviving the Genre." *Guardian*, Sept. 20, 2002, Friday Pages sec., 11.

Sandor, Andras. "Myths and the Fantastic." *New Literary History* 22 (1991): 339–58.

Saulo, Alfredo B. *Communism in the Philippines: An Introduction*. Quezon City: Ateneo de Manila University Press, 1990.

Schivelbusch, Wolfgang. *The Railway Journey: Trains and Travel in the 19th Century*. Trans. Anselm Hollo. Oxford: Basil Blackwell, 1977.

Scholes, Robert. Foreword to Todorov, *The Fantastic*, v–ix.

Sconce, Jeffrey. *Haunted Media: Electronic Presence from Telegraphy to Television*. Durham, N.C.: Duke University Press, 2000.

Sek Kei. "The Wandering Spook." In *Phantoms of the Hong Kong Cinema: Program Notes for the 13th Hong Kong International Film Festival*, 13–16. Hong Kong: Urban Council, 1987.

Shapiro, Michael J. "National Times and Other Times: Re-thinking Citizenship." *Cultural Studies* 14, no. 1 (2000): 79–98.

Sicam, Chula R. "'Manananggal' Season." *Manila Chronicle*, May 9–15, 1992, 31, 34.

Siebers, Tobin. *The Romantic Fantastic*. Ithaca, N.Y.: Cornell University Press, 1984.

Snowblood Apple Forums. www.mandiapple.com.

Snyder, Gabriel. "'Buffy' Effect: Teen Girls Buoy Screen Screamers." *Variety*, March 14–20, 2005, 6–7.

Sobchack, Vivian. "Bringing It All Back Home: Family Economy and Generic Exchange." In *The Dread of Difference: Gender and the Horror Film*, ed. Barry Keith Grant, 143–63. Austin: University of Texas Press, 1996.

———. "'Lounge Time': Postwar Crises and the Chronotope of Film Noir." In *Refiguring American Film Genres: History and Theory*, ed. Nick Browne, 129–70. Berkeley: University of California Press, 1998.

Spivak, Gayatri Chakravorty. "'In a Word': Interview" (with Ellen Rooney). In *The Second Wave: A Reader in Feminist Theory*, ed. Linda Nicholson, 356–78. New York: Routledge, 1997.

———. "The Politics of Translation." In *Outside in the Teaching Machine*, 179–200. New York: Routledge, 1993.

Stanley, T. L. "Like Jason, Horror Flicks Don't Stay Dead and Buried, but Keep on Rising; Popular, Cheap to Make, Classics and Sequels Hot Sellers in DVD, Theaters." *Advertising Age*, May 2, 2005, 4.

Stein, Elliott. "Manila's Angels." *Film Comment*, Sept.–Oct. 1983, 48–55.

Steinwand, Jonathan. "The Future of Nostalgia in Friedrich Schlegel's Gender Theory: Casting German Aesthetics beyond Ancient Greece and Modern Europe." In *Narratives of Nostalgia, Gender, and Nationalism*, ed. Jean Pickering and Suzanne Kehde, 9–29. New York: New York University Press, 1997.

Tejero, Constantino C. "'Dugo! Dugo!' The Manananggal of Tondo." *Sunday Inquirer Magazine*, May 24, 1992, 3–4, 6–7.

Telotte, J. P. "Beyond All Reason: The Nature of the Cult." *The Cult Film Experience*, ed. J. P. Telotte, 5–17. Austin: University of Texas Press, 1991.

Teo, Stephen. *Hong Kong Cinema: The Extra Dimensions*. London: British Film Institute, 1997.

———. "Hong Kong's Electric Shadow Show: From Survival to Discovery." In Law, *Fifty Years of Electric Shadows*, 18–24.

Thompson, E. P. "Time, Work-Discipline, and Industrial Capitalism." *Essays in Social History*, ed. M. W. Flinn and T. C. Smout, 39–77. Oxford: Clarendon, 1974.

Thornton, Sarah. *Club Cultures: Music, Media, and Subcultural Capital*. Hanover, N.H.: Wesleyan University Press, 1996.

Tigno, Jorge V. "Ties That Bind: The Past and Prospects of Philippine Labor Outmigration." *Pilipinas* 29 (fall 1997): 1–18.

Todorov, Tzvetan. *The Fantastic: A Structural Approach to a Literary Genre*. Trans. Richard Howard. Ithaca, N.Y.: Cornell University Press, 1975.

Tolentino, Rolando B. "Media and Ethnicity." *Plaridel: A Journal of Philippine Communication, Media, and Society* 3, no. 1 (February 2006): iii–viii.

Tomlinson, Hugh, and Barbara Habberjam. "Translators' Introduction." In Deleuze, *Bergsonism*, 7–12.

Trinh T. Minh-ha. *Woman, Native, Other: Writing Postcoloniality and Feminism*. Bloomington: Indiana University Press, 1989.

Vaño, Manolo O. "Folk Religion and Revolts in the Eastern Visayas." *Diliman Review* 43, nos. 3–4 (1995): 38–53.

Venida, Victor S. "The Santo and the Rural Aristocracy." *Philippine Studies* 44 (1996): 500–513.

Vera, Noel. "Butch Perez: Portrait of the Director as a Perfect Gentleman." Unpublished manuscript.

Vromen, Suzanne. "The Ambiguity of Nostalgia." *Yivo Annual* 21 (1993): 69–86.

Wai-yee Li. "The Late Ming Courtesan: Invention of a Cultural Ideal." In Widmer and Chang, *Writing Women in Late Imperial China*, 46–73.

Warner, Marina. "Women against Women in the Old Wives' Tale." In *Cinema and the Realms of Enchantment*, ed. Duncan Petrie, 63–78. London: British Film Institute, 1993.

Weber, Max. "Science as a Vocation." Trans. Michael John. In *Max Weber's "Science as a Vocation,"* ed. Peter Lassman, Irving Velody, and Herminio Martins, 3–31. London: Unwin Hyman, 1989.

Weber, Samuel. "Genealogy of Modernity: History, Myth and Allegory in Benjamin's *Origin of the German Mourning Play*." MLN 106, no. 3 (April 1991): 465–500.

Widmer, Ellen, and Kang-i Sun Chang, eds. *Writing Women in Late Imperial China*. Stanford: Stanford University Press, 1997.

Williams, Raymond. "Culture." In *Keywords: A Vocabulary of Culture and Society*, 87–93. New York: Oxford University Press, 1983.

Wills, David. "The French Remark: *Breathless* and Cinematic Citationality." In Horton and McDougal, *Play It Again, Sam*, 147–61.

Wong, Cindy Hing-yuk. "Cities, Cultures and Cassettes: Hong Kong Cinema and Transnational Audiences." *Postscript: Essays in Film and the Humanities* 19, no. 1 (fall 1999): 87–106.

Wood, Robin. "The American Nightmare: Horror in the 70s." In *Hollywood from Vietnam to Reagan*, 70–86. New York: Columbia University Press, 1986.

Xu, Gary G. *Sinascape: Contemporary Chinese Cinema*. Maryland: Rowman and Littlefield, 2007.

Yau, Esther C. M., ed. *At Full Speed: Hong Kong Cinema in a Borderless World*. Minneapolis: University of Minnesota Press, 2001.

———. "Border Crossing: Mainland China's Presence in Hong Kong Cinema." In *New Chinese Cinemas: Forms, Identities, Politics*, ed. Nick Browne, Paul G. Pickowicz, Vivian Sobchack, and Esther Yau, 180–201. Cambridge: Cambridge University Press, 1996.

———. "The Full Emptiness of the Decolonization Event: Two Virtual Worlds in/ of Hong Kong." Paper read at the Society for Cinema Studies conference, Chicago, March 9–12, 2000.

———. "Introduction: Hong Kong Cinema in a Borderless World." In Yau, *At Full Speed*, 1–28.

Yeh Yueh-Yu and Darrell William Davis. "Japan Hongscreen: Pan-Asian Cinemas and Flexible Accumulation." *Historical Journal of Film, Radio, and Television* 22, no. 1 (2002): 61–82.

Yu, Anthony C. "'Rest, Rest, Perturbed Spirit!' Ghosts in Traditional Chinese Prose Fiction." *Harvard Journal of Asiatic Studies* 47, no. 2 (1987): 397–434.

Yue, Audrey. "Preposterous Hong Kong Horror: *Rouge*'s (be)hindsight and *A* (sodomitical) *Chinese Ghost Story*. In *The Horror Reader*, ed. Ken Gelder, 364–73. London: Routledge, 2000.

Zeitlin, Judith T. "Embodying the Disembodied: Representations of Ghosts and the Feminine." In Widmer and Chang, *Writing Women in Late Imperial China*, 242–63.

———. *Historian of the Strange: Pu Songling and the Chinese Classical Tale*. Stanford: Stanford University Press, 1993.

INDEX

Page numbers in *italics* indicate illustrations.

anthropology (*cont.*)

    anachronism and, 16, 86–87, 248; nationalization and, 143; objectifying gaze of ethnography, 89–90

anthropometric photography, 93, *93*

anticolonialism and *Itim*, 4

Appadurai, Arjun, 159

apparatus: Baudry's theory of, 59; cinema as, 62, 63–66; Doane on cinematic time and, 269n71; as novelty, 63–64. *See also* cinematograph

Applause Pictures, 224–25

appropriation, deracinative, 216. *See also* deracination; remakes, Hollywood

Aquinas, Thomas, 107

Aquino, Corazon, 121, 141

Asian cinema and film festivals, 228, 301n100

"Asian horror films": Asianization of Hollywood and Hollywoodization of Asia, 232–33; cult cinephilia, 202–5, 228; cultural specificity vs. cultural neutrality, 223; generic-economic factors, 196–98; Hollywood remakes and, 194–99; naming of, 224; "new," 197; as regionalist-globalist phenomenon, 35, 40, 193–94, 197–98, 200, 204, 224–29, 231, 232; subcultural cult fandom, mainstreaming of, 228

Asia Shock, 204–5

astronomical time: as public time, 74

Aswang (1932), 114

Aswang (1992): domestic servants in, 129; guises of aswang in, 97–99, *98*, 115–16, *117*; photographic reproduction and, *116*; plot, 114–15; porous worlds in, 127–28; Reynes, Manilyn, in, 129

aswang complex and manananggal: in "Ang madre," 118–25, *122*, *124*, *125*; in CIA counterinsurgency psy-war

against Huks, 38, 101, 139–40; definition, orthography, and etymology of, 97–101, 275n1, 275n6; as demonization of babaylanes, 137–39; disenchanted view of, 282n89; enchantments of capital and, 134–37; ethnic and regional differences and types of, 138–39; in films (overview), 114, 120; generic porosity and rural and urban worlds, 127–31; as immiscible, 109; "Manananggal" (Balce), 130–31; "Manananggal" (Fojas), 119–20; mimetic capital and, 101; nationalization of, and immiscibility, 141–44; newspapers, tabloids, and media convergence, 113–14, 120–21, 123–26, *124*, *125*, 146; noncontemporaneous reception, permeable worlds, 144–48; nuns and, 280n63; racialized casting in aswang films, 120; sightings during 1992 Philippine elections, 96–97, 119–21, 141–42; sociological translations, 131–34; Spanish colonial missionary accounts and translations, 97, 133, 137–40

audiences: aswang and noncontemporaneous audiences, 37, 99–100, 113, 126, 145–46; early cinema and, 63, 65; genre and, 35; global and regional, 191–92, 199–201, 204, 216–33, 244; local Hong Kong, 291n76; national-popular, 204, 227, 229–30; nostalgia and, 159; *Rouge* and, 175–78; social, 104–5; terror and, 235, 264n99; verisimilitude and, 144. *See also* reception; spectatorship

Audition, The, 194

Austria, Amy, 289n49

autoreferentiality, textual, 102, 103, 148

babaylanes, 137–39, 283n100, 283n102, 284n121

Bliss Cua Lim is an associate
professor of film and media
studies and visual studies
at the University of
California, Irvine.

Library of Congress
Cataloging-in-Publication Data
Lim, Bliss Cua.
Translating time : cinema, the fantastic,
and temporal critique / Bliss Cua Lim.
p. cm.
Includes bibliographical references and
index.
ISBN 978-0-8223-4499-5 (cloth : alk. paper)
ISBN 978-0-8223-4510-7 (pbk. : alk. paper)
1. Fantasy films—History and criticism.
2. Time in motion pictures. 3. Horror
films—History and criticism.   ergson,
Henri, 1859–1941. I. Title.
PN1995.9.F36L56 2009
791.43'615—dc22   2009005702